HISTORY PRESERVED

A GUIDE TO

NEW YORK CITY LANDMARKS

AND HISTORIC DISTRICTS

By Harmon H. Goldstone

and Martha Dalrymple

SIMON AND SCHUSTER · NEW YORK

The authors and publisher are grateful to:

Mr. A. Gerald Doyle of the *Bronx Press-Review* for permission to reprint a letter from Bert Sack;

Harcourt Brace Jovanovich, Inc., for permission to reprint a selection from *Complete Poems 1913–1962,* by E. E. Cummings, originally published as *VV (Viva)*, copyright 1931 by Horace Liveright, Inc.;

Professor Stanley Milgram for permission to reprint an excerpt from "A Psychological Map of New York City," *City University Graduate Newsletter,* 1971;

The New York Times for permission to reprint an excerpt from an editorial of February 16, 1971, "All Snug in the Harbor," copyright © 1971 The New York Times Co.

SBN 671–21610–4
Library of Congress Catalog Card Number: 73–19096
Type design by Helen Barrow
Layout and graphics by Libra Graphic Services
Manufactured in the United States of America
Typography and binding by American Book–Stratford Press, Inc.
Printing by The Murray Printing Company

1   2   3   4   5   6   7   8   9   10

Acknowledgments

WE ARE grateful to the Landmarks Preservation Commission of the City of New York for the use of its Landmark and Historic District designation reports. These provided an invaluable point of departure for the discussion of individual structures and areas, and we have drawn freely on the material they contain. Where we have differed in interpretation we take responsibility for our own views, since this book is in no way an official publication of the Commission.

We are particularly appreciative of the time and effort expended by Alan Burnham, Frank B. Gilbert, James J. Heslin, Regina Kellerman, Richard J. Koke, Ellen Kramer, May Lewis, John H. Lindenbusch, Loring McMillen, Ellen Rosebrock, I. Barnett Shepherd, and William Wyckoff, who contributed information or were kind enough to read parts or all of the manuscript, and of the contribution of Vera Schneider, whose copy editing was inspired and invaluable. However, any errors or omissions are our responsibility.

We owe a debt of thanks to Hansi Bohm for the sketches of the Historic Districts and to John B. Bayley for the photographs which were made especially for this book. The maps of the Historic Districts and, unless otherwise credited, all photographs are reproduced with the permission of the Landmarks Preservation Commission.

H.H.G.
M.D.

TO THE MEMORY OF
James Felt

Contents

List of Maps

Introduction

OUR HOPE *is that this book can serve both for general reading and as a guide to officially designated Landmarks and Historic Districts in New York City.*

Chapter I spells out the ground rules and defines terms. Therefore it should be read at leisure or used as a reference section.

The other nine chapters are designed to serve as a guide. They are divided geographically by boroughs (in Manhattan by districts) and further subdivided by types of structures. Historic Districts, where they occur, are treated in sections by themselves at the end of each chapter. This book is not intended to serve as a block-by-block walking tour, but can serve very well as an introduction to the architecture and history of whatever part of the city you happen to be in.

The chronological chart on pages 533 ff, will serve as a further guide for those who want to follow all the Landmark examples of a particular architectural style or want to see examples of what was being built in a particular decade. Here again structures are subdivided by type. Any such system is somewhat arbitrary. We have further arbitrarily chosen to list structures in the category for which they were originally constructed, regardless of their present use.

We have used the following categories:

RESIDENTIAL *buildings include freestanding houses, row houses, apartment houses and hotels.*

ECCLESIASTICAL *structures include churches, synagogues, meeting houses and cemeteries.*

PUBLIC *buildings comprise government buildings, schools and colleges, libraries, railroad stations, theaters, clubs and museums, as well as park structures.*

COMMERCIAL *structures are confined to office buildings, banks and shops.*

UTILITARIAN *structures include factories, warehouses, bridges, forts, aqueducts, lighthouses and towers.*

Buildings and Historic Districts that were designated after this manuscript was completed have been added, in summary descriptions, to the chapter and section where they belong. They are also included on the maps and in the index but are not illustrated nor included in the Chronological Chart.

Architecture is a physical fact; history happened in actual places. We hope that the geographic arrangement will stimulate the reader to explore the city on foot, to seek out and examine the many vestiges of the city's great and enduring past. The purpose of this book is to encourage the reader to acquire a discriminating and appreciative eye.

A society requires antecedents . . . It tests its sense of identity, of regress or new achievement, against that past.

—GEORGE STEINER

LANDMARKS

History and Architecture

A S WORLD CITIES GO, New York has had only a brief history, but that history is dear to New Yorkers and is growing dearer every day that its remnants become rarer. Even as far back as 1831 a few citizens began to be concerned over the city's being stripped of its historic structures. On March 19 of that year the *New York Mirror,* which called itself a "Repository of Polite Literature and the Arts," carried a picture of an old Dutch house on Pearl Street with the caption "Built 1626, Rebuilt 1697, Demolished 1828." An editorial left no doubt how the editor felt:

> We present to our readers a correct and striking view of an ancient Dutch house, formerly familiarly known as old seventy-six and which was pulled down about three years ago, in compliance with that irreverence for antiquity which so grievously afflicts the people of this city, many of whom, we are credibly informed, demolish one house just for the pleasure of building another in its place. The original edifice was probably erected soon after the first settlement of New Amsterdam, say about 1626. It was, many years afterwards, partly destroyed by fire, and the date of 1697, it is believed, was that of the rebuilding.

And in 1845 Philip Hone, the prolific diarist, former mayor of New York and man about town, wrote: "Overturn, overturn, overturn! is the maxim of New York. The very bones of our ancestors are not permitted to lie quiet a quarter of a century, and one generation of men seem studious to remove all relics of those which preceded them."

But most New Yorkers accepted the loss of their past as the price of progress—that is, if they gave it any thought at all. They took as a matter of course, and actually rather relished, what Walt Whitman referred to in 1845 as "the pull-down-and-build-over-again spirit" of America. It was all part of the atmosphere that had characterized New York from the beginning as an exciting place in which to live, work and make money.

As the city grew older, however, and particularly during the prosperous years after the Civil War, when it became fashionable for wealthy Americans to travel in Europe, more and more of them felt, when they came back, that an important segment of American culture was being destroyed. Henry James, one of our more famous expatriates, returned to this country in 1904 and was appalled to see one of his boyhood homes in Boston demolished within a few weeks. "The act of obliteration had been breathlessly swift, and if I had often seen how fast history could be made I had doubtless never so felt that it could be unmade still faster."

If Henry James could write this way in 1904, what would he have said in 1941, when a federal survey of the entire United States found only 6,400 structures of architectural or historic importance still standing, or in 1963, when it was estimated that forty percent of even this short list had already been demolished?

But by that time something actually was being done to stem the tide of destruction. In 1949 the National Trust for Historic Preservation had been chartered by Congress, and in several states and cities protective ordinances had been written. It was not until April 19, 1965, however, that Mayor Robert F. Wagner signed the bill that brought the New York City Landmarks Preservation Commission into existence. Under the rather undramatic title of "Local Law No. 46 of the City of New York for the Year 1965," the City Charter and the Administrative Code were amended "in relation to the establishment and regulation of landmarks, landmark sites and historic districts."

The birth of New York City's Commission was not one of those events that just happen. It came about as the climax of years of work by a small group of idealists. Before lawmakers could be expected to take such a proposal seriously a constituency had to be built up in its support. The general public had to be made aware of the irreplaceable values being unnecessarily destroyed. Much credit for this task of public education belongs to the Municipal Art Society, a venerable private organization which, over the years, has been able to achieve, through the tenacious dedication of its members, far more than its size and limited resources would suggest. It was this organization that first sponsored Henry Hope Reed's famous architectural walking tours, which the Museum of the City of New York later took over and greatly extended. The society was also responsible for compiling a series of lists of the city's notable structures. These culminated in the publication in 1963 of Alan Burnham's book *New York Landmarks.*

The New York Community Trust is another organization that made an important contribution to the constituency, or lobby, in favor of legislation for landmark preservation. It played a significant role in public education by installing on outstanding buildings in the city bronze plaques briefly outlining the structures' historical and architectural importance. After the Landmarks Preservation Commission was established, the Community Trust turned over to it this task, and the funds to carry it out. It is hoped that in time each designated Landmark and all Historic Districts will be identified with plaques bearing the city's official seal.

But, above all, it was the voice of outraged citizens that made itself heard in City Hall. Sometimes they were well organized in groups such as the Brooklyn Heights Association, which was so anxious to protect its own neighborhood that it sought and obtained national recognition as an Historic District even before New York City's local law was enacted. Often it was a crisis over the imminent loss of an important building that focused public attention. There were public battles over Carnegie Hall, which was saved just in the nick of time, and over Pennsylvania Station and the Brokaw château on Fifth Avenue at 79th Street, both of which were lost. These served to shock New Yorkers into the realization that some permanent, orderly legal procedure must be set up if anything at all of our architectural heritage was going to be preserved.

The Municipal Art Society had been working quietly toward this end since the spring of 1961. James Felt, then chairman of the City Planning Commission, gave the project his sympathetic support and his expert guidance to Geoffrey Platt of the Municipal Art Society to steer it through the intricacies of municipal government. If four years seem like a long time between the start of this action and the final enactment of the landmarks legislation, it is well to remember the rather wistful remark which was recently attributed to Fidel Castro: "It is easier to wage guerrilla warfare than to govern."

The Landmarks Preservation Law transformed the process of landmark preservation from a series of hysterical skirmishes among aroused private citizens into an integral part of city government. The Landmarks Preservation Commission works closely with other city agencies so that when a Landmark or an Historic District is designated it means that it is the official policy of the City of New York to see that, if humanly possible, such a structure or area will be preserved and properly preserved.

While New York City was a late starter—about fifty cities in the United States had some form of landmarks legislation before our bill was passed—New York has worked hard to make up for lost time. In the nine years of its existence 378 individual structures have been designated Landmarks and twenty-three areas (containing in all over eight thousand buildings) have been declared Historic Districts. Within certain equitable limitations these structures and areas are all protected from the wrecking crew and from the misguided modernizer, however well-meaning. These designations attest to the importance of history preserved; they provide proof of past periods of architectural excellence; they demonstrate that New York is a city with roots and that she is proud of them.

Landmarks

According to the Landmarks Preservation Law of New York City, "Landmarks" are structures that "represent or reflect elements of the city's cultural, social, economic, political and architectural history." This is a pretty big order, and in actual practice a single structure seldom reflects all of the five aspects of the city that the law specifies. Sometimes a structure is designated because of its architectural *and* political history (for example, City Hall); sometimes purely for its architectural value (the Grecian Shelter in Prospect Park); and sometimes primarily for its social history (the Dunbar Apartments in

Harlem). Sometimes a structure, and particularly a monument (like the Statue of Liberty or the Soldiers' and Sailors' Monument), has not as yet been designated, simply because it is not endangered and the Commission, with limited resources, has tried to move first to protect threatened buildings.

Sometimes a structure is designated a Landmark when the Commission feels that its architecture, although not impressive in itself, is representative of an important period in the city's architectural development (for example, the Laing Stores). Occasionally a building is designated a Landmark primarily by virtue of some special role it has played. For example, J. P. Morgan and Company (now Morgan Guaranty) on Wall Street, while a handsome early-twentieth-century classical building, is more important for its effect upon world finance than upon world architecture. A Landmark may be almost anything: a bridge, a bank, a water tower, a home, an apartment, a theater, a school, a church, a cemetery, a club, a factory, an office building, a museum, even a tree. And Landmarks are located in all five boroughs. Although there will surely be additional designations in the future, it is apparent from the present list that a major portion of the city's most important old structures have already been spotted. Since the law provides that a structure must be at least thirty years old before it can be designated, worthy structures that will be coming of age during the years ahead will doubtless be candidates for future designation. As it happens, the thirty-year cutoff point worked out to be quite a natural one for a Commission established in 1965. Very few buildings were erected in New York City during the depression and war years of 1930 to 1945. What was built after the break was widely different from that which had gone before. The present list of Landmarks, therefore, marks the end of an epoch.

No two people setting out independently to write a history of New York City architecture, or a history of the city as reflected in its architecture, would choose exactly the same list of structures to illustrate their story. The present list of officially designated Landmarks and Historic Districts is the result of a nine-year sifting process by a staff and a Commission composed of individuals with widely differing qualifications. The list does not include many important buildings which had been razed before the Commission was established, nor does it include *every* structure that *every* citizen in the city would like to see preserved. It represents, rather, a consensus of what is worth saving balanced always against the realities of a fast-moving city always in need of space for new and modern purposes.

The arbitrary limitation of this book to a consideration of officially designated Landmarks and Historic Districts has one distinct advantage. Whatever the differences of opinion may be as to what should or should not have been included, the structures and areas discussed will, in all likelihood, still be standing for future generations to study and argue about.

Landmark Sites

A "Landmark Site" is simply the property that is designated along with each "Landmark." In the case of closely built-up sections of the city, the Landmark Site is often identical with the piece of ground on which the Landmark stands. In the case of a house surrounded by a garden or a church surrounded by a graveyard, the Landmark Site may be considerably larger.

Historic Districts

An "Historic District" must "have a special character or special historical or aesthetic interest or value" which makes it a distinct section of the city. Most important, these areas illustrate the way in which ordinary people lived and worked during various periods in the past. An Historic District does not necessarily have to remind us of some important historic event. Historic Districts illustrate a quiet type of history—a history without heroes.

When the Landmarks Preservation Law was being drafted, the idea of Historic Districts came almost as an afterthought. The obvious examples of Greenwich Village and Brooklyn Heights and perhaps a couple of others came to mind, and that was that. But, much to everyone's surprise, after the law was enacted and the Commission set up, pleas came from all over the city for designation not only of individual Landmarks, for which the Commission was prepared, but also of many more Historic Districts than had ever been anticipated.

Why are Historic Districts so popular? The Commission is under no illusion that the city is populated by architectural historians and antiquarians. The fact is that ordinary people, even New Yorkers, like the feeling that they belong. They see in the provisions for Historic Districts something that the framers of the law themselves had not foreseen—namely, that the designation of an Historic District would give its residents a sense of identity and of continuity that most of them unconsciously craved. In an era that has become increasingly rootless, people recognize in an Historic District a chance to preserve something of the best from the past and, in preserving it, an opportunity to share in a sense of community pride and achievement.

Very shortly after the Landmarks Preservation Commission was established, local organizations all over the city began to focus on a new activity. Some were old groups that had suddenly come to life, others were brand-new ones, stimulated by the possibility of having their neighborhoods designated. It is particularly interesting that these eager candidates are not only from wealthy areas which might have been expected to seek the protective provisions of the law. Many are from quite poor areas where little islands of community pride exist. The fact that the city government cares enough either to designate them or to consider them seriously for designation has had a remarkably stabilizing effect upon whole sections of the city.

The Landmarks Preservation Commission

The law provides that the Landmarks Preservation Commission shall consist of eleven members appointed by the mayor for three-year overlapping terms. The Commission must at all times be composed of at least three architects, one realtor, one city planner or landscape architect, and one historian who has specialized in the history of New York City. The remaining five commissioners may be laymen or additional professionals; almost always one or more are attorneys or are familiar with city government. In addition, the Commission must always contain at least one resident of each of the city's five boroughs. These provisions were written into the law in order to ensure broad-based, balanced and practical judgments. Except for the chairman, the commissioners serve the city without pay.

The Commission is assisted by a full-time paid staff of specialists:

architects, architectural historians, restoration specialists, and, of course, administrative, legal and clerical help. Its work, from the start, has been generously supported by the devoted services of enthusiastic volunteers, students, and members of the Urban Corps, students largely paid by the federal government to work in municipal agencies. Within the governmental structure the Commission and its staff are a component of the New York City Parks, Recreation and Cultural Affairs Administration.

Nominations for designation come from a variety of sources: from a concerned public, from members of the Commission and its staff, and from property owners. Nominations for Historic Districts usually come from an active community group that is proud of its neighborhood and wants to see it preserved.

The Commission holds public hearings on proposals for designation. From all the nominations that the Commission receives it selects those candidates that it considers, from a city-wide point of view, to be worthy of permanent preservation. This list of proposed structures and Historic Districts is duly advertised and property owners are notified so that anybody who wishes may come to the Board of Estimate Room in City Hall (incidentally, one of the most beautiful rooms in the United States) and be heard either for or against their designation.

In due course, after reviewing the testimony of the public hearing and studying the documentation, the Commission at one of its monthly meetings votes whether or not to designate a proposed structure or district. All designations by the Commission are subject to veto or modification, within ninety days, by the Board of Estimate, which is composed of the top elected city officials. The Board of Estimate reaches its decision after receiving an advisory report from the City Planning Commission. The Buildings, Fire, and Health Departments as well as the Board of Standards and Appeals are also notified of the Commission's designations and can raise objections, if they are so minded, before the Board of Estimate. All of this process is designed to ensure that the Landmarks Preservation Commission will not act capriciously or in reaction to purely local or ephemeral pressures. It also means that once a Landmark or Historic District designation passes this review, it carries with it the full weight of official city policy.

Once a building is declared a Landmark its exterior cannot be altered in any respect or added to without the approval of the Commission. The same holds true of structures within the boundaries of designated Historic Districts. The Commission's expert staff consults with owners on their proposed changes or additions and tries to work out plans that will meet the owner's needs and yet be appropriate to the architectural character and historic validity of the building and its surroundings.

The Commission holds monthly public hearings on all proposed exterior changes. As soon as it approves a change it issues a so-called certificate of appropriateness, and the owner is free to go ahead with his construction. If the Commission does not issue such a certificate and the owner tries to go ahead with his plans, the law provides appropriate penalties.

If an owner wishes to demolish his Landmark or a building in an Historic District there are provisions in the law to give the Commission time to find a workable solution: by locating a purchaser who wishes to maintain the building and is willing to pay the owner a fair price; by tax abatement or remission; by suggesting ingenious alternatives that will persuade an owner to adapt his business or economic needs to the building as it stands; or by permitting him to benefit from the sale of unused development rights. This last method, provided for in a 1968 amendment to the New York City Zoning Resolution, is an imaginative device through which the owner of a Landmark on a valuable site can get a fair return, roughly equivalent to the income that a new high rise on the property might bring him. By purchasing the unused development rights of the lot containing the Landmark, neighbors are allowed to build more than they would otherwise be permitted, and yet the total density of a given area remains just what the Zoning Resolution says it should be. The resolution also requires that the new building be designed to be as compatible as possible with the Landmark and that adequate provisions be made for maintenance of the Landmark.

The Landmarks Law establishes a fixed time limit on each step in the process of halting a demolition, so that, while the Commission is given the opportunity of working out an equitable solution, it cannot hold up a property owner indefinitely. The entire process, if each of the statutory steps is taken in succession, requires about one year. If, at the end of this time, no reasonable alternative has been found that is acceptable to the owner, and if the City itself does not wish to acquire the property either at a negotiated price or through condemnation proceedings, then the owner is free to demolish his structure. It is significant to note that, in the nine years of its experience with the hundreds of landmarks over which it has jurisdiction, only once has this end of the road been reached. While there was deep and general regret over the demolition of the Leonard Jerome Mansion on Madison Square—once the home of Winston Churchill's mother, Jennie— the way in which it was lost proved that the Landmarks Preservation Law is fair. If, with all the goodwill and effort in the world, there just is no viable future for an old building, then it seems better to treat a property owner equitably than to pretend that the economic realities of a dynamic city do not exist. The ultimate strength of a law can sometimes better be tested by its flexibility than by its rigidity.

One of the aims of the Commission is to keep the past a living and vibrant part of the present. As Ada Louise Huxtable says, you don't do it with hoopskirts.

The remaining sections of this chapter are not intended to be swallowed in one gulp. They are meant to provide a broad survey of a complicated period in architectural history, a period of rapid and overlapping changes. They describe the various architectural styles to be encountered and define names for these styles in the particular way we will be using them. The impatient reader can skip at once to Chapter Two and refer back to the remainder of Chapter One only when in need of it.

Architectural Vocabulary: Style and Fashion

In discussing architectural details it is necessary to use a certain number of special terms. Otherwise, long, clumsy circumlocutions would have to be resorted to. There is nothing mysterious about this technical vocabulary. Every profession, trade or sport, be it law, medicine, sailing or carpentry, has its own. It enables practitioners to communicate with one another quickly and precisely. Such a technical vocabulary can be very impressive to outsiders. One aspiring young architect so overawed the girl he was courting by an offhand reference to a "rabbeted astragal" that she married him.

When it comes to a vocabulary with which to describe architectural styles, we get into deeper water. The names given to the different styles may be compared in a very rough way to the names that ornithologists give to birds or ichthyologists to fish, but the classification of architectural styles is far less orderly. The terms are less precisely defined, and the choice of a particular system of classification depends more on the point of view of the classifier. In this book all we hope to do is give the interested amateur a series of convenient labels that will help him to identify what he sees from the sidewalk. But he should not delude himself that the pinning on of a label is all there is to architecture. Just as there are bird watchers who can identify a hundred species from their shape, color or song and yet know nothing of their physiology, evolution or ecology, so there are building spotters who can knowingly allude to "late Federal" or "neo-Grec" without having any idea of how the building was put together or where the designs came from or why they were used at a particular time and place.

The pitfall of relying blindly on superficial labels is nowhere more perilous than in the architecture of the nineteenth and early twentieth centuries. The hundred years from about 1830 to 1930 saw, in New York City alone, probably more different styles of architecture than can be found at any other place or point in history. It was a period of very rapid growth and change. The technological, economic and ideological revolutions that were transforming America from a spread-out agricultural society into a highly urbanized industrial one are reflected in its architecture. With its political and cultural roots cut loose from Europe, the new republic spent a century growing new ones. With the impatience of youth, it was willing to try anything, and did. Style succeeded style with such rapidity that, if the word were not so firmly embedded in the architectural vocabulary, it would be more accurate to describe many phases of the nineteenth-century architecture as "fashions" rather than as "styles." The kaleidoscopic shifts in tastes came and went, lingered in less sophisticated sections of the city, were revived and re-revived in others. There are abundant examples in which essentially identical buildings were given different faces, and there are even cases in which the "style" of a building was changed in mid-course of construction, just because something new and more fashionable was coming into vogue.

Classification of Styles

For the sake of simplicity—and aware of the risks there are in over-simplification—we have arbitrarily sorted all the different types of design that appear in New York City's Landmarks into three broad categories: the Classical Tradition, the Romantic Tradition and the Nonstylistic Tradition.

In the Classical Tradition we have included not only those buildings which, with their orders of columns, capitals and cornices, show a direct descent from Greece and Rome, but also those buildings whose arcades, balustrades, pediments and brackets include classical forms as they were modified during the Renaissance and post-Renaissance periods. The Classical Tradition is generally characterized by symmetry, tranquillity and monumentality.

The Romantic Tradition, on the other hand, is essentially asymmetrical, dynamic and picturesque. We include in it not only the Gothic and Romanesque styles, but also such apparently ill-assorted companions as Byzantine, Art Nouveau, and the Château style of Francis I, because they share the picturesqueness, exoticism and decorative quality which had such a wide appeal to nineteenth-century New Yorkers.

In the Nonstylistic Tradition we include everything that just went along by itself without bothering about history, aesthetics or literary ideas. It includes varieties of the local vernacular, the work that country carpenters or unsophisticated builders created, as well as the work of some great engineers. It includes fortifications, bridges, fences and such unclassifiable objects as cemeteries and trees.

These three traditions—the Classical, the Romantic and the Non-stylistic—can be traced through three centuries of the city's architecture. Sometimes one is in the ascendancy, sometimes another, and sometimes all three run along together.

It is important to distinguish clearly between the Revival styles characteristic of the first half of the nineteenth century and the Eclectic period that ran from the latter part of the nineteenth century well into the twentieth. The Revivals were broad movements, often nationwide, and were much inspired by philosophical, literary or political ideas. While there was some overlap, the Revivals generally came in successive waves. In the 1830s and 1840s everybody was doing Greek Revival; in the 1840s and 1850s Gothic Revival was the thing for churches, and, in the same period, townhouses had to be Italianate in order to be fashionable.

The products of Revival styles were sometimes naïve and show little understanding of the original function of the architectural forms they were reviving. Elements and details from one style were at times mixed with those from another. This untutored freshness and the evident enthusiasm with which builders plunged into the latest fashion give the Revivals much of their present appeal.

Eclecticism was quite another matter. As used to describe this period of architecture, Eclecticism means the free choice of any one of many styles for any one building. During the Revival periods almost all architects followed the particular style currently in fashion—Greek, Gothic, Italianate, etc.—while in the Eclectic period architects began to make individual selections from a wide range of styles for each individual building they designed. With one hand an architect might be designing a French château and with the other a Gothic church or an Italianate palazzo. Another architect might be designing a Roman bank and an Elizabethan half-timbered country manor at the same time.

This all came about because of a fundamental change in the training of designers of buildings. During the first half of the century the employment of professional architects had been the exception rather than the rule. Most buildings were designed by skilled carpenters and masons who relied heavily on a whole series of builders' guides, or pattern books, such as Asher Benjamin's *The Country Builder's Assistant* or his *The American Builder's Companion,* or perhaps Minard Lafever's *The Young Builder's General Instructor.* Such architects as there were, while rather more sophisticated, were only a step removed from the journeyman and were largely self-taught, from books or as apprentices to other architects. The lack of professionalism is exemplified in Alexander Jackson Davis' business card:

Formal training of American architects may be traced back to Richard Morris Hunt's enrollment in 1846 in the École des Beaux-Arts in Paris, which was the only place where professional training was then available. Many other American architects followed him there. However, professional schools of architecture were soon established in the United States: at the Massachusetts Institute of Technology, 1865; the University of Illinois, 1868; Cornell University, 1871; Syracuse University, 1873; and Columbia University, 1881. The new status of the architect as a professional was signalized by the formation in New York City in 1857 of the American Institute of Architects.

Simultaneous with this new professional approach came the development of photography. For the first time American architects not only saw the great works of Europe during their training or postgraduate travel, but could and did build up libraries of accurate, measured drawings and photographs on which to base their future practice.

Both the professional training and the accurate documentation of great buildings of the past gave to the architects of the Eclectic period, for the first time, scholarly resources for the correct reproduction of whatever style they chose. This did not necessarily mean that they were blindly making facsimile copies. The more creative of them might choose details from different buildings and combine them in fresh ways.

In addition to these new resources, the Eclectic architects had two other great assets—wealthy patrons and the availability of the finest craftsmanship the country has ever known. The clients, in the prosperous years between the close of the Civil War and the outbreak of World War I, traveled widely, so that in addition to being rich they were knowledgeable. When a merchant prince commissioned a man-

Greek Revival buildings are characterized by a flat, clean-shaven look. In row houses doorways are flanked by Ionic pilasters or columns and are crowned by flat entablatures. Simple rectangular panes replace the delicate leading of Federal sidelights and transoms. In more pretentious houses the doorway was sheltered by a portico supported by Doric or Ionic columns. A simple cornice ran across the top of the front wall; at most it was ornamented with a row of delicate dentils. Small horizontal windows to ventilate the attic were often inserted in the fascia board beneath the cornice. Roof slopes are quite flat, and dormers usually are a later addition. Smooth pressed bricks are set in running bond with narrow joints. Stone lintels are often crowned by a simple cap molding and are occasionally peaked with the effect of a very low pediment. The delicate wrought iron of the Federal style persists in part but is ornamented by small cast-iron copies of Greek fret, leaf and flower patterns.

For freestanding churches, public buildings and mansions a close copy of a Greek temple was attempted, though generally a portico of Doric or Ionic columns was confined to the front façade. Other compromises were made to meet functional requirements. Additional stories were inserted; flanking wings were added; and sometimes several temples were linked together by passageways. It was, in fact, the rigidity of the Greek-temple plan, essentially a one-story rectangle surrounded by columns, that spelled its doom. There was a limit to the compromises that were possible, and it was finally admitted that the simple box plan of a Greek temple just could not be adapted to meet the complex needs of nineteenth-century America. A more fluid and flexible style would be required. In addition, as the country prospered, the austerities of the Greek Revival style no longer satisfied a growing thirst for opulence.

ITALIANATE   The Italianate was the one Revival style that is never called a Revival by the architectural historians. In deference to them we will follow their accepted usage. Renaissance Italy provided the new inspiration. Architects began with the quite free adaptation of certain motifs from the early Florentine Renaissance: roundheaded arcaded windows, heavy projecting cornices supported on brackets, balconies and pediments supported on consoles, heavy stone or cast-iron balustrades and rusticated basements.

The Italianate coincides with the mass-quarrying of brownstone in

Connecticut and New Jersey. This new, easily worked material and the new style became so indissolubly wedded that the twenty- or twenty-five-foot-wide high-stooped "brownstone" *is* the Italianate in most New Yorkers' minds. A "brownstone" house is actually built of brick and simply covered with a four- or six-inch-thick facing of the new material, which is a form of sandstone. A detail worth noting is that at the same time sheet glass became available in big enough pieces so that each sash of a double-hung window could now be glazed with only two panes. This helped to increase the scale of Italianate houses in contrast to the multiple small panes that were used in the sash of Georgian, Federal or Greek Revival houses.

A later variety of the row-house plan in which the doorway was raised only a few steps above the sidewalk is sometimes referred to as "Anglo-Italianate" owing to its wide popularity in England.

One of the surprising developments of the Italianate was its adaptation to commerical structures. The rediscovery of the Italian Renaissance coincided with the development of cast-iron fronts where the repetition of arcaded windows, particularly characteristic of Venetian architecture, perfectly suited the requirements of the new structural techniques: prefabrication and interchange of a limited number of identical parts, maximum area of window openings and a concentration of wall loads on regularly spaced points of support.

FRENCH SECOND EMPIRE   In addition to reviving styles from past epochs, there were, in the last third of the nineteenth century, some direct importations of contemporary French styles. They had evolved in the classical tradition in France and came to New York with a very French accent indeed.

Earliest of the series and as popular in the United States of President Grant as it was in the France of Napoleon III—and for the same reasons—was the opulent and flamboyant French Second Empire style. It is easy to identify by the steep mansard roof, pierced by ornate dormers, that always crowns these buildings. What goes on below is like a fully orchestrated symphony—intricate, rich, yet firmly under control. Every resource is used to embellish these façades: carved friezes, keystones and pediments, ornate brackets, balustrades and balconies, and, above all, the decorative use of rustication. The quoins and the arch voussoirs were sometimes vermiculated (i.e., the stone looks as though it had been eaten by a worm—*vermis* in Latin), and ornamented bands were often carried right around the columns so that they seemed to be wearing horizontally striped socks.

''NEO-GREC'' The word "neo-Grec" is placed in quotation marks because the "Grec" has practically nothing to do with ancient Greece and the "neo" has nothing to do with our arbitrary choice of terms to identify the styles of the Eclectic period. It is simply the name given to a certain type of incised ornament and was popular in Paris in the 1870s. The motifs may be Greek, but they are just as likely to be simply geometric doodles of dots, circles, diamonds and squiggles. The designs are cut into smooth flat stone surfaces to a shallow uniform depth and look as though they had been drawn rather than carved. There is very little three-dimensional quality in this work as contrasted to the heavy modeling of the Italianate or the French Second Empire. It has a machine-made look that begins to express the industrial development of the country. Sometimes the designs were reproduced in cast iron to form heavy balustrades and newel posts.

BEAUX-ARTS Most significant of the French imports was the style that took its name from the great school which Napoleon I formed to train the painters, sculptors and architects of France in a joint course of study, the École des Beaux-Arts. One of the strong characteristics of this style is the union of the three arts; nowhere else are sculpture and painting such integral parts of the architectural design. Architectural forms are treated like sculpture, and a piece of sculpture can no more be eliminated from a Beaux-Arts façade than a column can. There is a predilection for paired columns, oval openings and a profusion of garlands and festoons. Other characteristics are its monumentality and the formal, axial organization of the plan and symmetry of elevations and sections. Beaux-Arts buildings are approached along malls and vistas; they are set on balustraded terraces and are surrounded by fountains, flagpoles and flights of stairs. For all their formality, however, these buildings are rarely dull; they are dramatic and exciting.

NEO—ITALIAN RENAISSANCE AND OTHER RENAISSANCE AND POST-RENAISSANCE STYLES Neo-Italian Renaissance was the earliest of the styles of the Eclectic period and one of the most popular. This can be largely attributed to the skill with which the newly formed firm of McKim, Mead & White launched the fashion. Members of the firm established the same close relationship with their clients that the great architects of the Italian Renaissance had had with their princely patrons. In addition to designing their mansions, clubs, churches, colleges and museums, the principals of the firm often scoured Italy for original mantels, doorways and furnishings.

Other architects of the Eclectic period favored other national manifestations of Renaissance and post-Renaissance architecture. They turned, for example, to the Italy of the seventeenth century, where the rather homogeneous character of the earlier Renaissance diverged, on the one hand, toward the Baroque and, on the other, toward the Palladian. Baroque designers thought of architecture as a form of drama; they used the play of light and shade and architectural and sculptural forms to obtain grandiose and vigorous effects. They were particularly conscious of the way a building related to its surroundings, and, though their details differ, they may be thought of as the aesthetic ancestors of the much later Beaux-Arts style. At the time, however, Italian Baroque had a direct influence on the post-Renaissance architecture of Spain, which was characterized by wide expanses of unadorned walls and concentrated spots of sparkling ornaments.

The followers of Palladio, in contrast, were purists. Their work was logical, staid and serene. Their influence was particularly strong in England, where the Palladian style—translated from stone and stucco into red brick with stone trim, reduced in scale and generally "domesticated"—became the main source of the eighteenth-century Georgian style.

In France the Renaissance period is divided into three distinct phases. The earliest, the "Francis I" style, is still so medieval in feeling that we have considered it in the Romantic Tradition. The latest, the Louis XV and Louis XVI (1715–1792), were so distinctive and so widely copied in the Eclectic period that we have considered them below under the special heading of "neo–French Classic." The middle period, Henry IV through Louis XIV (1589–1715) styles, while going through internal changes, is generally characterized by smaller scale than in Italy, by superimposed orders of columns, by steep roofs and dormers, and, above all, by rich decorations and the playful use of rustication which is often carried right around the columns themselves. The few Eclectic examples in New York are identified as "neo–French Renaissance."

German, Flemish and Dutch Renaissance buildings also have steep roofs, often enclosing two or three stories; windows occupy a great portion of the wall surface; dormers and highly decorated gables are prevalent; ornament is profuse and vigorous rather than refined. In Flemish and Dutch buildings stepped gables, ornamented with urns, scrolls and pinnacles are almost a trademark. Flemish and German buildings tended to be built of stone, while in Holland brick was commonly used with stone trim.

N E O - G E O R G I A N A N D N E O - F E D E R A L Slightly later Eclectics turned back for inspiration to styles that had already existed in the United States. The neo-Georgian and the neo-Federal are like their respective prototypes—only more so!

Sometimes, however, architects of neo-Georgian houses also turned directly to England for their details. The results were more elegant than if they had limited themselves to the simpler colonial American prototypes. To a lesser degree there was a certain borrowing of details from Adam and Regency London when designing neo-Federal houses. The original styles had all been contemporaries and quite naturally went well together.

As with the Italian Renaissance Eclectics, specialists in neo-Georgian and neo-Federal design became so fluent in their vocabularies that a few masters created some highly original and remarkably free designs. For the run-of-the-mill architect, however, Eclecticism was simply a convenient crutch—an excuse for slavish copying.

N E O – F R E N C H C L A S S I C As patrons began to tire of Italian and English sources, they took another look at France—not the flamboyant France of the Second Empire, the finicky detail of the "neo-Grec" or the overwhelming monumentality of the Beaux-Arts, but the understated fronts of the Louis XV and Louis XVI houses that made eighteenth-century Paris synonymous with aristocratic restraint. The quite different ideologies of republican, Directoire and Napoleonic France led still further in the direction of spartan simplicity. French architects by the eighteenth and early nineteenth centuries had refined the Classical Tradition to the point of mere suggestion. Columns had been reduced to flat pilasters. Large expanses of perfectly plain stonework were relieved by a slightly raised or recessed panel. Simple moldings were run around the top and the sides of windows; at the bottom, where the French doors came down to the floor, there was a simple balustrade or a wrought-iron guard. Ornament was confined to small delicate accents, a carved garland or a decorated keystone. Mansard roofs were usual, but now generally rose from behind a balustrade.

NEO–AMERICAN CLASSIC   The most widespread style of the Eclectic period in the Classical Tradition is the neo–American Classic that was adopted for the main buildings of the World's Columbian Exposition of 1893 in Chicago. Actually there are a few precursors that go back as far as 1875 which foreshadow the new movement. But it was the work of McKim, Mead & White, Daniel Burnham and Richard Morris Hunt at Chicago that really launched the style. The imposing grandeur of their row upon row of gleaming white columns, the domes and triumphal archways, sculptured pediments, terraces and balustrades, all on a monumental scale, had an aesthetic impact on the general public that no previously attempted style had ever had. And the United States was ready for it. As Henry Adams said of the American who visited the exposition, he "honestly . . . had the air of enjoying it as though it were all his own; he felt good; he was proud of it."

In the next two decades no city worthy of the name failed to build a town hall, a courthouse, a library or a railroad station that was not in some way reminiscent of the Parthenon, the Baths of Caracalla, the Arch of Septimus Severus or the Colosseum itself. In city planning, the 1893 exposition inspired the "City Beautiful" movement—that dream of great avenues and vistas leading to a visual climax.

More sober and restrained than the exuberant Beaux-Arts style, neo–American Classic architecture laid the same emphasis on formal, axial monumentality. It is appropriate that the Classical Tradition in this country should have closed with such a burst of glory. And there are many diehards who do not think it dead but merely dormant.

2 . THE ROMANTIC TRADITION

Unlike the Classical Tradition, the Romantic Tradition had no indigenous roots to link it to America's past. It was an artificial graft that was nourished by literary and philosophical ideas. It includes two important Revivals—Gothic and Romanesque.

GOTHIC REVIVAL The Gothic Revival can be traced back to literary and architectural sources in England: to Sir Horace Walpole and his Strawberry Hill, to William Beckford and his extraordinary concoction Fonthill Abbey, to the novels of Ann Radcliffe and Sir Walter Scott, and to such early how-to-do-it books as Batty Langley's 1747 *Gothic Architecture Improved by Rules and Proportions*. The immediate impetus in this country came from the romantic landscape plans and rural cottages designed by Alexander Jackson Davis. On the philosophical side, the Camden Society in Cambridge, England, decreed almost as dogma that the only appropriate setting for Episcopal worship was the English Gothic parish church. As a writer in the *North American Review* put it in 1836:

> . . . there is a style of architecture which belongs peculiarly to Christianity, and owes its existence even to this religion, whose very ornaments remind one of the joys of a life beyond the grave; whose lofty vaults and arches are crowded with the forms of prophets and martyrs and beautiful spirits, and seem to resound with the choral hymns of angels and archangels . . . these are the characteristics of the architecture of Christianity, the sublime, the glorious Gothic.

In both its domestic and its ecclesiastical applications, the "Gothicizing" meant the use of pointed windows and the application of crenellations, quatrefoil carvings, dormers, gables, crockets, tracery, buttresses and finials to buildings whose plans and structural systems seldom bore significant relation to the medieval buildings from which these forms had been borrowed. In row houses, where there was little room for such fantasies, Gothic details were generally confined to label moldings over the windows, pointed arched panels in the doors and ironwork, and, at times, a row of pointed corbel arches at the cornice line. Also, a heavy vertical muntin often gave the effect of a casement window without sacrificing the practical weather tightness of double-hung sash.

Although most historians date the beginning of the Gothic Revival in the United States in the late 1830s, there were a few much earlier harbingers of what was to come. As in the neo–American Classic style, there is no logical accounting for these early manifestations; they seem to have been born before their time.

ROMANESQUE REVIVAL   The Romanesque Revival began in an even more naïve fashion than the Gothic Revival. It often meant little more than the use of roundheaded openings and a prevalence of brick corbels. Roundheaded corbel arches were run up and down the gable ends of churches. With none of the glamour of Gothic, the Romanesque Revival style soon became relegated to commercial buildings, armories, stables and other utilitarian structures. Here it quietly developed its best inherent quality: the straightforward expression of the strength of heavy masonry bearing walls. The deeply recessed series of concentric, roundheaded arches, the broad and stubby piers, the wide stretches of unbroken wall surface, all were honest and effective as to both structure and style.

The Romantic Tradition flourished from the 1850s to the 1930s. Unhampered by the discipline of the classical orders, architects working in the Romantic Tradition felt free to create new decorative styles on their own. At times these were developed as a synthesis of elements at hand, at others they seem to spring, like Athena, fully armed from the head of Zeus.

VICTORIAN GOTHIC AND THE STICK STYLE   Some historians consider Victorian Gothic to be the most original stylistic creation of the nineteenth century. It is certainly unique to its era (1860–1880) and was, in its day, most extravagantly admired. It was subsequently vehemently denounced. In recent years its vivacity is again finding favor.

In distinction to the Gothic Revival, with its English sources, the inspiration for Victorian Gothic came from Ruskin's *Stones of Venice* (published in 1851) and Viollet-le-Duc's exhaustive studies of the Middle Ages. The style was characterized by a rich mixture of various materials—stone and brick of all sorts, colors and sizes, tile, ironwork, copper and polychrome slate. Forms were broken up as much as possible by gables, pinnacles, arcades, towers, bands, balconies, corbels and chimneys, in addition to a wide variety of portals, windows, bull's-eyes, niches and gargoyles. Wherever a free surface survived, it was at once covered by a textured pattern, preferably in polychrome. The result, if restless and indigestible, has, to us at least, a kind of con-

sistent charm. Victorian Gothic buildings often have a papery quality—as though they had been cut out of cardboard, painted and pasted
together by a group of imaginative children.

As far as New York City is concerned, the Stick style is hardly
more than a curiosity, since its application, roughly contemporary
with Victorian Gothic, was limited to country cottages and wooden
churches. Its main characteristic is the exposure, wherever possible, of
the structural framing system, and, in particular, of the diagonal
bracing members. This was done in the name of structural "truthful-
ness," but also, it is surmised, to obtain the greatest possible interplay
of intersecting triangular forms. No opportunity was lost to pile
dormers and towers on top of projecting gables and porches. Curtains
of jigsaw work, suspended from overhangs, cast rich shadows on the
little that was left of plain surfaces behind them.

QUEEN ANNE The Queen Anne style has as little to do with the
last Stuart monarch to sit on the British throne as "neo-Grec" has to
do with the Aegean Sea. It was the self-conscious creation of Richard
Norman Shaw, an English architect, who was searching for a cozy,
picturesque style that would be varied and inviting for country
houses. He combined Romanesque elements with details taken from
Elizabethan cottages and motifs from the Flemish Renaissance. This
style, which Alan Burnham calls a "potpourri," can be visualized as a
sort of domesticated Victorian Gothic, but without the pointed windows, quatrefoils or other Gothic details. There is, however, the same
restless multiplication of gables, towers, porches and chimneys, the
same mixture of different materials and fondness for pattern and
polychromy.

The style was introduced in the British Pavilion of the 1876
Philadelphia Centennial Exposition and caught on at once. Its adaptation to New York City row houses of the 1880s and 1890s was
particularly successful. Its wildest extravagances were somewhat tamed
by the limitations of having to build between party walls.

ART NOUVEAU AND ARTS DÉCORATIFS Like Queen Anne,
these styles were also self-conscious creations. The roots of the Art
Nouveau style, which flourished just around the turn of the century,
can be traced to the work of Victor Horta in Belgium, William Morris

in England, the Wiener Werkstätter in Vienna, Charles Mackintosh in Edinburgh, Louis Comfort Tiffany in New York, Antoni Gaudi in Barcelona and René Lalique in Paris. It was, as these sources suggest, an international movement in search of a new vocabulary to be applied primarily to furniture and the decorative arts. Its greatest successes were probably in the design of glassware and fabrics and in book and poster layout, but its unmistakable hallmark, a series of wavy lines converging and diverging in fluid flowerlike forms, can still be found in a few surviving examples of architecture.

The so-called Art Deco movement, like Art Nouveau, was also concerned with the decorative arts, but was much more limited in its inspiration and influence. It had an elegant discipline and placed a great emphasis on the refinements of details and finish. It took its name from the Paris Exposition des Arts Décoratifs of 1925, and by the 1930s it had run its course.

N E O - G O T H I C   While England had inspired the Gothic Revival and Venice the Victorian Gothic style, the Eclectic architects turned for their churches principally to thirteenth-century France, where the Gothic style had its fullest flowering. All the essentially Gothic elements—pointed windows, tracery, flying buttresses, compound piers, stilted vaulting, rose windows, etc.—are in the neo-Gothic style applied with a real understanding of their organic interdependence. In fact, a rare creative genius such as Bertram Goodhue learned the language so well that he could say entirely new and unexpected things in it without making a grammatical slip.

Neo-Gothic was also widely applied to the college campuses of the 1920s—the so-called Collegiate Gothic of English inspiration. It was somehow felt that the reproduction of the quadrangles of Oxford would automatically bring their much admired academic traditions with it. Closely related was the English Tudor style which was very popular for residential work. It was in fact the English counterpart of the work that was going on in France during the reign of Francis I.

N E O — F R A N C I S I   This style which we call neo–Francis I was also widely used for residences. It is also known as the early French Renaissance or the Château style.

It was during the reign of the "King of Gentlemen" (1515–1547) that skilled French stoneworkers began to add little Italian Renaissance details onto what were essentially French Gothic structures. The underlying buildings retained their picturesque, asymmetrical masses, their turrets, pinnacles, steep roofs, buttresses and clusters of towering chimneys; only some of the details were borrowed from Italy. The results were altogether charming, with the dreamlike quality of fairy-tale castles.

NEO-ROMANESQUE   Most historians consider what we call neo-Romanesque simply as a late phase of Romanesque Revival. However, we feel that the difference in fundamental approach between the two styles is distinct enough to warrant their consideration in separate categories.

Whereas neo-Gothic Eclecticism started out with a series of scholarly, accurate and rather dry works, with neo-Romanesque the course of events was just the reverse. This was because its earliest proponent, the great Boston architect Henry Hobson Richardson, was such a dominant and prolific genius that neo-Romanesque is frequently called Richardsonian Romanesque. There are, unfortunately no notable buildings of his in New York City, but the work of a number of very talented disciples serves well to illustrate the style.

The thing that first attracted Richardson to Romanesque architecture was the opportunity it afforded for the straightforward expression of structure and of the inherent qualities of different natural materials. Thus, in a building with masonry bearing walls, windows are limited in width by the capacity of their stone lintels to support the wall above them. If wider openings were wanted, the architect would use a series of windows separated by stubby piers, each carrying its own share of the weight. If still wider and higher openings were wanted, he would use great brick or stone archways to spread the load to the flanking bearing walls.

This emphasis on materials and their expressive use gives Richardson his position as one of the fathers of modern architecture. Decoration, if used at all, was applied sparingly and, again, always in a manner appropriate to the materials. Often the richness of a neo-Romanesque structure will depend solely on the relation of solids to voids and on the contrasting textures and colors of different materials. The effect is one of honesty and strength.

In addition to Richardson and his innovative followers there was another aspect to the neo-Romanesque style that might be called the scholarly approach. Architects following this path made a detailed study of Romanesque buildings in Europe. The neo-Romanesque structures they designed in New York show the same sort of deep understanding of the forms and details they selected as is seen in the best of the neo-Gothic buildings.

EXOTIC STYLES   In what sometimes seems like a frenzied search for novelty, there was almost nothing that architects in the closing years of the Eclectic period did not attempt. Among New York City Landmarks and in our Historic Districts, we run into such unexpected styles as Byzantine, Russian, Moorish and even East Indian.

Byzantine is characterized by polychromy and richly decorated but rather flat surfaces. The use of saucerlike domes, often set on low cylindrical drums, is universal in the case of churches. Arcades are common. They may be structural elements or merely decorative details.

The characteristic Russian church design spread northward from Byzantium and developed its own unmistakable onion-shaped dome. Often these domes are used in clusters: a large one over the center of a Greek-cross plan, and smaller ones over the four equal-length arms. The domes, frequently gilded, form a dramatic contrast to the usually rather simple walls beneath them.

Moorish can be considered as another offshoot of the Byzantine. Here, while the use of domes persisted—sometimes saucerlike and sometimes acorn-shaped—it was the decoration of a building's surface that was the architect's principal preoccupation. Every inch was covered with mosaic, tile or carving in low relief. The decoration was small in scale and was kept flat, so the planes of the underlying structure were not lost; they just seem to be covered with richly embroidered textiles.

With East Indian architecture the carving that covers every inch of a building's surface is carried out in deep relief. As a result, the underlying forms often seem to melt into one another, like a soap sculpture that has been left standing in water too long.

3. NONSTYLISTIC TRADITION

Simultaneous with the various styles which successively convulsed both the Classical and the Romantic Traditions, there has run a Nonstylistic Tradition through three centuries of building in New York City. In its quiet way this has often had as much to say about the way in which people lived and worked as its flashier contemporaries.

VERNACULAR   The one continuous thread in the Nonstylistic Tradition is what is widely referred to as "vernacular" architecture. The term has been borrowed from a term meaning, according to *Webster's New International Dictionary,* "the common mode of expression in a particular locality . . . the native as contrasted with the literary language of a place." It is an appropriate term to describe the work of builders who never thought of themselves as creating "architecture."

Examples of vernacular buildings that have come down to us from the seventeenth and eighteenth centuries are the farmhouses that once dotted a countryside which in 1679 was described as follows:

> Impossible to tell how many peach trees we passed, all laden with fruit to breaking down. . . . We came to a place surrounded with such trees from which so many had fallen off that the ground could not be discerned, and you could not put your foot down without trampling them; and, notwithstanding such large quantities had fallen off, the trees still were as full as they could bear. The hogs and other animals mostly feed on them. . . . We tasted here, for the first time, twaelft [striped bass]. . . . It was salted a little and then smoked, and, although it was now a year old, it was still perfectly good, and in flavor not inferior to smoked salmon. We drank here also, the first new cider, which was very fine.

While the peach trees have long since gone, there still can be found, in the Flatlands section of Brooklyn, in the Bronx, in Flushing and on Staten Island, a few of the houses of the men who planted the trees and caught the bass.

The so-called Dutch Colonial farmhouses are generally one and a half stories high and are readily identified by overshot roofs. Sometimes the projecting eaves are supported by an additional curved timber fastened to the roof rafter. When the projection extended too far, a row of supporting posts was added to form a veranda. This was particularly true of later examples. In either case the projecting eaves protected the door and windows from driving rain and snow. The roof characteristically ended in a gentle outward curve like a skijump. This attractive feature is unique to the style. Originally the Dutch used the garret only for storage, but in the eighteenth century they adapted a gambrel roof in order to get more headroom in what amounted to a second story.

Actually there appear to be no direct prototypes in Holland for these curved projecting eaves which we think of as so characteristically "Dutch." According to the best authorities, this is a form indigenous to New York City, Long Island, the lower Hudson Valley, northern New Jersey, and, oddly enough, Quebec. Its ancestry is cloudy and perhaps includes as many English, Flemish and French forebears as Dutch. In fact, this type of farmhouse did not reach its peak popularity until about 1800. With this word of warning, we shall continue to call this type of architecture "Dutch Colonial" only because of its close association with so many of the early Dutch settlers.

The typical farmhouses built by English settlers were more likely to consist of two stories and to have straight sloped gable-ended roofs with no projecting eaves. If there is a porch it was added as a separate structure. The more imposing survivors, the manor houses, were built of rubble fieldstone and reflect, in a simplified way, their Georgian models.

The same sort of simplified imitation of whatever style was currently in vogue can be traced right through the nineteenth century. There are unsophisticated imitations of Greek and Gothic Revival buildings and even of such elaborate fashions as the French Second Empire style. The nineteenth-century vernacular was, moreover, not limited to farmhouses or country estates. The vast majority of buildings, at least until the second half of the nineteenth century, were constructed without benefit of architect.

Whether or not a particular building is considered "stylistic" or "vernacular" is a matter of degree. A discriminating client and an experienced builder could produce adequate examples of the currently fashionable style. In less sophisticated hands, and particularly when masonry forms were copied in wood, the results could be quite naïve. It is these examples, which also often mix elements from several styles, that we describe as "vernacular."

A final guideline is the matter of date, whenever that can be independently established. Vernacular buildings of the nineteenth century, as might be expected, tend to lag about a dozen years after the style they are trying to imitate reached its peak of popularity in the center of the city.

ENGINEERING A second category of structures in the Nonstylistic Tradition includes those Landmarks which are primarily significant either for their method of construction or for their utility. They comprise some great accomplishments in the field of engineering, such as the suspension-bridge principle or the structural possibilities of cast iron. The many advances in nineteenth-century engineering and technology—in prefabricated columns and panels, in rolled sections, in reinforced concrete, in safe elevators, etc.—made the development of twentieth-century architecture possible. Sometimes these achievements go unnoticed because they are hidden by "stylistic" façades, but occasionally their expression is given naked display. In either case the achievements of civil and structural engineers have been recognized among New York City Landmarks.

The same recognition has been given to the military engineers who designed the successive pairs of forts that have guarded the waterway entrances to New York City. These structures, built solely of necessity and designed solely for utility, often have a scale, simplicity and power that give them dramatic aesthetic qualities. It is for these, as well as for their historic importance, that a number of the city's nineteenth-century forts have been designated as Landmarks.

MISCELLANEOUS Finally, the Nonstylistic category includes miscellaneous objects which defy classification. Cemeteries, trees, fences, gates, monuments are examples of the sort of thing that can have important historic and aesthetic qualities and should be preserved as part of the city's cultural heritage.

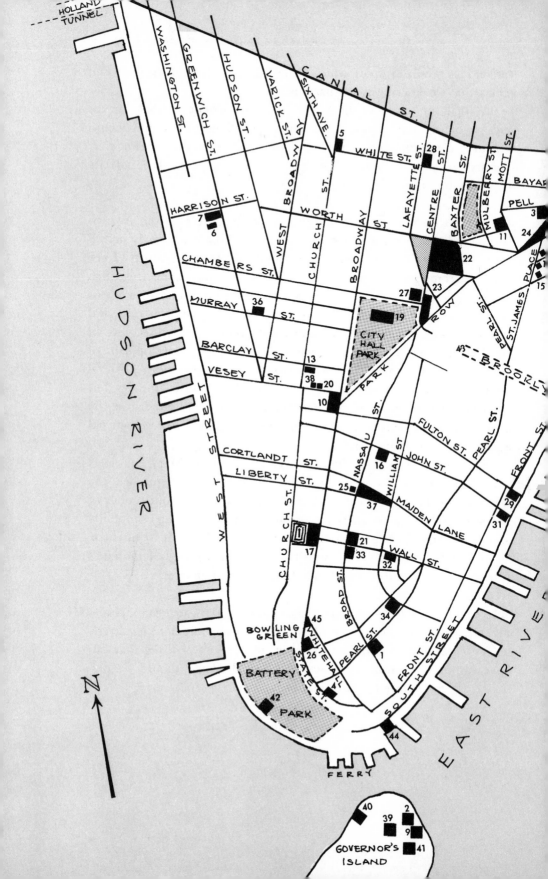

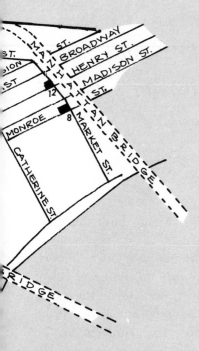

MANHATTAN

*From the Battery
to Canal Street
and Governor's Island*

CHAPTER TWO

MANHATTAN

From the Battery to Canal Street and Governor's Island

THE BATTERY: this is where it all began, both the geography and the history of New York City.

Giovanni da Verrazzano, an Italian in the employ of the French government, was the first white man to lay eyes on the lower tip of Manhattan, shortly after he had sailed up the Lower Bay in the spring of 1524. With some members of his crew he took to his boats and made his way through the Narrows into the Upper Bay. He went up the "very great river" and encountered a group of Indians "clothed with the feathers of birds of various colours" who welcomed the newcomers, "joyfully uttering very great exclamations of admiration."

A sudden storm, however, discouraged the explorers, who scurried for the safety of the mother ship, much to the dismay of the friendly Indians who were waiting on the island of Manhattan to welcome these strange adventurers.

Verrazzano staked France's claim to the rich new lands, and Francis I named the entire North American territory New France, although he never followed up his claim.

The next visitor from the Old World was Esteban Gomes, a Portuguese in the employ of the Spanish king. He arrived in New York Harbor early in 1525, a few months after Verrazzano. This time there were no curious Indians, friendly or otherwise, for their custom was to desert the cold, windy island during the winter months, using it mainly as a campsite during the hunting and fishing seasons.

There are old maps in existence indicating that various other explorers skirted in and around what was destined to become one of the greatest harbors in the world. But none left a significant mark until Henry Hudson, this time an English navigator in the employ of the Dutch East India Company, came along in his eighty-ton ship, the *Half Moon*. For some unexplained reason most of the early colonial powers employed foreign nationals to do their exploring.

Hudson is truly New York's own, since his influence lasted longer than that of his predecessors. One of the great glories of the city, the river that sweeps along its western boundary, is named after him. His explorations led to the first settlement of this part of the New World by the Dutch.

On September 2, 1609, Hudson anchored his little vessel in the Lower Bay. He was awed by the tremendous stream that rushed into the Upper Bay, which the ship's mate, Robert Juet, called a "great lake of water."

The Indians were as welcoming to Hudson as they had been to Verrazzano, for Juet reported that the inhabitants, wearing elk skins, "made strange gambols with dancing and singing." Hudson, following his mission from the Dutch East India Company, actually felt he was on the track of a new northwest passage to the East. He confidently headed the *Half Moon* upstream, exploring the gracious countryside and trading with the hospitable Indians. It was not until he was in the vicinity of Albany that Hudson reluctantly concluded that the mighty body of water was really a river, not a strait leading to the other side of the world.

The next year he sailed, this time for England, to the great bay in Canada that was eventually to bear his name. After wintering in James Bay, a mutinous crew deserted Hudson and some of his men, leaving them on the lonely shore. The abandoned navigator was never heard of again.

Fifteen years after Hudson's trip the first white settlers came to Manhattan. They set up their rude shelters probably on the site that the United States Custom House occupies on Broadway. From that moment in 1624 until today, when New York has grown to be the nation's largest and most predominant city, all true New Yorkers can exult with Walt Whitman when he wrote:

Walt Whitman am I, a Kosmos, of mighty Manhattan the son.

Mansions and Row Houses

It would be nice if, in this lower part of Manhattan, where it all began, we could still trace the city's early history through a series of private houses which might have been designated Landmarks. Unfortunately, this is not possible. Nothing at all is left from the Dutch period except a few fragments of old foundations.

Some aspects of early Dutch architecture have survived, however, in our own brownstones. The high front stoop (derived from the Dutch *stoep*) was a necessity in Holland, where a leak in one of the country's dikes could send water swirling around the burghers' houses. For this reason they raised their first floors well above ground level, which was actually below sea level. Although the sea was not the same threat in the New World, old habits were hard to change.

It is somewhat of a miracle that there is anything at all in the way of residential architecture still surviving in lower Manhattan, where the value of land is without doubt the highest in the world. Even in the early days the amount of usable land was severely limited—so limited that the ingenious colonists early started retrieving land by filling in the East River. Pearl Street, which really was Mother-of-Pearl Street because of the iridescent shells that covered the ground, marks the original waterfront. In the late 1600s the shore line was extended eastward and Water Street was created. In the mid-1780s it moved to Front Street and by 1800 to South Street, where it has remained. And currently serious plans are being developed to extend the shore line still farther into the river to make room for a proposed new waterfront development. Incidentally, some historians attribute the winding nature of Pearl Street to the fact that originally it curved around the foot of a hill which has long since been leveled.

To make maximum use of the scarce land, New Yorkers early introduced row houses in place of freestanding houses, which took up more room. The row house, which was destined to become a trademark of New York City, was not universally acclaimed. Mrs. Frances Trollope, in her book *Domestic Manners of the Americans,* published in 1832, was quite outspoken: "The great defect of the houses [of New York] is their uniformity—when you have seen one you have seen all." Nearly a century later, Edith Wharton, the aristocratic novelist of New York City, complained of the "intolerable ugliness of

New York, of its untouched streets and the narrow houses so lacking in external dignity, so crammed with smug and suffocating upholstery."

But, as we shall see in future chapters of this book, the eminently practical row house can rise to great architectural distinction.

Only two examples of an eighteenth-century private mansion survive in this lower part of the city, one a reconstruction on Pearl Street and the other an elegant small country house on Governor's Island.

Fraunces Tavern, at the corner of Pearl and Broad Streets, one of the most popular of New York City Landmarks, is actually a reconstruction of a building that was originally erected in the early eighteenth century. The Sons of the Revolution of the State of New York, who bought the property in 1904, did the reconstruction and maintained it. The original building was designed as a home for the merchant Stephen De Lancey, in 1719. The De Lanceys became probably the most powerful family in colonial New York, but later, as Loyalists, they were to lose their extensive real-estate holdings through confiscation; today only shabby Delancey Street, on the Lower East Side, remains to commemorate them.

In 1763 the De Lancey house became the Queen's Head Tavern, with Samuel Fraunces, a well-known West Indian innkeeper, as proprietor. He was later to become George Washington's chief steward. The tavern was popular and the scene of many significant events in the city's history. In 1768 what is now the New York State Chamber of Commerce was founded at a meeting held in the tavern, and in 1783 George Washington bade an emotional farewell to his officers at a banquet in the Long Room on the second floor. A contemporary account describes Washington's departure from the city:

> Genl Washington passed through the Corps of Light Infantry and walked to the White Hall, where a barge awaited to convey him to Paulus' Hook. The whole Company followed in mute and solemn procession, with dejected countenances, testifying to feelings of delicious melanc[h]oly which no language can describe. Having entered the barge, he turned to the Co., and waving his hat, bid them a silent adieu. They paid him the same affectionate compliment, and after the barge had left them, returned in the same solemn manner to the place where they had assembled.

Washington was just fifty-one years old and looked forward to a life of relaxed retirement at his pleasant estate, Mount Vernon on the Potomac. But just six years later he stood taking the oath of office as first President of the United States at the site of what is now the Federal Hall National Memorial, only five blocks away from the scene of his farewell dinner.

Taverns and other convivial drinking spots had been prevalent since New York's early days. In New Amsterdam, capital of the Dutch colony of New Netherland, life was hard and a man needed something to take his mind off his troubles. Peter Stuyvesant, the hot-tempered but puritanical director general of the colony, frequently lashed out at the purveyors of beer and spirits, complaining that they were contributing to the corruption of "the Common people and the [Dutch West India] Company's servants . . . still worse, the Youth." He even went so far as to order that no "new Alehouses, Taverns, or Tippling Places" could be inaugurated without the approval of the director general. But, like Prohibition nearly three centuries later, his moralizing made little impression on the thirsty and convivial New Yorker.

The west wall of Fraunces Tavern still contains some original Holland brick, and the rubblestone walls of the cellar could easily date back 250 years. The tall chimneys, the shed-roofed dormers, the balustrade crowning the hipped roof, and the ornamented entablature are all characteristic of the Georgian style. Houses of great formal dignity such as this were built in both England and the British colonies throughout the reigns of George I (1714–1727) and George II (1727–1760) and well into the reign of George III (1760–1820).

To see an original and much less pretentious example of the style, one has to take the ferry across the narrow part of the Upper Bay to Governor's Island. Here is an austere red brick house in the form of a Greek cross, said to have been built in the eighteenth century as a home for the British governors and known by the mellifluous appellation of "the Smiling Gardens of the Sovereigns of the Province." Though the Governor's House lacks the rich elegance of De Lancey's mansion, the same formal dignity, the Flemish bond of the brickwork, the hipped roof and the strongly vertical proportions of the windows place it in the same period and tradition. The pediment crowning the central wing and running back into the main roof is also typically Georgian.

1. *Fraunces Tavern*
   (former Stephen De Lancey House)
   54 Pearl Street, at Broad Street
   1719
   Reconstruction: 1907, William H. Mersereau

2. *Governor's House*
   Governor's Island
   Early 18th century

The Governor's House is one of the earliest buildings on the island. During the War of 1812 it served as a guardhouse and contained an infamous "Black Hole," a basement cell for solitary confinement. Legend has it that during the Revolution, when New York was held by the British, a secret tunnel large enough for a coach and four was built to connect the house with a private dock where a barge was anchored. This was to provide an escape hatch for the governor in case the rebellious Americans landed on the island.

One of the city's most interesting town houses is also the oldest row house that has survived on Manhattan. It dates from about 1785, shortly after the British evacuated New York City but before Washington was inaugurated as the first President. It formed the end of a row at the corner of Pell Street and the Bowery, on the edge of what is today's Chinatown. It was built by Edward Mooney, a well-to-do merchant and an important figure in the wholesale meat business. It still contains its original hand-hewn timbers, and the windows in the gable end on Pell Street are particularly interesting for their quarter-round shape and for the interlacing muntins that have survived in the roundheaded central windows. These features are characteristic of the incoming Federal style, whereas the splayed lintels and splayed double keystones at the heads of the other windows are typically Georgian.

The house is in a remarkable state of preservation and fortunately has been authentically restored by the present owner. It houses, among other tenants, an off-track betting parlor. The Off-Track Betting Corporation was doubly pleased with its choice of quarters when research dug up the fact that Mooney had been a breeder of racehorses. There are two bronze plaques on this house—the regular one in English and the other bearing the legend in Chinese.

The James Watson House at 7 State Street, the last to remain of an elegant row that once faced the Battery, is now part of the Roman Catholic Shrine of the Blessed Elizabeth Seton. The easterly, and oldest, portion of the house, two windows wide, was built in 1793 and is Georgian in feeling except for the typically Federal detail of two

3. (*Left*) *Edward Mooney House   18 Bowery, at Pell Street*
Between 1785 and 1789
Pell Street extension: 1807   Restoration: 1970–71

4. (*Right*) *James Watson House*
(now Rectory, Shrine of the Blessed Elizabeth Seton)   7 State Street
East portion: 1793   West portion: 1806, attributed to John McComb, Jr.
Restoration: 1965, Shanley & Sturges

marble plaques inserted in the brickwork over the second-story windows. The house is more famous, however, for the Federal wing of 1806 with its curved porch attributed to John McComb, Jr., its delicate Ionic columns and the graceful oval windows in the west wall. The attenuation of the columns, always characteristic of the Federal style, is particularly exaggerated here because they were actually made from ships' masts.

The Watson House and its neighbors were gentlemen's homes and show how, even when pressed shoulder to shoulder in rows, such houses could retain an air of elegance and individuality. Even today, surrounded by the sheer glass walls of modern office buildings, the Watson House more than holds its own. It gains by its very anachronism.

State Street was once one of the city's most fashionable streets and remained so until the beginning of the nineteenth century, when the merchant princes began moving uptown. These prosperous gentlemen were at one time known as "Peep-o'-Day Boys" because they got up at dawn to stare across the harbor at Staten Island, where signals were set to indicate the arrival of their ships as they were sighted in the Narrows.

Although Pearl Street is one of the city's oldest streets, State Street has contributed its share of glory to the town, beginning with the residence of Peter Stuyvesant, the second director general sent out by the Dutch government to run the struggling little colony. He early tired of living within the fort which was the first structure erected on the tip of the island. Stuyvesant first moved to a house at what is now the corner of State and Whitehall Streets, and shortly afterward he bought his "Bouwerie," or farm, a fairly large acreage out in the country. Although his town house has vanished, we shall see later what both Peter and his farm have contributed to modern New York.

More modest than the Watson House, and, for that reason, more extraordinary in its survival, is the tiny house at 2 White Street. Although it was completed in 1809, it really is more eighteenth-century in style and character than nineteenth-century. The gambrel roof, splayed lintels and double keystones of the second story are Georgian. The very flat pedimented dormers containing elliptical-headed openings are rare Federal survivals. There was probably always a shop on the ground floor, with the owner living above.

The same sort of Federal dormers are found at 37, 39 and 41 Harrison Street, although in these houses, dating from 1828, the second-story lintels with their incised panels are now also typically Federal in feeling. These three houses belong to a group of nine, at the corner of Washington and Harrison Streets, that are being restored as part of the Washington Market Urban Renewal. Six of the houses survive in their original locations, although much altered on the ground floor. Three others have been moved from nearby. The earliest of the group dates from 1796. Two were designed by John McComb, Jr., New York's first native-born architect. He himself lived in one of them for many years. Although originally built as homes for people of considerable means, these houses present very discreet and unostentatious exteriors. As the city grew and Washington Market moved northward, the houses became engulfed in a busy commercial environment. When they are restored for use as maisonette apartments, they will provide a delightful contrast to the towering new apartment buildings now under construction around them.

In his report urging the preservation of these buildings, Michael W. Gold, director of preservation for the Landmarks Preservation Commission, reveals with commendable frankness one of the philosophical tenets which guide the Commission:

> We are at pains to avoid being discredited by excessive use of superlatives, especially of the word "unique." It happens that this group of houses really is unique, and in the most important possible way; but let us say first what is not unique. The houses are not the oldest in the City, though they are among the oldest; they are not the best, though they are quite good; they are not in the best state of preservation, though among them are features which are not preserved anywhere else.
>
> What does make them unique is this: in aggregate they look strikingly unlike anything else in the City—more than any other bit of cityscape this group is redolent of an earlier time and a different way of life—and this is apparent not just to the trained observer, but to any layman however unsophisticated.
>
> Why this is so is less interesting than the fact that it is so, and not easily explained, but since this is a "technical report" we will try to account for it.
>
> In the first place they are two and a half stories high, and not the usual three or four. Almost all houses of this period were built to two and a half stories; however, all but a few were subsequently expanded either by adding a story to the top or by

5. *No. 2 White Street*
   1809

7. *Jonas Wood House during removal*
   25 Harrison Street
   (formerly at 314 Washington Street)
   c. 1804
   Restored: 1973, Oppenheimer, Brady
     and Associates

6. *Nos. 37, 39, 41 Harrison Street, before restoration*
   (formerly 329, 331, and 337 Washington Street)
   1828
   Restored: 1973, Oppenheimer, Brady and Associates

jacking the building up and adding a story to the bottom. These six survived probably because it was only the ground floor which was intensively used. The low height and general smallness of scale, especially in buildings which are nonetheless substantial, is quite unfamiliar in New York, much more unfamiliar in Manhattan.

In the second place they retain their original roof lines. This means that they all have gabled roofs and unaltered dormers. These too are so rare in New York as immediately to distinguish any building that retains them.

In the third place there are six of them (and if the other three are moved, nine). Two-and-a-half-story Federal houses complete with their gable roofs and unaltered dormers are rare enough in New York. A group of six, not to mention nine, is absolutely unique. Thus the fact that there are six (or nine) greatly strengthens the first two points. But it is not merely a matter of numbers. The important thing is that the preservation of an isolated Federal house, however valuable, or even several houses together, may be insufficient to accomplish our real task. Historic preservation, to be meaningful, must assure the survival of some buildings which are really expressive of values which once were common but now are not. Such an expression may very well be at variance with the preponderant contemporary values. A preserved building therefore is in very unequal competition with its environment. This is not always the case, but it is the case with our few remaining Federal-style houses. They all happen to be located in just that part of the City which is most uncongenial to them. They must, therefore, make an especially strong statement. This group of six houses on Washington and Harrison Streets, if restored, will be the strongest statement of Federal times in the City.

Not all New Yorkers, however, lived as simply as did the original owners of these buildings. While it is still restrained in its outward show, the detail and the doorway of the house at 51 Market Street are exceptionally fine examples of late Federal architecture, displaying an atmosphere of far greater prosperity. The doorway, crowned by a molded elliptical arch, is particularly characteristic, as are the attenuated fluted columns that flank it and the eight-panel door with leaded-glass sidelights and fanlight above. The simple iron railing of wrought iron, instead of the later cast iron, is another indication of the Federal style.

Fashions in architecture, like fashions in clothes, always seem to start at the center of things. As we move away from the center we find people are generally more conservative; they tend to hang on to last year's models. We will see this trend as the city spreads across the East River to Brooklyn and Queens, across the bay to Staten Island and across the Harlem River to the Bronx. The other four boroughs are often ten or more years behind Manhattan in picking up the latest architectural fashions.

This phenomenon is quite clearly illustrated by the Admiral's House on Governor's Island, not completed until 1840 but still very much in the then passé Federal style. The tall, slender columns of the portico closely recall the porch attributed to John McComb, Jr., at 7 State Street and built a generation earlier. The lunette window in the flat pedimented gable is still strictly Federal in its feeling. Note, however, that the crowning balustrade which topped the roof of the Georgian Fraunces Tavern has now been dropped to the lowest level of the roof—a Federal detail we will meet again.

Although the structure is called the Admiral's House in view of its present use by the Eastern-area commander of the Coast Guard, it was known for over 150 years as the Commanding General's Headquarters

8. *No. 51 Market Street*
1824–25

9. *Admiral's House   (originally Commanding General's Headquarters)*
Governor's Island
1840

and served as the home for such illustrious Army generals as Winfield
Scott, Leonard Wood, John J. Pershing, Hugh A. Drum, Omar N.
Bradley and Walter Bedell Smith.

Churches and Graveyards

Lower Manhattan is fortunate in having good surviving examples of
the major early ecclesiastical styles of architecture. Much the oldest,
and in many ways the most important, is St. Paul's Chapel on Broadway between Fulton and Vesey Streets. This was begun in 1764 by an
architect named Thomas McBean, who had been a student of James
Gibbs of London. The church strongly reflects Gibbs's masterpiece,
the Church of St. Martin's-in-the-Fields. It is built of locally cut stones
hardly larger than cobblestones.

During the construction of the chapel many people worried.
There were already some twenty churches in the city, and St. Paul's
was awfully far out of town! But they were pleased with the gracious
site. The front entrance, at the west, commanded a magnificent view
across the Hudson River, and the church backed on the Broad Way.

But within a few years the town had caught up with St. Paul's, and the growth of business and traffic finally forced the construction of a portico and entrance at the east, or Broadway, end of the church. Today most people enter the church through what was once the back door.

At the end of the century, in 1794, James Crommelin Lawrence added the handsome clock tower and spire at the west end of the church, again modeling it closely on St. Martin's-in-the-Fields.

The building as a whole is certainly one of the most distinguished Georgian edifices remaining in New York—distinguished not only for its architecture but particularly for its association with George Washington. Old Trinity Church on Broadway at the head of Wall Street had been destroyed in the fire of 1776, and so St. Paul's, the only other Episcopal church of prominence in the city, was used for the religious service following Washington's inauguration in 1789. Washington continued to worship in St. Paul's until the capital of the United States was moved to Philadelphia. The pew that the first President used is still preserved off the north aisle.

10. St. Paul's Chapel in 1821
   Broadway between Fulton
   and Vesey Streets
   1764–66, Thomas McBean
   Tower: 1794,
   James Crommelin Lawrence

Broadway is one of the city's historic thoroughfares. It started out as an Indian trail that led from the Battery to what is now City Hall Park. It was in 1789, while walking back and forth in front of President George Washington's Broadway home, that Thomas Jefferson and Alexander Hamilton made a deal whereby the young nation's permanent capital was to be located in the South, not in Harlem Heights, Brooklyn or Westchester County, all of which had been suggested.

In the earliest days people had their homes and churches as well as their businesses on lower Broadway. Some of the mansions on Broadway and the adjoining streets, like Wall Street, were of wondrous magnificence, with great Palladian windows, pillars and impressive entrances. Their interiors, kept gleaming by a liberal supply of servants, were equally opulent.

Even the vitriolic Mrs. Trollope was constrained to say: "I must . . . declare that I think New-York one of the finest cities I ever saw, and as much superior to every other in the Union (Philadelphia not excepted) as London to Liverpool, or Paris to Rouen. . . . Situated on an island, which I think it will one day cover, it rises, like Venice from the sea, . . ."

As the city began its march northward, private homes slowly gave way to commercial structures. A writer in the 1870s found Broadway "but little improved above Thirty-fourth Street, though it is believed the next few years will witness important changes in this quarter." He was right.

Broadway has in many ways responded to the heartbeat of the city through its glamour, through its tawdriness, through its poverty, through its affluence. For almost 350 years it has welcomed masses of people, sometimes joyous, sometimes sad, sometimes to honor living heroes, sometimes to mourn dead ones.

In the lower part of Manhattan are two unpretentious little churches that are quite similar although built almost a generation apart—the present Roman Catholic Church of the Transfiguration, at 25 Mott Street, and the Sea and Land Church at Henry and Market Streets. The former was built in 1801 and the latter in 1817. Both are built of the same rubble masonry as St. Paul's Chapel, but are far less sophisticated in their detailing. Both are in the Georgian tradition, as seen in the steeply pitched end gables. The rich entablature and the quoins are also typical Georgian details. Decidedly not Georgian and

11. *(Left) Church of the Transfiguration (R.C.)*
(Originally Lutheran Zion Church)   25 Mott Street, at Park Street
1801

12. *(Right) Sea and Land Church   61 Henry Street, at Market Street*
1817

very unexpected in the early 1800s are the pointed window heads. Since both buildings predate the Gothic Revival in the United States by a full generation, this detail may well be a sentimental recollection of the little Gothic parish churches that the builders doubtless remembered from their villages in England. Possibly they felt that any building intended for worship had to have pointed windows.

The Sea and Land Church, which is today the First Chinese Presbyterian Church, received its name in 1866 when it made a special effort to be of service to seamen. The Church of the Transfiguration is interesting as having been built by English Lutherans, though later used by other denominations. Today, located in the heart of Chinatown, the church serves a Roman Catholic parish.

The evolution of Mott and Pell Streets as the heart of Chinatown came long after the church was built. Not until the 1890s did China-town become the much publicized center of brothels, gambling houses, opium dens and tong warfare. In later years it developed into a rather staid community of middle-class shopkeepers and families, but today it is beginning to experience some of the anguish that affects other parts of the city—overcrowding, rebellious youth, frustrated taxpayers.

The next three churches stand in marked contrast. They date from the mid-1830s to the early 1840s and are beautiful examples of the Greek Revival style with all its elegance and restraint. They also illus-trate a marked technical advance over the earlier churches: finely dressed and carved ashlar has replaced rubble masonry. St. Peter's Roman Catholic Church at 22 Barclay Street is particularly note-worthy; it is built of granite, a very hard stone to work. The other two, Mariners' Temple at 12 Oliver Street and St. James' Roman Catholic Church at 32 James Street, are early examples of the use of the Connecticut brownstone that was soon to become the most popu-lar building material in mid-nineteenth-century New York. This form of sandstone was cheap and easy to cut and carve. Unfortunately, it did not weather well in the New York climate. The combination of heavy rains and wide annual fluctuations in temperature caused the surface to flake and the crisply cut details to crumble.

The Greek Revival style is just what its name implies—a revival in

the United States of the Greek colonnaded temple. St. Peter's, with its impressive six-column Ionic portico and low pediment, replaced the first Roman Catholic church in New York, which had been built in 1786.

Mariners' Temple, by Minard Lafever, built in 1842, and St. James' Church, attributed to Lafever and started in 1835, are very close to each other in style, though the former uses an Ionic order and the latter a Doric. In these two churches the front walls were brought forward at either side to line up with a central pair of columns. These flanking extensions were used to contain stairs to the gallery. The recessed entrance loggia emphasized the actual church entrance much more strongly than the six-column portico of St. Peter's had done.

The history of Mariners' Temple provides an interesting vignette of the city's development. Originally organized by Baptists in 1843 to serve seamen when their ships were in port, it moved from Cherry Street into its present building in 1863. During the period of heavy European immigration the Temple threw open its doors to immigrants of all faiths. Among the congregations that were organized within its walls were the First Swedish Church, the First Italian Church, the First Latvian Church, the Norwegian-Danish Mission, the First Russian Church and the First Chinese Church. After the turn of the century, until World War II, its main concern was work with homeless men living in the shabby hotels and rooming houses along

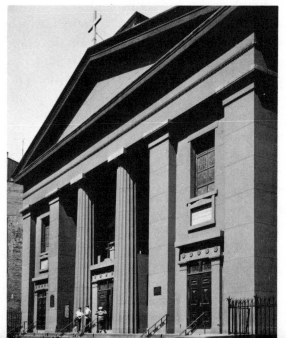

13. *(Left) St. Peter's Church (R.C.)*
22 Barclay Street,
at Church Street
1836–40, John R. Haggerty and
Thomas Thomas

14. *(Center) Mariners' Temple*
12 Oliver Street
1842, Minard Lafever

15. *(Right) St. James' Church (R.C.)*
32 James Street
1835–37, attributed to
Minard Lafever

the Bowery. Today urban renewal and redevelopment have brought in new low- and middle-income neighbors, largely black and Spanish-speaking.

The John Street United Methodist Church, at 44 John Street, though almost contemporary with these Greek Revival churches, is illustrative of what was then the new and was ultimately to become the very fashionable Italianate style. As in their Renaissance proto-types, windows are now crowned by semicircular arches. The Palladian motif—a roundheaded window flanked by two narrow square-headed ones—is a north-Italian detail that reached America after a long period of popularity in England.

The John Street Methodist Church, built in 1841, has survived, almost untouched, in the heart of the financial district. The present building is the third Methodist church erected on the same site and is also notable for its historic connection with two of the founding members of the sect in America, Philip Embury and Barbara Heck. One of its earliest sextons, Peter Williams, a former slave whom the congregation had bought for forty-seven pounds sterling, later went into the tobacco business, made a fortune and established the city's first Methodist church for blacks.

We now come to what is probably the city's most famous church and certainly the most dramatically situated—Trinity Church. The present structure is the third Episcopal church on this historic site on Broadway at the head of Wall Street. It was completed in 1846 from Richard Upjohn's design in the Gothic Revival style.

The inspiration for Upjohn's design has been traced to a drawing by the English architect A. W. Pugin for an imaginary church, which he published in 1841 in his *True Principles of Pointed or Christian Architecture,* though with the omission of Pugin's chancel. This was probably considered too popish for a Protestant Episcopal parish. The details are based on late English Gothic, or "Perpendicular," proto-types, though with little understanding of their original organic sig-nificance. The row of buttresses that flank the nave would, in a real Gothic church, have been needed to balance the lateral thrust of the stone roof vaults. In Trinity they are merely a decoration, since the "vaults" are made of plaster and are hung, like an ordinary plaster ceiling, from wooden roof trusses concealed above them. Yet the over-all result, though it may strike us as somewhat tight and dry, im-pressed contemporaries. Arthur D. Gilman, writing in 1844, said,

16. *John Street Methodist Church*
44 John Street
1841

17. *Trinity Church*
Broadway at Wall Street
1846, Richard Upjohn
Churchyard: 1681–

". . . in size, in the delicacy and propriety of its decoration, and in the beauty of its general effect, we are inclined to think that it surpasses any church erected in England since the revival of the pointed style." Even today, its beautiful spire holds its own among the soaring skyscrapers of the financial district.

In its historic churchyard lie buried, among others, Alexander Hamilton, Albert Gallatin and Robert Fulton. Fulton was a successful portrait painter as well as an inventor; the bas-relief on his monument is based on a self-portrait. A weathered brown slab marks the grave of Charlotte Temple, whose legendary and unhappy love affair was dramatized in 1801 in a two-volume novel, *The History of Charlotte Temple, Founded on Fact*. A British officer seduced her from her boarding school and then deserted her. Her desperate father finally found her in a garret where she and her baby were quietly starving to death. They were buried in Trinity Churchyard, and a few years later her remorseful lover put the brownstone marker on the grave.

Trinity Churchyard, covering two and a quarter acres, is a favorite lunchtime haunt for the office workers of the district, particularly in the spring. The flowering magnolias, the tulips and all the fourteen varieties of exotic trees and shrubs attract not only weary New Yorkers but also other birds. It is not at all uncommon to see a sedate attorney take binoculars from his briefcase to search the trees for arrivals from the South. One alert reporter for *The New York Times* recently recorded having seen two warblers, a black-throated blue and a vesper sparrow, early one morning.

Most notable architectural feature of the churchyard is the Martyrs' Monument, which was "erected by the Vestry to fulfill a public desire expressed in a meeting of citizens in 1852 to honor the memory of 'heroic men who sacrificed their lives in achieving the independence of the United States, many of whom died whilst in captivity in the old Sugar House [on Liberty Street] and are interred in Trinity Churchyard.' "

A modern and discordant note has recently appeared in this green refuge—drugs. Several arrests of people for allegedly selling drugs in the churchyard have led Trinity authorities to install, reluctantly, a three-foot-square blue-and-white sign: YOUR ATTENTION IS CALLED TO STATE AND FEDERAL LAWS PROHIBITING THE USE OR DISTRIBUTION OF DRUGS OR NARCOTICS.

The first Trinity Church was completed in 1697, paid for by taxation of all citizens regardless of religion, since the Church of England was considered the established religion of the colony. In addition, many people of means, including Jews and even Captain Kidd (the notorious pirate), made contributions to the construction fund. The church was given the privilege of taking over all unclaimed shipwrecks and all beached whales. The first church, like St. Paul's, faced the Hudson River rather than Broadway.

Although the Church of England has long since been placed on a par with other sects in this country, Trinity is still probably the wealthiest parish in the city because of the original grant of land, which has become increasingly valuable and to which have been added skilled investments in real estate.

Trinity has four chapels, or subsidiary congregations, throughout the city. Three of these are also Landmarks: St. Paul's Chapel, St. Augustine's Chapel and the Chapel of the Intercession. In a recent ruling, the church has begun to give its chapels more autonomy and has decided to spend its entire income (some five million dollars a year) on social and religious programs. Before this ruling, it spent only half its income on missionary functions. One of the officers of the church said, "We've been a good corporation. Now it's time to become a good church."

Little known is the tiny remnant of the Jewish Congregation Shearith Israel's first burial place near Chatham Square. Rather, it is

18. *First Shearith Israel
Cemetery
55–57 St. James Place
1683–1828*

the congregation's earliest surviving burial place, since the first one can no longer be located. The oldest gravestone is dated 1683, only a couple of years after the earliest legible stone in Trinity Churchyard. Perhaps the most touching is a memorial to Walter J. Judah:

STUDENT OF PHYSIC, WHO WORN DOWN
BY HIS EXERTIONS TO ALLEVIATE THE
SUFFERINGS OF HIS FELLOW CITIZENS
IN THAT DREADFUL CONTAGION
THAT VISITED THE CITY OF NEW YORK
IN 1798 FELL A VICTIM IN THE CAUSE
OF HUMANITY THE 5TH OF TISHRI
A.M. 5559 CORRESPONDING
WITH THE 15TH OF SEPTEMBER 1798
AET 20 YEARS 5 MONTHS AND 11 DAYS

And below, in Hebrew: "Here lies buried / The unmarried man . . . / Old in wisdom, tender in years."

Over the years, surrounding streets have been widened and new ones cut through. As a consequence, many people formerly buried here had to be moved to either West 11th Street or West 21st Street, Shearith Israel's second and third burial grounds in Manhattan.

Congregation Shearith Israel, which means "Remnant of Israel," is the oldest Jewish congregation in the United States and dates from September 12, 1654, when a group of recently landed Spanish and Portuguese Jews held a New Year service in New Amsterdam. It probably took place in secrecy, for the irascible Peter Stuyvesant was strongly opposed to the immigration of Jews, who, he said, would "infest" the colony. In view of the fact that many Jews owned shares in the Dutch West India Company, Stuyvesant was overruled by the home office. By the time of Stuyvesant's death (1672) the Jews were playing an active part in the civic and commercial affairs of the colony, although they were still forbidden to hold public office.

The earliest Jewish settlers in New York were mostly descendants of those exiled from Spain and Portugal in 1492. They had taken refuge in Holland and later in Brazil when the Dutch established colonies there. But in 1654 the Portuguese moved into Brazil and the Jews fled again, headed back for Holland. One ship carrying twenty-three refugees was captured by pirates, who stranded its passengers in the West Indies. The captain of a French ship, the *Saint Charles*, picked up the unfortunate little group and brought them to the nearest Dutch settlement, New Amsterdam.

Way downtown in the minuscule Peter Minuit Plaza east of Battery Park, a bronze plaque honors these twenty-three doughty settlers. It was erected by the State of New York in 1954, on the three-hundredth anniversary of their arrival.

Public Buildings

Government and public buildings take naturally to the classic styles. There is—or there was in more self-confident days—something very appealing in the association of government with the glory that was Greece and the grandeur that was Rome. Hence we find almost all of New York City's notable public buildings designed in the Classical Tradition.

This tradition, as we have seen in Chapter One, takes many forms. Most obvious are direct borrowings from ancient Greece or Rome. Less direct, though still in the Classical Tradition, are adaptations from the Renaissance and post-Renaissance architecture of Italy, England and France. A French architect, Joseph F. Mangin, collaborated with the New Yorker John McComb, Jr., in competing for the commission to design a new seat of municipal government in 1802. Their prize money was $350. They probably took for their main inspiration the Hôtel de Monaco in Paris, combining its Louis XVI classicism with the delicacy and elegance of our native Federal style. In 1956 the white Massachusetts marble front that had badly disintegrated was replaced with a stone-by-stone facsimile in less perishable Alabama limestone, and the crumbling brownstone basement was replaced with Missouri red granite.

City Hall, as we see it today, has been the seat of city government for almost a century and three quarters. It is only the third such building the city has ever had, and, in its restored condition, it should survive for another couple of centuries. Such continuity is rare anywhere in the United States, and particularly rare in New York City, which has so constantly rebuilt itself.

Up the sweeping flight of stairs and through the imposing entrance portico of City Hall have passed all the heroes and rogues that have made the city what it is. Kings and queens, princes and presidents, explorers and astronauts, soldiers and poets have been received here.

19. *City Hall*
City Hall Park
between
Broadway and
Park Row
1802–11, Joseph F.
Mangin and John
McComb, Jr.

The body of Abraham Lincoln lay in state in its rotunda while a grieving public paid tribute.

What we know today as City Hall Park has always served as the city's village green or town common, where things have happened. It was once owned by the Dutch West India Company and then became part of the common lands. It was a burial ground for paupers; it was the site of public executions until the gallows was moved to the "Five Points"; the Sons of Liberty erected "liberty poles" and demonstrated here during the pre-Revolutionary tension; the Declaration of Independence, rushed by courier from Philadelphia, was read here for the first time in New York. The park was the scene of bread riots when a financial panic threatened in 1837; in 1900 a grand ceremony marking the initiation of the subway system was held here; not so long ago it saw a bloody clash between antiwar youth and hard-hat construction workers.

Recently an archaeologist did some digging outside the mayor's window, trying to determine whether old maps were correct when they indicated that there had been a madhouse on the site in the eighteenth century. When told of what was going on, Mayor Lindsay's only comment was that he had suspected something like that for quite a while.

Jumping over a century and a quarter to the 1930 design that Cass Gilbert conceived for the New York County Lawyers' Association on

Vesey Street, the same sort of refined elegance is found in a neo-Federal example. The fact that it is carried out entirely in white stone with panels of delicate carving recalls the close affinity of our Federal style with the English Regency.

Borrowings that stem more directly from the classical can be found in three impressive public buildings in lower Manhattan.

The building now known as the Federal Hall National Memorial, on Wall and Nassau Streets at the head of Broad Street, was begun in 1834 by the architects Town & Davis, John Frazee and Samuel Thompson and is a pure Greek Doric temple with the unusual feature of having a second portico on the north side, facing William Street. It is on the site of the original Federal Hall where George Washington took his oath of office in 1789 and which for years had served as the seat of the city government. New York in that year still showed the scars of the Revolution. A devastating fire had destroyed almost everything west of Broadway. Firewood had been at a premium and many a splendid ornamental or fruit tree was mysteriously missing. Citizens who had fled the city during the war had returned to find their homes, their businesses, their churches in ashes or ruins. But in spite of everything there was an electric quality in the air as thousands flocked to Wall and Nassau to witness the birth of a nation.

20. *New York County Lawyers' Association*
14 Vesey Street
1930, Cass Gilbert

21. *Federal Hall National Memorial*
(former U.S. Custom House
and U.S. Subtreasury Building)
28 Wall Street, at Nassau Street
1834–42, Town & Davis, John Frazee and
Samuel Thompson

According to contemporary illustrations the original Federal Hall was an imposing two-and-a-half-story building with a colonnaded balcony on the second floor where the ceremony took place. Washington, surrounded by John Adams, Baron von Steuben, James Madison, Richard Henry Lee and Governor George Clinton, used a Bible borrowed at the last moment from a nearby Masonic lodge. Thousands of onlookers crowded into the streets and clung to rooftops, window ledges and other vantage points. They cheered their new President with such gusto and emotion that even that hardened old soldier's composure was shaken.

The building that is now on this site was completed in 1842 for the United States Customs Service. In 1862 it became a branch of the United States Treasury. Today it is a National Monument under the jurisdiction of the National Park Service; in the magnificent interior rotunda is a federal museum containing a wealth of historic exhibits, including the suit of brown homespun worn by Washington when he took the oath of office. Recently the Park Service has done a complete renovation of the interior and has also sponsored dance and dramatic performances on the broad flight of steps leading up from Wall Street for the pleasure and edification of the noonday crowds.

Again we jump almost a century, to Guy Lowell's 1912 design for the New York County Courthouse, home of the New York State Supreme Court, at 60 Centre Street. He took a Roman temple as his model for the central portico. The heroic scale of the richly carved Corinthian columns and the pediment crowded with carved figures and crowned by gigantic statues form a dramatic contrast to the modest restraint of the simple Doric order at Federal Hall. The portico of the County Courthouse is brought forward, three columns deep and ten columns wide; it has obviously been applied to the hexagonal building behind it solely to make an impression, while at Federal Hall the portico is an integral part of the building.

A much more imaginative example of the grand classic manner is seen in McKim, Mead & White's Municipal Building of 1914 at Centre and Chambers Streets. Here too the architects borrowed freely from Rome to create an imposing civic skyscraper, but they did it with exuberance and originality. The Municipal Building was designed to reflect and complement the little City Hall that stands just to the southwest. Despite the thirty-two-story difference in their height, they

22. *New York County*
Courthouse
60 Centre Street, on Foley
Square
1912, Guy Lowell

23. *Municipal Building*
Centre Street at Chambers
Street
1914, McKim, Mead &
White

make an effective pair. The detail of the carving of the great free-standing colonnade of the Municipal Building and the almost Baroque series of pinnacles, superimposed lanterns, urns, obelisks and figures which crown the top of the building are quite different in spirit from the academic application of classical details at the County Courthouse. Yet the two buildings belong to the same period of American Eclecticism, which, inspired by the 1893 World's Columbian Exposition at Chicago, sought, in the manner of Imperial Rome, to create the "City Beautiful." At the time of the Spanish–American War the United States was beginning to feel pretty imperial itself.

In the seventeenth century the entire area around the present Centre Street and Foley Square consisted of a lake called Collect Pond and a surrounding marshland. The pond was fed by fresh-water springs and was a favorite recreation spot for boaters and picnickers. In 1808 a work relief project was set up to drain the district. All went well until the land began to sink, whereupon the decent folk abandoned it to seek more salubrious locations. (Even to this day the sidewalks surrounding the New York State Building at Centre and Worth Streets have a distressing tendency to curl and buckle because of underground streams.) By the early part of the nineteenth century freed slaves, unfortunate immigrants and all sorts of unsavory characters moved into the abandoned buildings.

24. *Five Points in 1827*

An area just behind the County Courthouse came to be known as the Five Points because five streets converged here on what was then known as Paradise Square—an ironic misnomer, as it turned out. By the middle of the nineteenth century the Five Points had become one of the world's worst slums. New York's first gangs—the Plug Uglies, the Shirt Tails, the Forty Thieves and the Dead Rabbits, among others—had their birth here When Charles Dickens visited the United States in 1842, two policemen escorted him to the Five Points, where he found that

> poverty, wretchedness and vice are rife. The coarse and bloated faces at the door have counterparts at home and all the wide world over. Debauchery has made the very houses prematurely old. See how the rotten beams are tumbling down, and how the patched and broken windows seem to scowl dimly, like eyes that have been hurt in drunken frays.

But he found a few encouraging signs.

> So far, nearly every house is a low tavern; and on the bar-room walls are coloured prints of Washington and Queen Victoria of England and the American Eagle. Among the pigeon-holes that hold the bottles are pieces of plate-glass and coloured paper for there is, in some sort, a taste for decoration, even here.

To see a really triumphant taste for decoration, however, we turn to some buildings in the Beaux-Arts style. Notable examples are the Chamber of Commerce Building on Liberty Street, the United States Custom House on Bowling Green and the Surrogate's Court, or Hall of Records, on Chambers Street. All were built between 1899 and 1911, and all exemplify the luxuriant exuberance, the deeply penetrated surfaces and the integration of sculpture into the architectural composition that are so characteristic of Beaux-Arts design.

To appreciate the essential role that sculpture played in these compositions, it is necessary only to contrast the Chamber of Commerce Building as it first appeared, with its sculptured figures, to the stripped-down way that it looks today. Fortunately, the building still retains the bull's-eye windows, the paired columns, the profusion of carved garlands and ornaments, the deep arched openings and the copper-crested roof that are typical Beaux-Arts. Despite the richness of the style, there is an ordered control in these buildings. Each of them

25. *New York Chamber of Commerce*
65 Liberty Street
1901, James B. Baker

26. *Surrogate's Court (Hall of Records)*
31 Chambers Street
1899–1911, John R. Thomas and
Horgan & Slattery

27. *United States Custom House*
Bowling Green
1901–07, Cass Gilbert

has a clearly articulated bottom, middle and top. The Custom House and the Surrogate's Court balance the left and right sides around a dominant center, and one can sense how uncomfortable the architect of the Chamber of Commerce must have been when he was forced, by the exigencies of site and plan, to place his entrance unbalanced and off center.

Dolphins, masts, rudder, tridents, the caduceus of Mercury, the winged wheel, the stylized wave and other symbols of the sea embellish the exterior of the Custom House. In the window arches there are heads representing eight "races" of mankind: Caucasian, Hindu, Latin, Celtic, Mongolian, Eskimo, Slavic and African.

Four large sculptures, representing four continents, adorn the front of the building. They are the work of Daniel Chester French. Michael Stramiello, Jr., former regional commissioner of customs, describes them thus in a descriptive brochure:

> *ASIA.* Represented by the kneeling Hindu, the Chinese coolie and the suppliant woman bound by the injustice of the ages, with a tiger glaring into her face.
> *AMERICA.* Seated on a stone carved with barbaric inscriptions, holds the light of the torch of progress in one hand —the other hand is stretched protectingly over the figure of labor; an Indian peers over her shoulder; the eagle is seated by her side; and on her knees rest sheaves of grain.
> *EUROPE.* Seated on a throne carved with the emblem of achievement; the open book, the globe, and the ship prows stand for her exploits.
> *AFRICA.* Leaning against an Egyptian pillar, seated between a lion and a sphinx—her attitude is of a drowsiness and hopelessness.

The site of the Custom House, facing on Bowling Green, is a hallowed one for New Yorkers. It is believed that the first white settlers built their crude shelters near this spot during the summer of 1624. They had come nearly fifteen years after Henry Hudson had made his momentous discovery on behalf of the Dutch and nearly three years after the Pilgrims, who, intending to make landfall at Hudson's river, had by mistake landed at Cape Cod.

The first white settlers of Manhattan were alien residents of Holland—refugee Protestants, Walloons and Frenchmen—who arrived aboard the 260-ton ship *Nieu Nederlandt.* The captain sailed into the harbor, deposited eight men on the tip of the island and then proceeded up the river to found Fort Orange, which today is Albany.

We know little of these hardy artisans and farmers except that they survived the winter. There was ample fresh spring water, venison, fish and oysters, and they probably planted and harvested corn.

They were joined sometime later by six complete Dutch families from Holland—the men in their broad-brimmed hats, short jackets and bulky pantaloons, the women with snowy white caps and full swishing skirts. These families brought cows, sheep and horses with them and thus were able, with farming and stock raising, to augment the subsistence living of the original settlers.

Among these newcomers was Peter Minuit, who had been appointed director general of the colony by the Dutch West India Company. It was he who presided at the famous transaction with the Manhattan Indians, whose principal village was at the north tip of the island, on what became known as Spuyten Duyvil Creek; however, they laid claim to the island's entire twenty-two-mile length. For sixty guilders (twenty-four dollars) in trinkets, Minuit took title to what was to become the world's most valuable piece of real estate.

The first thing the new group of white settlers did was build a fort, where the U.S. Custom House stands today. There were some houses inside the fort, and others clustered around the outside. The colony was called New Netherland and the town New Amsterdam. News of its favorable location spread, and the colony grew. By 1626 the little settlement numbered nearly forty houses.

The Custom House and all the other public buildings we have been discussing, despite their stylistic differences, are all clearly in the Classical Tradition. One example, and a delightful one, is not. Napoleon Le Brun's Firehouse for Engine Company No. 31 at 87 Lafayette Street is an enchanting echo of the very early French Renaissance style. As in the châteaux of the time of Francis I, there is a certain lip service paid to classical details if one looks closely at the firehouse, but the entire spirit of the building, with its corner tower, its steep roof, its rich and varied dormers and its stone and metal crestings, is as romantic as a fairy story. With the Vanderbilt château gone from Fifth Avenue and the Schwab mansion from Riverside Drive, this is about the best example left us of a charming and fanciful style. From our present-day perspective of great stretches of avenues chilly with chrome and glass, it seems almost incredible that as recently as 1895

28. *Firehouse, Engine
Company No. 31
87 Lafayette Street
1895, Napoleon Le Brun
and Sons*

such a wealth of imagination could have been expended on so utilitarian a structure as a firehouse.

As a matter of fact, the fire-fighting organization and apparatus of the city has always had a certain flair and dash. The first fire company was organized in 1658. It was called the Rattle Watch, because people had rattles which they twisted to summon help when fire broke out. The watch was composed of eight men who were on duty from nine at night until "morning drum beat." Later companies rejoiced in such names as Old Maid's Boys, Fly by Nights, Lucky Thirteen, White Ghost, Drybones and Dock Rats, while their pet engines were affectionately labeled "Hope," "Wreath of Roses," "Old Brass Back" and "Honey Bee." The early equipment consisted of 250 fire buckets imported from Holland. In 1731 New York got its first two shiny hand-drawn fire engines from London. They were housed in sheds behind the then City Hall and drew constant crowds of admiring citizens. Though the Fire Department was incorporated in 1798, volunteers continued to serve for a long time.

Charles Dickens describes the arrival of a fire company on the scene of a fire:

> In a dash the volunteers in their red shirts and helmets—from oyster shells and half-finished clam soup, from newly begun games of billiards, from the theatre, . . . from the mad drollery of the Christy minstrels, from gin slings, from barroom, from sulphurous pistol galleries, from studios, from dissecting rooms, from half-shuttered shops, from conversazioni and lectures —from everywhere . . . breathless, hot, eager, daring, shouting, mad.

Commercial Buildings

New York City has from the start been a place where the main interest of most people was money. Its settlers, for the most part, were not refugees from religious persecution, like the Pilgrims, nor were they colonizers of an outpost for the mother country, like the English along the South Atlantic coast. New Amsterdam was a private venture set up by the Dutch for the sole purpose of trade. It is true that under Dutch rule some disputes about rights and freedoms broke out between the trading company and the rugged individualists who had crossed the treacherous North Atlantic to achieve a better life and were determined to have it. But these disputes were generally over the percentage of the take.

The trader, the merchant, the shipper, the broker and the banker have generally been more prominent than the manufacturer. New York has never been a company town or a place identified with a single product. The variety of its industries, the mixture of its population and their native skills have combined with the natural advantages of its great port to make New York primarily a place where goods change hands.

A visitor from London, John Lambert, wrote about the New York scene in 1807: "Everything was in motion; all was life, bustle and activity. The people were scampering in all directions to trade with each other. . . . Every thought, word, look and action of the multitudes seemed to be absorbed in commerce."

It is particularly appropriate that the earliest commercial buildings to have survived on the crowded tip of lower Manhattan should be closely identified both with the history of shipping and with what was, until very recently, an actual marketplace. Schermerhorn Row, which extends along Fulton Street between South and Front Streets, was one of the earliest and is now the last surviving commercial row of Federal-style warehouses built in New York City. These twelve buildings were all built at the same time, between 1811 and 1812, by the same man, Peter Schermerhorn, a prominent merchant who ran a prosperous ship chandler business at 243 Water Street. Except for Nos. 2 and 12 Fulton Street, and Nos. 91 and 92 South Street, around the corner, all these buildings retain their original steep-pitched roofs. The dormers were added somewhat later. They still show some of their original Flemish-bond brickwork and splayed lintels. Sweet's Restaurant, now at No. 2 Fulton Street, has been in the block ever since 1845. During the decade 1850–60 it was a favorite haunt of "blackbirders" who consummated many slave-running deals here before the Civil War. This building and its neighbor on South Street were still owned by Schermerhorns as late as 1939. Other tenants in the block have included grocers, merchants, plumbers, woodenware dealers, agricultural-equipment tradesmen, saloonkeepers and chinaware merchants.

As early as the 1720s the Schermerhorn family had owned property on Pearl Street between Fulton and Beekman Streets. Pearl Street had marked Manhattan's original shore line. As this line was extended eastward—to Water Street, then to Front Street, and finally, by 1800, to South Street—the owners of contiguous properties acquired "water lots" which were first used for wharves and docking slips. Many of the old names still survive: Coenties Slip, Old Slip, Burling Slip. Later these lots were filled in; in fact, the last series of grants were made on condition that the lots be filled. This was an early instance of city

29. *Schermerhorn Row   2–18 Fulton Street (and, not shown, 91, 92 South*
     and 195 Front Streets)
     1811–12
     Raising of 12 Fulton Street: mid–19th century

government acting in cooperation with private business for their common benefit. Schermerhorn Row stands as a witness to this early partnership.

It also stands as testimony to a much later government intervention, again with both public and private benefit. In 1968 this historic block seemed destined for demolition, but it was saved by the dramatic intervention of the Landmarks Preservation Commission. At a hastily called emergency meeting, the Commission voted to designate the entire block of buildings (including 189–195 Front Street and 159–171 John Street), thus saving it from the iron ball. At the same time, through the cooperation of other City agencies, arrangements were made to sell to private developers of adjacent properties the unused development rights of the Landmark buildings.

The city now owns the Schermerhorn property. Present plans for its future call for architectural restoration and the installation of the New York State Maritime Museum. It will be a major component of the South Street Seaport, a private nonprofit organization formed in 1967 to preserve and restore New York's nineteenth-century waterfront.

The goal of the South Street Seaport is to tell the story of the men in ships and to weave back into the fabric of the city's life some of the excitement that led to South Street's becoming known as the "Street of Ships." During the days of the clipper ship and the packet boat the whole area bristled with ships' masts and spars, while the bowsprits of some of the larger vessels projected far across the street. When the steamboat arrived, the South Street docks lost out to those on the West Side of the island, where the Hudson provided the depth the new vessels required.

South Street Seaport has acquired several old vessels, including the original Ambrose Lightship, the wooden-hulled Gloucester fishing schooner *Caviare*, the full-rigged merchantman *Wavertree*, and the *Alexander Hamilton*, last of the Hudson River Day Line sidewheelers. They are being restored and are tied up at the Fulton Street docks, where they are open to the public.

Another reconstruction that is planned for the Seaport is an unpretentious little building dating from 1826 which shows that a typical late-Federal-style commercial establishment looked not very different from a residence of the same period. In fact, the merchant tenant lived upstairs above his shop. It stood originally at 71 Pearl Street, on what had long been thought to be the site of the original Stadhuis, or City Hall, of New Amsterdam.

The Stadhuis had originally been built as an inn and was acquired by the City in 1653. Here was conducted all the City's business, including the dispensing of justice. It is said that in 1670 the English governor, Francis Lovelace, built a new inn next to the Stadhuis and had a door cut through the wall to connect inn and courtroom, thus considerably lubricating the course of justice.

The building became the first City Hall when New Amsterdam received its municipal charter, giving the inhabitants a form of self-government which was in many ways more democratic than the later

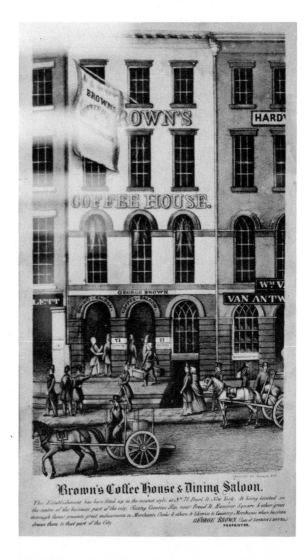

30. *Former 71 Pearl Street (Probably to be reerected at South Street Seaport) 1826 Planned reconstruction: 1970s*

English one. The people drew up a list of suitable individuals who might represent them, and the director general of the colony appointed officials from that list. Under English rule, the citizens had no say whatever in appointments of local officials.

When the banking house of Lehman Brothers began to acquire property in the area in 1968 for a new skyscraper headquarters, it agreed to pay for archeological excavation of the Pearl Street site, which culminated in 1971 in the confirmation that this was indeed where the Stadhuis once stood. The old foundations were revealed, and many artifacts, including clay pipes, bottles, glasses and plates, were retrieved.

In addition, Lehman Brothers made possible the careful disassembly and storage of the 71 Pearl Street façade. The arched windows on both the first and second floors are the last such examples remaining in Manhattan. Originally a two-and-a-half-story house, it was altered in 1826 to a four-story structure housing Brown's Coffee House and Dining Saloon. A 1965 restoration returned the building to its original two-and-a-half-story height and exposed the original warm red brick; it is in this form that it is planned to be rebuilt at the South Street Seaport.

Just north of Schermerhorn Row and across Fulton Street was the malodorous and bustling Fulton Fish Market, which is being incorporated into the new Hunts Point Market in the Bronx. The Fulton Fish Market was established in 1821 to "supply the common people with the necessities of life at a reasonable price." Not only fish, but also cheap finery, books, ice cream, candy and even hardware and dry goods could be found here. And, of course, the oyster bars! Young bloods, elegant ladies dressed in the latest fashion, statesmen, politicians, even the clergy gathered in the rather rough wooden rooms to enjoy the succulent shellfish on the half shell or in stews.

Commercial buildings generally followed the same sequence of architectural styles that were popular for residences and public buildings. Just across Burling Slip from the Schermerhorn block, at 170–176 John Street, is one of the finest and also one of the last surviving examples of the extremely simple type of Greek Revival commercial buildings whose severe granite fronts once lined the waterfront of New York.

Other commercial Landmarks, dating from 1811 to 1849, are

31. *No. 170–176 John Street
1840*

found on the north side of Burling Slip. They include 159–171 John Street and extend around the corner to 189 Front Street. Two very early buildings, Nos. 191 and 193 Front Street, date from before 1793 but have been extensively altered. The trapezoidal shape of Burling Slip itself still suggests the days before the docking basin was filled in.

All of this area along the East River, from Brooklyn Bridge to the Battery, including the Schermerhorn block and the South Street Seaport, is scheduled to be part of a projected development called Manhattan Landing, destined to have parks, commercial buildings, a four-hundred-room hotel, a department store, a marina and apartments for eight thousand to nine thousand families. Sponsors of the project, who include private individuals and banks as well as the City, hope to make the area a twenty-four-hour-a-day community, where people can live, work and be entertained.

A recent move in this direction was a Fourth of July celebration that brought thousands to the financial district, usually dismally empty on a holiday. Things started at the South Street Seaport, where a map for a do-it-yourself walking tour and a country music concert were available. There was dancing on John Street, vespers at Trinity, a brass fanfare and a drama performance on the steps of Federal Hall, a dance recital on the steps of the Custom House and singing and picnicking at Castle Clinton in Battery Park. All of this was topped off with a fireboat water display off the Battery.

Much richer and more sophisticated, though exactly contemporary with these waterfront classical buildings, is the lower portion of what is now the First National City Bank at 55 Wall Street, which was built between 1836 and 1842, from designs by Isaiah Rogers, as the Merchants' Exchange and was later used as the U.S. Custom House. The fine row of monolithic Ionic columns resting on a basement is very severe, very classical. This building has a special interest because in 1907 a second story, a superimposed row of Corinthian columns, was skillfully added by McKim, Mead & White when the building was taken over by the bank. There are, of course, classical precedents for the superimposition of one order upon another, and McKim, Mead & White, with their classical expertise, achieved such harmony here that few would suspect that the two parts of this building were designed almost a century apart.

Farther west, and on the same south side of Wall Street, is Trowbridge & Livingston's famous corner building which they designed in 1913 for J. P. Morgan and Company, now occupied by the Morgan Guaranty Trust Company. Though almost contemporary with McKim, Mead & White's work for the First National City Bank and conceived in the same spirit of scholarly classicism that the Chicago World's Columbian Exposition of 1893 had inspired, the finished effect is totally different. Where the McKim, Mead & White colonnade is vigorous and powerful and depends for its impact on the shadows created by deep recesses and bold projections, the Morgan Bank is all smooth-surfaced elegance and refinement. It achieves its effect by contrasting concentrated areas of richly carved, delicate detail against wide expanses that are left perfectly plain. The lower story is, in fact, so austerely stripped down that, if one ignores the ornate bronze window grilles, the treatment is surprisingly reminiscent of the severely utilitarian granite front of 170–176 John Street.

After the original Greek Revival fashion had run its course, the next strong influence on commercial buildings was the Italianate. India House, built in the early 1850s on Hanover Square, is a good prototype. It was designed to be the home of the Hanover Bank and

32. *First National City Bank
(former Merchants'
Exchange and U.S.
Custom House)
55 Wall Street
Lower portion: 1836–42,
Isaiah Rogers
Upper portion: 1907,
McKim, Mead & White*

33. *J. P. Morgan and Company Building
(now Morgan Guaranty Trust Company)
23 Wall Street
1913, Trowbridge & Livingston*

34. *India House
(former Hanover
Bank, New York
Cotton Exchange,
and W. R. Grace
and Company)
1 Hanover Square
1851–54*

later served as headquarters of the New York Cotton Exchange and of W. R. Grace and Company. Today it is a club containing a fine maritime collection. The strongly rusticated basement, the smooth brownstone of the main part of the building, the cornice supported on brackets, the brackets under the second- and third-story windowsills, the use of triangular and segmental arched pediments over the first- and second-story windows, and the long consoles that support the latter are some of the typical details that were repeated again and again on the rows of brownstone houses that were to be built on block after block of the city during the next thirty years.

But Italianate details were not limited to brownstones. They were also applied to an altogether new and highly original sort of structure that was quietly being developed in the mid-century by a few far-sighted engineers. The nineteenth century was not only a period of aesthetic disorientation—a century in search of its soul—but also a time of extraordinary technological development. It is to this development that the creation of cast-iron architecture belongs. This was a uniquely American creation and principally identified with New York City.

The oldest surviving examples of cast-iron construction in this country are James Bogardus' Laing Stores, which were erected at the northwest corner of Washington and Murray Streets in 1848. These were also the second-oldest application of the new technology to the creation of self-supporting prefabricated "screen wall" façades.

While the floors and roofs of this series of five stores were supported by wood beams resting on brick bearing walls, each section of the street façade was a prefabricated unit of cast iron, made in a shop and then assembled on the site very much like an Erector set. This cast-iron front was the lightest type of construction so far achieved, and permitted the use of slender uprights and much greater window space than conventional masonry methods. On the Murray Street side of No. 258 Washington Street, the cast-iron front also carried a part of the load from the floor joists; this was a very significant advance in structural technique.

At the time of its construction the *New York Evening Post* described the process thus: "Each piece may be put up as fast as it is brought to the ground. They may be taken down, removed and put up again in a short time like any other casting." Prophetically enough, a century and a quarter later, in 1970, the Laing Stores were taken down just as intended. It is planned that they will be reerected just two blocks away for the new Manhattan Community College, which is part of the Washington Market Urban Renewal Project.

The preservation of these buildings is a good example of various city and federal agencies acting together in the public interest. These structures were exactly in the middle of a huge area slated for demolition. The Landmarks Preservation Commission presented the case for preservation to the City's Housing and Development Administration and also to the United States Department of Housing and Urban Development. Both agreed to see what could be done. The City University of New York, which had plans for an entire new campus in the

35. *Laing Stores*
Former location: 258–262
   Washington Street and 97
   Murray Street
Future location: Manhattan
   Community College, on the
   westerly half of a superblock on
   West Street
1848, James Bogardus
Reerection: 1970s, Caudill,
   Rowlett & Scott

area, then agreed to incorporate the Landmarks into their plans. Finally, the approval of the Board of Estimate was obtained. An architectural historian was selected to supervise the dismantling process, complete with full photographic documentation, a written log and a complete set of measured and detailed drawings. The dismantled pieces were carefully rustproofed and stored awaiting their moment of resurrection.

The Bogardus method of construction was particularly suited to the Italianate style and had a special affinity to the sort of architecture that had been developed in Venice during the Renaissance. Venice is one of Italy's most northerly cities and has rather dismal winters. Her architects naturally tried to provide as much daylight as possible in their buildings. Since building sites were scarce and expensive, Venetian structures—even the palaces—were built shoulder to shoulder, with only the narrow front and rear walls available for any windows at all. This was all the more reason to make them as open to daylight as possible. Fortunately, Venice, protected from attack by its lagoon, could afford this openness—unlike Rome, Florence or Milan, whose palaces also had to serve as fortresses.

There were many fascinating parallels in nineteenth-century New York to this fifteenth-century Venetian experience. Land here also was scarce and expensive; daylight, before the invention of electricity, was at a premium; and open fronts were feasible because the city was relatively safe. But, above all, there was a structural parallel. Because they were built on mud, Venetian buildings had to be supported on piles, with the concentration of loads on as few points as possible. In New York the use of cast-iron columns led to the same concentration of loads at isolated points. In both cases the intervening spaces could be filled in with large windows or non-load-bearing panels. Also, the repetitive character of a series of superimposed arcades—so typical of the Venetian Renaissance—lent itself admirably to the economies of cast iron, for obviously the more pieces you cast from one mold, the less expensive is the whole process.

All of these characteristics, both stylistic and structural, are well illustrated by a fine example at 75 Murray Street. The building fills every inch of its valuable twenty-five-foot lot. Its third and fourth stories, with their typically Venetian detail, are absolutely identical because the parts were cast from the same mold; the second story

36. *No. 75 Murray Street*
c. 1865

differs only in having slightly longer column shafts; the fifth story differs only by being crowned with a heavily decorated Italianate entablature. The upper two stories retain the original subdivision of their window openings: a pair of semicircular arches with a bull's-eye filling the space between them. This motif, inspired by the Palazzo Vendramini in Venice, will be encountered again and again in Italianate designs.

The isolated structural columns with light panels between them and the prefabrication of repetitive units are direct precursors of the skeleton construction and metal-and-glass curtain walls of our twentieth-century skyscrapers.

In contrast, the much later example of Florentine Renaissance inspiration, the Federal Reserve Bank on Liberty Street, reverted to an earlier masonry bearing-wall construction. It is an imposing structure, with the monumental scale of its rusticated stonework and the superb craftsmanship of the triplex lanterns that the great ironworker Samuel Yellin executed. Modeled as it is on the Palazzo Strozzi, it is a good example of how architects of the Eclectic period approached problems of design.

In its function as a bank for banks, the Federal Reserve building has five underground levels which house offices of foreign nations as well as the vaults where their gold is stored. This bullion is moved from nation to nation as the balance of trade fluctuates, without ever leaving the building.

The Federal Reserve is now embarked on a new project, a $60,000,000 forty-story office tower on land adjacent to its old building. The new structure will be perched thirteen stories above ground and will straddle an open landscaped plaza which has been designed to dramatize the adjacent Landmark, the little John Street United Methodist Church.

While most architects of the Eclectic period were turning out scholarly exercises in neo-Federal, neo-Romanesque or neo-Gothic, a few pioneers were trying to create an entirely new "style" which they felt might be more in keeping with new problems and technology. One of the first attempts now goes by the name of Art Nouveau. One of the few examples in New York is the old New York Evening Post Building at 20 Vesey Street, designed by Robert D. Kohn in 1906. There is a strong expression of the vertical with plain masonry piers rising in unbroken contrast to the decorative bay windows that separate them. At the top the design bursts into an efflorescence of arches, balconies and heroic statues standing on corbeled pedestals. Two of its statues were executed by Gutzon Borglum. In later years both Louis Sullivan and Frank Lloyd Wright, each in his own way, strove to develop the same sort of integration of architecture and decoration.

Forts, a Bridge and a Fence

The first permanent defenses of Manhattan Island consisted, in 1626, of a blockhouse surrounded by a wooden stockade. This was replaced

37. (*Left*) *Federal Reserve Bank   33 Liberty Street
1924, York & Sawyer*

38. (*Right*) *Old* New York Evening Post *Building   20 Vesey Street
1906, Robert D. Kohn*

in 1635 by Fort Amsterdam, on the site of the present United States Custom House. It consisted of a bastioned earthwork topped by a stockade and included within its enclosure the governor's residence, the chamber of the provincial Council, the Dutch Reformed Church of St. Nicholas, barracks, a guardhouse and an armory, but, oddly enough, no water supply. In the event of an Indian raid the entire population of the surrounding community could seek shelter within its confines.

The position of the Dutch in New Netherland, between English settlers to the north in New England and to the south in Maryland and Virginia, was a constant source of unease during Peter Stuyvesant's regime. The Dutch West India Company was cool to his pleas for help in defense. When war broke out between England and Holland, the two mother countries, it seemed bound to spread to the colonies. It was then that Stuyvesant ordered a fortified wall to be built along what is today Wall Street, to protect the colony from the Indians and also from any possible land attack by the English. It was made of heavy flat planks which proved so attractive to the good citizens as firewood that within a couple of years the wall was in a state of total disrepair. During the entire period that the Dutch controlled New Amsterdam the town never grew north of Wall Street.

On March 22, 1664, Charles II of England conferred upon his brother James, Duke of York and Albany, "all the land from the west side of the Connectecutte River to the east side of the de la Ware Bay," as well as part of Maine, all of Long Island, Martha's Vineyard and Nantucket. Regardless of the Dutch claims in New Netherland, the Duke of York promptly sailed to take possession of his new estates. Stuyvesant and his people, lulled into a false sense of security by the rumor that the Duke's forces were headed for Boston, relaxed. The palisade along Wall Street had fallen to pieces, and the colonists, feeling that the mother country, not the colony, should pay for the defense of New Netherland, did not replace it. But perhaps the most compelling reason for the disaster that the Dutch were to suffer was their underlying feeling of hopelessness, for the English far outnumbered the Dutch in America. By the mid–seventeenth century there were nearly 100,000 English colonists in New England, Maryland and Virginia, matched against a mere 10,000 Dutch in all of New Netherland. As Stuyvesant himself put it, the English "are able to deprive us of the country when they please."

The fort on the Battery proved to be of little effect against an outside invader. The mere sight of two English warships anchored in the channel between the fort and Governor's Island caused such a flurry on September 5, 1664, that the colony surrendered without a shot being fired. The burgomasters, in advising the West India Company of events, said the defeat had all happened "through God's pleasure thus unexpectedly," primarily because of the company's "neglect and forgetfulness."

In 1667 the Dutch and the English made their peace and signed a solemn treaty, the Peace of Breda. The Dutch, with what they no doubt thought was great canniness, ceded to the British the colony they called New Amsterdam and kept for themselves the colony of Surinam on the north coast of South America. This is probably one of history's great errors of judgment.

It is only from old maps, prints and records that we can learn where these earliest fortifications were or what they looked like. The defenses of New York Harbor that survive as Landmarks all date from the period following the Revolutionary War. Coastal defenses were then conceived as paired forts on either side of a strategic waterway. The first such pair were Fort Jay on Governor's Island and Castle Clinton on the Manhattan shore.

*39. Fort Jay
Governor's Island
1794–98
Rebuilt 1806*

Although Governor's Island is now used by the United States Coast Guard and is not accessible to the general public, it is legally part of the borough of Manhattan and is considered part of lower Manhattan for Landmark purposes. A look at the map will show its strategic position in relation to Manhattan and the rest of the Upper Bay. After the English captured New Amsterdam, Governor's Island was used "for the benefit and accommodation of His Majestie's Governors for the time being." Hence the name.

The island has had a checkered career since the Indians sold it to the Dutch for two ax heads, a string of beads and a few nails—cheaper than Manhattan but, in view of present-day real-estate values, not as good a buy. It was the headquarters for both Dutch and English governors and has since been a quarantine station, a pheasant preserve, a garrisoned fortress, a summer resort, a recruiting depot, a prison, an embarkation port and a flying field. It was a United States Army installation for a century and a half and since 1966 has been the headquarters of the Coast Guard's Eastern Area, with a fleet of cutters, icebreakers, buoy tenders and tugs, and a working force of six thousand.

Fort Jay was started in 1794 when war with France threatened. Three years later so little progress had been made that Governor De Witt Clinton of New York complained that federal appropriations were inadequate for the needs of the city—a complaint that has a painfully familiar and contemporary ring. He called on patriotic students and faculty members of Columbia College, along with members of various trade groups, to volunteer their labor for the construction of what he considered the city's most important point of defense. The volunteer labor force must have been extraordinarily responsive, for the fort was completed in less than a year and named for the then Secretary of Foreign Affairs, John Jay. It was rebuilt in 1806, after which it was renamed Fort Columbus. But in 1904 the old name Fort Jay was restored.

Like so many other early fortifications in this country, Fort Jay owes its inspiration to the great French architect Sébastien de Vauban, who was military engineer extraordinary to Louis XIV. It is a star-shaped irregular pentagon—a form designed not for aesthetic reasons, but for the very practical one that it permitted the defender to subject any invader to a flanking fire as he approached between points of the star.

The fort is on a knoll near the northern end of the island and has an impressive stone entrance gateway which shows considerable French influence. The gateway is surmounted by a flamboyant sculptured trophy composed of flags, cannon, small weapons, banded fasces with a liberty cap, and, dominating it all, a spread eagle. The fort was protected by a dry moat; the chains at the entrance are all that remain of the original drawbridge. The fort once boasted a hundred guns, and its massive walls sheltered a quadrangle of officers' quarters. Its fearsome appearance and bristling guns must have had their effect, for no enemy has ever tried to assault it, not even the British in the War of 1812. Today the fort, which stands forty feet above high tide, is surrounded by a nine-hole golf course, while the dry moat provides some of the game's worst sand traps.

After the completion of Fort Jay, New Yorkers were fairly relaxed about their safety, but the shelling, in 1807, of the U.S.S. *Chesapeake* off Norfolk, Virginia, by an English cruiser shocked them into what a contemporary commentator called "fortification fever." Fort Jay was rebuilt and was reinforced by the circular Castle Williams on the northwest corner of Governor's Island, while the construction of the matching fort, Castle Clinton on Manhattan, was started.

Projecting out into the water and now enjoying a spectacular view of Manhattan's skyscrapers, the massive, round Castle Williams (1807–11) was named after its designer, Lieutenant Colonel Jonathan Williams, chief engineer of the Army. Its walls, made of Newark red sandstone, are some forty feet high and seven to eight feet thick. The stones in the outer walls are dovetailed so that no stone can be removed without being broken to pieces. (Incidentally, the old South Brooklyn Savings Bank in the Cobble Hill Historic District of Brooklyn used a similar security technique as late as 1871: cannonballs were inserted as locks between the stones of its underground vault.)

Castle Williams, known on various occasions as the "Tower" or the "Cheesebox," had guns on its three levels. During the Civil War some one thousand Confederate prisoners were kept in the castle, and later it was used as a maximum-security military prison. Today it houses a teen-agers' canteen.

40. *Castle Williams. Governor's Island* (*early view*)
1807–11, Lt. Col. Jonathan Williams

Another prison was the Blockhouse, a simple square structure in the Greek Revival style which was erected on Governor's Island in 1843 from plans by Martin E. Thompson.

Most familiar to New Yorkers of any of these buildings is Castle Clinton at the tip of Manhattan. It was designed by John McComb, Jr., who, as we have said, was New York's first native-born architect. As late as 1810 he listed himself in the City Directory as a "mason and master-builder," which in itself was a masterpiece of understatement. He changed his listing to "architect" in 1811, by which time he was firmly established in his professional capacity. In addition to his important public buildings, McComb designed many private homes.

41. Blockhouse
Governor's Island
1843, Martin E. Thompson

42. Castle Clinton (early view)
(later Castle Garden, Emigrant
Landing Depot, and Aquarium)
The Battery
1807, John McComb, Jr.
Restoration: 1968–

When Castle Clinton was originally built, it was offshore at the end of a two-hundred-foot causeway. The intervening water has since been filled in, and the fort now sits squarely in Battery Park. Built in a ring form, open to the sky, it had massive sandstone walls, measuring eight feet thick at the gun ports. The gateway was, in all probability, copied from Vauban. Like its sister forts on Governor's Island, none of Castle Clinton's threatening twenty-eight guns ever fired a shot, but its menacing posture no doubt had a deterring effect during the War of 1812.

Actually, Castle Clinton has played a more interesting role in the social and cultural life of the city than in its military history. In 1823 the federal government ceded it to New York City, which promptly changed its name to Castle Garden, decorated it with plants and flowers and leased it out as a "place of resort." Band concerts, fireworks, public receptions and occasional balloon ascensions delighted the crowds that gathered nightly in this open-air garden. The Marquis de Lafayette was enthusiastically received here when he arrived from France on his return visit in 1824. At the conclusion of his triumphal American tour, Lafayette was again honored at the Garden. It was covered with a vast awning for the occasion. The *Evening Post* called it "the most magnificent fete given under cover in the world." At various times Presidents Andrew Jackson, John Tyler, James K. Polk and Franklin Pierce were welcomed here by their New York constituents.

In 1845 Castle Garden was permanently roofed over and became a home for opera and lighter musical entertainment; and, perhaps more important, the Garden cellars were filled "with the most delicious fluids so that the audience may be at once regaled with the choicest Italian music and the most inspiring mint juleps." September 11, 1850, witnessed the musical event of the century when the greatest of showmen, P. T. Barnum, brought Jenny Lind, the "Swedish Nightingale," to the Battery shore. An overflow crowd of six thousand attended.

However, a less frivolous future lay ahead, for in 1855 Castle Garden was converted into an "Emigrant Landing Depot" to cope with the flood tide of mid-century migration from Europe. For the first time, an attempt was made to protect bewildered newcomers from the rapacious sharpers who roamed the public wharves. Here at the depot they could get reliable information, a fair exchange of currency, even medical attention and a chance at a job. More than seven million immigrants, mostly Irish and German, passed through Castle Garden during the next thirty-five years, after which it was replaced by new and more commodious quarters on Ellis Island.

Again the castle was altered and its function changed. In 1896 it was transformed by McKim, Mead & White into the New York City Aquarium. During the next forty-five years, some ninety million persons filed through it, making it probably the most popular public display in the history of the city. In 1941 a variety of circumstances—pollution of the harbor water, interference with the approaches to the Brooklyn–Battery Tunnel and lack of space for expansion—combined to force a decision to move the Aquarium to Coney Island.

For a time it seemed that the old building was doomed to demolition. But determined New Yorkers intervened, and, in 1946, Congress declared it a national monument. It was turned over to the National Park Service, which restored it to its original fortress form and opened it to the public.

These three examples of military architecture—Fort Jay, Castle Williams and Castle Clinton—are vigorous examples of the strict expression of function. The purpose of the structures was to mount guns and to protect the gunners, with no nonsense wasted in the way of decoration. The same straightforward approach is well illustrated by another Landmark of lower Manhattan: Brooklyn Bridge. This is, in some ways, New York's most famous structure. Its Manhattan approach rests on historic ground. For there, at what was No. 3 Cherry Street, was the nation's first White House, rented by George Washington when he was President-elect. Although it was a large house, on Franklin Square, there was not enough room for the eighteen servants that George and Martha kept, and the stables were quite inadequate for that country squire's elaborate equipages. His cream-colored coach, ornamented with cupids and festoons of flowers and drawn by six prancing horses with painted hoofs, was a familiar sight in the streets of the town. Washington went to his inauguration from Cherry Street but shortly afterward found more central and more commodious quarters at 39 Broadway, just south of where Trinity Church stands today.

Kenneth Clark, the noted English critic, has said that "all modern

43. Brooklyn Bridge
City Hall Park, Manhattan, to Cadman Plaza, Brooklyn
1867–83, John A. and Washington A. Roebling

New York, heroic New York, started with Brooklyn Bridge." Certainly it is a world milestone in the history of civil engineering. Its enduring beauty lies in the honest contrast between the compressive strength of the great pylons and the tensile strength of the delicate tracery of the woven suspension cables. The push of the pylons and the pull of the cables make the drama. Each part of the bridge expresses, in terms of its materials, its particular role in supporting the great span. The bridge, which opened with great fanfare on May 24, 1883, also has a fascinating story to tell of creative imagination, courage and persistence in the face of established inertia, and, finally, of human tragedy.

John A. Roebling, German-born, many-sided genius, was the designer. In 1857, when he first proposed to build a bridge across the East River (a distance of 6,016 feet), his suggestion was greeted with incredulity or indifference by the city fathers of both New York and

Brooklyn, which was then a separate city. However, after the Civil War, a small group of farsighted Brooklyn citizens agreed to push the idea, and, what is more important, to support it financially. The state legislature granted a charter, thirty-nine businessmen invested, Congress passed a bill authorizing the construction, and, on January 2, 1870, work began.

But just six months before work had actually started, Roebling was standing on a Brooklyn wharf when a ferryboat crushed his foot. Despite the amputation of his toes, lockjaw set in and the designer died at the age of sixty-three.

His thirty-two-year-old son, Washington Roebling, who had worked closely with his father, was appointed chief engineer. But in 1872 the young man was carried from a caisson suffering from the bends. For the rest of his ninety-year life he was partially paralyzed and largely an invalid. But this did not deter him from carrying out his father's dream.

The Roeblings introduced a completely novel system of pulley-and-reel which permitted the creation of the great cables as they were being installed in their final position. A witness described the process as resembling a giant spider spinning her web.

The Brooklyn Bridge has garnered many firsts. It was the longest suspension bridge in the world and remained so for twenty years; it was the first to span the East River; one of the first to use pneumatic caissons for working underwater; the first to use steel cables; it had for many years the longest span of any bridge on earth. It has probably inspired more poetry, prose, paintings and legends than any other engineering structure in the world. And to walk or to bicycle across it still affords one of the real spectaculars of the modern city.

When the bridge was inaugurated, the official account of the ceremony recorded that it was done "with befitting pomp and ceremonial" and that "throughout the Union, from the rocky headlands of Maine to the golden shores of the Pacific and from the gleaming waters of the St. Lawrence to the vast expanse of the Mexican Gulf, the opening ceremonies were regarded with intelligent concern and approval." In 1973, grateful city fathers celebrated the bridge's ninetieth birthday by painting it with the colors that historians believe were the original ones ordered by Roebling—silver and two shades of buff.

While the opening of the Brooklyn Bridge marked the beginning of a new era, it also marked the end of an old one. Ferry service had been an essential factor in the life of early Manhattan and was largely concentrated on the lower tip of the island. At its peak, seventeen lines plied between Manhattan and Brooklyn alone. The piers of the City's Department of Marine and Aviation, formerly the Manhattan terminus of the South Brooklyn Ferry—built in 1907–1909 and in active service until 1938—are the last surviving witnesses of this vanished period. They are now used by the Coast Guard for service to Governor's Island and also house the offices of the Department of Marine and Aviation.

44. *Old South Brooklyn Ferry Piers*
(now piers of the Department of Marine and Aviation)
11 South Street
1909

Architecturally, these piers stand in extreme contrast to the Brooklyn Bridge and the military structures that have been described. In the piers the basic functional form has been accepted as a skeleton to which an exuberant architectural display has been attached. This is not to imply that the architect did not understand the function; rather, he dramatized it. He did so with the sophisticated vocabulary of the then popular Beaux-Arts style.

To ships approaching the tip of Manhattan, the monumental arched openings of this ferry terminal were indeed the "gateway to the city." The three steel arches look like three colossal tunnels leading into the downtown canyons. Over three hundred feet wide, the bold curves of the archways are in marked contrast to the rectangles of the cityscape that looms behind them. Even today, with no more Brooklyn ferries and with most foreign visitors arriving by plane, a rare experience awaits the New Yorker or the tourist who will invest ten cents for a round-trip ferry ride to Staten Island; he will see the city from its most dramatic approach.

As a quiet coda to all these great and grandiose structures, one of the oldest of lower-Manhattan Landmarks is so inconspicuous as to be often overlooked. This is the simple iron fence around Bowling Green, which was once actually what its name implies, a green for

45. Bowling Green Fence
   Bowling Green
   1771, Richard Sharpe,
      Peter T. Curtenius,
      Gilbert Forbes,
      Andrew Lyall
   Restoration: 1970s

bowling. The fence was erected in 1771 to protect the gilded equestrian statue of George III and also to ensure that the green should not become "a receptacle of all the filth and dirt of the neighborhood." It was estimated it would cost £800, but the final bill was £843.

The statue of the King which used to stand in front of what is now the U.S. Custom House became the hated symbol of tyranny as revolutionary tensions mounted. It was pulled down and hacked apart by a crowd of soldiers and civilians on July 9, 1776, the day the Declaration of Independence reached New York from Philadelphia. The fence fared somewhat better than the statue, although it too was partially destroyed at the time and the ornaments which originally capped the posts (variously described as royal crowns or iron balls) were broken off by patriots and melted down for ammunition. It is said that the melted pieces of the statue were molded into 42,000 bullets by the patriotic wife and daughter of the governor of Connecticut. With an unexcelled penchant for detail, the rumor insists that four hundred British soldiers were killed by these bullets. The fence was repaired after the Revolution, and old prints show that graceful lamps were installed at intervals above the posts.

The Bowling Green Fence had a difficult time. When the subway was being constructed in 1914, this fence was removed entirely. In 1919 it was returned to the park. Currently, plans are under way for a major enlargement of the Bowling Green subway station. When the work is completed, the subway entrance will be eliminated from the park, and Bowling Green itself—which was the city's first public park— will be restored, together with the refurbished fence and a surrounding walk paved in bluestone. There will be new shrubs, flowers, benches and once again a fountain. There are no plans, however, to re-erect the statue of George III.

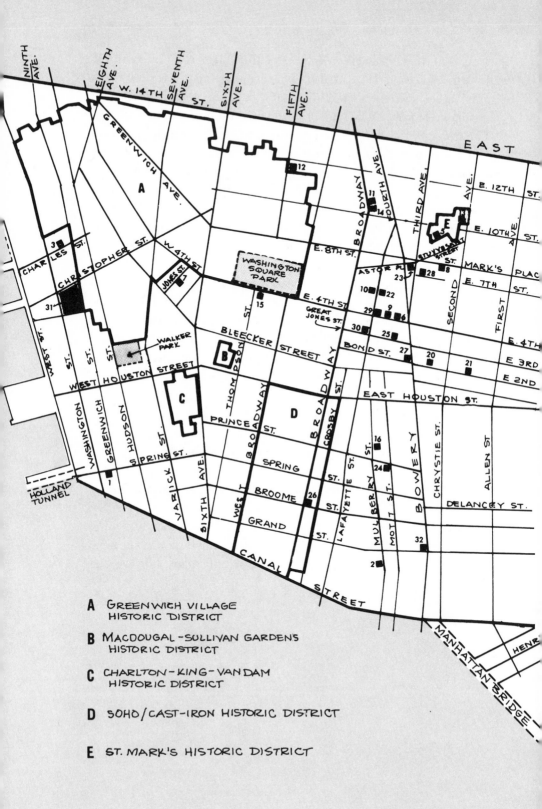

A GREENWICH VILLAGE
HISTORIC DISTRICT

B MACDOUGAL-SULLIVAN GARDENS
HISTORIC DISTRICT

C CHARLTON-KING-VANDAM
HISTORIC DISTRICT

D SOHO/CAST-IRON HISTORIC DISTRICT

E ST. MARK'S HISTORIC DISTRICT

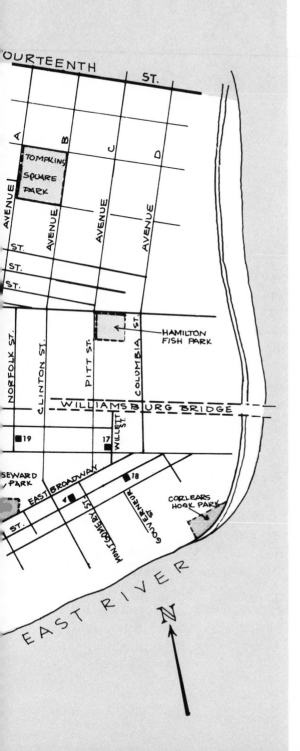

MANHATTAN

*From Canal Street
to 14th Street*

CHAPTER THREE

MANHATTAN

From Canal Street to 14th Street

B<small>Y THE BEGINNING</small> of the 1800s the city extended as far north as Canal Street. As could be surmised, there originally was a canal where Canal Street now is. In fact, there were several canals in the city, including one along Broad Street. These helped to make the raw little colony seem more like home to the Dutchmen, for old Amsterdam, lying below sea level, was riddled with waterways.

Between 1805 and 1840 the whole central spine of the town along Broadway between Canal and 14th Streets had been built up, and the population rose to over 300,000. The city was growing up.

This area between Canal and 14th Streets is where Manhattan abruptly widens to its greatest spread. The bulge on the East River comprises the Lower East Side, where the melting pot had its real genesis and where some of the country's true genius was nurtured. Tomkins Square was originally laid out as a drill ground. Here the Jewish rialto started; today it is a resort for dissident youth—junkies, Black Panthers and flower people. There is the once gently elegant Astor Place and Lafayette Street area, which bristles with Landmarks, and the St. Mark's Historic District. Beyond this is the famous SoHo Cast-Iron area, Greenwich Village and two other gracious Historic Districts.

Most cities grow outward from a central core, adding layer after layer like an onion. But Manhattan is a narrow island, wedged between two swift-flowing rivers. (The East River is actually a tidal strait connecting New York Bay with Long Island Sound.) When Manhattan needed to grow, there was no place to go but up—at first up to the north and later up to the sky. Because of its limitations of space, the city has, from the very beginning, simply rebuilt itself. What once had been quiet residential areas were replaced by commercial or industrial agglomerations—often in successive or alternating waves. And our own day is seeing this process come around in a full circle as many decaying industrial and commercial areas are being reclaimed for residential use.

Row Houses and a Rectory

It is this history of cyclical development that accounts for the fact that even in densely developed business and manufacturing sections we find odd little residential remnants—houses that are a reminder that people actually once lived here. These are lonely survivors and are now often sadly altered from their original condition. One has to put them all together in order to create a composite picture of what any one of them really looked like.

The earliest are the James Brown House, 326 Spring Street, dating from 1817, and the Stephen Van Rensselaer House, 149 Mulberry Street, completed in 1816. Both show the high-shouldered gambrel roof which was a characteristic of many little Federal houses that once dotted the city. The dormers on the Van Rensselaer House with their delicate pilasters and round heads are typical of the style, whereas the dormers on the James Brown house are a later modification. Though built at exactly the same time, the lintels of the Van Rensselaer House are, with their flat incised panels, typically Federal in style while those of the James Brown House, with flared ends and double-flared key-stones, are a throwback to the earlier Georgian period.

The lintels and probably the sills of the late (1834) Federal house at 131 Charles Street, as well as the heavy cornice over the front door, are mid-Victorian additions, but the main wood cornice with its row of "guttae" (little cone-shaped pegs that hang like drops, which is what the word means) beneath the frieze is a miraculous survival of Federal elegance. This little house is in a fine state of repair, and, with an ailanthus tree in its front yard, makes a pleasant break among the lofts and warehouses. The eight-panel front doors of the Charles Street house and of the house at 265 Henry Street are also remarkable survivals of the Federal period. Both are flanked by attenuated Ionic colonnettes; both are surmounted by leaded-glass transoms enframed by richly carved moldings; but the Henry Street house has the added feature of leaded-glass sidelights and the typical Federal detail of a break in the entablature just over the front door itself. In still grander Federal doorways, the leaded-glass transom took the form of a semi-elliptical fanlight. A beautiful example can be seen at 59 Morton Street in Greenwich Village.

At 265 Henry Street, the typical Federal wrought-iron railings have survived; the open box newels and the acorns—symbols of hospitality—that top the areaway posts are characteristic. So are the shuttered window blinds. Yet, even here, the cornice over the doorway and the window lintels are later additions.

The flanking houses, at 263 and 267 Henry Street, though practically contemporary with No. 265, have been much modified by later changes. These three houses together are of historic importance as the home, since its founding by Lillian Wald in 1893, of the Henry Street Settlement House.

The Settlement was one of the earliest attempts to alleviate the intolerable living conditions of slum dwellers on the Lower East Side. Miss Wald, a graduate nurse and settlement worker who lived uptown but worked downtown, persuaded some wealthy friends to finance a small establishment on Henry Street to serve as a volunteer nursing service and social center. Here were generated over the years some of the country's most fundamental health and social programs, among them district nursing, school nurses, the United States Children's Bureau and the whole concept of public-health nursing.

Nos. 83, 85 and 116 Sullivan Street (not pictured) are Federal-style houses, all by unknown architects. They illustrate well what has frequently been called the "architecture of good breeding." The doorway was the most important architectural feature of a Federal house. Despite minor alterations to the door panels at No. 85, both it and No. 83 are equally notable for their complete Federal doorways. The unique enframement of the front door of No. 116 is its claim to fame. Instead of having the usual leaded-glass treatment, the carved wood frames of the sidelights simulate sash curtains drawn through a series of rings.

1. *James Brown House*
   326 Spring Street
   1817

2. *Stephen Van Rensselaer House*
   149 Mulberry Street
   (originally at 153 Mulberry Street)
   1816
   Moved 1841

3. *No. 131 Charles Street*
   1834

4. *Henry Street Settlement*
   265 Henry Street
   1827
   Restored 1964

By picking a cornice here, a doorway or a dormer there, a railing, a lintel or a shutter from someplace else, it is possible to piece together what a Federal-style town house originally looked like. One unfailing clue for brick buildings is the use of Flemish bond. No matter how many details were later added or modified, this common denominator is found in all the surviving examples, for the simple reason that it was deemed a structural necessity. It consisted of alternating "headers" (bricks laid so that the end faces out) and "stretchers" (bricks laid with the side facing out) on each course. It was felt that this was the only method of ensuring that the expensive face brick would be firmly tied to the cheaper common brick laid behind it and that the entire wall, usually twelve inches thick, would support the floor and roof loads it had to carry. Later it was found that stone lintels and sills were sufficient to tie the face of a brick wall to its back-up, and in Greek Revival houses running bond—consisting only of stretchers—was used. This saved a lot of money, since twenty-five percent less of the costly face brick was necessary.

It may be interesting to note how the Federal style was applied to such simple dwellings as that of David Christie, a stonecutter, at 131 Charles Street—it cost him $2,600 in 1834—as well as to the very elegant mansion at 21 Stuyvesant Street which a great-grandson of Governor Peter Stuyvesant built in 1803 as a wedding gift for his

*5. Stuyvesant-Fish House
21 Stuyvesant Street
1803–04*

daughter Elizabeth when she married Nicholas Fish. At the age of eighteen Fish had been commissioned as a major—believed to be the youngest in the history of the United States Army—and he had fought with distinction throughout the Revolutionary War. He was a close friend of Alexander Hamilton and entertained General Lafayette at 21 Stuyvesant Street on the occasion of the latter's triumphant tour of America in 1824, fifty years after the Revolution. Nicholas Fish's son, Hamilton Fish, who was born in this house, became governor of New York State. The house is superbly maintained, and many original features survive in the interior. The exterior, however, has been much stripped down and altered.

The next fashion in architecture to be adopted in New York City houses was the Greek Revival style; whole rows of them survive in the City's Historic Districts. The few individually designated examples are particularly interesting because they illustrate a number of transitional features between the Federal and Greek Revival periods.

In addition to the change from Flemish to running bond, an economy of this period is the shift from wrought iron to cast iron for ornamental details. Cast iron is exactly what it says. Molten metal is cast in molds; it can be highly ornate and yet be reproduced in large quantities quite cheaply. Wrought iron, in contrast, must be hammered out by hand, one piece at a time. While it is much stronger and more delicate than cast iron, it requires the skill and time of expert craftsmen.

These shifts in techniques are comparable to the shift that was being made at the same time from cut glass to pressed glass. All are indicative of the nineteenth-century search for ways to produce cheaply and in large quantity the things that formerly only the wealthy could afford.

The 1844–1845 house at 37 East 4th Street and the nearly identical triplets at 26, 28 and 30 Jones Street show the new running-bond brickwork, but the Daniel Le Roy House at 20 St. Mark's Place and the Old Merchant's House at 29 East 4th Street, built about ten or fifteen years earlier, still retain the old Flemish bond. The earlier houses, however, give a good idea of the new forms of Greek Revival lintels—either flat with square ends as on the Old Merchant's House or slightly pedimented and often with a reverse rise at the ends. In the finer houses they were capped by a simple projecting molding.

6. *No. 37 East 4th Street*
1845

7. *Nos. 26, 28, 30 Jones Street*
1844

The splayed lintels on the Jones Street houses are misleading. Actually they have nothing to do with the Georgian prototypes they suggest but are the result of ill-advised restoration. Originally these lintels had typically Greek Revival "cap moldings," but when they deteriorated (as they have at 37 East 4th Street) the mason simply shaved them off flush with the flat stone below. An awkward triangular gap was left between the square end of the lintel and the stone lug where the original cap molding had returned into the brickwork. The mason filled in this triangle with the same white stucco which he spread over the entire surface. The splayed end we see is the result. These houses are all that are left of what was undoubtedly a block-long row of similar structures. Today, with the exception of the three survivals, the block is rather nondescript, even ramshackle.

No. 37 East 4th Street has the characteristic Greek Revival attic windows. Nearly always horizontal in proportion, these windows are often set into the flat frieze or fascia bond that runs just below the cornice. This house also has the paired Ionic columns supporting a full entablature over the front door that is typical of a grand Greek Revival house; No. 28 Jones Street illustrates a less pretentious treatment. And it can be noted that the elaborate leaded-glass transoms and sidelights of Federal days are things of the past; they have been replaced by simple panels divided into small panes. The Federal fluted colonnettes have been replaced by flat pilasters, and the elaborate broken entablature has become an austerely simple frieze with a simple row of dentils providing the only ornamentation.

The unusual doorways at the Old Merchant's House and the Daniel Le Roy House trouble architectural historians. They seem to have little to do with either the Federal or the Greek Revival style but rather to have been inspired by some of the great houses built in England during the late seventeenth and early eighteenth centuries. Similar examples may be found at 28 Bedford Square in London, at Cleve Manor in Virginia and in the Hooper House in Danvers, Massachusetts. All have the same heavy blocks interrupting the rich surrounding moldings of the arched enframements crowned with multiple splayed keystones. In the Old Merchant's House paneled blocks have also been inserted around the basement windows.

If its door enframement is unusual, the panels of the stoop railings and the ornaments which cap the areaway fence of the Old Merchant's House are good illustrations of the incoming use of repetitive cast-iron

8. Daniel Le Roy House
20 St. Mark's Place
1832

decorations. They are used here in combination with wrought-iron stoop railings and handsome urn-shaped newels.

The Old Merchant's House, which is open to the public as a museum, belonged to Seabury Tredwell. A trapdoor to a cellar with access to the East River leads one to believe that Tredwell, a well-known abolitionist, might have used the house as part of the underground railway. His daughter Gertrude was born in the house in 1840 and died there in 1933, at the age of ninety-three. The interior has been well preserved and is remarkable in retaining most of its original furniture and fittings. Funds have recently been provided from various sources for a complete renovation and restoration of the house.

No. 37 East 4th Street was built by Samuel Tredwell Skidmore, a distant cousin of Seabury Tredwell. Skidmore was a well-to-do citizen who made his fortune in the wholesale rug business and served as vestryman and senior warden of Trinity Church. Skidmore, with his wife and eight children, lived here for almost four decades.

In the 1840s East 4th Street was one of the most fashionable residential streets of the city, sharing with its neighbors on Lafayette Street some of the glamour of high society. With the inexorable growth of the city, however, the private homes made way for commercial establishments, until by the early twentieth century the only residential survivals were the two homes of the Tredwell cousins, Nos. 29 and 37.

Three other important residential structures are to be found within a few blocks of one another: Colonnade Row, a Greek Revival example in a class by itself, Grace Church Rectory, one of the first and also one of the best residences in the Gothic Revival style, and the Salmagundi Club, a prototype of the Italianate which was to dominate the city's architecture during much of the balance of the century.

La Grange Terrace, on Lafayette Street, more popularly known as Colonnade Row, was built from 1831 to 1833 and now contains only four of the nine original buildings. In one of them is an off-Broadway theater which proudly housed a long-run phenomenally successful production, *The Dirtiest Show in Town*.

While contemporary with the Greek Revival period, the richly carved two-story-high row of Corinthian columns as well as the strong base, with its deep joints, betray a Roman inspiration. True, the Corinthian columns and the entablature have been copied from a

9. *Old Merchant's House*
   29 East 4th Street
   1831–32, attributed to Minard
   Lafever

10. *La Grange Terrace, or Colonnade*
   Row (early view)
   428–434 Lafayette Street
   1831–33

Greek order rather than a Roman one, but the proportions and spacing of the columns are more Roman than Greek. Then, too, there is certainly no Greek precedent for the rusticated ground story on which the columns rest. The treatment seems much closer to the sort of free classicism that Thomas Jefferson employed in his 1785 State Capitol at Richmond.

This is a style that Jefferson almost single-handedly tried to establish on American soil. He felt that nothing would be more appropriate to symbolize our emerging republic than the restraint and dignified grandeur of Republican Rome. His own designs for the State Capitol in Richmond, for his home at Monticello and for the University of Virginia in Charlottesville are strong statements of his convictions.

Perhaps the best solution to the Colonnade Row question is not to worry about a proper label but simply to enjoy it for what it is. Certainly La Grange Terrace is one of the finest examples in New York of the treatment of a row of individual houses as a single architectural unit, as had so successfully been done in London and Bath.

The design of Colonnade Row has frequently been attributed to Alexander Jackson Davis because James Dakin of the firm of Town, Davis & Dakin was responsible for the design of many of the interiors. But there is no evidence that either Davis or Dakin had any connection with the exterior design. Mrs. Regina Kellerman, the architectural historian, has, in an unpublished paper, tentatively attributed the overall design of the buildings to Robert Higham, a long-forgotten architect of the period. The work is obviously from the hand of a very skillful architect and quite an original one.

John Jacob Astor, Jr., Edwin D. Morgan, a governor of New York State, and Warren Delano, grandfather of President Franklin Delano Roosevelt, were residents at one time or another of these buildings. The most romantic story connected with the row concerns the David Gardiner family, who lived in one of the houses. One weekend in 1844, Mr. Gardiner, who also owned Gardiner's Island, and his young daughter Julia were guests of President John Tyler on a pleasure excursion aboard the gunboat *Princeton*. There was an explosion during the excursion and Gardiner was killed. Three months later Julia eloped with Tyler, a recent widower and the father of seven children, some of whom were older than their new stepmother. Julia was a dashing society belle, and during the nine months she held sway in the White House she created considerable stir in the nation's capital. Some of her later years were spent in another Landmark, the Gardiner-Tyler House on Staten Island.

Just a few blocks away from the magnificence of Colonnade Row is the enchanting little Grace Church Rectory on Broadway opposite East 11th Street. This house, by James Renwick, Jr., is one of the

11. Grace Church Rectory   804 Broadway
1846, James Renwick, Jr.

12. Salmagundi Club
(former Irad Hawley House)
47 Fifth Avenue
1853

earliest Gothic Revival residences in Manhattan and illustrates his somewhat naïve struggle to break away from classical symmetry. In actuality, the house consists of two gabled wings of equal width balanced on either side of a central porch. But in order to make it seem asymmetrical the bay windows on either side of the porch are treated quite differently. This was obviously a romantic afterthought and had nothing to do with the requirements of the plan.

The Salmagundi Club, at 47 Fifth Avenue, was erected in 1853 and is notable as one of the first brownstone mansions designed in the newly fashionable Italianate style. The characteristics of the style show clearly in the heavy pediment over the arched doorway, in the richly carved consoles that support this pediment and in the little brackets that carry the individual cornices over each of the French windows of the main floor. The moldings around all the rest of the windows were later stripped off, but the main cornice along the top of the building is still supported on its original heavy paired brackets.

The Salmagundi Club is the last of the brownstone mansions that once lined Fifth Avenue almost solidly from Washington Square to Central Park—"Two Miles of Millionaires." The mansion was built for Irad Hawley, president of the Pennsylvania Coal Company. The

club, which was organized in 1871 for "the promotion of social inter-
course among artists and the advancement of art," bought the building in 1917 and has kept it in a state of impeccable preservation. The
name of the club was taken from a series of satirical essays written by a
group of young bloods led by Washington Irving and later published
under the title *Salmagundi,* which had been taken from the name of a
spicy stew of chopped meat, anchovies, eggs, onions and oil. And this
in turn had come from the Italian *salami conditi,* or pickled sausages.

Churches, Cemeteries and a Synagogue

Between Canal and 14th Streets there are three large and important
churches that almost exactly span the nineteenth century, dating from
the beginning, the middle and the end. The area also has four smaller
and less well-known churches that date from the first half of the nineteenth century. The Greenwich Village Historic District contains
others which, like everything else in that large, heterogeneous district,
represent all styles, sizes and types.

Earliest of the three great churches is St. Mark's-in-the-Bowery,
dating from 1799, the central body of which is quite similar to St.
Paul's Chapel, the only surviving church in Manhattan that predates
it. St. Mark's is built of the same small, almost cobblestone-sized rough
masonry, with smooth trim around the windows—late Georgian in
feeling and very simple and austere. Two additions have been made to
the church, and, though they date from two quite different periods,
they harmonize remarkably well. In 1828, at the height of the Greek
Revival period, the famous architect Ithiel Town added a square
belfry, a clock tower and a spire atop the main pediment. A generation later a cast-iron portico was built across the front of the church in
the newly fashionable Italianate style. With its narrow arches, flanked
by engaged columns, and with its paired columns at the corners, the
composition is quite Palladian in feeling.

The fact that the late-Georgian, Greek Revival and Italianate
portions of St. Mark's-in-the-Bowery are so harmonious demonstrates
that these styles are in fact variations on a single theme: the Classical
Tradition.

The church was built on old Peter Stuyvesant's "Bouwerie," or

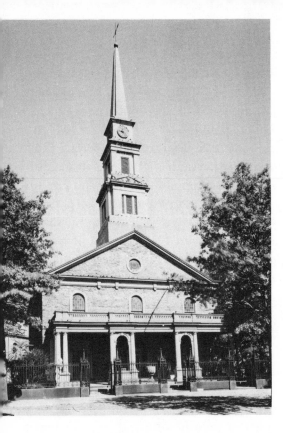

13. *St. Mark's-in-the-Bowery*
Second Avenue at 10th Street
1799
Steeple: 1828, Ithiel Town
Portico: 1854

farm, and near the site of his private chapel. After the English took over New Amsterdam in 1664, Peter continued to live in his beloved Bouwerie, often entertaining the English governor himself. Peter was buried here when he died in 1672, at the age of eighty, as were six generations of subsequent Stuyvesants. The Dutch and English names of many other families famous in the city's history can still be read on the flat tombstones in the surrounding churchyard, the whole of which is enclosed by a very handsome iron fence erected in 1838.

The last direct descendant of Peter was Augustus Van Horne Stuyvesant, Jr., an eighth-generation Stuyvesant born in 1870, who lived in a Fifth Avenue mansion, with a summer home in Newport, and increased his already sizable fortune by astute dealings in Manhattan real estate. He spent the last twenty-five years of his life as a complete recluse, venturing out of his mansion only to pay his weekly respects to his ancestors at St. Mark's. He died in 1953 and was buried beside them.

Despite its venerable antecedents, the church has at times been a little advanced in the theological field. Dr. William Norman Guthrie, who was pastor in the 1920s, preached the essential unity of all religions. He introduced a Body and Soul Clinic, American Indian chants and Greek folk dancing, all of which deeply offended the more conservative members of his congregation.

This same spirit of enterprise has persisted into recent years, during which the composition of the parish has changed considerably. Instead of a prosperous middle-class community, the church now serves an underprivileged population. In an attempt to keep youngsters off the streets and out of trouble, the pastor had the tree-shaded churchyard in which grass never grew covered with paving blocks, the work being done by local boys. It is now used as a playground. The church has also been the scene of some pretty far-out religious services in the modern idiom. Some parishioners resent the use of an historic church for such manifestations of the taste of today's youth, but others have recognized that, with changing social conditions, the role of the church must change if it is going to survive.

Like so many churches in changing neighborhoods, St. Mark's has severe financial woes. Recently it had to go, hat in hand, to its parishioners for money in order to obey the Board of Health edict to exterminate the friendly pigeons who were nesting and reproducing in the ironwork.

In 1843 young James Renwick, Jr.—who was only twenty-five at the time—was commissioned to design Grace Church at the head of Broadway, on the corner of 10th Street. This was a particularly prominent site, because Broadway changes direction at that point.

For many years Grace Church dominated all northward views of New York City. The building was built in white marble, quarried at Sing Sing (now Ossining) on the Hudson. The stonework is used almost like lace. The tracery of the windows, the pinnacles, the piers and the crenellations along the roof are freely designed and delicately executed. The spire was originally constructed of wood, which led to rumors that the foundations of the church were not strong enough to support one of marble. The rumor was finally put to rest in 1863 when members of the building committee declared that there was "no truth in the ridiculous story" and that Renwick himself had "advised us strongly to put up a spire of stone. The difficulty in the way of carrying out his views was not the want of a foundation, but the want of funds." Ironically, thirty-seven years later when the wooden spire

14. *Grace Church*
800 Broadway, at 10th Street
1843–45, James Renwick, Jr.

was replaced by one of marble, it cost more than two-thirds the original cost of the entire church.

The church has always been highly fashionable. In the 1880s the editor of the *Home Journal* described Society as made up of those "who keep carriages, live above Bleecker, are subscribers to the opera, go to Grace Church, have a town house and a country house and give balls."

The sexton of the church, one Isaac Hull Brown, who had an undertaking and rent-a-carriage business on the side, became indispensable to the leaders of Society. He made up their guest lists, delivered the invitations, selected the menu, flowers and music, and, on the big evening, was at the curb to greet the guests—many of whom arrived in carriages he had rented to them. An observer of the mores and foibles of New York in 1872 comments: "A wedding over which he presides is sure to be a great success. A wonderful man is Brown. . . . There is no sharper, shrewder man in New York and no one who estimates his customers more correctly. . . . Fat and sleek and smooth of tongue he can be a very despot when he chooses."

Allen Churchill quotes a poem written by an anonymous contemporary who commemorates Brown's versatility:

> *Oh, glorious Brown! thou medley strange*
> *of churchyard, ball-room, saint and sinner!*
> *Flying by morn through Fashion's range,*
> *And burying mortals after dinner!*
> *Walking one day with invitations—*
> *Passing the next at consecrations;*
> *Tossing the sod at eve on coffins;*
> *With one hand drying the tears of orphans,*
> *And one unclasping ball-room carriage,*
> *Or cutting plum cake up for marriage;*
> *Dusting by day the pew and missal,*
> *Sounding by night the ball-room whistle.*
> *Admitted free through Fashion's wicket,*
> *And skilled at psalms, at punch and cricket.*

With the completion of Renwick's Grace Church in 1846, a year and a half after the completion of Upjohn's Trinity, Gothic became truly established as *the* appropriate style for ecclesiastical architecture, and in particular for Episcopal churches. Grace Church was much freer in its details than Trinity, and its white marble had a sparkle that brownstone could not equal. Both churches, however, have the same symmetrical plan with a square tower serving as the entrance to the nave. Though the later work of Renwick and Upjohn was to go through various phases and modifications, both had a dominant influence on the great church-building decades of the 1840s and 1850s.

The third important church in this part of the city illustrates how radically tastes had changed by the end of the century. The Judson Memorial Baptist Church and the adjoining Judson Hall and Bell Tower, on the south side of Washington Square, were designed by McKim, Mead & White in the neo–Italian Renaissance manner, one of several styles this famous firm was to introduce during the Eclectic period. The little clusters of round arched windows in the belfry blend beautifully, despite a change of scale, with the arches of the church itself. All these buildings are constructed in warm yellow Roman brick, relieved by terra-cotta bands and moldings and by panels of richly colored marble. The craftsmanship is superb. The stained-glass windows were executed by John La Farge.

15. *Judson Memorial Church   Washington Square South at Thompson*
    Street
   1892, McKim, Mead & White
   Judson Hall and Tower   52–54 Washington Square South
   1890–95, McKim, Mead & White
   The Judson   51 Washington Square South
   1877, John G. Prague

The small houses of worship that dot the area between Canal and 14th Streets are illustrative not only of a variety of much simpler styles but also of the variety of denominations that have existed in New York from its earliest days. Unlike some of the other colonies, New York, though not without a struggle, early achieved religious tolerance, and as populations moved and shifted frequently, the church of one denomination was often taken over by another.

The earliest of this group is the oldest Roman Catholic edifice in New York City. Old St. Patrick's Cathedral, at Mott and Prince Streets, was begun in 1809, a year after the Diocese of New York was established by Pope Pius VII. The work was interrupted due to the War of 1812, but Joseph Mangin, co-architect of City Hall, which was contemporary with St. Patrick's, was able to complete it by 1815.

A casual glance at Old St. Patrick's would hardly suggest its significance in the history of American architecture. All one sees today, except for some pointed windows along the nave, is the front that was added in 1868 when the church was rebuilt after a disastrous fire. One has to look at an old print to appreciate that the original building

16. Old St. Patrick's Cathedral
Mott and Prince Streets
1809–15, Joseph F. Mangin
Rebuilt 1868 (left, original
appearance and, right, today)

constructed by Mangin was actually a very early attempt to design something in the Gothic style. There is nothing quite like it anywhere except for the 1807 Chapel of St. Mary's Seminary in Baltimore, which has been called "the first church of the Gothic Revival to be executed in America." Both buildings go considerably further than the "Gothic survival" pointed windows that have been noted in connection with the Georgian design of the Church of the Transfiguration and the Sea and Land Church. There was a real attempt, in the original front of Old St. Patrick's, to compose a tripartite Gothic façade. A large window with elaborate tracery filled the central gable. The full classical entablature and balustrade which topped the walls were used simply because the architects knew of no other way in which to finish a building. Yet despite these naïve incongruities, Mangin must be credited with something as original at Old St. Patrick's as he usually is credited, in association with McComb, with something as beautiful as City Hall.

New York was created an archdiocese in 1850, and the church remained the seat of the archdiocese until 1879, when the much grander St. Patrick's Cathedral on Fifth Avenue was completed. Recently, a $200,000 restoration of the old church was celebrated with a rededication by Terence Cardinal Cooke, who commented that the church should henceforth be known as "Young St. Patrick's."

The adjoining walled cemetery encloses the graves of many well-known parishioners, including Pierre Toussaint, a black New Yorker who was born a slave in Haiti and who has been proposed for sainthood.

Bialystoker Synagogue, at 7 Willett Street, and St. Augustine's Chapel, nearby at 290 Henry Street, have much in common, with their fieldstone masonry construction and late-Federal-style details, even though the synagogue has round-topped windows and those of the chapel are pointed. Both types of windows derive from English precedents of the early nineteenth century. The Bialystoker Synagogue was originally a Methodist Episcopal church; St. Augustine's Chapel, now part of Trinity Church Parish, was originally the All Saints' Free Church.

The last of this group, at 60 Norfolk Street, was originally built as a Baptist church in 1850. It is a restrained example of the Gothic Revival style. In 1860, when the Baptists moved north, the Methodists

18. *St. Augustine's Chapel*
(originally All Saints'
Free Church)
290 Henry Street
1829

17. *Bialystoker Synagogue (originally*
Willett Street M. E. Church)
7–13 Willett Street
1826

19. *Beth Hamedrash Hagodol*
Synagogue
(originally Norfolk Street
Baptist Church)
60–64 Norfolk Street
1850

took it over for the next quarter of a century. They, in turn, were replaced by Russian Jews, who had been settling for some time on the Lower East Side. The church was rededicated as Beth Hamedrash Hagodol Synagogue and still serves the oldest congregation of Russian Orthodox Jews to have been organized in this country. Around it has focused much of the life of this very colorful neighborhood.

Two of New York's least-known Landmarks are the once fashionable burying grounds near 2nd Street and Second Avenue. Both were laid out as a result of a city ordinance that no further burials were to take place below Canal Street, under penalty of a fine of $250. The earlier of the two, the New York Marble Cemetery, is hidden in the interior of the block bounded by Second Avenue, the Bowery, and 2nd and 3rd Streets and is entered from an alley on Second Avenue. Actually, this is an invisible Landmark, since the burial vaults are underground and all that the visitor peering through the gates can see is a small green lawn, with plaques set into the high surrounding walls.

The New York Marble Cemetery was strictly a commercial venture by a group of businessmen who bought half an acre of land and on it built 156 underground vaults of Tuckahoe marble. These were sold to the city's leading families. In those days Second Avenue was a fashionable section, and the promoters cunningly located their cemetery in the center of the block, leaving room for fine houses on the street fronts. The lucky 156 were determined to be buried not only in Manhattan but in the most exclusive residential area.

Dr. Valentine Mott, a prominent surgeon, Dr. Gardiner Spring, pastor of the Brick Presbyterian Church, Uriah Scribner and his son Charles, the publishers, and Peter Lorillard, who established the Landmark Lorillard Snuff Mill in the Bronx and later founded a thriving tobacco empire, were among those who, looking forward to the future, bought the original vaults. Of this original group, however, only the Scribners were ever buried there. Subsequent interments included members of some of New York's first families—Varicks, Beekmans, Howes, Van Zandts and Hoyts.

This, the first nonsectarian public cemetery in the city, was opened in 1830. It was so popular, if that's the proper word, that it was followed a year later by another, around the corner on 2nd Street. This one, the New York *City* Marble Cemetery, is aboveground and can be seen through a handsome iron fence, between Second and First Avenues. The policy was the same: nonsectarian, open to anybody who wished to buy a vault, though the vaults here are marked by many handsome monuments and headstones. Among the dignitaries interred here are Preserved Fish, the well-known merchant, and Marinus Willett, a hero of the Revolutionary War. Here also are

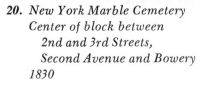

20. *New York Marble Cemetery*
    Center of block between
    2nd and 3rd Streets,
    Second Avenue and Bowery
    1830

21. *New York City Marble Cemetery*
    52–74 East 2nd Street
    1831

buried members of one branch of the Roosevelt family, including James Henry Roosevelt, who founded Roosevelt Hospital, as well as members of the Kip family, who gave their name to Kip's Bay.

Both cemeteries today are supported by endowments administered by boards of trustees. In time, Second Avenue lost out to Fifth Avenue as the city's most elegant thoroughfare, and today these small plots are oases in a shabby neighborhood.

Public Buildings

The mid-nineteenth-century interest in all things Italian found expression in two public buildings in the area of Astor Place—the Astor Library and Cooper Union.

Astor Place was named after the first John Jacob Astor, who arrived in New York in 1784, a twenty-one-year-old immigrant from Germany, with twenty-five dollars in his pocket, a thick German accent and a driving ambition. In his heyday a contemporary described him as "tall and heavily built with a decided German look, a dull un-intellectual face and a cold reserved manner."

In 1789 Astor made his first real-estate investment—a parcel of land between the Bowery and Elizabeth Street which he acquired for forty-seven pounds. He died at the age of eighty-five, leaving a fortune made from fur trading and dealing in Manhattan real estate. His sons were destined to make the name Astor synonymous with Society.

Apparently dissatisfied with his accomplishments, Astor is said to have muttered while lying on his deathbed, "Could I begin life again I would buy every foot of Manhattan Island." In spite of his regrets, Astor did pretty well for himself. During the middle years of the century he was known as "the landlord of New York" because of the rich income he received from such places as the Five Points. He weathered the 1837 Panic nicely by picking up mortgages and promptly foreclosing on them.

Astor's name was perpetuated in some of the city's theaters, hotels and streets. One of the city's great tragedies occurred on Astor Place. The growth of gang activities during the 1840s, resulting from deep-seated social unrest and a growing xenophobia, culminated in the Astor Place Riot of 1849. The Astor Place Opera House stood between Astor Place and 8th Street at Lafayette Street. A silly feud between the rather plebeian American actor Edwin Forrest and the aging British tragedian William Macready fanned the fires of hate among the gangs and their followers. Cries of "America for the Americans!" and "Workingmen! Shall Americans or English rule in this city?" greeted the announcement that Macready was to play *Macbeth* at the Astor Place Opera House.

Warned ahead of time, the city authorities had police and militia on hand for the performance. Rioters of the so-called Native American Party forced their way into the theater; others threw rocks through the windows, bringing down the great crystal chandelier. Macready escaped, but the fighters outside were joined by thousands of sympathizers until the police were completely outnumbered. Finally the militia fired point-blank on the crowd. The bloody aftermath was twenty-two killed, 150 wounded and eighty-six arrested.

The New York correspondent of the Philadelphia *Ledger,* appalled at the implications of the riot, reported that there was a "feeling that there is now in our country, in New York City, what every good patriot hitherto has considered it his duty to deny—a *high* and a *low* class."

New York is no stranger to riots. Beginning back in 1712, when rebelling black slaves were firmly routed by an armed militia, through our own day violent protest has been a way of life in New York. In 1741, the two thousand Negro slaves of the city, aroused by the auction and mistreatment of a shipload of blacks, set fire to the governor's house and touched off rioting that resulted in hundreds of hangings, burnings at the stake and arrests. In 1765 New York patriots, like their New England brethren, protested the Stamp Act, with bloody results: "The first man that either distributes or makes use of stamped paper, let him take care of his house, person, and effects." In 1788 mobs, incensed by stories of body-snatching by medical students, marched on the New York Hospital calling for the blood of the doctors who were desecrating the graves of their loved ones. Again the rioters were put down by the military. Just fourteen years after the Astor Place riots, the Draft Riots of 1863 paralyzed the city. These four bloody days of protest against conscription for service in the Union Army resulted in the death of more than twelve hundred rioters and in three million dollars' worth of damage throughout the city.

The only public benefaction that the original John Jacob Astor made was the Astor Library at 425 Lafayette Street, the first great library in this country to be made available to the public. Later the Astor merged with the Lenox Library and the Tilden Trust, to form the New York Public Library, which, despite its name, is still largely dependent on private financial support. Theoretically, Astor set his library up for the poor, but, since the hours were only from ten to four, most workingmen couldn't make use of it. Furthermore, books could not be taken from the reading room, and pen and ink could not be used in taking notes.

The Astor Library was built over a period of more than thirty years by three different architects, who carried through the original design so meticulously that it is impossible, from a mere inspection, to tell where one began and another left off. The conception was of a north-Italian palace of the early Renaissance period, but the smallness of the scale and a certain fussiness of detail betray its mid-Victorian origins. The over-all impression is one of elegance and charm rather than boldness and strength.

The building has had a long and eventful life. When the library moved in 1911 to its new home in Bryant Park, the Lafayette Street building became the home of the Hebrew Immigrant Aid Society, during the period of the great influx of immigrants from Eastern Europe. In 1965 the society decided to dispose of the building and had signed a contract for its sale for $550,000 just as the Landmarks

22. *Astor Library (later Hebrew Immigrant Aid Society and now the*
    Public Theatre)
    425 Lafayette Street
    South wing: 1849–53, Alexander Saeltzer
    Center section: 1856–59, Griffith Thomas
    North wing: 1879–81, Thomas Stent
    Reconversion: 1966, Giorgio Cavaglieri

Preservation Commission came into existence. At its first public hearing, in September 1965, the Commission heard designation pleas for fifteen Manhattan buildings, including the Astor Library. The building was designated a Landmark, despite protests of the society that this would ruin the proposed sale. At this moment, Joseph Papp, director of the Shakespeare Festival Public Theatre, which had been giving free performances outdoors in Central Park, called the Commission and asked if there were a Landmark which he could use for an indoor theater. And there, by chance, was the Astor Library. Papp, by some miracle, found the $550,000. He even persuaded the prospective purchaser, who had been going to tear it down, to make a contribution.

The library has now embarked on a whole new life as the Public Theatre. The entire interior has been reconstructed by architect Giorgio Cavaglieri into a series of dramatically modern stages for various types of productions.

Contemporary with the Astor Library and not far away is the Foundation Building of Cooper Union on Cooper Square, an adaptation by the architect Frederick A. Petersen of Italianate motifs to a freestanding building of monumental size. It was opened in 1859.

23. *Foundation Building, Cooper Union*
   (original appearance, from a rendering)
   Cooper Square between Astor Place and 7th Street
   1853–59, Frederick A. Petersen
   (6th, 7th and 8th stories added 1880–95, Leopold Eidlitz
   Reconstruction: 1972–73, John Hejduk)

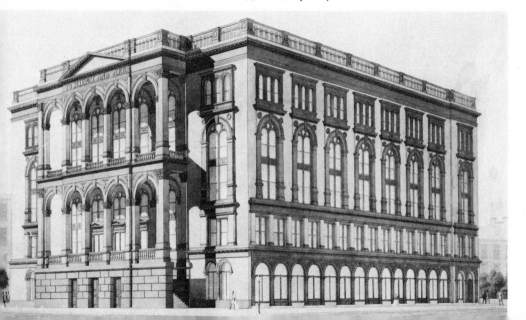

Subsequent additions have not helped the original design, but the building is very important in other ways—to the history of structural technology and to the history of American education.

Peter Cooper was a very different character from John Jacob Astor. Cooper was one of the greatest technical and social pioneers of the century. A contemporary described his face, though sharp and thin, as "one of the most thoroughly amiable and benevolent countenances to be met with in New York. It is emphatically the face of a good man."

Cooper developed his own rolling mills in New Jersey and successfully produced some of the first rolled wrought-iron sections to be used in building construction. They were incorporated into the Cooper Union Foundation Building, and some are still to be seen, exposed in the basement ceiling. In this development he adapted the rollers that had been turning out railroad rails to the making of new shapes. The first new section, a T with a round bulb at the end of the leg, did not look very different from the rail from which it had evolved. But the bulb was soon widened into a more efficient second flange, and the H and I sections with which we are familiar today were soon being produced. When these were rolled in steel instead of wrought iron, skyscraper construction became possible. The Cooper Union building also contains a prototype for that other invention essential to the skyscraper—the elevator. Incorporated in the structure, and still there, is a round shaft intended for a passenger elevator, constructed several years before the elevator itself became safe and feasible for human use in this country. Eventually a square elevator was installed, but a current planned renovation of the interior of the building includes the installation of a round cage to fit the original shaft.

As a social pioneer, Peter Cooper's contribution has been equally far-reaching. His endowment of Cooper Union created one of the earliest free institutions of education in the country, with emphasis on the trades and useful arts to equip students with the means of earning a living. The admission of women to the Union, in this mid-19th-century period, was also a great advance. It was in the auditorium of Cooper Union in 1860 that Abraham Lincoln gave the speech which is credited with launching him on the career that led to the Presidency.

In quite a different mood, two other public buildings in the area have been designated Landmarks for their architectural qualities. Around the corner from Old St. Patrick's Cathedral is its associated

24. *Old St. Patrick's Convent and
    Girls' School
    32 Prince Street, at Mott Street
    1826*

25. *Firehouse, Engine Company
    No. 33
    44 Great Jones Street
    1898, Ernest Flagg and
    W. B. Chambers*

convent and school. Though not completed until 1826, Old St. Patrick's Convent and Girls' School was conservatively designed in the late Federal style. Its main doorway closely rivals the one at 59 Morton Street in Greenwich Village as the finest surviving example of this restrained but elegant style.

Seventy years later, elegance was still appreciated for public purposes. Ernest Flagg's little firehouse at 44 Great Jones Street is full of fun, full of exuberance, full of the imaginative creation that found here a happy expression in the Beaux-Arts style. It is still actively used as a firehouse—for Engine Company 33—and lends a note of gaiety to its neighborhood of loft buildings.

Commercial Buildings

Within this area of the city, between Canal and 14th Streets, seven notable commercial buildings graphically illustrate the difference between "fashion" and "style." In some of them the forthright display of the materials with which they are built—the cast iron, the bricks, the stone masonry—and the direct expression of how these different materials are put together constitute "style." In the others, a "fashion" has been superimposed on the structure. In these latter cases some other mode might as readily have been selected, since "fashion" bears no essential relationship to the underlying structure or material.

The first group to be considered are the Haughwout Building at 488 Broadway, the Bouwerie Lane Theatre, originally the Bond Street Savings Bank, at Broadway and Bond Street, and the First Ukrainian Assembly of God (originally built for the Metropolitan Savings Bank) at 9 East 7th Street.

Oldest in date (completed in 1857) and the most important from many points of view is the Haughwout Building, without doubt the masterpiece of the cast-iron prefabricated system first developed by James Bogardus. John Gaynor, the architect of the building, used sections cast for him by Bogardus' rival and competitor, Daniel Badger. All the floor loads have been concentrated on evenly spaced cast-iron columns that carry them directly down to the ground. Between the columns, windows and cast-iron spandrel panels have been hung as a curtain. They keep out the weather and let in a maximum amount of daylight, but they carry no part of the load.

26. *Haughwout Building*
488–492 Broadway,
at Broome Street
1857, John P. Gaynor

Gaynor chose the style of Sansovino's Library of St. Mark in Venice as his model. As we have seen, there are many affinities between what architects were doing in sixteenth-century Venice and what architects and engineers were doing in mid-nineteenth-century New York. There are minor differences, however; in cast iron the columns could be considerably thinner than in stone, and the economy of making many castings from the same mold encouraged the repetition of the same details from bay to bay and from story to story.

While the Cooper Union Foundation Building had provided a shaft for a nonexistent elevator, the Haughwout Building—designed as an elegant retail store for china, silver, glassware, clocks and chandeliers—actually had Elisha Otis' first elevator. It was supported by cables over a drum, the operating principle of all modern elevators. Thus in its frame-and-curtain-wall construction, and in its pioneering use of an elevator, the Haughwout Building is a true prototype of the twentieth-century skyscraper.

The present Bouwerie Lane Theatre, built a generation later, in 1874, is also a cast-iron building, though no one would guess it by looking at it. It was built originally for the Bond Street Savings Bank and later became the German Exchange Bank. Still later it was used as a loft building, until 1963, when it was remodeled to become the off-Broadway theater it is today.

Here the architect has quite arbitrarily used the French Second Empire style, which was then very fashionable. The entire impression of the building is of a great stone structure, with its heavy quoins apparently bracing the corners, its pediments, its ponderous cornice, and its emphasis on the horizontal. As a purely aesthetic exercise the building is satisfactory. There is a subtle balance between the narrow façade on the Bowery and the long façade on Bond Street. The architect has made full use of a rich vocabulary: sometimes the columns flanking the windows are single, sometimes they are double; rusticated piers recall the quoins in an interesting rhythm; the central second-story windows are emphasized with pediments and roundheaded windows are played against flatheaded ones. All of these devices, however, are unrelated to the underlying structural system that is so clearly expressed in the Haughwout Building. They are merely surface imitations in cast iron of a character that would be perfectly appropriate to a building supported on masonry bearing walls.

This is immediately apparent in a comparison between the

27. *Bond Street Savings Bank*
(now Bouwerie Lane Theatre)
330 Bowery, at Bond Street
1874, Henry Engelbert

28. *Metropolitan Savings Bank*
(now First Ukrainian Assembly of God)
9 East 7th Street
1867, Carl Pfeiffer

Bouwerie Lane Theatre and the all-marble Metropolitan Savings Bank (now the First Ukrainian Assembly of God), built only seven years earlier and in the same French Second Empire manner. The use of quoins to emphasize corners, the breaks in the façade, the balustrades beneath the principal windows, the cornices at each story level are all similar. The treatment of the main entrance, with a pedimented window above it, is practically identical. Yet the Metropolitan Savings Bank is a stone building. Its floor loads are carried by thick masonry walls down to a continuous footing that rests on the ground—the complete antithesis of the point support system characteristic of cast-iron construction.

Both the Haughwout Building and the Metropolitan Savings Bank are good examples of what we have called "style." Both are straight-forward expressions of their structural systems and the materials of which they are made—in the Haughwout Building cast iron and in the Metropolitan Savings Bank stone. The Bouwerie Lane Theatre, on the other hand, is a good example of what we have called "fashion." It is really a cast-iron building disguised to look like a masonry-bearing-wall building. Superficially the Metropolitan Savings Bank and the Bouwerie Lane Theatre look alike, yet the former is an honest expression of its stone construction. On the other hand, the theater and the Haughwout Building, which do not resemble each other at all, have the same basic cast-iron structure.

A similar contrast in structural expression can be drawn between the De Vinne Press Building at 393 Lafayette Street and the loft building across the street at No. 376. Both buildings in this case are supported by brick bearing walls. The De Vinne Press, designed by Babb, Cook & Willard in 1885, immediately suggests the strength and solidity of the walls. One senses, almost physically, the weight of the printing presses and the great rolls of stored paper. The arched window heads, whether half round or segmental, show clearly how the load of the wall above is being spread to the flanking piers. Where great archways have been extended up through two or three floors, the thickness of the bearing walls is dramatically contrasted to the flat, thin screens of steel and glass that fill the openings and which obviously play no role in carrying the load.

Theodore De Vinne, after whom the building is named, was a distinguished scholar, founder and president of the Grolier Club, and author of many books on the history and the art of printing. He was responsible for the production of *Scribner's Monthly, St. Nicholas* magazine and *Century* magazine. His *Century Dictionary* and his edition of the Book of Common Prayer are landmarks in New York City's proud tradition in the production of fine books. This building stands as a monument to honesty and restraint in architectural expression and in the art of printing.

Henry J. Hardenbergh's nearby building at 376 Lafayette Street, built three years after the De Vinne Press, demonstrates a markedly different approach. Hardenbergh, architect of the Plaza Hotel and the Dakota Apartments, was not primarily interested in the expression of structure. Here he designed for general commercial use a romantic, dramatic building, rich with ornament and a wealth of sculptured details. In contrast to the bold treatment of the great masonry arches of the De Vinne Press, here the intervening screen wall is subdivided by little iron colonnettes, by decorated spandrel panels and by an actual offset in the plane itself. The masonry piers between the arches are also broken by buttresses, carved pinnacles and sculptured impost blocks. This multiplicity of forms disguises the underlying structure.

The same two attitudes toward architecture can be traced through to the end of the century. On the far West Side, occupying the entire city block bounded by Washington, Christopher, Greenwich and Barrow Streets, is the United States Federal Building. Built in 1899, it has the same structural vigor and integrity as the De Vinne Press Building. It too has masonry bearing walls. Its great arches and massive piers at street level are eloquent of the load they carry.

Back on the East Side, there is McKim, Mead & White's Bowery Savings Bank, at 130 Bowery. This is a fine example of the use of a Roman Corinthian order, surmounted by a handsome pediment, skillfully detailed and very much in the spirit of the Chicago World's Exposition of 1893. This was the period of the union of sculpture,

29. *DeVinne Press Building*
393–399 Lafayette Street,
at East 4th Street
1885, Babb, Cook & Willard

30. *No. 376–380 Lafayette Street*
1888, Henry J. Hardenbergh

31. *United States Federal Building*
641 Washington Street,
at Christopher Street
1899, W. J. Edbrooke

32. *Bowery Savings Bank*
130 Bowery
1894, McKim, Mead & White

architecture and the decorative arts and crafts. The availability of a very high level of craftsmanship made it possible to carry out such opulent work. But here architecture is considered primarily as the composition of a façade. There is not the primary interest in the expression of structure or in the display of the inherent qualities of different materials, as in the Haughwout Building, the De Vinne Press Building or the U.S. Federal Building. McKim, Mead & White were looking backward to the grandeur that was Rome, while some of their less elegant contemporaries were looking forward to the twentieth century.

The city itself was looking forward. In 1895 New York City included only Manhattan Island and The Bronx. Two years later it was recognized that the metropolitan area really extended across the East River to Brooklyn and Queens and over the bay to Staten Island. So a new city charter was enacted and on January 1, 1898, the present five-borough Greater New York City was born. With the great increase in population (to 3,400,000) that these additions brought, New York easily outstripped its nearest contenders, Philadelphia and Chicago, for the title of largest city in the United States.

With this honor came both progress and problems. No less an authority than Winston Churchill, then a brash young man of twenty on his first trip to the country of his mother's birth, wrote:

> So far I think the means of communication in New York have struck me the most. The comfort and convenience of elevated railways—tramways, cable cars and ferries, harmoniously fitted into a perfect system accessible alike to the richest and the poorest—is extraordinary. And when one reflects that such benefits have been secured to the people not by confiscation of the property of the rich or by arbitrary taxation but simply by business enterprise—out of which the promoters themselves have made colossal fortunes, one cannot fail to be impressed with the excellence of the active system.
>
> New York is full of contradictions and contrasts. . . . I come to the conclusion that the first class men of America are in the counting house and the less brilliant men in the government.

Historic Districts

With St. Mark's, Greenwich Village, Charlton-King-Vandam, Mac-Dougal-Sullivan Gardens and the SoHo Cast-Iron District within its boundaries, the mile-and-a-quarter slice of Manhattan between Canal and 14th Streets can boast of as many Historic Districts as any other section of the city. Each of these districts, despite erosions and intrusions, has managed to maintain a certain architectural integrity and a continuous sense of neighborhood identity. Each of them has a history and a character that not only set it apart from its surroundings but make it unique.

ST. MARK'S

The St. Mark's Historic District, for example, provides a link back to the original "Pegleg" Peter Stuyvesant, the hotheaded but honest director general of the little Dutch colony of New Netherland. He has left a legendary trail that has been celebrated in literature and song. Although he bullied his subjects, he brought some reforms and in general did what he believed was in their best interests. It was Stuyve-

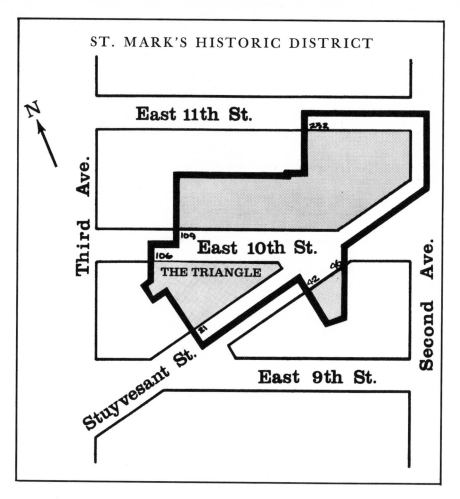

ST. MARK'S HISTORIC DISTRICT

East 11th St.

East 10th St.

THE TRIANGLE

East 9th St.

Third Ave.

Second Ave.

Stuyvesant St.

N

sant who introduced the first intimation of representative government when he set up a "Board of Nine Men" to cooperate in promoting the public welfare. However, he was usually the first to flout the board's wishes.

Early in his tour of duty Stuyvesant grew tired of living in the cramped quarters allotted to the director general within the fort and, as we have seen, moved to a house at the present corner of State and Whitehall Streets. Later, in 1651, he purchased from the Dutch West India Company the "Great Bouwerie," a tract of land extending from about the present 5th Street to 17th Street along the East River and westward to what is now Fourth Avenue. The foundations of what is believed to have been Peter Stuyvesant's actual house were uncovered in 1854 when the cellar was excavated for the building that now stands at 129 East 10th Street.

By the 1780s the Stuyvesant property had been inherited by Peter's great-grandson, Petrus. Finding himself land poor, and anticipating the eventual disposal of some of his property, Petrus had a complete street plan prepared. How much of it was actually built we do not know, but old maps show a grid, with the four streets running due north and south named for his daughters and the east–west streets named for various male members of his family. Only Stuyvesant Street itself survives; it continues to run due east and west in stubborn opposition to the surrounding Manhattan grid, which follows the axis of the island instead of the exact points of the compass.

Two of the early buildings in the district have been separately described: the Stuyvesant-Fish House at 21 Stuyvesant Street and St. Mark's-in-the-Bowery, for which Petrus Stuyvesant donated the land and £800 toward its construction. Older than either of these is the house which Petrus had built for his eldest son, Nicholas William, on the occasion of the latter's marriage in 1795. Though the house was subsequently considerably altered, certain Georgian traces still survive at 44 Stuyvesant Street—in the almost square windows with splayed lintels and in the proportions of the doorway.

Except for these structures, and their important associations with the Stuyvesant family, the dominant interest of the St. Mark's Historic District is the famous "Triangle" of sixteen houses that runs around

The Triangle   St. Mark's Historic District

the corner from the north side of Stuyvesant Street to the south side of
10th Street. The group was planned and built as a unit in 1861. It
stands on land which had once been Elizabeth Fish's garden and which
was conveyed by her son Hamilton to one Matthias Banta with the
stipulation that there was to be built upon the land

> no brewery, distillery, slaughter house, blacksmith shop, forge,
> furnace, soap, candle, starch, varnish, vitriol, glue, ink or tur-
> pentine factory, or any factory for tanning, dressing or prepar-
> ing skins, hides or leather, or any cow or livery stables or cattle
> yard, or any other dangerous, noxious or offensive establish-
> ments whatsoever, or any houses generally known as tenement
> houses, or any other stable of any kind.

Before the enactment, in 1916, of New York City's Zoning Resolution—the first in the United States—such restrictive covenants were the
only means available to property owners to protect the future character of a neighborhood.

The name of James Renwick, Jr., has traditionally been associated
with the design of the Triangle, and, since Matthias Banta's father was
a masonry contractor who worked on other Renwick buildings, the
attribution is possible. Until the late nineteenth century few architects' names can be positively connected with the design of speculative
row houses. These were considered journeymen's jobs in that their
designs were impersonal. The Triangle provides a fine illustration of the Italianate style, carried out in pressed red brick with light
sandstone trim. The workmanship is of high quality, and, except for
the loss of most of the original iron fences and railings, the houses are
in an excellent state of preservation.

GREENWICH VILLAGE

In contrast to the tidy conciseness of the St. Mark's Historic District,
Greenwich Village is not only the largest Historic District to have
been designated in New York City, it is also the most heterogeneous.
In fact, its fascination for generations of residents and visitors has been
in its contrasts and contradictions. Here are still to be found streets
that have, as Henry James put it, "a kind of established repose—a
riper, richer, more honorable look—the look of having had something

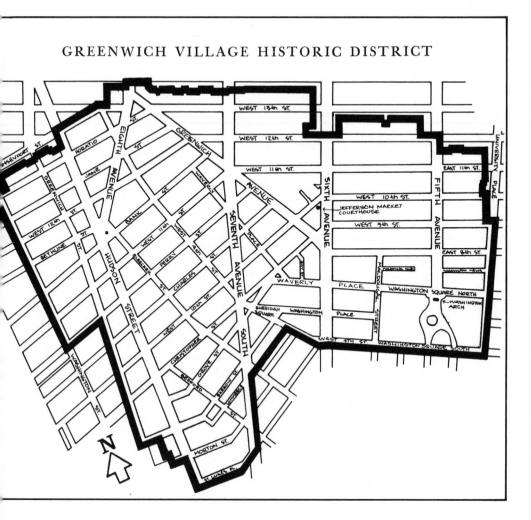

of a history." And here also are the derelicts whom e e cummings, another Village resident, observed

> *down*
> *to*
> *smoking*
> *found*
> *Butts*

It would make an interesting study in urban psychology to examine whether diversity of architecture is the cause or the consequence of variety in social structure and opinion. Certainly there are few parts of the city whose buildings offer such a range from hauteur to honky-tonk, from quaintness to commercialism, from the attractive to the unappetizing. Certainly there are few other neighborhoods in which no possible topic—not excluding motherhood—can be raised in public discussion without the immediate conflict of half a dozen points of view. And yet somehow, and perhaps because of, the vitality of its contradictions, the community and its architecture create a unique entity. Though residents will differ violently in their definitions of the boundaries, quality, character, or future of the Village, any true Villager, interviewed at random, will defend with passion his concept of what the Village really is.

The roots of this diversity may be found in history; at least history suggests some clues. In the 1790s the large country estates in Greenwich Village belonging to wealthy pre-Revolutionary landholders began to be broken up. These estates had been refuges for those colonists who wanted to escape the heat and commercial hubbub downtown. They were sold off in lots or, as in the case of land owned by Trinity Parish and Sailors' Snug Harbor, subdivided and developed under long leaseholds. Streets were laid out, following the meandering paths already established. Some of the irregularities of block size mark the boundaries of old estates. The district was rapidly built up with rows of modest houses, occupied primarily by weavers, butchers, craftsmen, suppliers to the building trades, sailmakers and carters who found it convenient to live near the Hudson River, on which much of their business depended. The unpaved roads of the eighteenth century were so rough that as much heavy freight as possible was transported by water.

A great impetus to the rapid development of Greenwich Village was the succession of smallpox, yellow-fever and cholera epidemics that struck the city in the 1790s and early 1800s. Lower Manhattan was practically deserted; everybody who could afford to fled to the healthy open country. Many families lived in tents. Soon the more prosperous substituted permanent homes for such makeshift arrangements. But these too were simple, small houses, often built in rows of three or four. The owners came to Greenwich as a temporary haven.

The result of this early intensive development was that when the Commissioners' Plan was adopted in 1811, the irregular streets of Greenwich Village were already so heavily built up that the City simply could not afford to superimpose the new grid pattern. Thus as early as a century and a half ago there was already something different about Greenwich Village.

Henry Hope Reed, in his article "The Vision Spurned," comments on the Commissioners' Plan:

> In explaining why they had limited themselves to rectilinear and rectangular streets or "whether they should adopt a grid in preference to some of those supposed improvements, by circles, ovals and stars, which certainly embellish a plan, whatever their effects as to convenience and utility" the planners stated that ". . . a city is to be composed of the habitations of men and that strait [*sic*] sided and right angled houses are the most cheap to build, and the most convenient to live in."

Reed concludes: "There is a familiar ring to this, as in our own time when 'necessity' is offered to explain away mediocrity."

Original plans provided a total of some 170 acres for parks and open spaces in the city, but most of these got swallowed up in the heady increase of real-estate values. Washington Square is one of the few to have survived.

Another element of diversity for Greenwich Village came with great suddenness. What had been, since 1789, a paupers' burial ground was converted in 1826 into a parade ground, and within the next couple of years the entire south side of what is now Washington Square was built up with elegant rows of Greek Revival houses. Since not a single one of these houses survives, it is necessary, in order to visualize what Washington Square once looked like, to imagine the south side filled with houses quite similar to "the Row" of 1832–33 that still stands on the north side, east of Fifth Avenue.

The east side of the square was soon dominated by the original Gothic Revival building of New York University, and the west side was soon filled in by a mixture of Greek Revival and Italianate row houses. These were definitely not houses for craftsmen or tradesmen, nor were they temporary refuges to be occupied only during the unhealthy summer months. They were the homes of the wealthy and fashionable who were being crowded out by the encroachments of commerce on the old residential sections. The new neighborhood of the fashionable and wealthy spread rapidly up Fifth Avenue and through the side streets between University Place and Sixth Avenue, where it met the earlier settlements of the unfashionable and poor. As if to signalize the union of the old-timers with the newcomers, the public market which, since 1812, had been located near the Hudson River end of Christopher Street moved in 1833 to a triangular area bounded by Sixth Avenue, Greenwich Avenue and West 10th Street, where, as the Jefferson Market, it served both the old and the new sections of the Village.

By the 1850s the Village was solidly built up. To some extent its boundaries gave way after the Civil War to commercial development in the east and the north, and, in the 1880s and 1890s, to tenements housing a new Italian population along the blocks south of Washington Square and to warehouses and industrial plants along the Hudson behind the docks, but its inner core remained residential simply because people liked living there.

As fashionable families moved away to greener pastures—around Gramercy Park, Madison Square and upper Fifth Avenue—many of their great houses were divided into flats and studios, their stables converted into little houses. The low scale, the crooked streets and the cheap rents appealed to artists and writers. Poe wrote, lived and drank here; Horace Greeley and Walt Whitman chose it for their homes. Later came Henry James, who was born on Washington Place, Mark Twain, Ida Tarbell, Theodore Dreiser and Edna St. Vincent Millay. John Masefield, English poet laureate, made a living in the Village by scrubbing saloon floors. The fine arts were also well represented in the Village. The early painters of the Hudson River School, Bierstadt, Church and Kensett, lived here, as did John La Farge; they were followed by the Impressionists Ernest Lawson and Robert Henri, and by the Ashcan School: Glackens, Sloan and Hopper. Greenwich Village was, in fact, the first American Bohemia. It provided during the years before World War I the same stimulating atmosphere for painters and writers that Paris was to offer to the expatriates of the 1920s.

So strong had the sense of identity become in the Village that, as early as 1916, local residents, in league with some sympathetic realtors, were able to have the central blocks of the Village protected for residential use by the newly enacted Zoning Resolution. They were not strong enough, however, to block the cutting through of Seventh Avenue South below Greenwich Avenue after World War I or the opening of Sixth Avenue below Carmine Street in the 1920s. These developments, and the new subways that came with them, doubtless improved the City's handling of traffic and transit, but they left irreparable scars. In fact, Seventh Avenue South today, fifty years later, still shows these scars: exposed party walls of bisected buildings and tiny overgrown triangular plots of land, too small for real development. However, these scars have succeeded in hardening resistance against future "improvements." A proposal in the 1950s to carry Fifth Avenue as a throughway across Washington Square was successfully blocked, as was a later proposal for an urban-renewal project along the Hudson River. Further protective zoning was achieved in the Zoning Resolution of 1962, and finally, in the spring of 1969, the protection of the long-sought Historic District designation was won.

No matter how violent their internal differences may be, Villagers can generally be counted on to fight with tenacity for the right to retain all the variety they have inherited. This spirit of the place is certainly reflected in its architecture. Practically every style and character of nineteenth- and twentieth-century architecture can be found in Greenwich Village, and sometimes with variations that are *only* to be found here.

Washington Arch   Greenwich Village Historic District

Much of the fascination of the place is the unexpected. Among house styles, charming rows of little Federal houses can still be found on Grove Street and on Gay Street. Very grand Greek Revival houses survive on Washington Square North. No. 20, west of Fifth Avenue, is the earliest one to have been built; the best-preserved row is east of Fifth Avenue. These houses were built in 1832–33 on land belonging to Sailors' Snug Harbor. The long-term leases provide an early example of design control. The lessee agreed to build within two years "a good and substantial dwelling house, of the width of said lot, three or more stories high, in brick or stone, covered [i.e., the roof] with slate or metal," the front to be twelve feet back of and parallel to Washington Square North and "to be finished in such style as may be approved by" the lessor. The stables behind these houses, on Washington Mews, as well as those on Macdougal Alley, are now all converted into mini-houses and studios that enjoy a sense of withdrawal from the city.

Fine examples of the brownstone Italianate style are remarkably well preserved along St. Luke's Place. They were built in 1852–54 on land leased from Trinity Church. Jimmy Walker, once the swinging mayor of New York City, lived at No. 11, and the playground on the south side of the street is named in his honor. The ill-fated Starr Faithfull left her home at No. 12 one June morning in 1931 to do some shopping and was never seen alive again. Her strangled body was washed ashore two days later on a lonely Long Island beach.

Distinguished illustrations of the Anglo-Italianate style can be found between Fifth and Sixth Avenues on the north side of 9th Street (Nos. 19–23) and on the south side of 10th Street (Nos. 20–38). Both groups have been attributed, without proof, to James Renwick, Jr., but there is no doubt in anyone's mind as to their architectural distinction. The 10th Street row, or "terrace," of ten brownstones, dating from 1856–58, has been compared in elegance to the great row of Greek Revival houses built a generation earlier on the north side of Washington Square. There are fine examples of the French Second Empire style at 70 and 76 Perry Street and, in the next block, at 59 Charles Street. At 243–247 Waverly Place, between West 11th and Bank Streets, three little brick houses built in 1888 illustrate how late the Romanesque Revival style lingered, even in the hands of so sophisticated an architect as William B. Tuthill. There is even a house with East Indian detail which Lockwood de Forrest had built for himself at 7 East 10th Street.

The narrowest house in the city, only nine and a half feet wide, is at 75½ Bedford Street, where Edna St. Vincent Millay lived. It is next door to the oldest surviving house in the Village, dating from 1799–1800, at the corner of Commerce and Bedford Streets. What would have been the newest house in the Village was to have filled in the gap at 18 West 11th Street where a fine Greek Revival house was destroyed by a tragic explosion in March 1969. (Some young would-be revolutionaries had been using the basement to manufacture bombs; something triggered the explosion, destroying the house, killing three persons and impelling two young girls to flee to parts unknown from which to date they have not returned.) A young architect, Hugh Hardy, prepared a contemporary design for the house he proposed to build. Although the design maintained the setback line, the cornice line, the upper-story windows, the color and the stoop projection of its neighbors, a storm of controversy arose among those who felt that new buildings in old districts should copy historic styles, those who felt that to each epoch belongs its own expression, those who objected to this particular design because it straddled the issue and those who held every shade of opinion in between. The Landmarks Preservation Commission concluded that as long as a building does not do violence to the mass, materials and scale of its neighbors, the architect of the 1970s has the same obligation to create a good design in his own terms as the architect of the 1840s. The Commission, by a narrow margin, decided in favor of the proposed design. Building and financing costs proved prohibitive, however, and plans for the construction of the house were abandoned. And so a hundred years from now some future commission will not be able to judge whether the decision was right or wrong.

Another time in which the Landmarks Preservation Commission had to exercise judgment between an exact copy and a sensitive modern adaptation was in the case of a design by architect Edgar Tafel for a new church for St. John's in the Village, whose 125-year-old Greek Revival structure had burned to the ground in 1972. Tafel prepared a contemporary design, reflecting elements of Greek Revival style, that related admirably to its neighbors and to the Historic District generally. The Commission enthusiastically approved the proposed design.

On 12th Street, between Fifth and Sixth Avenues, three different approaches to this complicated and controversial dilemma are dramatically demonstrated. Joseph Urban in his 1930 design for the New School for Social Research loudly proclaimed his independence of past tradition by erecting a black-and-white horizontally striped structure in a style then considered the latest thing. This building was, in fact, one of the first "modern" façades built in New York. Edgar Tafel's 1958 Church House annex to the Gothic Revival First Presbyterian Church of 1844–46, although of contemporary design, is far more respectful of its neighbors. Its dark-brown Roman brick picks up the tonality of the brownstone church, and the use of a quatrefoil motif in the terra-cotta balcony recalls the roof cresting of the church.

Across the street is the seven-story apartment house, Butterfield House, which Meyer, Whittlesey & Glass designed in 1959. With no actual imitation of anything specific from its surroundings, this design achieves, through its scale, delicacy of form and elegance of detail—in its own idiom—an extraordinary harmony with its neighbors. Butterfield House is, in fact, one of the most distinguished apartment-house designs anywhere in the city. A comparison with the neo-Georgian apartment houses along lower Fifth Avenue illustrates how much better good architecture of different epochs can harmonize than do heavy-handed efforts to achieve superficial similarity. Even the rather flamboyant Beaux-Arts style apartment house at 43 Fifth Avenue, though hardly "appropriate" to Greenwich Village, is somehow more satisfying simply by being true to itself.

The range in church styles in Greenwich Village is as varied as the house styles. St. Luke's on Hudson Street is a charming little country church built in 1821–22 to accommodate the ever-growing population that was pushing northward on the island. It was originally known as St. Luke's-in-the-Fields because of its rural setting. In 1890 the congregation moved to a new church way uptown at Convent Avenue and 141st Street, and in 1892 Trinity bought the little downtown church and made it a chapel of Trinity Parish.

James N. Wells, a carpenter who rose to become a man of wealth and influence in the city, designed St. Luke's in the Federal style. He also designed the entire surrounding block bounded by Christopher, Barrow, Greenwich and Hudson Streets. A series of small town houses and an impressive vicarage and parish house shielded the church burial ground and garden from public view—a delightful bit of early site-planning. The burial ground has vanished and the row of thirteen two-and-a-half-story houses on Greenwich Street was demolished in the 1950s to make room for St. Luke's School.

Quite a different Wells—Joseph C., the English-born architect, who was later to be one of the founders of the American Institute of Architects—designed the Gothic Revival First Presbyterian Church on Fifth Avenue between 11th and 12th Streets. It is just one block above Richard Upjohn's Church of the Ascension, built in 1840–41, which was the prototype of a series of imposing Gothic Revival churches. The Church of the Ascension pointed the way not only to Wells's building but also to Renwick's Grace Church and Upjohn's own Trinity Church a few years later. The Church of the Ascension is particularly famous for the altar mural and stained glass by John La Farge.

Since St. John's in the Village burned down, the only remaining church in the form of a Greek Revival temple is St. Joseph's, an imposing Roman Catholic edifice on the corner of Sixth Avenue and Washington Place.

But towering over the Village, both physically and symbolically, is the Jefferson Market Courthouse at Sixth Avenue and 10th Street. It towers because of its central location, its dominant height, its aesthetic history and its emotional focus. The courthouse was built between 1874 and 1877 on the site of the old marketplace. At the same time the market moved into a new structure erected adjoining the courthouse on the south. This extraordinary complex, of which only the court-house remains, was the creation of Frederick Clarke Withers and Calvert Vaux. With its gables, its turrets, its banded brick and stone-work, its carvings and polychromy, its belfry and its balconies, the Jefferson Market Courthouse is the epitome of Victorian Gothic. In a poll of architects taken in the 1880s, it was listed fifth among the ten most beautiful buildings in the United States.

But times and tastes change, and not many years ago so notable a critic as Ada Louise Huxtable was quoted as saying, "If you can save that you can save anything!" For there was, at that time, a very real

Jefferson Market Courthouse
(early view)
Greenwich Village Historic Distr

threat that it would be torn down. It had seen service as a courthouse and a police academy, but it had been boarded up for years and was serving only the pigeons who flew in and out of the broken stained-glass windows. When faced with the threat of losing something it was used to, the Village rallied under the leadership of Margot Gayle, a devoted local resident, and, with extraordinary unanimity, first got the huge four-faced clock running again and then fought for funds in the City's budget to have the building converted into a regional public library. The Village won, and the architect Giorgio Cavaglieri, with great sensitivity and skill, remodeled the courthouse for its new purpose.

Now "Old Jeff" bravely faces its second century at the crossroads of Greenwich Village, where the elegant mansions to the east meet the charming alleys and little houses to the west, where the truck traffic of Sixth Avenue meets the razzle-dazzle of West 8th Street, and where hippies and yippies and winos and homos and grandes dames and just people are all mixed up together and want to keep things the way they are.

CHARLTON-KING-VANDAM

Though a casual glance at the map might suggest that Charlton-King-Vandam and Macdougal-Sullivan Gardens were leftover appendages of Greenwich Village, these two small areas of the city qualify as Historic Districts in their own right and for quite separate reasons.

Charlton-King-Vandam is on the site originally occupied by the famous "Richmond Hill," a great Georgian mansion built before the Revolution for a British major. Washington used it as his headquarters for a period during the war, and later it became home for the first Vice-President, John Adams, when New York was the capital of the country. Mrs. Adams has left us a nostalgic description of what the area looked like in 1789:

> In natural beauty it might vie with the most delicious spot I ever saw. It is a mile and a half distant from the city of New York. The house stands upon an eminence; at an agreeable distance flows the noble Hudson, bearing upon its bosom innumerable small vessels laden with the fruitful productions of the adjacent country. Upon my right hand are fields beautifully variegated with grass and grain, to a great extent, like the valley of Honiton in Devonshire. Upon my left the city opens to view, intercepted here and there by a rising ground and an ancient oak. In front, beyond the Hudson, the Jersey shores present the exuberance of a rich well-cultivated soil. In the background is a large flower-garden, enclosed with a hedge and some very handsome trees. Venerable oaks and broken ground covered with wild shrubs surround me, giving a natural beauty to the spot which is truly enchanting. A lovely variety of birds serenade me morning and evening, rejoicing in their liberty and security.

Later, Aaron Burr bought the property and for several years used it for lavish entertaining in furtherance of his soaring ambitions. By

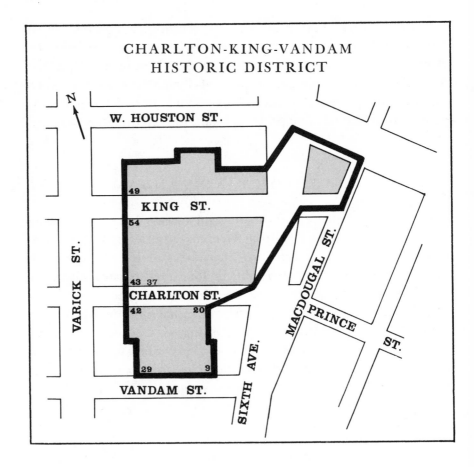

1797, caught between the growing city in the south and the spread of Greenwich Village from the north, Burr had the property mapped into its present system of streets. Before work could commence on the subdivision, however, Burr had fought his fatal duel with Hamilton and had found it prudent to leave New York for a while. John Jacob Astor, always with an eye to real-estate opportunities, took over the development in 1817. The great mansion was rolled downhill to the southeast corner of Charlton and Varick Streets, and the hill was leveled —quite a feat in those pre-bulldozer days. Twenty-five-by-100-foot lots were sold off and the greater part of the present houses built in the 1820s. They were bought by prosperous builders, lawyers and merchants who wanted to live near the Greenwich Street wharves and markets.

The district has a great degree of homogeneity and contains the largest concentration of Federal-style houses to be found in the city. The north side of Vandam Street contains an unbroken row, with Nos. 23 through 29 very close to their original state. The north side of Charlton Street contains a still longer row—Nos. 25 through 39 being particularly interesting—in addition to four Greek Revival houses that replaced Federal originals after a fire in 1840. Many of the Charlton Street houses had stables or servants' quarters in rear buildings that faced onto an alley. An access passageway to the stable still exists at No. 25.

King Street is more varied, a happy jumble. Nos. 20, 40, 42 and 44, perfectly preserved examples of the Greek Revival style, are inter-

*House on Charlton Street
(No. 37)
Charlton-King-Vandam
Historic District*

spersed with Federal houses and, incongruously, with some apartment houses dating from later days. At the corner of King and MacDougal Streets is one of the rare early-19th-century shop fronts to have survived anywhere in the city.

The charm of this Historic District seems almost enhanced by the concentration of industrial and commercial buildings and the heavy truck traffic on Varick Street. The district acts as though such things didn't exist and goes on its serene way, secure in its innate gentility.

MACDOUGAL-SULLIVAN GARDENS

On the other side of Houston Street and running through from Macdougal to Sullivan Street is one of the city's smallest Historic Districts, consisting of less than two dozen houses and a common garden between them. It too has had an interesting history. The land originally belonged to Nicholas Low, a prominent banker and political figure in post-Revolutionary New York. After his death his sons subdivided the property and built a number of row houses as an investment. Those on Macdougal Street were finished in 1844 and those on Sullivan in 1850. All were designed in the fashionable Greek Revival style, but unfortunately were drastically altered in the 1920s. It is for their backs rather than their fronts and for their significance in real-estate history that the district has been designated.

Instead of selling off the individual lots, as was the usual practice, the Low heirs kept their property intact and leased the houses for long periods of time. They held on to the property for 125 years. Around the turn of the century the neighborhood began to change as Italian immigrants crowded into the area. Instead of demolishing their houses in order to build tenements for quick profit, the Lows let the original houses stand—deteriorating, to be sure, but still bringing in some income.

In 1920 William Sloane Coffin, a grandson of the founder of W. & J. Sloane and Company and later president of the Metropolitan Museum of Art, conceived the idea of offering an alternative to highrise apartments or the suburbs. He felt that attractive, moderately priced housing could be provided through the renovation of essentially sound old row houses. He formed a corporation, "Hearth and Home," to test his theories, bought the entire block surrounded by

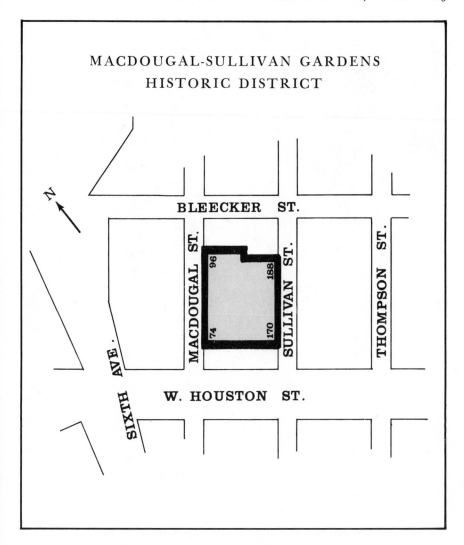

MACDOUGAL-SULLIVAN GARDENS
HISTORIC DISTRICT

BLEECKER ST.

MACDOUGAL ST.

SULLIVAN ST.

THOMPSON ST.

SIXTH AVE.

W. HOUSTON ST.

Macdougal, West Houston, Sullivan and Bleecker Streets and split up the old houses into duplex, simplex and efficiency apartments. (As usual, costs were higher than expected, and the houses on Bleecker and West Houston Streets were sold to help finance the rehabilitation of the Macdougal and Sullivan buildings.) Modern plumbing, wiring and kitchen equipment were installed in the remaining buildings. Most important, however, was the radical idea of throwing together the individual back yards into a garden for the common use of all the abutting houses. After the renovation was finished, the individual

Macdougal-Sullivan Gardens

houses were sold, mostly to writers, artists, musicians, even a few to businessmen, with the stipulation that maintenance and enjoyment of the central garden be continued on a joint basis.

A permanent organization of residents was set up in 1921 and still functions. Half a century later, this imaginative experiment in creating a new life for an old neighborhood is as attractive as ever. Except for Turtle Bay Gardens, it has had few imitators. The main obstacle to copying it is, of course, the difficulty and expense of putting together a comparable assemblage of back-to-back houses from dozens of different property owners. The heirs of Nicholas Low may have clung to their land out of conservatism or simple inertia, but the unexpected outcome of their inaction became one of the city's most attractive illustrations of urban renewal.

SOHO CAST-IRON HISTORIC DISTRICT

This district is nearly rectangular in shape and is bounded by Canal Street, Broadway, Howard Street, Crosby Street, East and West

Houston Streets and West Broadway. The "SoHo" part of the name is an acronym of *So*uth of *Ho*uston, adopted by the artists who moved, in the 1960s, into the area to take advantage of low rents and high-ceilinged, uninterrupted space for their larger and larger canvases. The "Cast Iron" part of the name refers to a now unique assemblage of buildings that can be considered in many ways the direct ancestors of the twentieth-century skyscraper. The Haughwout Building (also designated earlier as an individual Landmark) and the Arnold Constable and Company store were among the earliest retail stores in the country—dating from the 1850s—to use cast-iron construction. Most of the storefronts were imitative of the masonry façades of the 1850s, '60s and '70s, reflecting the Italianate style so popular in contemporary architecture, as well as the French Renaissance, French Second Empire and neo-Grec. The popularity of cast iron in the second half of the nineteenth century was due to the fact that cast-iron façades could provide at less cost a lot more opulent ornamentation than those of brick or stone—an important factor during those days of the conspicuous display of wealth. Another factor was the time element. Cast-iron forms could be produced rapidly, while it would take stonecarvers months to achieve the same results. Painting the cast-iron fronts was a simple and cheap method of maintenance, plus giving the owner wonderful leeway in the choice of colors. By the 1880s the popularity of cast iron had begun to wane. The development of steel skeleton construction permitting buildings of much greater height and serious questions about the resistance of unprotected cast iron to fire were among the causes of its decline.

Though cast-iron buildings give the district its unique importance in the history of American architecture, the area also contains many notable examples of stone and brick commercial building of the second half of the nineteenth century.

In the Dutch colonial period the district had been an area of farms and forts. It was also the site of one of the earliest settlements of freed black slaves. In the early days of the Republic it became a favored residential area as life on the island of Manhattan moved northward. By 1850 changes came rapidly. Broadway metamorphosed into a boulevard of marble, cast-iron and brownstone commercial palazzos—retail stores, hotels, theaters. A notorious red-light district sprang up along Greene Street. By the end of the nineteenth century growth

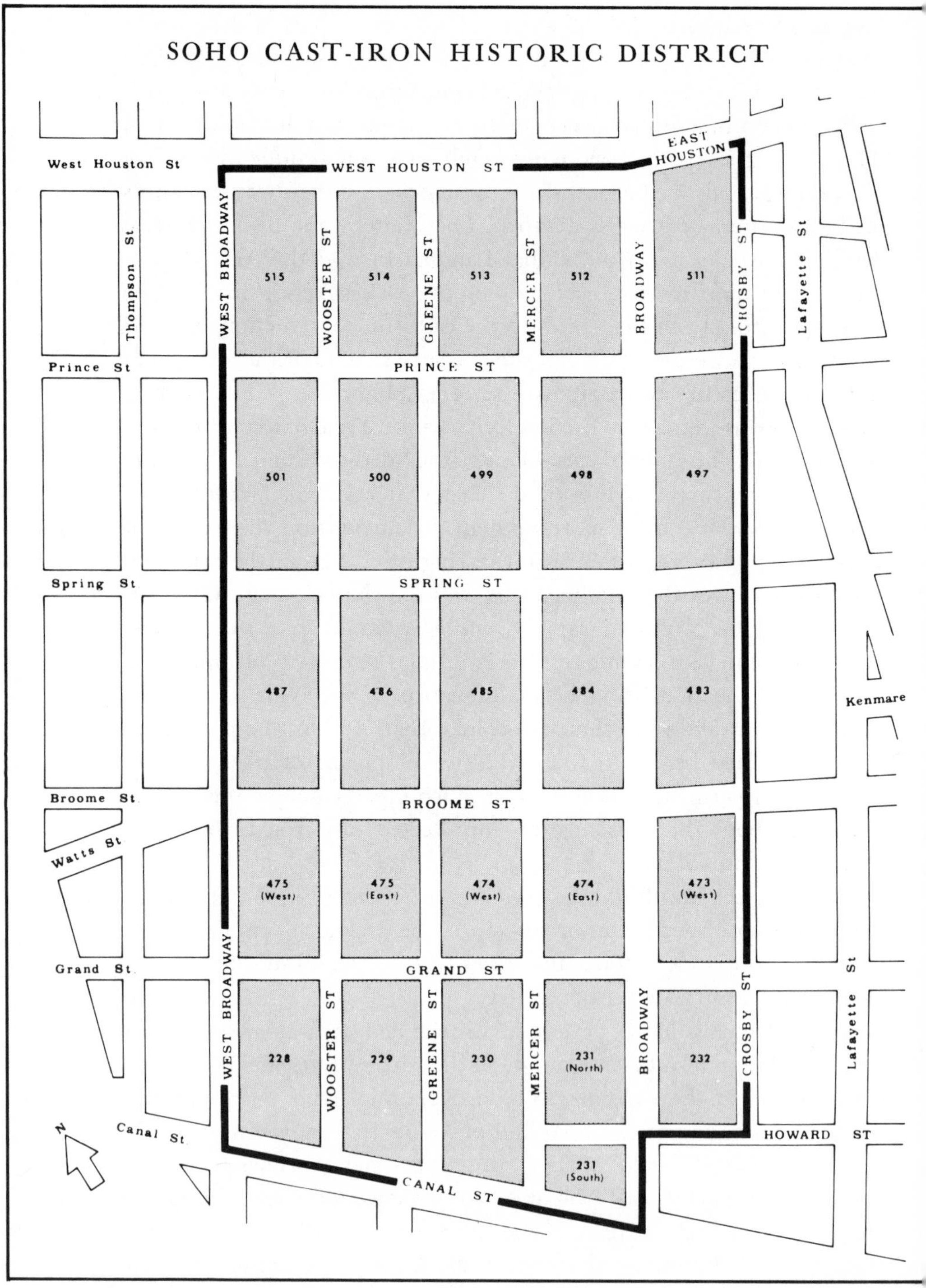

SOHO CAST-IRON HISTORIC DISTRICT

West Houston St

WEST HOUSTON ST

EAST HOUSTON

Thompson St

WEST BROADWAY

WOOSTER ST

GREENE ST

MERCER ST

BROADWAY

CROSBY ST

Lafayette St

515

514

513

512

511

Prince St

PRINCE ST

501

500

499

498

497

Spring St

SPRING ST

487

486

485

484

483

Broome St

BROOME ST

Kenmare

Watts St

475 (West)

475 (East)

474 (West)

474 (East)

473 (West)

Grand St

GRAND ST

WEST BROADWAY

WOOSTER ST

GREENE ST

MERCER ST

BROADWAY

CROSBY ST

Lafayette St

228

229

230

231 (North)

232

Canal St

HOWARD ST

N

CANAL ST

231 (South)

ceased and the district entered a long period of decay—sixty years of a limbo of economically marginal commercial enterprises. In the 1960s some innovative zoning changes permitted artists to move into the area without seriously conflicting with the small industries which contribute an important element to the city's economy. The result is that the district today is one of the country's most exciting creative centers; it is humming, day and night.

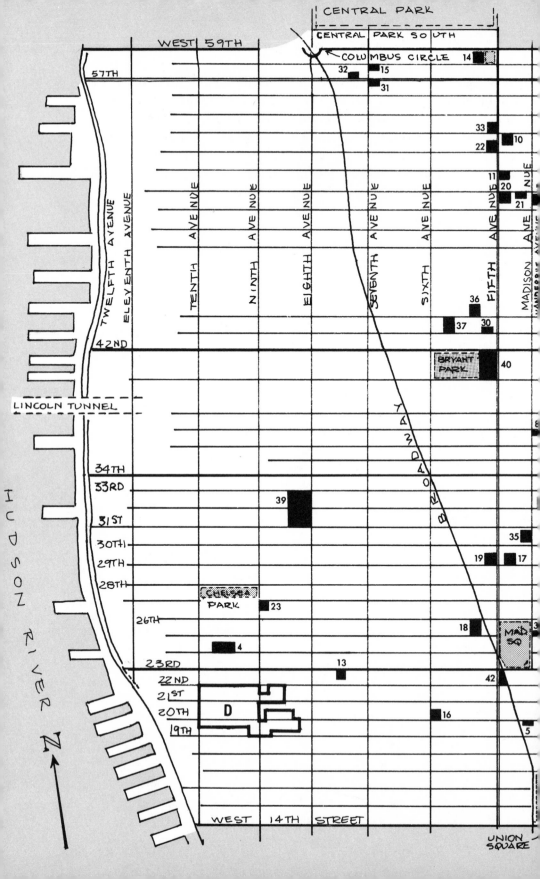

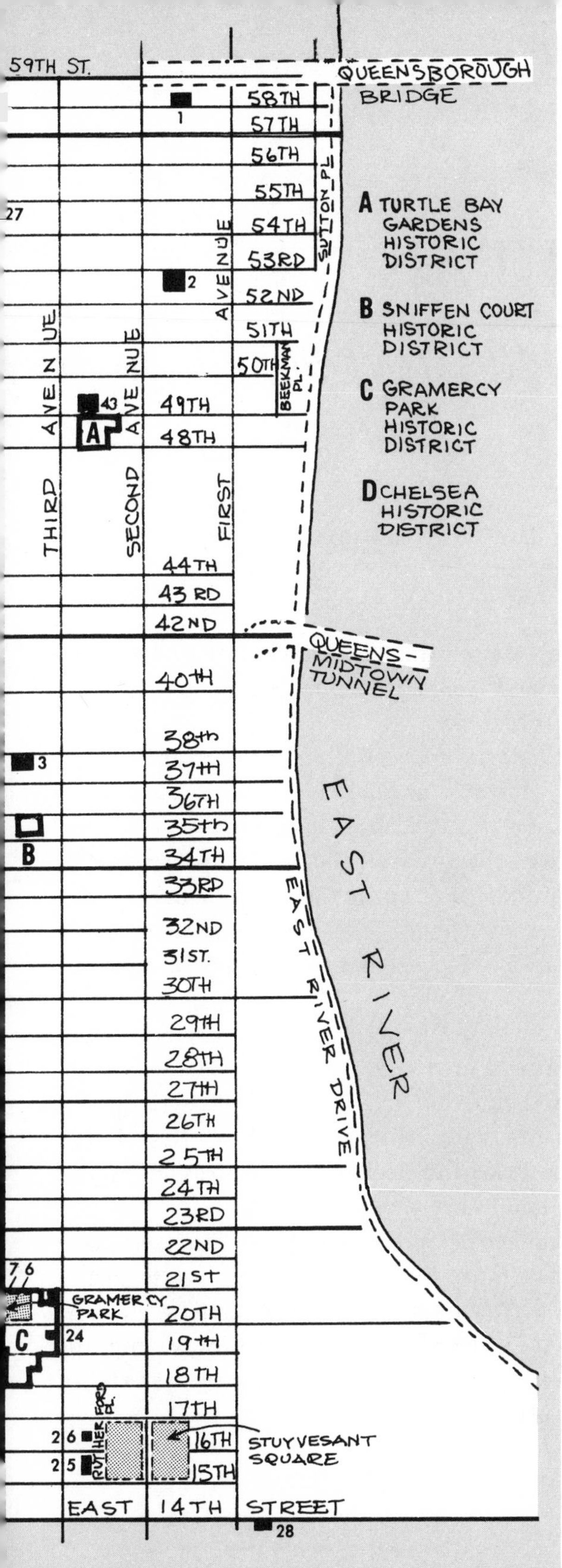

MANHATTAN

From 14th Street
to 59th Street

59TH ST.

QUEENSBOROUGH BRIDGE

58TH
57TH
56TH
55TH
54TH
53RD
52ND
51TH
50TH
49TH
48TH
44TH
43RD
42ND

A TURTLE BAY GARDENS HISTORIC DISTRICT

B SNIFFEN COURT HISTORIC DISTRICT

C GRAMERCY PARK HISTORIC DISTRICT

D CHELSEA HISTORIC DISTRICT

27

THIRD AVENUE
SECOND AVENUE
FIRST AVENUE
AVENUE
SUTTON PL.
BEEKMAN PL.

1
2
43
A

QUEENS-MIDTOWN TUNNEL

40TH
38TH
37TH
36TH
35TH
34TH
33RD
32ND
31ST.
30TH
29TH
28TH
27TH
26TH
25TH
24TH
23RD
22ND
21ST
20TH
19TH
18TH
17TH
16TH
15TH

3
B

EAST RIVER

EAST RIVER DRIVE

7 6
GRAMERCY PARK
24
C
26
25
RUTHERFORD PL.
STUYVESANT SQUARE

EAST 14TH STREET

28

CHAPTER FOUR

MANHATTAN

From 14th Street to 59th Street

THIS IS THE HEART of Manhattan Island. It sweeps across from river to river and from 14th up to 59th Street. In many ways it is the climax of this great city.

On the West Side is Chelsea, just beginning to return to its original role of a community clustered around the General Theological Seminary; the garment district, packed from curb to curb with hand trucks on which thousands of coats, dresses and jackets swing jauntily; Times Square, once the proud center of the theater, now the home of prostitutes and lurid peep-show movies; Hell's Kitchen, the successor to the ill-famed Five Points; and Rockefeller Center, the village green of modern New York.

On the East Side the Gashouse District, named for the great round gas storage tanks that once dotted the area, abuts on Stuyvesant Square, where hospitals and churches give the area a deceptive air of well-bred placidity. Gramercy Park, Murray Hill, Kip's Bay, Turtle Bay and the elegant Sutton Place and Beekman Place areas add to this section's extraordinary flair and variety.

The shopping area had moved progressively uptown from 14th Street in the 1870s to 23rd Street in the 1890s, and, in the early part of the 1900s, to 34th Street, where it still has an anchor. Between these crosstown streets the shops generally followed Broadway, and the nine-block stretch from Union Square to Madison Square was known in the 1870s as the Ladies' Mile.

In 1906, however, Benjamin Altman outraged the solid citizens who lived in their fine mansions on Fifth Avenue by opening a handsome new store at the corner of 34th Street. So sensitive was Altman to the protests that he hid the function of his emporium behind a Florentine façade and did not even put his name on the outside. After this, the shopping area began to run more vertically than horizontally—up Fifth Avenue and later up Madison Avenue, from 34th Street to 57th Street, where it is again spreading east and west. These successive centers were all located on the wide streets—14th, 23rd, 34th, 42nd and 57th—which were laid out one hundred feet wide instead of the usual sixty feet.

The shopping section has now practically ended at 57th Street, with the area above remaining residential. Under the influence of the new Zoning Resolution and some conscious city planning, retail business is now moving east to Second and Third Avenues, reclaimed and greatly raised in value since the elevated tracks came down, and west to Sixth and Seventh Avenues and to an underutilized far West Side. It is also making a leap to East 86th Street.

Row Houses, Mansions, Hotels and an Apartment House

There are many interesting survivors of the time when this heart of the city was entirely a residential area.

To begin with, there are a few quaint and tiny relics of a past age. The two little modest houses that huddle under the giant shadow of the Queensborough Bridge on East 58th Street are in the simple vernacular of the 1850s with some slight Greek Revival reminiscences. They are both set back from the street, and one has a tree growing defiantly out of its foundation. These two-story survivors are quite typical of the hundreds of modest semi-suburban houses that dotted the uptown cross streets of mid-nineteenth-century Manhattan. A huge apartment building going up on Second Avenue is indebted to one of these little houses for the sale of its development rights.

There is also an enchanting little wooden house at 312 East 53rd Street. Its mansard roof and heavy door and window enframements

*1. Nos. 311 and 313 East 58th Street
1856–57*

echo in miniature the French Second Empire style. The heavy central muntin of the double-hung windows imitates the look of a French casement without sacrificing the practical air- and water-tightness of double-hung sash. In 1968 the owner was offered the incredible sum of $185,000 for the house, for which he had paid $41,000 in 1952. The offer came from a developer who was interested in assembling property for an apartment building. The owner not only refused to sell for a profit of over 350 percent, but asked the Landmarks Preservation Commission to designate his house so that its future might be assured.

A third example of this type of modest survivor, much altered, is at 152 East 38th Street in Murray Hill. This house was built in the 1850s and was transformed in 1934–35 into the neo-Federal style with good taste and charm. It is set back from the street by a forecourt and a landscaped garden. Originally built as a gatehouse for an estate that belonged to a member of President Van Buren's family, the house was sold by his descendants in 1929 to the publisher Cass Canfield, who remodeled it.

No original Federal architecture survives in this section of the city. Probably few examples ever existed, for the simple reason that Manhattan north of 14th Street was still open country by the time this style went out of fashion. All of the earliest survivors are in the Greek Revival style, and most of these are in the Chelsea Historic District.

Just north of Chelsea, and now cut off from it by the full-block sixteen-story mass of London Terrace, an apartment building erected in 1930, there is an interesting row of transitional buildings on West 24th Street between Ninth and Tenth Avenues—transitional between the Greek Revival, which was going out of fashion, and the Italianate, which was just coming in. They were built in 1849–50 by Philo V. Beebe, a carpenter. As soon as he finished one pair of houses and sold them, he started another immediately adjacent. These twelve charming three-story houses with their pleasant little front gardens, fifteen feet deep, provide the neighborhood with a much needed human scale. Their paired front doors and stoops combine to give a sense of unity to the whole. The houses have been substantially altered over the years, many with neo-Grec, Queen Anne and neo-Federal additions.

When the 24th Street houses were built there was a very different sort of London Terrace opposite them. The original London Terrace consisted of a row of town houses set back some twenty-five feet and shaded by a canopy of large trees. They were owned by rich merchants. Just back of them, on 23rd Street, was a row of little houses, known as the Chelsea Cottages, which were intended for the employees of the merchants. The surviving row on the north side of 24th Street was planned for middle-class professional and business people, of an economic level between the two groups to the south. Here was

2. No. 312 East 53rd Street
1866

3. No. 152 East 38th Street
1857
Altered 1934

true economic and class integration. And flowing serenely along the western end of the rows was the Hudson River, which has long since been pushed westward by land fill.

4. Nos. 437–459 West 24th Street
1849–50

Nos. 326, 328 and 330 East 18th Street (not pictured), built in the 1850s, are rare survivors in Manhattan. Their unusual deep front yards add greatly to the charm and character of these little vernacular houses. Much of the original cast-iron work of the stoops and verandas has survived. Nos. 326 and 328 were conceived as a pair. The buildings, still used as individual private residences, are built on land that once was part of Peter Stuyvesant's "Bouwerie." They reflect a vernacular interpretation of the Italianate style which was popular in the mid-nineteenth century.

In addition to these relatively modest row houses, there have survived in the midtown area a number of the great mansions. These structures represent almost every architectural style of the nineteenth century. Most of them are no longer used as private homes, because nobody, in these days of taxes and scarcity of servants, can manage to keep them up. That they have thus far escaped the wrecker's iron ball is due to the fact that other users and other uses have been found for them.

A good example of how the Gothic Revival style was applied to the residence of a prosperous merchant is seen at 28 East 20th Street, where Theodore Roosevelt was born and brought up. Roosevelt was the descendant of one of the old Dutch families of Manhattan, and is so far the only native-born New Yorker to achieve the Presidency.

Originally there were two houses on this site, built by Teddy's grandfather for two of his sons. Theodore was born on October 27, 1858, in an upstairs front bedroom. He was a frail child, plagued by asthma. His father, Theodore Senior, fitted up a gymnasium on the upstairs porch and encouraged the boy to practice push-ups. "You have the mind, but haven't got the body." Within a year Theodore Junior had so improved that asthma was never again to bother him.

New York was a thriving city of 750,000 people during Roosevelt's boyhood. Like the rest of the country, the city was caught up in the

5. *Theodore Roosevelt House*
28 East 20th Street
1848
1923 restoration:
  Theodate Pope Riddle

tensions of the Civil War, which must have been particularly trying for the Roosevelt family, with a Yankee father and a mother from Georgia. Young Teddy never liked city life. His heart was always in the country, and yet he has left some vivid pictures of city life during his youth. He was strangely prophetic when he wrote in his autobiography:

> While still a small boy I began to take an interest in natural history. I remember distinctly the first day that I started on my career as a zoologist. I was walking up Broadway and as I passed the market to which I used sometimes to be sent before breakfast to get strawberries, I suddenly saw a dead seal laid out on a slab of wood. That seal filled me with every possible feeling of romance and adventure. . . . As long as that seal remained there I haunted the neighborhood of the market day after day. I measured it and I recall that, not having a tape measure I had to do my best to get the girth with a folding pocket foot-rule, a difficult undertaking. I carefully made a record of the utterly useless measurements and at once began to write a natural history of my own. . . . I think . . . I did get the seal's skull, and with two of my cousins promptly started what we ambitiously called the "Roosevelt Museum of Natural History."

In Chapter Six we shall see how such a museum came into being. Although it was called the American Museum of Natural History, it does have an impressive wing called the Theodore Roosevelt Memorial, dedicated in 1931 by a distant cousin, Franklin Delano Roosevelt.

The family moved in 1873 to a larger house on 57th Street, and the 20th Street dwelling began a slow and sad decline. It was severely altered for commercial purposes, even losing its two top stories. But in 1919, a few months after Roosevelt's death, the Women's Roosevelt Memorial Association (later merged with the Theodore Roosevelt Association) bought it and also the adjoining house where Roosevelt's uncle had lived. The two buildings were restored and remodeled with skill by one of the country's early women architects, Theodate Pope Riddle. In 1962 President Kennedy signed a bill naming the house a National Historic Site, and today it is administered by the National Park Service as a museum. It survives incongruously amidst huge, grim warehouses.

One block east, at 16 Gramercy Park South, the same sort of inverted-U "label" moldings as at the Roosevelt House crown the

6. *The Players   16 Gramercy Park South*
1845
Porch and remodeling: 1880, Stanford White

windows of the second and third stories. They are all that remain to
suggest that this house too, when it was built in 1845, was Gothic
Revival in style. Everything else was changed in 1888 when Edwin
Booth, the country's foremost actor, bought the building with the idea
of making it into an actors' club. The house was among the earliest
brownstone fronts to have been built in the city.

When Booth took over, eyebrows all around Gramercy Park went
up in honest horror. For the square was then the epitome of elegance,
of genteel society, the exclusive preserve of the best families. Mrs.
Stuyvesant Fish was one of the residents before she created her Italian
palace uptown. Samuel J. Tilden owned the house next door to No.
16; from it he built an underground passageway to 19th Street so that
he could escape politicians and bores.

But Booth persisted and persuaded his good friend Stanford White to make the old home suitable for club purposes. Neighbors gasped when the stoop came down and a two-story porch went up. When magnificent wrought-iron lanterns and evergreens in tubs appeared, Mrs. Fish called for her smelling salts. The new work was a scholarly copy of an Italian Renaissance prototype. Stanford White, whose famous firm did so much to establish both the neo–Italian Renaissance style and the Eclectic approach, was personally responsible for this particular design. It is one of the few works, of the many to which his name is linked, that can definitely be attributed to his own hand.

The Players, as the new club was called, was inaugurated on New Year's Eve, with Booth making a little speech as he presented the title of the house to the members. Either the attitude of his neighbors had changed or he chose to ignore them, for, writing his daughter about the dedication ceremony, Booth said, "All the exclusive neighbors in this conservative quarter are pleased instead of offended by the innovation of a club-house in the midst of their respectable mansions." The ceremony is repeated every year on New Year's Eve, Founders' Night. Booth's memory is further preserved by a statue of him, garbed in a toga, in the center of Gramercy Square.

The membership list of the Players constitutes a Who's Who of the theater, the arts and letters. For Booth felt that actors should mix with others. Even bankers and lawyers are included, as patrons of the arts. Frank Sullivan characterized the qualification of a patron as "solvency in case any of the real members need a touch." Joseph Jefferson, John Drew, General William Tecumseh Sherman, Thomas Bailey Aldrich and Mark Twain were among the original incorporators. Elihu Root, J. P. Morgan and Grover Cleveland frequently lunched at the club. Don Marquis, Otis Skinner, Walter Hampden, Irvin S. Cobb, John Barrymore and Booth Tarkington were others who have left their mark on the Players.

The club rooms bear quotations, mainly from Shakespeare, appropriate to each room's use: in the bar, "Well, you are to call at all the ale-houses and bid those that are drunk get them to bed"; in the dining room, "Dear Actors, eat no onions or garlic, for we are to utter sweet breath"; on the menu, "Why muse you, sir? 'tis dinner-time"; and in the ladies' room, "It droppeth as the gentle rain from Heaven."

Right next door to the Players, the National Arts Club shows what had happened to Gothic architecture by the second half of the nine-teenth century. No. 15 Gramercy Park South, originally two modest connecting houses, had been built in 1845. Their present appearance is due to the 1874 remodeling by Calvert Vaux, architect of the Jefferson Market Courthouse.

In this Victorian Gothic style, the simple drip moldings of the 1840s have been replaced by bands and panels of carving, a multi-plicity of pilasters and colonnettes, and a restless shifting of surfaces and broken silhouettes. Little sculptured heads appear in the tri-angular pediment over the doorway and in the segmental panels over many of the windows. There are contrasts in stone color, in horizontal bands and in the radiating voussoirs over the arched windows—and rosettes everywhere. This is the type of luxuriant architecture that John Ruskin so greatly admired and that he preached in *The Stones of Venice*.

The houses were remodeled for Samuel Jones Tilden, once gover-nor of New York, a prominent lawyer and statesman and an active participant in the overthrow of the Tweed Ring. Headed by Boss William Marcy Tweed, the ring, through systematic graft and favor-

*7. National Arts Club
(originally Samuel J.
Tilden House)
15 Gramercy Park South
1845
Remodeled: 1874,
Calvert Vaux*

itism, milked the city of millions of dollars—variously estimated at between $40,000,000 and $200,000,000 for the period 1869–1871 alone. After his exposure, Tweed was brought to trial and found guilty, and eventually he died in prison.

After serving as governor, Tilden was nominated as Democratic Presidential candidate opposing Rutherford B. Hayes. On a bleak November day in 1876 Tilden, from the balcony of his Gramercy Park house, graciously acknowledged the plaudits of the crowd who had come to celebrate his election. However, a special electoral commission later gave the prize to Hayes. Although Tilden had received the larger popular vote, Hayes received one more electoral vote—185 to 184—from the electoral commission.

Tilden, a wealthy bachelor and a scholar, established a substantial trust fund which, after his death, permitted the merger of the Astor and Lenox Libraries to form the nucleus of the great collection of the New York Public Library. The National Arts Club bought his house in 1906. (The Players had apparently behaved so well that there was no outcry against the establishment of this second club on the periphery of elegant Gramercy Park.)

The National Arts Club had been formed in 1898 by Charles de Kay, literary and art critic for *The New York Times,* "to provide exhibition facilities for such lines of art as might not otherwise be provided for." True to its trust, the club has provided a haven for some of the country's outstanding artists, writers and people of the theater.

Theodore Roosevelt, after he left the White House and while he was editor of *Outlook,* used the club for a daily luncheon conference. William Allen White, the sage of Kansas, made the club his headquarters when he could bear to leave his beloved Emporia for an occasional visit to New York. Such artists as George Bellows, Frederic Remington, Saint-Gaudens, Daniel Chester French, Malvina Hoffman and Paul Manship have been on the club's roster. And art patrons such as J. P. Morgan, Henry Frick, Benjamin Altman, Jules Bache, Gertrude Vanderbilt Whitney and Thomas J. Watson have been members. With commendable pride the club publication, shortly after the outbreak of World War II, boasted, "The National Arts Club was the first and still is among the few to welcome women on the same professional footing as men."

The Victorian Gothic style that Tilden had chosen for his house never had a wide appeal among the great merchant princes who rose to power after the Civil War. They turned rather to the Italian palazzo as a model for their imposing mansions. Perhaps the parallel between the taste of the Italian *condottieri*—mercenaries who served the highest bidder, whether prince or republic, and who built some of the original palazzi in the fourteenth and fifteenth centuries—and the robber barons of the Grant-to-Garfield era is not altogether accidental.

J. P. Morgan, Jr.'s house on Madison Avenue and 37th Street is one of the earliest examples of a freestanding Italianate mansion and one of the last to survive. It had originally been built in 1852, as one of the three that occupied the west side of the block on Madison between 36th and 37th Streets. Morgan liked to get away from his downtown office and frequently used his town house to transact little business deals—like saving the credit rating of New York City and supplying a billion and a half in loans to the Allies in World War I. The Lutheran Church in America bought J. P. Morgan, Jr.'s house in 1944 as a national headquarters and remodeled it to suit its needs, adding a wing in 1958. In 1965, because of a great increase in both its number of congregations and its membership, the church wanted to expand its headquarters space and decided to demolish the Morgan house to make way for a modern office building. It applied for a

8. *J. P. Morgan, Jr., House*
(now Lutheran Church
in America Building)
231 Madison Avenue,
at 37th Street
1852

zoning change from residential use to commercial. The Murray Hill neighborhood fought this request, and it was not approved by the City Planning Commission. After the Landmarks Preservation Commission designated the structure in late 1965, the church brought suit against the City, charging that the designation worked an undue hardship on it. The suit is still in the courts.

Though the Morgan house is fully Italianate in its feeling, the really princely style was not developed until 1882–86, when McKim, Mead & White launched the neo–Italian Renaissance style with the superb U-shaped block on the east side of Madison Avenue, between 50th and 51st Streets, known as the Villard Houses. Although the structure looks like a single building, there are actually four different houses, skillfully designed to look like one. They surround a courtyard which was originally used as a turn-around for carriages. The inspiration for the design came largely from the Palazzo della Cancelleria in Rome, though particular details can be traced to other specific sources. The Villard Houses are among the finest examples of the Eclectic period in New York City. This epoch, in which architects made an arbitrary choice, building by building, of a particular style, has been somewhat scorned in recent years. Eclecticism will someday receive a

9. *Villard Houses*   (*Roman Catholic Archdiocese of New York*)
   451–455 Madison Avenue   *1882–84, McKim, Mead & White*
   24 East 51st Street   *1886, Babb, Cook & Willard*
   29½ East 50th Street   *1909, McKim, Mead & White*

new evaluation. The weak examples will be sifted from the good. And the good Eclectic designers will be found to be not unlike the good classical musicians: they both accepted rigid rules of harmony and some strict rules of composition; they did not break new ground, but, working within self-imposed disciplines, they created some beautiful buildings and some beautiful music.

The history of the Villard Houses has been largely connected with the publishing business and the Roman Catholic Archdiocese of New York. They were built originally by Henry Villard, a journalist, born in Bavaria, who became the owner of the *New York Evening Post.* His wife was the daughter of the abolitionist William Lloyd Garrison, and their son, Oswald Garrison Villard, was publisher and editor of *The Nation* for many years.

Villard himself occupied the mansion at the corner of Madison Avenue and 50th Street and sold the others to friends. A couple of years after the group was completed, the firm of Babb, Cook & Willard added No. 24 East 51st Street onto the northeast corner of the property. Their use of materials and details similar to those in the Villard Houses makes it seem an integral part of the whole complex. A later resident of the 50th Street corner, Whitelaw Reid, publisher of the *New York Tribune,* had McKim, Mead & White enlarge his wing in 1909 with an eight-story addition on 50th Street.

In the 1940s the archdiocese acquired the two central buildings and the south wing, and in 1946 Random House purchased the mansion at the 51st Street corner. Here Bennett Cerf and his colleagues held sway until 1969, when, in the interest of efficiency, they moved to a glass-and-aluminum structure a couple of blocks east. When Random House vacated the north wing, Henry J. Gaisman purchased it and gave it to the archdiocese.

It is a minor miracle that this magnificent architectural island still survives in the center of midtown Manhattan. Its two projecting wings balance the rectory and Cardinal's residence that flank the Lady chapel of St. Patrick's Cathedral on the other side of the avenue. These buildings, which were designed by James Renwick, Jr., architect of the cathedral, are in the late Gothic Revival style and are Landmarks in their own right. Plans recently under serious consideration for the transformation of Madison Avenue into a pedestrian mall took full advantage of this monumental composition. Its location on the highest point of the avenue between 42nd and 59th Streets made it a particularly appropriate climax to the proposed design.

A third mansion in the neo–Italian Renaissance style is the William R. Moore House, off Fifth Avenue on 54th Street. It also was designed by McKim, Mead & White just at the close of the century. Moore was a Chicago industrialist and a founder of the United States Steel Corporation, the American Can Company and the National Biscuit Company. The Israel Cultural Center, an organization devoted to furthering the arts of Israel and cultural interchange between that country and the United States, bought it in 1966.

It is a curious and ecumenical coincidence, and one particularly characteristic of New York City, that these three great houses owe their architectural survival to representatives of three great faiths— Protestant, Catholic and Jewish.

Still a fourth, this time not ecumenical, is the nearby Morton F. Plant house at Fifth Avenue and 52nd Street, a neo–Italian Renaissance private residence designed by Robert W. Gibson in 1903. It was superbly remodeled in 1917 as an American headquarters for Cartier, the jeweler. The richness and intimacy of what was a private palace make an appropriate setting for the merchandising of small objects of great beauty and value.

Plant was an investment banker, yachtsman and baseball-club owner who relished his preeminence on the avenue. But, after a few years, bothered by the increasing traffic and noise in the street outside his windows, he decided to move to a quieter neighborhood uptown. Pierre Cartier, the jeweler, who had opened a New York branch of the French firm in 1907, needed to expand. He and Plant struck a bargain—a string of matched black and white Oriental pearls for Mrs. Plant and a fine new home for the jewels of Cartier. The pearls were said to be worth over a million at the time (1917), but on Mrs. Plant's death in 1956 they were sold for $151,000.

Pierre Cartier's family had been jewelers since the eighteenth century, when they had supplied baubles to the Pompadours, the Du Barrys and the Marie Antoinettes of the French court. When Edward VII of England ordered an elaborate creation for his delicately beautiful Queen, Alexandra, the firm's international reputation was assured. Indian maharajahs and burgeoning American millionaires followed the King's lead and sought Cartier's aid—the former to have their crown jewels remounted and the latter to have their crown jewels created.

New York City's Cartier Building embodies a felicitous example of each of three phases in the life of that durable thoroughfare Fifth Avenue. It served as a town house for twelve years. Then it became the epitome of the luxury retail trade. Currently the unused development rights of the property are being incorporated into a skyscraper which the Greek magnate Aristotle Onassis is building on the remainder of the block front. This new building in itself will represent the sophistication of modern zoning concepts. It will combine retail sales space on the lower floors, offices in the middle and apartments at the top—each section of the building with its own entrance. There will be an arcaded pedestrian walkway through the middle of the block from 51st to 52nd Street. Most importantly, however, the new building will preserve the beautiful Plant-Cartier Landmark, surrounded by an appropriately designed plaza.

There is one town house in the midtown area, and only one, that looks ahead rather than backward. This is the original Grolier Club at

10. *William R. Moore House*
(now the Israel
Cultural Center)
4 East 54th Street
1898–1900,
McKim, Mead & White

11. *Cartier, Inc.* *(originally Morton F. Plant House)*
651–653 Fifth Avenue *1903–05, Robert W. Gibson*
4 East 52nd Street *1905, Charles P. H. Gilbert*
Remodeled as shop: *1917, William W. Bosworth*

29 East 32nd Street. It was designed by Charles W. Romeyn in 1890 in a most imaginative interpretation of the neo-Romanesque style. Like other pioneer architects, widely scattered around the world, Romeyn was groping for a new style—a style that would be uniquely expressive of the incoming new century.

The Grolier Club, named for the sixteenth-century French bibliophile Jean Grolier, is dedicated to the art of book production. When the building was sold in 1968 to Mr. Gilbert Kiamie, the club moved to new quarters uptown where it continues its scholarly tradition.

Two distinguished hotels and one apartment house have also been designated as midtown Manhattan Landmarks. Oldest is the Hotel Chelsea on West 23rd Street, built in 1883 by Hubert, Pirsson and Company. The tier after tier of richly decorated iron balconies constitute the most remarkable feature of this eleven-story structure. Above them the banding of stone- and brickwork, the broken surfaces, the bays and gables, the decorated panels and the rosettes are reminiscent of the Victorian Gothic of the National Arts Club.

This ninety-year-old durable dowager of 23rd Street began as a cooperative apartment hotel sponsored by a group of artists who wanted studio accommodations in a good neighborhood. Chelsea was then fashionable and the center of the theater district. Though she has lived through many vicissitudes, the venerable old lady has always provided a haven for artists, writers and musicians, whether classical, contemporary or far out. Its register lists as residents and transients hundreds of the famous and great from the date of its opening through today: Mark Twain, Sarah Bernhardt, O. Henry, Edgar Lee Masters, John Sloan, Thomas Wolfe, Yevgeny Yevtushenko, Brendan Behan, James T. Farrell, Arthur Miller, Larry Rivers, Charles Jackson, Arthur C. Clarke, Jane Fonda and Jackson Pollock. Virgil Thompson has lived there for years.

The Plaza Hotel, built between 1905 and 1907 from the plans of Henry J. Hardenbergh, who also designed the Dakota Apartments, was and still is one of the great hotels of the world. Its site is beyond compare, on an open plaza off Fifth Avenue at Central Park South, overlooking the park, with the Pulitzer Fountain in the square immediately facing it.

The details of the French Renaissance period that inspired the design have been adapted with great imagination. The use of a rounded tower to turn the corner is particularly skillful. The building

12. *Old Grolier Club*
(now Gilbert Kiamie House)
29 East 32nd Street
1890, Charles W. Romeyn

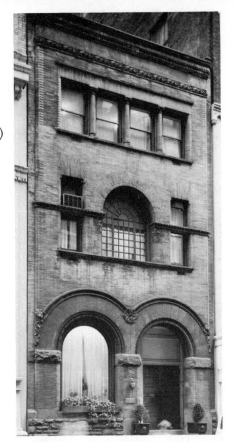

3. *Hotel Chelsea*
222 West 23rd Street
1883, Hubert, Pirsson and Company

14. *The Plaza Hotel*
Fifth Avenue and Central Park South
1905–07, Henry J. Hardenbergh

is exceptional in New York in that two of its façades can be seen at the same time from a considerable distance. Its balconies, balustrades, loggias, piled-up roofs, dormers, chimneys, all contribute to the richness of the design. Yet the details never run away with the over-all composition, which is carefully controlled with an almost classic discipline. Each façade has a dominant central portion flanked by left- and right-hand elements; each façade has a clearly defined base, middle and top.

When the Plaza opened its doors on October 1, 1907, the man who had been waiting sixty years to ascend the throne of England, and whose name was synonymous with the Age of Elegance, had been King Edward VII for just six years. His reign was to end three years later, but the graciousness and sumptuousness that characterized his era were to be found at the Plaza for many years afterward. The hotel has been the scene of the city's most elaborate debuts, most elegant dinner parties, most lavish balls and most extravagant weddings. It has also been the home of the great, the talented and the ambitious.

The hotel has never displayed its name on the building. A modest bronze Landmark plaque which was installed in 1963 by the New York Community Trust is the only indication that this is *the* Plaza. Despite this, as Eve Brown, author of *The Plaza, Its Life and Times,* says:

> From the cotillion to the bunny hug, to the Charleston, to the frug; from diademed dowager to dancing deb; from Lillian Russell to Eloise; from Elinor Glyn to Eleanor Roosevelt; from Groucho to Gromyko; from Billie Burke to Brigitte Bardot; from Caruso to Ringo; from High Society to Hollywood— through all phases of transition, The Plaza has managed always to be in tune with the times, its dignity unruffled, its good taste unimpaired.

Unique in the city and dating from the same period as the Plaza are the Alwyn Court Apartments, at 58th Street and Seventh Avenue. Here the architects, Harde & Short, took advantage of an inexpensive material, terra cotta, a cast clay that was glazed and fired. A single mold could be used time after time to repeat the same design. Once the original mold was paid for, casting additional terra-cotta blocks was relatively inexpensive. The amount of decoration was limited only by the architects' imagination. At Alwyn Court they covered every inch of their building with the intricate ornamentation typical

15. *Alwyn Court Apartments*
182 West 58th Street
1907–09, Harde & Short

of the Francis I style. The crowned salamander over the main doorway is the symbol of the King, one of the great Renaissance patrons of the arts.

Churches, Meeting Houses and a Synagogue

The last place in the world one would think of going to study the development of nineteenth- and early-twentieth-century ecclesiastical architecture would be the commercial heart of New York City. Yet here are to be found key examples of almost every style. There is a particularly significant series of churches that illustrate the fascinating history of the Gothic Revival in America. Of course, when these churches were built they were surrounded by residential neighborhoods. With the conservatism of ecclesiastical establishments, they have lingered on, sometimes with shifting parishes, sometimes with great economic difficulties, but they have survived and one can still trace in this unlikely location the full sequence of styles and fashions in church building.

St. Peter's Episcopal Church in the Chelsea Historic District (see illustration on page 233), on the south side of 20th Street in the middle of the block between Eighth and Ninth Avenues, is so modest that you have to look sharply or you will miss it. Although St. Peter's has not been individually designated a Landmark, it is described here because it is the earliest example in the United States of the sort of English Gothic parish church that was to spread by the hundreds across the country in the ensuing decades. It was built in 1836–38. Phoebe B. Stanton in *The Gothic Revival and American Church Architecture* credits St. Peter's with marking "the beginning of serious revivalism."

Clement Clarke Moore, who is more widely known for his "A Visit from Saint Nicholas," had rented the land to the newly established parish in 1832 at the rate of seven cents per year. A group of three buildings, a church flanked by a chapel and a rectory, were designed by Moore himself in the formal Greek Revival style just then coming into fashion. The chapel (now the rectory) just west of the church was actually built, in 1831–32, in the form of a simplified Greek temple with engaged brick pilasters rather than the freestanding Doric portico that the original drawings indicate. Possibly the change was made to save money or possibly to permit the church itself to dominate the two flanking buildings. In either event the result is unusual: a Greek-temple design carried out with pilasters instead of freestanding columns.

The story has it that foundations for the church, which was to have been a rectangular Greek temple, were already in place when one of the vestrymen came back from a trip to England so filled with enthusiasm for the Gothic churches he had seen that he persuaded the parish to change its plans. With not much to go on except some sketches and drawings and perhaps a copy of *An Essay on Gothic Architecture,* which Bishop John H. Hopkins of Vermont had published in 1836, Moore, with the assistance of an architect-builder, James W. Smith, created the first Gothic church in America. Of course, it was actually Gothic only in the applied details. A comparison with the little Federal-style St. Luke's in the Greenwich Village Historic District, built only fourteen years earlier, shows how essentially similar the two buildings are—even to the square front tower through which the church is entered. The tower at St. Peter's was originally flanked by two handsome wooden porches, which unfortunately started to fall apart and had to be taken down a few years ago. The rest of the church, however, survives. It was consecrated in 1838. The iron fence and gates are the originals from St. Paul's Chapel on Broadway, which were replaced at about the time St. Peter's was built. They were donated to the new chapel by Trinity Parish.

The third member of what Moore planned as a cluster of Greek temples was not built until 1871. What he had originally conceived to be the rectory became the parish hall and was designed in the Victorian Gothic style. Yet somehow this strange *ménage à trois* with its complicated history still seems to thrive on West 20th Street.

The Episcopal Church of the Holy Communion, built in 1844–46 at the northeast corner of Sixth Avenue and 20th Street by the great ecclesiastical architect Richard Upjohn, exhibits a deeper understanding of the Gothic style than that of Moore and Smith and reveals for the first time the essentially romantic asymmetrical character of an English parish church. The tower has been moved off center to the southwest corner of the plot, where the street and the avenue meet. Instead of the simple rectangle of St. Peter's, the church itself has been given a fully developed cruciform plan, and the sisters' house, with its own tower and gable, has been tucked into the north corner on Sixth Avenue.

16. *Church of the Holy Communion   Sixth Avenue and 20th Street*
   Church: 1844–46, Richard Upjohn
   Sisters' House: 1850, Richard Upjohn
   Chapel: 1879, Richard Upjohn

Holy Communion represents an abrupt shift by Upjohn from the formal and imposing style of the earlier Trinity Church. This, as well as Grace Church, by his great rival, James Renwick, Jr., had been much inspired by the ideas of the English architect A. W. Pugin. While Renwick was to continue in the grand manner of Pugin, Upjohn had come strongly under the influence of the Cambridge Camden Society and its American offshoot, the New York Ecclesiological Society. Their doctrine was that the only appropriate models for Episcopal worship were the little country parish churches of England. So strongly was doctrine intertwined with style that Upjohn, in 1846, refused a commission to design a Unitarian church in Boston because he felt, as a devout Episcopalian, disqualified to carry it out.

Holy Communion also made history when it decreed that the pews would be free to all and not sold to those who could afford them, as had been the custom in all New York churches up to that time. The first rector, Dr. William A. Muhlenberg, founder and guiding light of the Ecclesiological Society, wanted to see a church hospital in the city, and on St. Luke's Day in 1846 he asked that half the morning collection be set aside for such a purpose. Thirty dollars was the result. When a parishioner chided the good doctor, "When do you expect your hospital to be finished at this rate?" Dr. Muhlenberg replied, "Never, if I never make a beginning." Soon St. Luke's Hospital became the concern of Episcopalians throughout the city, and in 1858 a fine new hospital at the corner of 54th Street and Fifth Avenue replaced the initial facilities in the Holy Communion Sisters' House. Many years later it moved to its present extensive quarters on Morningside Heights.

The Church of the Holy Communion was located in what was once one of the city's wealthiest parishes. Its worshipers included John Jacob Astor, Cornelius Vanderbilt and Jay Gould. Today the congregation has shrunk to a bare 150 and includes only a few descendants of some of the founding families.

The influence of the English parish church is again seen in the Little Church Around the Corner, also called the Actors' Church, but officially known as the Church of the Transfiguration. It was designed by an unidentified architect in 1849. The church, with its guild hall, Lady chapel, mortuary chapel and above all its lich gate, stands serene in its miniature garden, in the shadow of the Empire State Building.

17. *Church of the Transfiguration   (Episcopal)*
("Little Church Around the Corner")   1 East 29th Street
Church, Rectory, Guild Hall: 1849–61
Lich Gate: 1896, Frederick C. Withers
Lady Chapel, Mortuary Chapel: 1906–08

The lich gate was designed by Frederick C. Withers and built in 1896 as the gift of Mrs. Franklin Hughes Delano, a great-aunt of F.D.R. Lich gates, more common in England than in the United States, provided a covered resting place at the entrance to a churchyard where the pallbearers could rest the coffin while waiting for the burial service to begin. "Lich" in Old English means corpse.

The great American actor Joseph Jefferson gave the church its popular sobriquet in 1870. An actor friend, George Holland, had died and Jefferson went to a fashionable church in the neighborhood to arrange for the funeral service. When the rector learned that the deceased had been an actor, he politely declined but suggested that there was a "little church around the corner where the matter might be arranged." Whereupon Jefferson, with deep feeling, replied, "Thank God for the little church around the corner."

From that day there has been a special bond between the stage and this church. Sir Henry Irving, Dame Ellen Terry and Sarah Bernhardt attended services here at one time or another. There are memorial windows to some of the most distinguished of American actors: Jefferson, Richard Mansfield, John Drew and Edwin Booth. A bronze plaque designed by Paul Manship honors Otis Skinner, and the Actors' Memorial Window in the transept pays homage to all members of the theatrical profession who have died, sung and unsung. In 1923 the Episcopal Actors' Guild of America (a nondenominational membership group despite its name) was organized under the presidency of George Arliss and set up headquarters in a large second-story room in the guild hall.

The church has also been one of the city's favorite places for weddings. Indeed, at one time it boasted that it "now solemnizes more marriages than any other church in the world (but does not marry divorced persons) ."

The rectories of both the Church of the Holy Communion and the Little Church Around the Corner are of special interest. While each was designed as a subsidiary part of a larger composition, they stand in their own right as good examples of Gothic Revival domestic architecture. Their open sites permitted these little freestanding houses to develop to the full a truly Gothic spirit of gables, chimneys and picturesque details.

Another church by Richard Upjohn illustrates the transition between the early Gothic Revival and Victorian Gothic. It was originally built at 15 West 25th Street as an uptown offshoot of Trinity Parish, but today it is the Serbian Orthodox Cathedral of St. Sava, the spiritual home of hundreds of Croatian families who have found refuge in the United States in the last two decades.

From the front the cathedral presents a very bold Gothic presence, though the little pinnacles that flank the main gable begin to have that spidery look that was to become a Victorian Gothic trademark. The triangular gables of the clergy house in the rear give an impression of a paper-cutout fantasy that is almost fully Victorian. Five years after the 1855 completion of the church a parish house designed by Jacob Wrey Mould was built to the east. Here all the Ruskinian flourishes of bands of contrasting masonry, carved panels, little open belfries and pinnacles, ornamental brick and polychromy are in the full swing of the Victorian Gothic style.

The Marble Collegiate Reformed Church, Fifth Avenue and 29th

18. SERBIAN ORTHODOX CATHEDRAL OF ST. SAVA
(originally Trinity Chapel)

a. Cathedral
15 West 25th Street
1850–55, Richard Upjohn

b. Clergy House (right) and
Rear of Cathedral
16 West 26th Street
1850–55, Richard Upjohn

c. Parish House
13 West 25th Street
1860, Jacob Wrey Mould

Street, dating from about the same period, provides an amusing illustration of how little meaning labels sometimes have. The architect, Samuel A. Warner, apparently thought he was designing a Romanesque church and said as much. This was a new style that was just coming into fashion. It is true that there are round heads to the windows instead of pointed arches, and that little strings of corbeled brackets support the water tables and other projecting surfaces. These are quite correct details of the Romanesque style, but their application here is entirely superficial. The proportions of the building, its strong verticality, its spindly pinnacles and the general fussiness of its forms are essentially Gothic Revival.

The Collegiate Reformed Dutch Church is the oldest denomination to have been established in the city. It was founded in 1628, and for many years the congregation worshiped in a dilapidated little wooden house on the shore of the East River. Peter Minuit, the third governor of New Netherland and the lucky man who bought Manhattan from the Indians, was one of the first elders of the church. By 1642 the church had progressed to a small stone building inside the fort of New Amsterdam, where it occupied one fourth of the fort's space. Its fortunes steadily ascended, as did its location: its homes slowly moved up the island until in 1854 the present Marble Collegiate Church was built on Fifth Avenue at 29th Street. It was called "Marble," obviously, because its exterior is entirely of marble, and "Collegiate" because its ministers, usually three in number, serve on an equal basis and are called "colleagues." Sometimes it is known rather irreverently as the "Church of the Holy Rooster" because of the large gilded cock that crowns its spire.

The church has in recent years, under the energetic leadership of Dr. Norman Vincent Peale, prolific author and indefatigable traveler to places in the news, presented a sharp and very up-to-date image to the public. Recently it made news by inviting the colorful and persuasive Roman Catholic Archbishop Fulton J. Sheen to preach at a regular service.

James Renwick, Jr.'s Cathedral of St. Patrick on Fifth Avenue between 50th and 51st Streets is in a number of ways the most important Gothic church built in New York City in the nineteenth century. In the first place, it is far and away the largest. With an interior space 306 feet long by 108 feet high, it is truly a cathedral in scale and is an

19. *Marble Collegiate Reformed Church*
Fifth Avenue and 29th Street
1851–54, Samuel A. Warner

20. *St. Patrick's Cathedral*
Fifth Avenue, 50th to 51st Street
1858–79, 1888, James Renwick, Jr.

appropriate symbol for the wealthiest Roman Catholic archdiocese in the United States. It was twenty-one years under construction—from the laying of the cornerstone in 1858 by the Right Reverend John Hughes, the first Catholic Archbishop of New York, to its dedication in 1879 by John Cardinal McCloskey, the first American to receive the red hat. The spires were not completed until nine years afterward; rising 330 feet from the sidewalk, they dominated the skyline of midtown Manhattan for half a century.

St. Patrick's also occupies a pivotal point in the architectural history of American Gothic. When, in 1853, Renwick started making studies for the great edifice, he not only was older than when he had designed Grace Church but also seems to have been somewhat over-awed by the sheer magnitude of the commission. Whatever the cause, there is surely a certain dryness in the result. Then, too, there is—particularly in the detailing of the little pinnacles and in the rather flat lacework that fills the steep-sided pediments—just a hint of the Victorian Gothic style which was then coming into being. It should be recalled that St. Patrick's was being designed while Upjohn's St. Sava was being built. Renwick was never one to let his rival steal a march on him. On the whole, however, St. Patrick's Cathedral, with its rather free and casual mixture of French and English Gothic elements, can be considered the climax of the Gothic Revival style.

St. Patrick's also illustrates the later Eclectic approach with its Lady chapel, which Charles T. Mathews added in 1906. This is a beautiful and very correct French Gothic design. The lacy *flèche* which punctuates the eastern end of the great cathedral with an exclamation point is a particularly happy inspiration.

The full story of Gothic architecture in New York did not end,

21. *Cardinal's Residence and Lady Chapel, St. Patrick's Cathedral West side of Madison Avenue, 50th to 51st Street*
Residence: 1880, James Renwick, Jr.
Lady Chapel: 1906, Charles T. Mathews
Rectory (not shown) : 1880, James Renwick, Jr.

however, in scholarly Eclecticism. It had a last and brilliant flowering in the work of one man, Bertram Grosvenor Goodhue. His work is so personal, so original, that whether he worked with a Gothic vocabulary or with the elements of some other period, Goodhue has to be considered outside all categories. He had the unique ability to project himself back into an epoch and to absorb so thoroughly not only its superficial elements but also its inner impulses that he could then create from them something completely new and completely his own.

Many people, both professional critics and the man in the street, feel that Goodhue's St. Thomas' Episcopal Church on Fifth Avenue at 53rd Street is the most beautiful church in the city. Both outside and inside, the wealth of imaginative detail seems both immediately familiar and yet highly original. The strongly asymmetrical composition, with the bold tower on the corner and the deeply recessed main portal thrown off center, is somehow in perfect balance and yet like no other church anywhere. There is a diametric play of plain surfaces against richly carved ones. Some of the detail, particularly at the portal, seems pure French of the thirteenth century. The straight rows of saints in their niches suggest Notre Dame de Paris. Yet the abrupt way in which the tower is squared off with crenellations is very English. The truth of the matter is that the design is pure Goodhue.

St. Thomas' separated from Trinity in 1823, when the congregation held its first independent service. In 1826 it moved into its own church building at Broadway and Houston Street, which was destroyed by fire in 1851. A second church on the same site, consecrated in 1852, was abandoned in 1866 because of fast-encroaching slums, and a new edifice was planned for the present Fifth Avenue site. Opened in 1870, this new church was also destroyed by fire in 1905. But enough of the structure was left to permit the building of a large temporary chapel within the walls. It seated twelve hundred people. For eight years, construction of the new church went on over and around the temporary chapel while services were carried on as usual. In 1914, when the new church was ready, the temporary shell was removed and services were transferred to the new building without skipping a prayer or a hymn.

Actually quite a lot of material was salvaged from the original church. The present carillon of twenty-one bells was cast in England in 1928 from the metal of the original bells, which had been damaged

22. *St. Thomas' Church*
Fifth Avenue and 53rd Street
1909–14, Cram, Goodhue & Ferguson

beyond repair. The baptismal font is decorated with a number of little medallions saved from the old font.

Many generations of the city's most fashionable brides have passed through the "Brides' Door," located to the south of the main portal. It was through its predecessor that a weeping Consuelo Vanderbilt marched to her wedding to the Duke of Marlborough, cousin of Winston Churchill—one of the sensations of the day and the high point of that early American custom, acquiring a title for the poor little rich girl. It was rumored that the Duke received, in addition to his bride, $2,500,000 in railroad stocks and an annual income of $100,000 for life. In the ornamental carving over the present Brides' Door it is not too difficult to make out a dollar sign that has been skillfully chiseled next to a lovers' knot.

Ecclesiastical architecture in New York in the nineteenth century was not exclusively Gothic. There were several competing styles. There are two good and quite different examples in the Italianate style. The earlier one, which goes back to 1848, is Minard Lafever's Church of the Holy Apostles at Ninth Avenue and 28th Street. Lafever, who is much better known for his Greek Revival and Gothic Revival churches, shows equal versatility in handling this quite different style with originality and restraint.

Its outstanding feature is the handsome spire. The transitions between the square brick tower and the octagonal belfry and between the belfry and the steeple are skillfully achieved with shallow arched pediments. Instead of being engulfed by the monstrous housing units that now surround it, this little church seems enhanced by them; its gemlike qualities shine by contrast.

The Episcopal congregation of the Church of the Holy Apostles was organized in 1844; the cornerstone of the church was laid in 1846; and it opened for worship in 1848. In 1966, shortly after the church had been designated a New York City Landmark, it was discovered that the priceless stained-glass windows (the work of William Jay Bolton, the first and finest stained-glass artist in this country) were seriously endangered by time and weather. A quick fund-raising campaign and the generosity of neighborhood groups made it possible for the church to carry out an emergency program to seal and protect the windows, while a more extensive campaign for funds was launched to permit complete restoration.

King & Kellum's Friends' Meeting House on East 20th Street, off Gramercy Park, was built a decade later than the Church of the Holy Apostles. Austere, as are all Quaker meeting houses, this one achieves a dignified richness from the contrast between the plain wall surfaces and the arched pediment that is supported on consoles over the wide central doorway. A beautifully proportioned triangular pediment crowns the building as a whole.

The Society of Friends has been active in Manhattan since 1687, when it met in the homes of its members. In 1696 they built their first meeting house, a little frame structure on what is now Liberty Place. In 1827 a schism developed when the followers of Elias Hicks seceded. The so-called Hicksites built a meeting house at Rutherford Place on Stuyvesant Square, and the orthodox group constructed their meeting

23. *Church of the Holy Apostles*
Ninth Avenue and 28th Street
1846–48, Minard Lafever
Transepts: 1858,
Richard Upjohn & Son

24. *Friends' Meeting House*
(now United Federation of Teachers)
144 East 20th Street
1859, King & Kellum

house on Gramercy Square. In 1958 the schism was healed and the two groups combined in the Stuyvesant Square quarters. Religious services were discontinued in the Gramercy Park building, but for a while it remained headquarters for Quaker charities.

In 1965 the society gave an option on the property to a developer who wanted to build a thirty-story apartment house on the site. The Gramercy Park neighborhood rallied to save the historic structure. Among the most active groups to oppose demolition were the Professional Theater Wing, which recruited the many theatrical people who lived in the area, as well as members of the Players. Plans were even made to organize a community theater in the building as a tryout spot for Broadway hopefuls. Eventually, the property was acquired by the United Federation of Teachers, to be used for community activities as well as for some of the union's headquarters operations.

This will not be the first time that the meeting house has been used for purposes other than religious worship. Before the Civil War the third floor of the building had been used as a refuge for Southern Negroes smuggled north by the Underground Railway. The slaves were given some sort of rehabilitation before being sent on to make their way in a new world. Also, a small effort initiated here by members of the society to assist travelers in distress resulted in the formation of the Travelers' Aid Society in 1905.

The Friends' Meeting House and Seminary on Rutherford Place, facing Stuyvesant Square, were built in 1861 in very restrained Greek Revival style, austere to the point of being simple vernacular. This is the simplicity and also the conservatism that Quakers have always favored.

Next to the meeting house on Rutherford Place, but quite different in spirit, is the early Romanesque Revival St. George's Episcopal Church, which Blesch & Eidlitz designed in 1846. This is strong and easily recognizable Romanesque architecture as contrasted with the Marble Collegiate Church, which was actually begun five years after St. George's. Originally there were spires on the two towers, but they

25. *Friends' Meeting House and Seminary*
15 Rutherford Place, 226 East 16th Street
1861, Charles T. Bunting, builder

became unsafe and had to be demolished in the late 1880s. It is not at all certain that the design with its squat vigorous proportions did not actually gain from the loss.

It was at St. George's Church that J. P. Morgan, as an elder, ruled with such an iron hand that it was known as "Morgan's Church." However, in recent years the church has had hard sledding with a steadily dwindling congregation.

As the century neared its close and as the potentials of one style after another were explored, developed, modified and abandoned, there was a restless searching for new styles and new interests that would captivate public taste. This Eclecticism was not always a mere search for new fashions. At times there were carefully thought-out reasons for the selection of a particular style.

For example, Henry Fernbach, the architect of the Central Synagogue at Lexington Avenue and 55th Street (1871–72), although he used a conventional Latin-cross ground plan, felt that Gothic architecture, so closely identified with Christian churches, would not be appropriate to what was one of the earliest, if not the earliest, reformed Jewish congregation in New York. So he turned to the Near East and gave the city its finest example of neo-Moorish architecture. Two striking octagonal towers surmounted by onion-shaped domes dominate the front of the synagogue. The north elevation has six fine

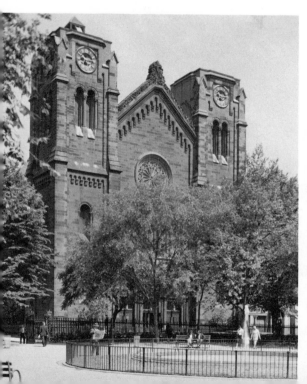

stained-glass windows set in horseshoe-shaped Moorish arches. The building is now New York State's oldest Jewish house of worship in continuous use by the same congregation. Its Moorish style was widely adopted for many subsequent synagogues.

The Roman Catholic Immaculate Conception Church, on East 14th Street, is one of the only two churches in the city built in the charming neo–Francis I style. The same sort of hunger for intimacy and human warmth in church architecture that fifty years earlier had led the Ecclesiological Society to turn for inspiration to the English parish church seems to have inspired the architects of what was originally an offshoot of Grace Church Parish. Known then as Grace Chapel and Hospital on 14th Street, it was built to provide free pews for those less fortunate financially than the members of Grace Church itself. What was, in effect, another "little church around the corner" provided a much needed service to the Protestant newcomer from northern Europe who was part of the huge tide of immigration at the end of the nineteenth century. When the tide subsided, the church had served its purpose. The buildings were bought in 1943 by the Roman Catholics, who now make use of them to serve a new community.

It is particularly appropriate to close this survey of midtown Manhattan ecclesiastical architecture with what is not only the latest

26. *St. George's Church*
    Rutherford Place and
    East 16th Street
    1846–56, Blesch & Eidlitz
    Restored after fire 1867
    Spires removed 1888

27. *Central Synagogue*
    652 Lexington Avenue,
    at 55th Street
    1871–72, Henry Fernbach

28. *Immaculate Conception Church*
    (originally Grace Chapel)
    406–412 East 14th Street
    1894, Barney & Chapman

Landmark church in date but also the most magnificent. St. Bartholomew's occupies the whole eastern block front of Park Avenue from 50th to 51st Street. The architect, Bertram Grosvenor Goodhue, this time looked for inspiration to Byzantium. It seems incredible that the same man who worked so creatively in the Gothic style of St. Thomas' could, a few blocks away and a few years later, be just as original and expressive in this totally different style.

Not the least notable feature of the building is the magnificent porch, which had been designed in 1902 by McKim, Mead & White for an earlier building of St. Bartholomew's congregation. It had been adapted from a Provençal Romanesque church near Arles and was moved bodily to its present location. This porch is not Byzantine, of course, but the skill used by Goodhue in combining it with the main body of the new church shows again how he could weave together many styles, making of them something uniquely his own. Whereas

29. *St. Bartholomew's Church   Park Avenue, 50th to 51st Street*
1917–19, Bertram G. Goodhue
Porch from former church: 1902, McKim, Mead & White
Community House (partially shown)   109 East 50th Street
1926–28, Mayers, Murray & Philip

the mood of St. Thomas' is full of the withdrawn and inward-looking mystery of the Middle Ages, St. Bartholomew's—with the rich texture of intermittent bands of limestone interrupting its warm salmon-colored brick, with its spots of beautifully executed carving, and, above all, with its great low polychrome dome—is all outgoing opulence. Superbly situated amid its terraced gardens, it exudes the warmth of the Mediterranean skies.

St. Bartholomew's was organized as a congregation in 1835 when "a number of gentlemen residing in the Bowery and vicinity deemed it expedient to establish a new Episcopal congregation." Its first home was in Lafayette Place, at Great Jones Street, in the heart of the 250,000 people who then made up New York. By 1871 Manhattan's population had increased to 800,000, and the march northward left the Lafayette Place structure not only too small but too far off the beaten track for its modern needs. So a splendid, large new structure was erected at Madison Avenue and 44th Street. It was for this church that McKim, Mead & White designed the porch, a memorial gift of the family of Cornelius Vanderbilt.

The inexorable march continued, and by 1917 the population center had again moved uptown and the Madison Avenue quarters were found to be inadequate. The present church was begun in 1917 and completed in 1919. St. Bartholomew's Community House was added after Goodhue's death in 1924 by his associates, Mayers, Murray & Philip, in the same materials and following the spirit of the master.

Public Buildings, Clubs, a Concert Hall and a Railway Terminal

The Landmark public buildings of midtown Manhattan are interesting for two reasons. The large ones provide excellent examples, few though they are, of what truly monumental architecture is. The smaller ones closely follow the same four styles of the Eclectic period that were the most popular choices for the great mansions built on the Upper East Side during the closing years of the nineteenth century and the opening decades of the twentieth—which makes them all "neo," or new, versions of Italian Renaissance, French Renaissance,

Georgian and Federal. This is really not very surprising. The same men who were building their private palaces along Fifth and Park Avenues were the club members and patrons of the arts responsible also for the public buildings. The residential and the public buildings quite simply reflect the same taste.

One of the purest examples of the neo–Italian Renaissance style is the building that McKim, Mead & White designed in 1889–91 for the Century Association on West 43rd Street. It combines granite, terra cotta and yellow brick in quite a free and elegant adaptation of an Italian palazzo. The Palladian window above the main doorway was originally an open loggia, and the appearance of the building was weakened when it was glassed in. This symmetrical façade is essentially a linear composition and does not express the actual volumes of the rooms behind.

The Century, long considered the city's most cultural club, was founded by William Cullen Bryant, who called it the Century because it was originally supposed to hold its membership to one hundred, a figure that has long since been exceeded. Among its members have been many of the city's practitioners in the fields of arts and letters, as well as scholars, jurists, architects and amateurs of the arts.

William B. Tuthill also chose the neo–Italian Renaissance style for his great concert auditorium, Carnegie Hall, at 57th Street and Seventh Avenue. It is less successful than the Century because of its awkward mass, in which the eleven-story studio building overshadows the hall itself.

Carnegie Hall has had a sort of Perils-of-Pauline existence that could happen only in New York. Leopold Damrosch decided, back in the 1880s, that his Oratorio Society needed a proper auditorium. None of the available concert and recital halls was suitable, and the society was forced to give concerts in the showroom of a piano store. Damrosch, who also founded the New York Symphony Society, infected his son Walter with the fever of building a music hall worthy of the city. Young Damrosch, who inherited the directorship of both groups, approached Andrew Carnegie, Scottish philanthropist and steel tycoon, with the proposal that he make possible a suitable hall.

Although Carnegie much preferred the bagpipes of his native Scotland to choral and symphonic music, he was also aware of the social importance of a certain amount of culture and agreed to put up two

30. *The Century Association*
7 West 43rd Street
1889–91, McKim, Mead & White

31. *Carnegie Hall (early view)*
57th Street and Seventh Avenue
1889–91, William B. Tuthill

million dollars to construct the building. His gesture was not entirely philanthropic, for he looked forward to the Hall's becoming a paying proposition. He voiced his pride and wishful thinking when the cornerstone was laid in 1890: "It is built to stand for ages and during these ages it is probable that this Hall will intertwine itself with the history of our country."

The gala opening was held on the evening of May 9, 1891, with the famed Russian composer Peter Ilich Tchaikovsky on the podium conducting some of his own works. Tchaikovsky paid tribute to the acoustics of the hall, as have thousands of others, by declaring it "magnificent."

In 1892 the New York Philharmonic Orchestra made its debut in Carnegie Hall, where it was to play for seventy years until it moved to Lincoln Center. Paderewski, Joseph Lhevinne, Efrem Zimbalist, Mischa Elman and Toscanini are among the great artists who have been heard at Carnegie. Benny Goodman, with his clarinet, startled the sober-sided Philharmonic sponsors but delighted their youngsters.

Although Carnegie Hall was a *succès d'estime,* it did not pay for itself. Its operating costs consistently exceeded its income, even though it played to full houses. With much grumbling, Carnegie underwrote its annual deficits. Then he got bored. Its future was in considerable doubt until private subscriptions came to the rescue. Another financial crisis arose in 1925, but a syndicate purchased the building and made several alterations which helped to put the hall back on its financial feet.

Yet another cliff-hanger developed in 1960 when the owners wanted to demolish it in order to erect an office building. Musicians and music-lovers, led by the violinist Isaac Stern, rallied under the slogan "Save Carnegie Hall." The plush Lincoln Center, which was to include Philharmonic Hall as a new home of the orchestra, was being completed, and the prophets of doom said that since the city could not support two great concert halls, Carnegie had to go. But the dedicated savers persisted: New York City won a battle in Albany which permitted it to buy the building, the Carnegie Hall Corporation was organized and the hall was back in business. Today, both Carnegie Hall and Philharmonic Hall (now Avery Fisher Hall) in Lincoln Center are fully booked.

Henry J. Hardenbergh used the neo–Francis I idiom for the

American Fine Arts Society Building, also on 57th Street, a little west of Carnegie. Architecturally, it is more successful than the concert hall because its scale and style harmonize.

This structure has for years been the home of the famed Art Students' League. The American Fine Arts Society was incorporated in 1889 by three component organizations, the Society of American Artists (which was later absorbed into the National Academy of Design), the Architectural League of New York and the Art Students' League. To provide galleries, studios and classrooms for their activities the three groups bought the site on 57th Street, commissioned the building and in 1892 moved in. Practically all of the major fine-arts exhibitions in the city were held in the building's galleries until 1941, when the Art Students' League acquired full interest in the building and converted the ground-floor galleries into studios, to accommodate an ever-growing body of students.

32. The American Fine Arts Society
215 West 57th Street
1891–92, Henry J. Hardenbergh

McKim, Mead & White's University Club at 54th Street and Fifth Avenue continues the tradition of the Italian Renaissance palazzo which the firm had launched so brilliantly with the Villard Houses. It demonstrates a superb understanding of the sixteenth-century idiom and yet with some remarkably free elements. It is not a copy of any one building but combines details taken from many. It displays almost the same sort of creative freedom that Goodhue did with the Gothic style just a block away at St. Thomas' Church. Different individuals have different favorites—and certainly McKim, Mead & White, at the height of their powers, maintained an extraordinarily high quality of design in building after building. Many people feel the Villard Houses are the firm's masterpieces, but, by any set of criteria, the University Club is certainly one of the great buildings of the city.

The library that the same firm designed for J. P. Morgan on East 36th Street is also among its finest works. Built entirely of white marble with an austere blank surface broken only by a deep Palladian porch and a pair of flanking niches, the Morgan Library suggests the purity of the early fifteenth century in Florence, the days of Fra Angelico and Botticelli, rather than the mature magnificence of a century later, the epoch of Michelangelo, which the University Club reflects. The Morgan Library was designed by Charles McKim himself. The white marble was put together in dry form, with the blocks ground so perfectly that no mortar was needed to set them. You cannot insert a penknife between the stones. This type of dry-masonry construction has been used very rarely in the history of architecture, primarily because it is very rare to obtain the highly skilled workmanship it requires. It was used in the building of the Parthenon and also in some ancient Egyptian and Incan works. The essential prerequisite is an unlimited supply of time and labor rather than the sophistication of modern tools.

An interesting footnote to the artistic ego of architects is the bas-relief of a sphinx halfway up the building. Morgan was adamant that his library not be "blemished" with the architect's signature, so the sculptor used McKim's profile for the head of the sphinx. There is no record of what Morgan said or whether he even noticed it.

Just after the turn of the century there appeared a revival of interest in the Georgian and Federal styles. After almost a hundred years of reviving, adapting or imitating the architecture of classical

33. *University Club*
1 West 54th Street, at Fifth Avenue
1897–99, McKim, Mead & White

34. Morgan Library
33 East 36th Street
1903–06, McKim, Mead & White
Annex: 1928, Benjamin W. Morris

Greece and Rome, of Gothic Europe, of Renaissance Italy and France, of Byzantium and even Moorish North Africa, it was a natural reaction to search the American past for inspiration closer to home.

Again it was those protean Eclectics McKim, Mead & White who led the way. Their neo-Federal building at 120 Madison Avenue, built in 1905, was the original home of the Colony Club and made history before women's lib had even been dreamed of and long before women got the vote. The Colony was the first private women's club in New York to build itself a clubhouse. It was primarily a social club, with overtones of good works—namely, patronage of the arts. Mrs. Borden Harriman and Miss Anne Morgan, with other social and civic leaders of the city, were founding members. There were many raised eye-brows at the news that this social-cum-arts club had a bar. But the club flourished and so did the arts.

The architects must have had quite a problem when presented all the requirements: a swimming pool, assembly rooms, a gymnasium, restaurants, a roof garden, rooms for transients and a bar—all within a building which, it was hoped, would retain something of a domestic character. They succeeded in satisfying the ladies with six stories and a basement. The result was somewhat out of scale for the neo-Federal style, but nevertheless rather graceful and elegant.

The Colony Club later moved to grander quarters on Park Avenue and 62nd Street, and in 1963 the American Academy of Dramatic Arts bought the Madison Avenue structure. The Academy was founded in 1884 and is the oldest school of professional dramatic training in the English-speaking world. For nearly ninety years it has produced some of the greatest American stars, among them Spencer Tracy, Edward G. Robinson, Rosalind Russell, Agnes Moorehead, Kirk Douglas, Lauren Bacall.

35. American Academy of
Dramatic Arts
(originally the Colony Club)
120 Madison Avenue
1905, McKim, Mead & White

36. *The Harvard Club*
(early view)
27 West 44th Street
1893–94, 1903, 1915:
McKim, Mead & White

The grander neo-Georgian style seemed more appropriately masculine for the Harvard Club, which McKim, Mead & White designed in 1903–04 on West 44th Street. Its semi-Palladian motif on the second floor, carried out in white limestone against a background of dark red "Harvard brick," resulted in a very handsome building. There were many subsequent additions by McKim, Mead & White, most notably the great Harvard Hall on the 45th Street side, which is three stories high and is one of the most impressive interior spaces in the city.

There is something about government and the law that calls for classicism. The very concepts of law and order evoke Rome, and Rome at once suggests columns. This tradition is well illustrated by three fine examples in midtown Manhattan.

Earliest of these was Cyrus L. W. Eidlitz's 1895 building, also on 44th Street, for the Association of the Bar of the City of New York, in which he used massive Doric columns at the lower story and very simple engaged pilasters against the blank wall of the reading room and library above. This building runs through from street to street and, like the Harvard Club, which it faces, has been added to in many different stages.

Stung by the accusations against the legal profession for its complacency in the face of shocking post–Civil War corruption in the courts, the lawyers of the city banded together in 1870 to form the Association of the Bar of the City of New York (how lawyerlike to choose this wordy name). In less than two years, under the prodding of Samuel J. Tilden, the Bar Association exposed the Tweed Ring and sponsored many impeachment proceedings against venal judges. In the more than a century since then the Bar Association has pursued its role as the city's conscience in all matters affecting the judiciary and the practice of law. Its original home was in a private house on West 27th Street, where its six hundred members enjoyed a pleasant gentlemen's-club atmosphere. In 1874 it moved to West 29th Street, where it remained until its present home was completed in 1895.

When the building committee turned over the key to the new structure to the president, West 44th Street was a quiet uptown street in a fashionable residential district, where morning-coated members could walk leisurely from their homes or drive their carriages to the Association. Although he had long since gone to his reward, Boss Tweed, during his heyday, had lived around the corner at 43rd Street and Fifth Avenue. The Association today has nearly ten thousand members, and the leisurely atmosphere of the street has vanished.

Much more magnificent than the Association of the Bar building is James Lord's Brown building for the Appellate Division of the New York State Supreme Court at 25th Street and Madison Avenue. This is a truly Roman building, all of white marble, with a great hexastyle pedimented entrance on 25th Street and four engaged columns on the narrow end, which faces on the square. The detail of the building is superb, and it is particularly remarkable for its sculpture. The seated figures flanking the main doorway and the heroic statues of the great lawgivers that stand on pedestals around the parapet give it a richness that one does not normally associate with a solemn courthouse. One third of the total construction cost is supposed to have been spent in decoration. There are very few buildings of our day, or, in fact, of any day, of which this can be said. The interiors are equally lavish, with fine paneling, murals and marble floors.

37. *Association of the Bar*
      of the City of New York
      42 West 44th Street
      1895, Cyrus L. W. Eidlitz

38. *Appellate Division,*
      New York State Supreme Court
      25th Street and Madison Avenue
      1896–1900, James Brown Lord

39. *U.S. General Post Office   Eighth Avenue, 31st to 33rd Street*
      1910–13, McKim, Mead & White

Finally, in this classical series, McKim, Mead & White produced the General Post Office, which stands on Eighth Avenue between 31st and 33rd Streets. Here they really went in for columns. There are twenty of them, standing fifty-three feet high. The main façade, including the end pavilions, extends almost five hundred feet and is tremendously imposing. It was even more effective when it was balanced across the street by the façade of Pennsylvania Railroad Station, the firm's great and much lamented masterpiece.

Impressive though such a monumental Roman structure is, it has a certain coldness about it that is altogether lacking in that equally monumental style that evolved in Paris during the second half of the 19th century at the École des Beaux-Arts. Where the Roman style overawes with its scale and power, the Beaux-Arts style has an exuberance and a vitality that accords particularly well with the dynamic quality of a modern city.

New York is fortunate in having two wonderful examples of the style, the main building of the New York Public Library and Grand Central Terminal. The library, on Fifth Avenue between 40th and 42nd Streets, is one of the city's real treasures—both artistically and intellectually. Guarded by its famous stone lions (and every true New Yorker knows that they roar only when a virgin passes), it looms up on the site formerly occupied by the Croton Reservoir. The reservoir, which had been completed in 1842, held twenty million gallons of water, brought down from the Croton River, some forty miles north. Heavy battered-stone walls, resembling an Egyptian temple, surrounded it. On top of these high walls was a wide roadway where the city's fashionable promenaded on fine days.

In 1895 it was proposed that a merger of the city's library facilities be effected among the Astor Library bequeathed by John Jacob Astor, with an endowment of $1,700,000, the Lenox collection, assembled by and provided with $505,500 by James Lenox, a book collector and philanthropist, and the Tilden Trust, with a fund estimated at $2,000,000 donated by Samuel J. Tilden. To house these great collections, it was decided to replace the reservoir with a monumental new building befitting the caliber of the books it was to contain.

Today the library has eighty-two thriving branches, six mobile units that take their wares to the remotest corners of the five boroughs and a total of eight million volumes—in three thousand languages and

***40.** New York Public Library
Fifth Avenue,
   40th to 42nd Street
1898–1911,
   Carrère & Hastings*

dialects. In addition, there are countless periodicals, newspapers, manuscripts, maps, microcopies and prints. In the main building, which is devoted to research, there are eighty miles of bookshelves and a reading room that covers two city blocks and accommodates more than five thousand readers every day. It contains Washington's Farewell Address in his own handwriting, the first Gutenberg Bible brought to this country, and Jefferson's draft on the Declaration of Independence.

The New York Public Library is public only in use. It has always depended upon endowments and private donations, and with today's rising costs it has found itself in a serious financial situation. It has had to curtail services, restrict hours of use and severely cut its acquisitions program. As usual, the citizens of New York are responding to the needs of one of their cherished institutions. A savings bank is donating double the cost of gifts the bank ordinarily offers new depositors if they forgo their presents. Actors and musicians from all over the country have contributed their time and talent to raise money for the Performing Arts branch in Lincoln Center. But this is still not enough.

Carrère & Hastings' sumptuous building was dedicated on May 23, 1911, thirteen years after it was started. Set back a considerable distance from Fifth Avenue, it rests on a wide terrace extending the full length of the Fifth Avenue side. A generous and inviting flight of steps leads to three deep-set archways flanked by coupled Corinthian columns. Surmounting the colonnade, six sculptured figures stand on a ledge above the ornately decorated cornice. On either side of the central pavilion wall, niches contain sculptured figures and fountains. The flanking wings terminate in pedimented pavilions at 40th and 42nd Streets.

Whitney Warren's south façade of Grand Central Terminal is similar to the library. It has a great order of doubled columns (a characteristic Beaux-Arts touch) framing what amounts to a triple triumphal archway. It again demonstrates the integration of sculpture with architecture. To appreciate their interdependence it is only necessary to compare the south façade of Grand Central Terminal with the Appellate Division Courthouse. Delightful though the figures of the lawgivers on the courthouse are, they could step down from their pedestals without being missed. But if Mercury, Hercules or Minerva should fly off from the Grand Central clock, the climax of the whole composition would fall apart.

41. *Grand Central Terminal*
42nd Street at Vanderbilt
1903–13, Reed & Stem and
Warren & Wetmore

Since some 400,000 people pass through the station every day, the terminal is both literally and figuratively the gateway to the city. Its importance as a symbol is greatly enhanced in that it is the only monumental building in the city with an adequate axial approach. The half-mile-long vista up the 140-foot width of Park Avenue, which would be commonplace in Paris, is rare in New York. Think what the 42nd Street Library or the main front of the Metropolitan Museum of Art might have looked like if given such a setting, instead of being approached along sixty-foot-wide side streets.

Unfortunately, the vista from the north, framed by the strong and uniform cornice line of the apartment buildings and hotels that lined Park Avenue before the Second World War, has been lost beyond recapture. The apartment houses were replaced by metal-and-glass office buildings, which, taking advantage of the new zoning bonuses for plazas, were set forward or back to obtain maximum utilization of their high-rent tower space. The street line that used to frame and flow past the romantic silhouette of the New York Central Office Building (now the New York General Building) has been completely broken up. Then Walter Gropius, who had devoted a lifetime to teaching the social responsibility of the architect, gave Park Avenue the *coup de grâce* by creating the Pan American Building, which smothers the north vista with a monstrous bland blanket. While the Pan American Building has not helped the south vista, neither has it completely destroyed it. It is all the more urgent to save what remains. It is also the more urgent since Pennsylvania Station was lost before a Landmarks Preservation Commission existed to fight for it.

Of Pennsylvania Station and of what has replaced it, Vincent Scully says: "It was academic building at its best, rational and ordered according to a pattern of use and a blessed sense of civic excess. . . . Through it one entered the city like a god . . . One scuttles in now like a rat." Grand Central Terminal not only has that "blessed sense of civic excess" but functions supremely well both within itself and as a part of the city.

In 1832 the New York and Harlem Railroad began running steam trains on its right of way on what was originally Fourth Avenue, and shortly afterward it made a cut through Murray Hill between 32nd and 42nd Streets. The Common Council banned steam operation below 42nd Street in 1854 because of the smoke and noise pollution, so the railroad leased its right of way below 42nd Street to the Metropolitan Street Railroad Company for local public transportation—at first horsecars, then streetcars and then motor buses. In time the cut was bridged and finally made into an arched tunnel. In 1871 the first Grand Central Depot, a splendid structure of iron and glass, was opened. It was replaced by the present Landmark, Grand Central Terminal, in 1913.

In 1902 the railroad, by now the New York Central Railroad, was faced with a state order, either to electrify all its urban rails by 1910 or to remove its terminal to the outskirts of the city. Many railroads in other cities, faced with the same problem at the same time, chose the latter alternative—the easy way out. The Central chose the bolder solution that made it possible in twenty years to convert over two and a half miles of Fourth Avenue (renamed Park Avenue) from a noisy, dirty open-cut eyesore into one of the great residential boulevards of the world. The fact that the terminal, serving two major railroads, remained in the heart of the city was an enormous stimulus to the development of midtown Manhattan. The retention of air rights over an underground railroad yard extending from 42nd Street to 59th Street gave the New York Central a most profitable potential for the development of midtown hotels, shops and office buildings. The underground concourse that connects all of these with both the station and three subway systems has become a city in itself and was the inspiration for the concourse system built later under Rockefeller Center.

It was William J. Wilgus, a brilliant railroad engineer, who worked out the multilevel track system through which commuter service was separated from the long-haul trains and from freight and baggage handling. He also devised a loop at the lower level that permits certain trains to turn around under the station without backing out to a yard. The one missing link in the system—and it was due more to corporate rigidity than to a failure of engineering imagination—was a direct track connection between Grand Central and Pennsylvania Stations.

The engineering firm Reed & Stem, of St. Paul, Minnesota, won the nationwide competition for the design of Grand Central Terminal largely on the basis of their imaginative use of ramps to separate vehicular from pedestrian traffic and both from the freight operations and rail and subway lines. The ingenuity of their solution has stood the test of time.

In 1968, the Penn Central Transportation Company, which then operated Grand Central, and an English developer of office buildings applied to the Landmarks Preservation Commission for a "certificate of no exterior effect" for a fifty-five-story office tower cantilevered above the roof of the Beaux-Arts façade. The Commission did not agree that a fifty-five-story office building would have "no exterior effect." Penn Central then filed a request for a "certificate of appropriateness" for the tower, which the Commission found would be "nothing more than an aesthetic joke. . . . The tower would overwhelm the Terminal by its sheer mass . . . and would reduce the Landmark itself to the status of a curiosity." An alternative scheme proposed by Penn Central and the developer would have replaced the entire south portion of the terminal with an office tower reaching to the ground. The Commission found that it was not "appropriate" to preserve Landmarks by tearing them down.

Penn Central and the developer filed suit against the City in late 1969, charging that the Landmarks Preservation Law is unconstitutional and that the action of the Commission had deprived them of millions of dollars of revenue from one of the most valuable office building sites in New York City. The City countered that equivalent revenue was available through the transfer of development rights. The matter is still before the courts.

Commercial Buildings

Surprisingly, in this great commercial center of New York, the climax of the city, there is only one office building that is a designated Landmark, and, in marked contrast to it, one little enclave of residences converted into shops that has a story of its own.

There are several reasons for this paucity of commercial Landmarks where one might have expected the most. The vast majority of commercial buildings are erected for speculative purposes, and, rewarding though they may be economically, not many have historic or architectural value. Of the few that do qualify as possible Landmarks, some are too new (the law specifies that a Landmark must be at least thirty years old). Most of the rest either fill a viable economic niche, are unsuitable for conversion to new purposes, or are not in any danger of demolition.

The twenty-story Flatiron Building, at 23rd Street where Broadway and Fifth Avenue meet, was designed in 1902 by the great Chicago architect Daniel H. Burnham. It was one of the tall buildings of its time and one of the early examples in New York City to be entirely supported on a steel skeleton frame. The stonework and terra cotta with which it is covered are only a skin to keep out the weather. As Buckminster Fuller recently remarked about it, "architects were still pretending there was no steel." And yet he is also quoted as claiming the Flatiron Building as one of his favorites. Perhaps he likes it because it looks like a great ship sailing up the avenue, or else he sees, with X-ray eyes, through the neo–French Renaissance details of the exterior to the boldness of the underlying structure that shows up only on old photographs of the building under construction. There is heavy diagonal wind-bracing at the corner of each bay. The building was so narrow that many people felt it might topple over with the wind. It never toppled, and the wind remained. In those days when women wore long skirts that barely cleared the ground, the windy 23rd Street corner was an admirable place for ankle-watching. Police were constantly shooing away the loungers, and it is said that the expression "twenty-three skidoo" originated with this activity at the base of the Flatiron Building.

The Flatiron Building is the last visible remnant of the city's onetime most glamorous spot, Madison Square. During the 1890s Ward McAllister's Four Hundred dined and danced here at Delmonico's, attended all the fashionable doings at the great Madison Square Garden and lived in nearby mansions. The Garden itself, which stood where the New York Life Insurance Building now rises, was designed by Stanford White, with its tower copied from the Giralda in Spain and topped by Saint-Gaudens' statue of Diana. It was the scene of a variety of events. People flocked to see Wild West shows, political conventions, circuses, prize fights, horse shows, automobile shows (the country's first) and even mass meetings of the Christian Endeavor Society. Ironically, in 1906 the Garden's architect was killed in the roof garden of the building by Harry K. Thaw, the millionaire husband of the actress Evelyn Nesbit; he had accused White of paying undue attentions to his beautiful wife. This was the outstanding scandal of the decade.

Madison Square is also the locale of the only designated Landmark

42. *The Flatiron Building in*
construction
Broadway and Fifth Avenue at
23rd Street
(viewed from 22nd Street)
1902, D. H. Burnham and Co.
The Flatiron in 1973
(from an etching by Richard Haas)

that the Commission could not save from demolition, the Leonard Jerome house, at 26th Street. Here Winston Churchill's mother, Jenny, lived as a girl. It took a full year of searching for a buyer before the Commission reluctantly agreed that the financial hardship of the owner justified demolition. With the best will on the part of everyone concerned it proved impossible to devise a viable future use for the building.

The erection of the Flatiron Building, originally named the Fuller Building, was the beginning of the end for the old Madison Square as the playground of society. The commercial era of midtown Manhattan was just beginning, pushing, as always, the older residential sections of the city ahead of it.

One tiny enclave on East 49th Street, between Second and Third Avenues, called Amster Yard, illustrates one way in which bits and pieces of the old city can survive alongside the new, and how some sense of the past can be preserved, not in a glass case but as an active part of the commercial community.

Amster Yard was made up originally of small workshops and modest houses of the 1869–70 period, built on the site of what is said to have been the terminal stop of the Boston stagecoach that ran on the old Boston Post Road. James Amster, a designer, bought the property in 1945, after the El on Second Avenue had come down, and converted it, with the expert assistance of Harold Sterner, from a ripe

43. Amster Yard
211–215 East 49th Street
1869–70
Conversion to shops:
1945, Harold Sterner

slum into a little mid-nineteenth-century version of what would, in present-day parlance, be called a shopping mall. Amster Yard is entered through an arcade from 49th Street. The buildings on the irregularly shaped courtyard vary in height from one to four stories. They all blend harmoniously and are related in scale, size, proportion, materials and color. The style of the complex, made up of offices, shops and apartments grouped around an attractively landscaped garden, can best be described as late-nineteenth-century vernacular.

Not only has the modest but imaginative enterprise survived, but its long-range future may eventually be assured through the sale of the unused development rights over the Landmark to an office building on the Third Avenue block front.

Historic Districts

This midsection of the city contains four Historic Districts that vary widely in size and style. Two are in the Twenties—one on the East Side and one on the West Side. They were both built around a central square and were laid out in the 1830s and 1840s. They illustrate certain aspects of good city planning, which is one of the reasons why they have survived. One is the Chelsea Historic District, bounded roughly by West 20th Street and West 22nd Street, Tenth Avenue and a point midway between Eighth and Ninth Avenues. The other is the Gramercy Park Historic District, between Park Avenue South, Third Avenue, and East 18th and 21st Streets.

Two other little enclaves in this part of New York have been designated Historic Districts. One faces on a cobbled courtyard, the other on an interior garden. They share a certain sense of withdrawal from the surrounding city.

CHELSEA

Most people associate Clement Clarke Moore only with "A Visit from Saint Nicholas" and the agony of having to stand up in front of a Christmas party and stumbling through " 'Twas the night before Christmas . . ." But actually this scholarly professor of Greek and Biblical learning and author of a lexicon of the Hebrew language was

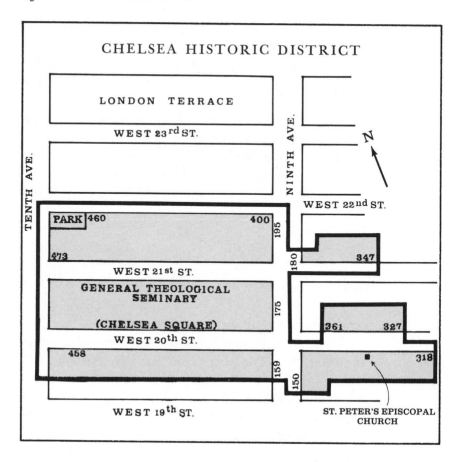

an early and eminently successful city planner as well as an amateur architect.

The land which comprises the Chelsea Historic District had come down in Moore's family from his maternal grandfather, Captain Thomas Clarke, who had acquired it in 1750 and named it for the Chelsea section of London. Moore at first used it only as a summer home, maintaining his permanent residence at the corner of Charlton and Macdougal Streets.

The Commissioners' Plan of 1811 for the grid pattern of Manhattan streets spelled the doom of Moore's idyllic pastoral acres. Rather than let himself be swamped by the city's rush northward, he moved permanently into the area and laid out a very intelligent and farsighted plan. He donated the entire block from 20th to 21st Street, Ninth to Tenth Avenue, to the General Theological Seminary, and laid out lots for rows of town houses around the open square on which he envisioned the seminary buildings.

In 1835, Moore offered lots for sale with this admonition: "Purchasers of lots on this map will be required to build fireproof houses of good quality. Those on the avenue lots to be three stories and those on the cross streets, two stories in height. All kinds of nuisances will be prohibited. . . ."

The essence of his agreement with purchasers was that there be a uniform setback of ten feet, with the space forever unobstructed except for the necessary platforms, fences, etc. The houses were to cover the entire frontage of the lot; there were to be no alleys, no stables, no manufactories. While some of these provisions had been written into similar covenants in the St. Mark's Historic District and on Washington Square, Moore is credited with having combined them all and also with having originated what would now be called "design control." The provision that new houses be designed to match their neighbors would, if literally enforced, have resulted in deadly monotony. Liberally interpreted, as it was, to mean compatible with their neighbors, it resulted in just that sort of variation on a theme that makes the Chelsea blocks so charming. It is a provision which, if voluntarily observed by architects today, would result in far more good urban design than the mandates of any possible design control board could accomplish.

Chelsea never quite fulfilled the hopes of its initial residents by becoming a very fashionable neighborhood, but it remained comfortable and middle-class, even when its neighbor to the north, Hell's Kitchen, was making heavy inroads into it. Today Chelsea, like so many other slightly old-fashioned sections of the city, is being rediscovered as an eminently livable area.

The oldest house in the Chelsea Historic District was built in 1829–30 at 404 West 20th Street; all that remains to indicate its original Federal style is the Flemish bond of the brickwork and a glimpse of the original clapboard side wall.

The chief distinction of Chelsea is its Greek Revival rows. These were built for speculation—for sale, rental or investment—but they had enduring qualities. The first to make its appearance, and still among the finest, is what is known as Cushman Row, Nos. 406 to 418 West 20th Street, facing the seminary. It was built in 1839–40 for Don

Alonzo Cushman, a successful dry-goods merchant who was an early associate of Moore's. Except for the northeast side of Washington Square, this is the finest Greek Revival row that has survived in the city. The ten-foot front yards and the superb ironwork, much of which is still intact, are particularly notable.

There are two great Greek Revival mansions in Chelsea. No. 436-38 West 22nd Street is a double house. It is known as the Forrest House because the great Shakespearian actor Edwin Forrest bought it, apparently to escape from his family-in-law, who had taken over his house downtown. Sometime later, it was acquired by Christian Herter, the designer and head of Herter Brothers, whose firm did many famous interiors for the wealthy of the day. The building has now been converted into an apartment house.

Farther east in the same block is the other double house built by James N. Wells, who was associated with Clement Moore in the development of the area. This splendid mansion is the only five-bay Greek Revival house surviving in Manhattan. Incidentally, this is the same James Wells who was earlier responsible for the delightful group of Federal-style buildings surrounding St. Luke's Chapel in Greenwich Village. His real-estate firm is still active today on West 23rd Street.

In addition to St. Peter's Episcopal Church, whose importance to the development of the Gothic Revival style has already been discussed, Chelsea contains an interesting early example of secular Gothic Revival architecture in the West Hall of the General Theological Seminary. This was built in 1836 and at that time was matched by a building to the east that has since been demolished. Together with James Renwick, Jr.'s Smallpox Hospital, the shell of which still stands on the southern tip of Welfare (now Roosevelt) Island, and with St. John's Residence Hall at Fordham University, West Hall is one of the few remaining examples that illustrate how the Gothic Revival was applied to institutional as well as to church and residential buildings.

Of the many rows of Italianate design, three are of particular interest. On West 20th Street the group from No. 438 to 450, built between 1853 and 1855, illustrates both the English-basement type, with entrance at sidewalk level, and the more usual high-stooped type. No. 442 retains most of its original details. On West 21st Street the brick-and-brownstone houses, Nos. 465 to 473, were built in 1853 and

St. Peter's Episcopal Church and Rectory
Chelsea Historic District

comprise one of the best-designed and best-preserved rows of early Italianate houses in Manhattan. Nos. 400 through 412 West 22nd Street were built three years later; they are only fourteen feet wide and illustrate how charming this usually pompous style can be when adapted to modest dwellings.

GRAMERCY PARK

Five long crosstown blocks due east of Chelsea is the Gramercy Park Historic District, an area that was planned as a fashionable residential neighborhood 150 years ago and has remained one ever since.

The district was originally named by the Dutch "Krom Moerasje," meaning "little crooked stream," after a rivulet that twisted from

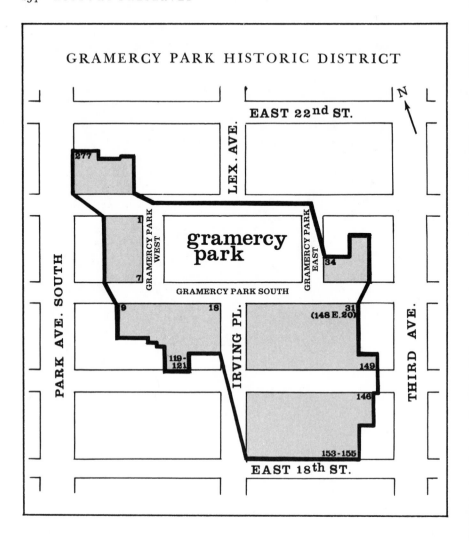

GRAMERCY PARK HISTORIC DISTRICT

Madison Square to the East River near 18th Street. In time the name became corrupted to Crommesshie and finally to Gramercy.

When Samuel B. Ruggles, one of the city's first major real-estate operators, bought the land in 1831, it was a swamp. He drained it and provided a private park, 520 feet by 184 feet, for the exclusive use of those who bought the surrounding lots. He promptly sold sixty-six of them to the cream of New York society.

The park was enclosed by an eight-foot-high fence, and it is said that golden keys were provided to the lucky purchasers. To this day the tenants of the fine houses around the park are its joint owners, are responsible for its maintenance and are the only ones to have keys (no longer of gold).

There is a great lack of the small neighborhood parks in New York that make London so pleasant to live in. A map prepared by the city surveyor in 1838 proposed eighteen small parks, with a total area of 170 acres. By the time Central Park was decided upon, with its magnificently generous 840 acres, over 70 acres of the original 170 had been removed from the map. What no one realized at the time was that a dense metropolis needs both large and small open spaces: large areas laid out for active sports and landscaped for a change of scene, and small areas close to home where children can play, where old people can sit and where neighbors can breathe. That is what makes Gramercy Park—New York's only surviving private square—so welcome, even though most of us have to enjoy it through iron palings.

Unlike Chelsea, there are few surviving examples of the Greek Revival period in the Gramercy Park Historic District, although three houses, Nos. 3, 4 and 5 on the west side of the square, are particularly delightful examples, with their ornate cast-iron porches and balconies.

Gramercy Park West

Their design is attributed to the architect Alexander Jackson Davis. Nos. 1 and 2, though built only a few years later, are already in the newly fashionable Italianate style of the mid-century. The fact that they were also built in red brick and that they maintained the same cornice line as their neighbors makes Gramercy Park West remarkably cohesive. James Harper, mayor of New York City from 1844 to 1847, lived at No. 4. A pair of iron-mounted lamps still mark the house, a reminder of the days when his Honor wished to be easily available in case of nighttime emergencies. The famous physician Dr. Valentine Mott lived at No. 1, the beautiful house on the corner of 21st Street. Just down the block, in Calvary Church at the corner of Park Avenue South, Edith Newbold Jones, a young girl who had been born on West 23rd Street, made an unhappy marriage to the Boston banker Edward Wharton; later she made the name Wharton famous in American literature. Here also Eleanor Roosevelt was baptized and here her uncle Theodore worshiped.

Calvary Church was the ambitious project of James Renwick, Jr. He designed it on the scale of a great cathedral with tripartite nave and transepts. He intended to crown the structure with two openwork stone spires but they were never built. Such a grandiose scheme seems pretentious for a lot which is only 117 by 142 feet.

The National Arts Club, the Players and the Friends' Meeting House, with their assortment of Gothic Revival, Victorian Gothic, Italianate and neo–Italian Renaissance, get along remarkably well on the south side of the park. The corner house, No. 19 Gramercy Park South, was altered in 1887 for Stuyvesant Fish, whose father, Hamilton Fish, had been born in another Landmark house at 21 Stuyvesant Street.

At No. 34 Gramercy Park East stands one of the earliest of the city's apartment houses, or "French Flats" as they were first called in order to make them sound genteel. It was built in 1883 and its original elevator is still in operation, though somewhat slow and creaky after ninety years of service.

The elegant atmosphere of Gramercy Park soon overflowed down Irving Place, which was cut through to 14th Street in 1833. The present Historic District follows Irving Place for a couple of blocks and into some of the abutting side streets. Nineteenth Street, as it extends eastward to Third Avenue, has a character all its own. Mid-nineteenth-century houses on both sides of the street, as well as a few former stables, were remodeled in the taste of the 1920s. The rows of trees and flowering window boxes, the mixture of styles, textures, patterns and colors have earned for it the name "Block Beautiful." It deserves something better.

SNIFFEN COURT

Sniffen Court is a blind alley off East 36th Street, between Lexington and Third Avenues. Its ten tiny houses were originally stables for the great houses on Murray Hill. They are in the vernacular of the period, with suggestions of the early Romanesque Revival. Like the mews off Washington Square, they were converted in the 1920s into mini-houses, studios, a little theater and offices. The studio of the sculptress Malvina Hoffman once overlooked the end of the row. It is

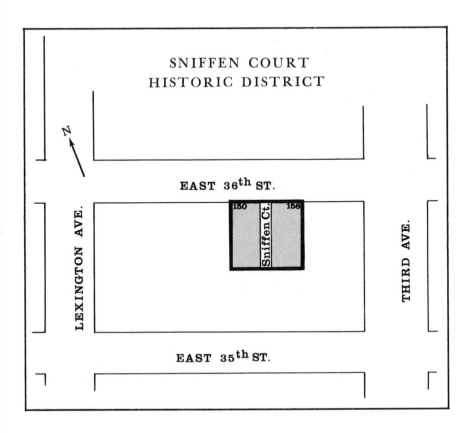

Sniffen Court

interesting to stand on East 36th Street and watch the passersby. Nine out of ten—harried executives on their way to meetings, secretaries late for work, housewives rushing to the supermarket—will stop and look and then resume their way, refreshed.

TURTLE BAY GARDENS

Another enclave, Turtle Bay Gardens, on 48th and 49th Streets between Second and Third Avenues, is so private that most passersby are not even aware of its existence. One theory has it that the name derives from a cove in the East River between 45th and 48th Streets, now the site of the United Nations, where turtles once abounded. Another is that it is an English corruption of *Deutal*, the Dutch word for a slightly bent blade. Still another is that it came from the shape of the bay, which looked like a turtle. Whatever its origin, the name Turtle Bay was in common usage in wills and deeds as early as 1712.

From the sidewalks, all one sees are some four-story Italianate houses of the 1860s with their original high-stoop entrances replaced by English basements, with most of the heavy trim shaved off and the brownstone surfaces painted or stuccoed. Yet the regular rhythm of the well-proportioned openings, the generally uniform height of the houses and the occasional accent of a pediment above a window or a well-designed iron balcony give the rows a certain quiet urbanity. Their real interest, however, is the common garden they share in the center of the block, very similar to the Macdougal-Sullivan Gardens.

Through the years the midtown area along the East River metamorphosed from a rural retreat to a fine residential area and then, with the blight of the Second and Third Avenue Elevateds, into a slum. It was here that the Dead End Kids flourished. After World War I a few pioneers, such as Anne Morgan, moved into the section on the

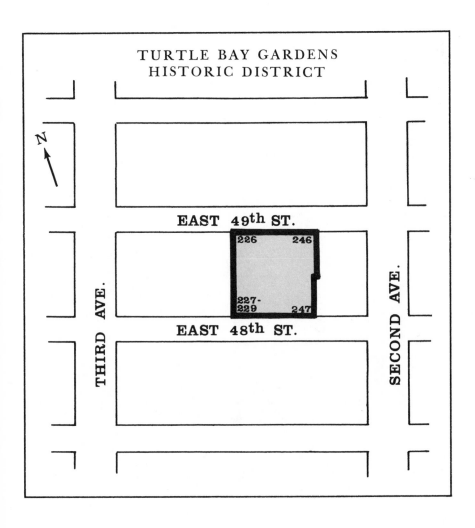

river, and bit by bit chic was restored to the area. Rooming houses were reconverted to private homes, secondhand stores became antique shops, saloons became cocktail lounges. Fashionable groups of private homes like Beekman Place and Sutton Place and high-rise luxury apartments have completed the transformation.

In an action that seems almost clairvoyant, a Mrs. Walton Martin, in 1919–20, bought ten houses on 48th Street and the ten on 49th Street that backed up to them. She tore down all the fences that separated the back yards, filled in the swampy areas and created a delightful Italian garden down the entire center of the block to be shared by all the abutting houses. Each individual house still retains a rather shallow private terrace. This provided the distinct advantage of permitting the owners to turn their backs on the sordid neighborhood around them.

Mrs. Martin also made some architectural changes. No two houses are alike, although all the kitchens are on the street side while the living rooms face the garden. Cast-iron turtles decorate the street railings and also are found in the garden itself. The individual homeowners maintain the garden on a cooperative basis and also

Turtle Bay Gardens

voluntarily submit to certain design controls over the exterior of their houses and the upkeep of their private terraces. The original covenant to which owners subscribed, and which has been altered only slightly over the years, provided that no more than one additional floor could be added and that that had to be well set back from both front and rear; that no extension exceeding one story in height or ten feet in depth be added to the rear; that no fence or railing other than an ornamental iron railing be erected in the front; that no fence be built in the rear; that no laundry and no garbage cans be allowed in the rear; that no house be used as a boardinghouse or hotel; and that no business be conducted on the premises. There has been a relaxation of the last restriction to the extent that a professional person—a lawyer, architect or doctor of medicine—may have his office on the premises and display an "unilluminated sign not exceeding in dimensions three inches by fifteen inches."

Large apartment houses have recently been built at either end of the block on Second and Third Avenues. Instead of ruining the garden, they actually enhance it, by shielding it from the traffic noises of the two busy avenues. In summer the trees are so thick that you are unaware of the soaring neighbors, and in winter the residents just don't go outdoors.

Perhaps Turtle Bay Gardens is a bit like a stage set, but, in providing a pleasant way of life in the heart of the city, these houses have been enormously popular, and rightly so. Leopold Stokowsky, Mary Martin, Judge Learned Hand, Katharine Hepburn and E. B. White, the sage of *The New Yorker,* have lived in Turtle Bay Gardens.

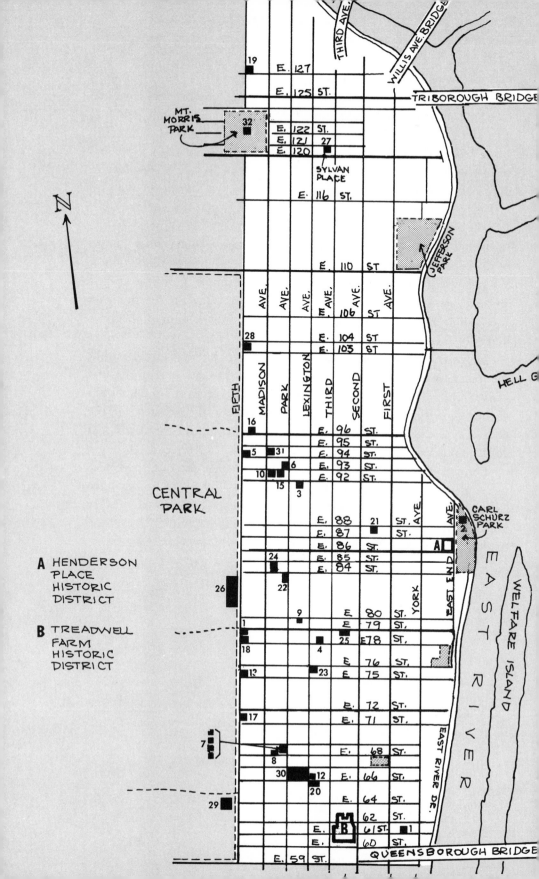

STORIA

MANHATTAN

East Side Above 59th Street

CHAPTER FIVE

MANHATTAN

East Side Above 59th Street

THIS SECTION of New York City is primarily residential. The area below 96th Street contains more handsome mansions, luxurious apartment houses and residential hotels than any other section of the city. Interspersed with the homes of the wealthy are churches, clubs, museums and a swarm of specialty shops and boutiques. With a few vestigial exceptions, this is a relatively modern area.

All of the great private mansions were built between 1900 and 1930. Most are now used for charitable or religious purposes, or by learned societies, clubs, museums and schools, or to house foreign delegations, or as headquarters for national and international organizations. Others have been subdivided into rather elegant residential cooperatives.

The big apartment houses and hotels were built after the mansions. A few predate World War I, but the majority were constructed between 1918 and 1932, when all building was stopped by the depression. Isolated blocks of row houses survive, from the late 1860s through the 1880s, and two groups of these have been designated as Historic Districts. The churches were mostly built between 1890 and 1920.

The reasons for the late development of the Upper East Side are twofold. Until work was started on Central Park in 1857, everything north of 59th Street was open country except for scattered villages like Yorkville and Harlem on the east and Bloomingdale and Manhattan-ville on the west. Pictures of the region of the future park in this period show scrubby farms, squatters' shanties, and goats roaming along upper Fifth Avenue. Even after the park was opened—and it was not extended to 110th Street until 1863—the open cut along Park Avenue, with its noisy and dirty steam trains, was a blighting barrier for any expansion of new building beyond a thin fringe west of Park Avenue. The explosive development of the Upper East Side as a fashionable residential neighborhood was the immediate consequence of the electrification of the New York Central lines and the decking over of Park Avenue in 1907.

Mansions, Row Houses, a Stable and an Apartment House

Two vestiges of the early, rural days, both dating from 1799, survive as Landmark reminders of how totally different this part of Manhattan was not so very long ago.

The Abigail Adams Smith House, at 421 East 61st Street, which is now headquarters of the Colonial Dames of America, was the coach house and stable of a twenty-three-acre estate originally built by Colonel William S. Smith. Smith had met John Adams' daughter, Abigail, at the American Legation when Adams was envoy to the Court of St. James's. The young couple were married in London in 1786. Colonel Smith and Abigail planned a fine country estate in New York on the acreage he purchased in 1795 and called "Mount Vernon on the East River," in honor of George Washington. But financial disaster overtook Smith, and he was forced to discontinue his building projects in 1798 and to sell the whole property, which lost its Mount Vernon name and became popularly known as "Smith's Folly." Abigail Adams Smith never lived in her fine country house. The coach house and stable was probably completed in 1799 by the new owner, William T. Robinson, who did not himself live long in the main mansion. The latter subsequently became an inn, famous for green turtle soup made from the plump turtles that throve in the East River, and was used by a school before it burned to the ground in 1826.

But the "ornamental stable," as it was called, remained and soon became the Mount Vernon Hotel, noted for its gaiety and good cheer, and a favorite stopping-off place for both New Yorkers and foreigners. In 1833 it became a private home, but, with the advance of the city and a concentration of gas tanks and warehouses in the neighborhood, it fell into disuse. It was bought in 1924 by the Colonial Dames of America. The ladies, known as the "Gashouse Dames" because of their environment, have maintained the house as a museum open to the public. A recent routine repair job revealed some serious structural deterioration, which led to further discouraging discoveries—a dangerously weak roof, leaking chimney flues, obsolete wiring, a hazardous heating system, termites and rotting timbers. The Dames collected an emergency repair fund and performed major surgery on the old building, with the result that the future of the museum is now permanently assured. The building is a good example of Federal stonework, with brick inserts around the windows of the attic story.

Identical in period, and of even greater historic importance, is Gracie Mansion, which has been the official residence of the mayors of New York City since Fiorello La Guardia's administration in 1942.

Originally on this site, projecting out into the East River between what are now 86th and 90th Streets, was a 1774 house belonging to a Loyalist, Jacob Walton. It was surrounded by fortifications known as Thompson's Battery, and in the battle for Manhattan in September 1776 the house and fort were set on fire by British bombardment from Long Island. The land was subsequently bought by Archibald Gracie, a wealthy merchant of Scottish descent, who, at the very end of the eighteenth century, built a beautiful Federal-style country villa looking out toward Hell Gate, the treacherous channel in the East River between Manhattan, Long Island and the present Ward's Island.

1. *Abigail Adams Smith House (now headquarters, Colonial Dames of America) 421 East 61st Street 1799 Restored 1924*

Gracie lived here in great style and entertained, among others, the future king of the French, Louis Philippe, the Marquis de Lafayette, John Quincy Adams, Alexander Hamilton, Washington Irving and De Witt Clinton.

The house became the property of a series of owners after financial reverses forced Gracie to sell it in 1819. Finally, in 1887, the City purchased it and added the property to what is now Carl Schurz Park. Schurz was a German American who served as a general of volunteers in the Civil War. He also was United States Senator from Missouri, Secretary of the Interior, and, as editor of the *New York Evening Post,* an important force among liberals in the Republican Party.

The Museum of the City of New York, incorporated in 1923, occupied the mansion until the museum moved to its new quarters on upper Fifth Avenue. In 1942 the building became what the Department of Parks called the "Mayor's House"—a name no New Yorker ever uses. After the City had decided to provide a home for its mayor, several possibilities were suggested, including the seventy-five-room French château that had been built by Charles M. Schwab on Riverside Drive. When the down-to-earth Little Flower heard this suggestion he exploded, "What! Me in *that?*" and opted for Gracie Mansion.

The only major addition to the mansion since 1810 has been a reception wing which was completed in 1966. The wing contains a ballroom, a formal dining room, a drawing room and a conference room for official entertaining. Under the guidance of a committee chaired by James Grote Van Derpool, the wing was designed by Mott B. Schmidt to harmonize with the original structure. Its furnishings are a veritable treasure of eighteenth- and early-nineteenth-century originals.

According to tradition, Gracie Mansion may have been designed

2. *Gracie Mansion*
   East End Avenue
   and 88th Street,
   in Carl Schurz Park
   1799–1801, 1810
   Susan B. Wagner Wing:
   1966, Mott B. Schmidt

by the noted French architect Major Charles L'Enfant, who made the master plan for the District of Columbia. The Chinese Chippendale railings are particularly notable, as is the main doorway with its leaded-glass sidelights and semicircular lunette above—both characteristic details of the Federal style.

There are also a few survivors from the 1860s, 1870s and 1880s, built before this section of the city became fashionable. Among these are two quaint little wooden houses on East 92nd Street, between Park and Lexington Avenues, built in 1859 and 1871. They are slightly Italianate in their feeling, with cornices on brackets. One has a high porch reached by a steep flight of wooden steps. The other is set back from the street line, with its porch at ground level. Both houses have great charm and reflect in clapboard some of the same details of the more elaborate brick houses that were being built at the same time.

Five of the latter type, from an original row of eleven, survive on 78th Street between Lexington and Third Avenues. They were built for speculation by Henry Armstrong in 1861, at which time they were very definitely on the wrong side of the tracks. Despite this disadvantage they seem remarkably spacious and gracious. The original Italianate feeling is most apparent in the heavy cornices supported by a combination of ornate brackets alternating with three modillions. In addition to the uniform cornice height, a stone band that runs along at the parlor-floor level gives the group a fine sense of unity. The houses are unusual for the period and style because they are built of red brick instead of the then popular brownstone. This must have made them seem, at the time, somewhat provincial and old-fashioned; now it adds to their charm. Despite minor additions and changes, the row is remarkably well preserved.

While these vestiges of country estates, small wooden houses and row houses of the nineteenth century are interesting remnants of an earlier day, it is the great mansions of the twentieth century that give the Upper East Side its distinctive character. Almost without exception they were designed in one of four styles in the Classical Tradition: neo-Georgian, neo-Federal, neo–Italian Renaissance and neo–French Classic. These four styles were the same ones that the same wealthy men chose for their clubhouses or for the public buildings that were being built at the same time in mid-Manhattan. Residential

3. Nos. 122 and 120
   East 92nd Street in 1885
   1859 and 1871

4. Nos. 157, 159, 161,
   163-165 East 78th Street
   1861

architecture was, during this Eclectic period, very much a matter of fashion, and all four of these "neo" styles ran concurrently. A man selected the style of his house as a lady would choose a dress or a hat. All four styles were fashionable: the choice depended on which did the most for the owner—which showed off to best advantage his impeccable taste, which was best suited to the size and social needs of his family.

The neo-Georgian and neo-Federal styles are exemplified by two notable corner mansions and two fine rows of town houses.

The earlier of the two mansions, both of which were designed by Delano & Aldrich, is the Willard Straight House at Fifth Avenue and

94th Street. This palatial Federal-style house was completed in 1915 for Straight, who was a diplomat, a financier and an editor. After his death in 1918 the building passed through the hands of several owners, including the legendary white-haired, green-eyed Mona Williams, queen of the international set. The National Audubon Society, the oldest and largest conservation association in the country, used the building as its headquarters from 1952 to 1972. Typical Federal details are the arched doorway, the flat lintels with their recessed panels, the two contrasting white marble belt courses, the row of bull's-eye windows beneath the simple cornice, and the delicate balustrade which crowns the whole.

A few years after the Straight mansion was built, the same firm designed the large house on the northeast corner of Park Avenue and 93rd Street for Francis F. Palmer. It was later bought by George F. Baker, Jr., who added an L-shaped ballroom wing, and a garage and

*6. George F. Baker, Jr., House
(now the Synod of Bishops
of the Russian Orthodox
Church Outside of Russia)
69-75 East 93rd Street, at Park Avenue
1917–18, Delano & Aldrich
Addition: 1928, Delano & Aldrich*

*5. Willard Straight House
1130 Fifth Avenue, at 94th Street
1913–15, Delano & Aldrich*

7. *Nos. 680, 684, 686, 690 Park Avenue:*

Percy R. Pyne House (now the Center for Inter-American Relations)
1909–11, McKim, Mead & White

Oliver D. Filley House (now the Spanish Institute)
1925–26, McKim, Mead & White

William Sloane House (now the Italian Cultural Institute)
1916–19, Delano & Aldrich

Henry P. Davison House (now the Consulate General of Italy)
1916–17, Walker & Gillette

dower house to the west. In 1958 the Synod of the Bishops of the Russian Orthodox Church Outside of Russia bought the building, where it now maintains its headquarters and a school. Many elements of this mansion follow closely the neo-Federal spirit of the Willard Straight House, but here the steep slate roof with its two levels of dormers has Georgian overtones. In such assured hands as those of Delano & Aldrich, elements of both styles were often mingled.

A remarkable row of houses on the west side of Park Avenue between 68th and 69th Streets, sometimes known as the Pyne-Davison Row, illustrates the same stylistic freedom. The houses are predominantly neo-Federal in style but have many characteristically neo-Georgian details, thus again illustrating the self-confidence and skill of these talented Eclectic architects. Even more remarkable is the fact that each of the architects of the four houses on Park Avenue and the one around the corner on 68th Street respected the designs of his professional confreres. Four firms in all worked on the buildings, which were built at various times between 1909 and 1926.

In this row, a remarkable unity is achieved with variety and imagination. The house that set the key was the Percy R. Pyne residence on the corner of Park Avenue and 68th Street, which McKim, Mead & White designed in 1909. This and the house adjoining it on Park Avenue, which McKim, Mead & White did for Pyne's son-in-law, Oliver D. Filley, plus the house around the corner on 68th Street, which Trowbridge & Livingston designed for Mrs. J. William Clark in 1913, were threatened toward the end of 1965 by a developer who intended to tear them down and replace them with a thirty-one-story apartment house. At this critical juncture the Marquesa de Cuevas, a granddaughter of John D. Rockefeller, Sr., in a magnanimous gesture, bought the properties, which she eventually turned over to three public institutions. The Clark House is now occupied by Automation House, a nonprofit organization devoted to developing community TV stations and open access to TV channels for the general public. The Pyne House, which had for a time been the Soviet Mission to the United Nations and was famous for one of Premier Nikita Khrushchev's more flamboyant public appearances, is now the Center for Inter-American Relations, and the Filley House is occupied by the Spanish Institute.

Farther north on the block are the William Sloane House, designed by Delano & Aldrich, who tied their details very closely to the McKim, Mead & White house adjoining it, and the Henry P. Davison House on the corner of 69th Street, which was designed by Walker & Gillette. The Sloane House is now the Italian Cultural Institute, and the Davison House is the home of the Italian Consulate General. It is only through their use by such diplomatic and cultural organizations that these five great houses have been able to survive.

Another row of houses—less well known because less prominently located—on the south side of East 80th Street between Park and Lexington Avenues, also illustrates the fact that good architects can

respect their neighbors without sacrificing their own individuality and can create a harmonious combination that is the essence of good urban design.

The earliest of these was the Lewis Spencer Morris House, which Cross & Cross designed in 1922 at 116 East 80th Street in the simple red brick of the neo-Federal style. A few years later, Mott B. Schmidt designed No. 130 for Vincent Astor; it is now the home of the Junior League of the City of New York. Despite the fact that Schmidt's design is carried out entirely in a mellow-toned limestone instead of red brick, it is still in the neo-Federal style. Its sophistication suggests the Regency period in England. They get on very well together at either end of the row.

Subsequently the gap between these two houses was filled in by two more, the George Whitney House, by Cross & Cross, and the Clarence Dillon House, by Schmidt. Both houses were built in 1930 and were considered among the most elegant houses of their day. The Whitney House, while still basically neo-Federal, is more elaborate than its Morris neighbor. The pedimented central window and the raising of the balustrade to the top of the slate roof, above the dormers, are quite Georgian in feeling. The Dillon House, with its brick quoins, its splayed lintels and keystones and its heavily pedimented doorway, is pure neo-Georgian. The two architects, working between two existing and distinguished structures, managed to achieve a welcome unity and yet retain their own individual stamp. Thus, by a sensitive approach to the block as a whole, they succeeded in creating something quite special out of what would otherwise have been just another side street.

Another fine example of the "American Adam" style is the house which Walker & Gillette designed for William Goadby Loew on East

10. *William Goadby Loew House*
56 East 93rd Street
(now Smithers Alcoholism Center,
* The Roosevelt Hospital)*
1932, Walker & Gillette

93rd Street. It is across the street from the house of George F. Baker, Jr., who was Loew's father-in-law. The façade of smoothly dressed white limestone is elegant and restrained. In a welcoming gesture, the central portion of the building curves inward in a shallow arc; a driveway crosses the sidewalk and follows the same curve to the entrance portico. The shallow radial fluting above the bull's-eye and Palladian windows was a favorite detail of the Adam brothers.

William Goadby Loew was a wealthy stockbroker, sportsman and clubman. With his villa at Newport, his estate at Old Westbury, Long Island, and his own racing stable, he was one of the last of a vanished breed. Symbolically enough, his town house in New York, completed in 1932, was the last great mansion to have been built in the city. It subsequently became the home of the wonder-boy inventor of the Aquacade, the theatrical producer and art collector Billy Rose. For a number of years it was the residence of the ambassador from the Republic of Algeria to the United Nations, and recently it was purchased by The Roosevelt Hospital to be used as a therapy center for alcoholics.

The Sara Delano Roosevelt Memorial House at 47–49 East 65th Street (not pictured) is a fine example of an early twentieth-century neo-Georgian townhouse. In 1905 the late President Franklin Delano Roosevelt's mother commissioned Charles A. Platt to design, as a wedding present for her recently married son, a double house that she could share with him. Sara Delano Roosevelt lived in No. 47 and Franklin and Eleanor moved into No. 49 in the fall of 1908. Although Roosevelt and his young family moved frequently, they lived in the 65th Street residence whenever his duties as a lawyer and an officer of an insurance firm brought him to the city. It was in the fourth floor front bedroom in 1921 that Franklin began his arduous convalescence from the crippling attack of poliomyelitis that almost ended his public career. After 1928 he spent only brief periods at No. 49. This was the year he was first elected Governor of New York and the year that marked the beginning of a political career that was to culminate in the presidency four years later. His mother, Sara, continued to live at No. 47 until her death in 1941. The following year a group of citizens bought the double house for use by the students of nearby Hunter College as a social and interfaith center.

The Payne Whitney House, located on Fifth Avenue between 78th and 79th Streets and now belonging to the French government, is the earliest of the neo–Italian Renaissance places this far uptown. Although it is in the middle of the block, it is practically a freestanding house, since the lot between it and the adjoining Duke Mansion has always been kept open as a grassy lawn. This provided the architects (McKim, Mead & White again) with empty space instead of a blank party wall to work with. The extraordinary aspect of this gem of a house is the ornate façade, carved with great delicacy and precision, in granite. Granite is not commonly used as a building material because it is so difficult to work, but it has proven to be very resistant to New York's corrosive atmosphere.

There is an apartment house on the northeast corner of 66th Street and Lexington Avenue that is almost contemporaneous with the Payne Whitney House. This distinguished building, designed by Charles Adams Platt, shows how the neo–Italian Renaissance style was skillfully adapted to make an eleven-story building seem hardly taller than its five-story neighbors. This is achieved by some very clever devices. The heavily rusticated base is actually three stories high, and the fifth- and sixth-story windows are tied together by being framed in stone to make them look as though they were one. The great pedimented doorways run the full height of the three-story-high base. A series of horizontal bands and cornices break up the remaining height of the building, while the windows of the entablature are lost within the shadows of the great overhanging cornice. This building is considered one of the finest examples we have of the neo–Italian Renaissance style in an apartment house.

Quite similar in feeling but more in scale with the traditional Italian palazzo is the freestanding house at 75th Street and Fifth Avenue that H. D. Hale and J. G. Rogers designed at about the same time for Edward S. Harkness; it is now the headquarters of the Commonwealth Fund. This, like the Payne Whitney House, presents its narrow end to Fifth Avenue and its long, seven-window front to the side street. Superbly detailed with great restraint, it is built of white Tennessee marble. One of its special interests is an optical illusion. There seem to be paired pilasters between the windows of the ground floor, but a second look shows that actually only the capitals and bases exist. The eye supplies the shafts. Another attraction is the intricate

11. *Payne Whitney House*
(now the French Embassy Cultural Division)
972 Fifth Avenue
1902–04, McKim, Mead & White

12. *No. 131-135 East 66th Street*
1905–07, Charles A. Platt with
Simonson, Pollard & Steinam

13. *Edward S. Harkness House*
(now the Commonwealth
Fund)
1 East 75th Street
1907–09, H. D. Hale and
J. G. Rogers

and lacy wrought-iron fence, which has Italian Renaissance precedents and is one of the most extraordinary pieces of craftsmanship in the city.

More modest in character and contained within party walls is the handsome John S. Rogers House on 79th Street, which Trowbridge & Livingston designed just after the First World War. This traditional Italian palazzo in white limestone now houses the New York Society Library, which in itself is one of the most interesting organizations in the city.

*14. The New York Society Library
(originally the
John S. Rogers House)
53 East 79th Street
1916–17, Trowbridge & Livingston*

The library was started in 1754, almost one hundred years before the New York Public Library, by half a dozen enterprising New Yorkers who enlisted more than a hundred other subscribers at five pounds each, plus a yearly assessment of ten shillings. They persuaded Lieutenant Governor James De Lancey to set aside a room in the then City Hall to house their collection of 650 books. This City Hall, the second of the three that New York has had, was the one that stood on Wall Street at the head of Broad Street (where Town & Davis' Federal Hall National Memorial now stands) —the building on whose balcony George Washington later took the oath as first President of the United States. Some years before this event—in 1772, in fact—King George III granted the New York Society Library a charter that began: "Whereas our loving subjects . . . conceiving a public library would be useful as well as ornamental to our said city of New York . . ." No description of that first little room has come down to us, so we cannot determine how ornamental the library was. But the home it occupies today on East 79th Street more than justifies George's confidence.

The Revolution caused a slight hiatus in the library's operation, as the minutes record: "The accidents of the late war having nearly destroyed the former Library, no meeting of the proprietors for the choice of Trustees was held from the last Tuesday in April, 1774, until Tuesday, ye 20 December, 1788."

After the Revolution, in 1789, the state legislature confirmed the King's charter, and the library moved back into the old City Hall, which had recently become known as Federal Hall. Since the First Congress of the United States was meeting in the building at the time and the solons made frequent use of the collection, there would seem to be some justification for the New York Society's claim that it was the first Library of Congress. President George Washington, Vice-President John Adams, Aaron Burr, Alexander Hamilton and John Jay were among the early clients.

In 1793, when the library had grown to five thousand volumes, it moved into its own quarters on Nassau Street. After several other moves it located on University Place, where it remained for eighty-one years until it acquired its present home in 1936. The reading room on the ground floor is open to the public, although only member sub-scribers are permitted to take books out and to use the more extensive reference collections upstairs.

The neo–French Classic style is illuminated by several examples. Next door to the Loew House on East 93rd Street is the Mrs. Graham Fair Vanderbilt House, which was finished in 1931. The severity of its plain surfaces and the beautifully detailed stonework get along very well with its "American Adam" neighbor, providing one more illustration of the fact that for a harmonious street scene a

similarity of mass, material and scale are far more important than a slavish uniformity of style. John Russell Pope, who also designed the Jefferson Memorial and the National Gallery of Art in Washington, D.C., designed this residence for Mrs. Vanderbilt in the most austere tradition of the Louis XV style. It is now occupied by the Rumanian Mission to the United Nations.

Much more playful, but still in the same vocabulary, is the house a few blocks away which the architect Ogden Codman designed for his own use. Its multiplicity of shutters, wrought-iron balconies, dormer windows, mansard roof and porte-cochère leading to a courtyard and garage in the rear give it a gaiety that comes as a welcome relief in view of the somewhat pompous pre–World War I period in which it was built. After passing through the hands of various owners, including the Nippon Club, the mansion was bought by the Manhattan Country School in 1966. The house stands on today's dividing line between the fashionable Upper East Side and unfashionable Spanish Harlem—an area where the school's founders felt a realistic attempt at integration could best be achieved.

Much more modest is the R. Livingston Beekman House, now the

15. *(Left) Mrs. Graham Fair Vanderbilt House*
(now the Rumanian Mission to the United Nations)
60 East 93rd Street
1930–31, John Russell Pope

16. *(Center) Ogden Codman House*
(now the Manhattan Country School)
7 East 96th Street
1912–13, Ogden Codman

17. *(Right) R. Livingston Beekman House*
(now the Yugoslavian Mission to the United Nations)
854 Fifth Avenue
1903–05, Warren & Wetmore

home of the Yugoslavian Mission to the United Nations, on Fifth Avenue between 66th and 67th Streets. It is only two windows wide, and yet in this narrow space the architects, Warren & Wetmore, achieved a great deal of dignity and a suggestion of monumentality. The house gives the impression that if the façade could be multiplied several times the result would be a palace.

Such a palace was actually achieved in what is known as the James B. Duke House, on the corner of 78th Street and Fifth Avenue. It adjoins the Payne Whitney House and is now used as the graduate school of the Institute of Fine Arts of New York University. This superb example of the neo–French Classic style was designed by Horace Trumbauer and was built of a fine white limestone. The texture of the stone is so fine and the carved detail so delicate that it gives the impression of marble.

The mansion was finished in 1912 for the tobacco magnate, who was brought up on a farm in North Carolina, growing, curing and selling tobacco. By the 1880s he had become a dominant figure in the industry. In 1890 he became president of the American Tobacco Company, made up of the six principal cigarette manufacturers of the

18. *James B. Duke Mansion*
   (now the New York University Institute of Fine Arts)
   1 East 78th Street, at Fifth Avenue
   1909–12, Horace Trumbauer

country. When the Supreme Court, in 1911, ordered its dissolution under the antitrust laws, Duke, undaunted, promptly set about creating his own competing companies. He lived in the 78th Street palace until his death in 1925. Doris Duke, his only child, and her mother gave the property to New York University in 1957.

The Frick Collection, 1 East 70th Street (not pictured), occupies the entire blockfront on Fifth Avenue between 70th and 71st Streets. Designed by Carrère & Hastings, who were also architects for the New York Public Library on Fifth Avenue and 42nd Street, this mansion was completed in 1914 for Henry Clay Frick, the steel magnate. Although it was planned to be Frick's home, provision was made from the start to house his great collection of art. Frick, who died in 1919, left the mansion to his wife for her lifetime. After her death in 1931, the architect John Russell Pope altered the building to make it suitable for museum purposes. He adhered faithfully to the Louis XVI character established by Carrère & Hastings and added the Frick Art Reference Library at 10 East 71st Street. The trustees are now creating a formal French garden on property east of the museum on 70th Street.

The Lewis G. Morris House (now the New World Foundation Building), at 100 East 85th Street (not pictured), was built in 1914. It is noteworthy for the ingenious use the architect, Ernest Flagg, made of a long narrow corner plot—twenty-five feet on Park Avenue by eighty-two feet on East 85th Street. Actually the building seems to be two houses separated by a square open court. The major, or western, portion is on the Park Avenue side, while the eastern portion, containing a garage, presents a gable end to the street. The entrance is through the courtyard, where a stone staircase leads up to a handsome arched doorway. The house, designed in a rather free version of the neo-Federal style, was built as the residence of Lewis Gouverneur Morris, a descendant of the family that has contributed much to American history. When he died his daughters sold the building to the New World Foundation with the stipulation that it would be used only for the advancement of health, education, welfare and civil rights and that it be maintained as a Landmark.

Churches

The churches that were built in the late nineteenth and early twentieth centuries to serve the new residential communities on the Upper East Side continued the Romantic Tradition that flourished between 14th and 59th Streets. There are also in this Eclectic period a few examples in the Classic Tradition.

The romantic type of church is typified by St. Andrew's, at Fifth Avenue and 127th Street, one of nine important individual Landmarks that have been designated in Harlem. This church was originally built a few blocks away, at Park Avenue and 128th Street, in 1873. In 1889–91 it was taken apart stone by stone, moved to the present site and reerected facing in the opposite direction and with three bays added to the length of the nave.

The church is a rather unusual example of Victorian Gothic in that it is constructed of rock-faced granite and lacks the characteristic polychromy. A strong clock tower and heavy buttresses give it a rural and vigorous appearance.

The congregation had been organized in 1829, but its early growth was slow and its future uncertain because it was so far out of town. But

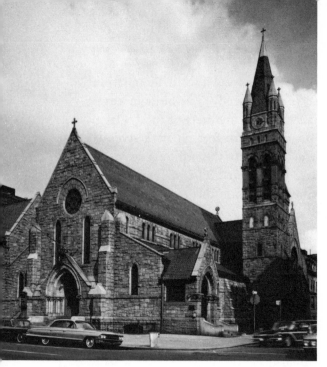

19. *St. Andrew's Church*
2067 Fifth Avenue, at 127th Stree
(originally at Park Avenue
and 128th Street)
1873, Henry B. Congdon
Moved and enlarged 1889–91

by the time the present church was completed this area was changing from a charming countryside to a fashionable semiurban community. The elevated railroad had made its appearance on Third Avenue and greatly stimulated the move north. Rows of brownstones began to appear; in 1889 Oscar Hammerstein opened an opera house on 125th Street.

Considerably later is Bertram Goodhue's neo-Gothic Church of St. Vincent Ferrer on Lexington Avenue at 66th Street. This is the third building of the Dominican Brothers to be erected on or near the present site. Initial plans, by a different architect, were for a miniature St. Patrick's Cathedral, which would have looked rather crowded on the confined site. The Brothers were not satisfied with this proposal, and, having seen the Episcopal Church of St. Thomas that Goodhue had recently completed on Fifth Avenue and 53rd Street, they invited him to design a church for them, giving him a completely free hand. Goodhue is supposed to have said that he considered St. Vincent Ferrer's to be his best work in the ecclesiastical field.

Despite its conventional Latin cross plan, it presents an even freer use of the Gothic vocabulary than St. Thomas'. The entrance porch, with its flanking buttresses, picks up the roof line of the side entrances. While this treatment provided a fine enframement for Lee Lawrie's

Crucifixion panel over the entrance portal, its strong horizontality diminishes the soaring quality that is the essence of Gothic architecture. As a result the magnificent rose window, though containing some of the finest stained glass in the country, seems cramped. A 150-foot-high *flèche* over the crossing was never built. This might have relieved some of the stubbiness of the church's present appearance. While it is hard to agree with Goodhue's reputed evaluation of his own work, this church, like everything this masterful architect touched, reveals a boldly creative imagination.

One of the most interesting groups of ecclesiastical buildings on the Upper East Side is the Episcopal Church of the Holy Trinity and

20. *Church of St. Vincent Ferrer (R.C.)   869 Lexington Avenue, at 66th Street 1916–18, Bertram G. Goodhue*

St. Christopher House and Parsonage on East 88th Street between First and Second Avenues. This remarkably homogeneous group of buildings is little known, because of its out-of-the-way location. The original Holy Trinity was located at Madison Avenue and 42nd Street. In 1897 Miss Serena Rhinelander, in memory of her father and grandfather, made a gift to the Episcopal Diocese of New York of part of the old Rhinelander farm that had been in the family since 1798. The family fortune was based on ninety-nine-year leases of prime acreage on the Lower West Side entered into in the 1790s by William Rhinelander. An obliging Common Council granted him rights to all the Hudson River frontage on which his property abutted. As the city grew, this area became the source of a handsome income, much of which was reinvested in land.

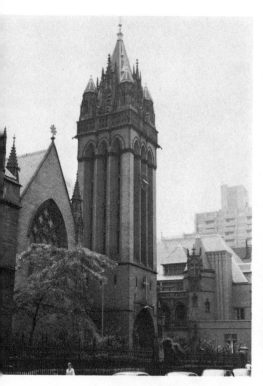

21. *Holy Trinity Church and St. Christopher House*
312-316 East 88th Street
1897, Barney & Chapman

The architects, Barney & Chapman, had just finished what is now the Immaculate Conception Church on East 14th Street in the early neo–Francis I style. They continued the same tradition here with a magnificent neo-Gothic belfry. The church is in the form of a Latin cross running the long way of the street. The chancel, at the east end, is connected directly with the parsonage. At its western end, a cloistered walk connects the church with the parish house, named for Saint Christopher. All three buildings are constructed in a combination of golden-brown brick and terra cotta. The asymmetrical grouping around a courtyard and the rich and fanciful detail are fully in the spirit of the delightfully fresh and informal châteaux that Francis I built along the Loire Valley.

In quite a different vein, two Roman Catholic churches on the Upper East Side reflect the self-confident opulence of the decades that just preceded the First World War. They turn for inspiration to seventeenth-century Rome, the period of the Counter Reformation when the Church was using a powerful and imposing architectural style to reassert its authority.

The earlier of these churches, at Park Avenue and 84th Street, is dedicated to Saint Ignatius Loyola, a Spanish soldier who was to become leader of the Counter Reformation and founder of the Jesuits. The present edifice rests on a lower church, built in the mid-1880s and dedicated to Saint Lawrence O'Toole, titular saint of the oldest parish in Yorkville. The parish had been established in 1851 to serve the Irish Catholics who came to work on the Croton Aqueduct and on the Harlem River Railroad. As can still be seen at the basement level along 84th Street, the rough-cut, heavy stone buttresses were intended to support a church in the Gothic Revival style. After the Jesuits took over the parish they petitioned the Pope to rededicate the church to their own patron saint. The main altar was dedicated to Saint Ignatius and that in the lower church to Saint Lawrence O'Toole as co–titular saint.

The present edifice was built between 1895 and 1900. It was designed in the typical formal Jesuit tradition. Incidentally, two planned bell towers were never completed, giving the church an unfinished appearance. The church ties in beautifully with Regis High School, just across the street, which is directed by the same order. The church, which now serves a wealthy and fashionable

22. *Church of St. Ignatius Loyola (R.C.)*
980 Park Avenue, at 84th Street
1895–1900, Schickel & Ditmars

23. *St. Jean Baptiste Church (R.C.)*
1067-1071 Lexington Avenue
1910–13, Nicholas Serracino

parish, provided the last haven for the great but controversial Jesuit anthropologist-philosopher Pierre Teilhard de Chardin until his death in 1955.

The building of the St. Jean Baptiste Church, Lexington Avenue on the southeast corner of 76th Street, was largely the result of the contributions of a single patron, Thomas Fortune Ryan. A large group of French Canadians who had settled in the area and found it too far and too inconvenient to make the trip to Canal Street, where the only French Catholic church in the city was located, opened a little mission chapel over a stable in the neighborhood in 1881. A few years later the congregation managed to build a small church on the north side of 76th Street between Lexington and Third Avenues. Ryan, a devout Catholic and a man of unassuming ways, preferred the little Church of St. Jean to the more luxurious ones nearer his Fifth Avenue mansion. One day he arrived late for the service and found standing room only. Dutifully, if uncomfortably, he stayed through the Mass and then approached the attending priest.

"How much would it cost to build a new church?" he asked.

The priest made a quick calculation. "At least three hundred thousand dollars."

"O.K. Get some plans and I will pay for it," said Ryan.

The final cost was $600,000. When Ryan died in 1928, his funeral service, a simple low requiem Mass, was held in St. Jean Baptiste's.

It was built in 1910 by an Italian architect, Nicholas Serracino, and is in the post–Italian Renaissance, or Baroque, style, with a great freestanding Corinthian portico, two bell towers, and a dome over the crossing. Such an ambitious combination of imposing elements suffers considerably from its setting—half a block front on a busy avenue and overshadowed by apartment houses.

Public Buildings

With few exceptions the public buildings of the Upper East Side are in the Classical Tradition.

The Regis High School, on East 84th Street, by McGinnis & Walsh, is an example of the ingenious adaptation of a classical canon to meet contemporary needs. By the use of a monumental Ionic order, extending through three stories, this five-story building is brought into scale with St. Ignatius Loyola Church across the street. Yet its

24. *The Regis High School*
55 East 84th Street
1913–17, Maginnis & Walsh

large windows are both expressive of and functional for the school within. The north side of the building, which runs through to 85th Street, is expressive of the large auditorium inside: the great blank wall of the hall is flanked by projecting end bays containing the fire stairs. Most of the classrooms open onto an interior court which is not visible from the street.

The Yorkville Branch of the New York Public Library, on East 79th Street, is a particularly distinguished example of the dozens of

25. Yorkville Branch,
*   New York Public Library*
222 East 79th Street
1902, James Brown Lord

local libraries which Andrew Carnegie built in English-speaking countries just after the turn of the century. Carnegie, whose first job was that of a bobbin boy in a cotton factory, had a passion for education and self-betterment. In 1868, when he was thirty-three, he wrote a memorandum: "Thirty-three and an income of $50,000 per annum . . . I will resign business at thirty-five but during the ensuing two years I wish to spend the afternoons receiving instruction and in reading systematically." He actually did not retire at thirty-five, but by the time he had amassed his fortune in steel he had also developed a well-articulated philosophy of wealth:

> This then, is held to be the duty of the man of wealth: to set an example of modest, unostentatious living, shunning display or extravagance; to provide moderately for the wants of those dependent upon him; and, after doing so, to consider all surplus revenues which come to him simply as trust funds which he is called upon to administer, the man of wealth thus becoming the mere trustee and agent for his poorer brethren.

Among his endowments, which include the Carnegie Corporation, the Carnegie Endowment for International Peace and the Carnegie Foundation for the Advancement of Teaching, was a contribution of $5,200,000 to New York City in 1901 for branch libraries. Sixty-five were built on sites furnished by the City.

The Yorkville building was the creation of James Brown Lord, who designed it in the Palladian manner of the late Italian Renaissance. It has a combination of strength and refinement, of restraint and grace. This particular branch library has the added interest of being the place where Thomas Masaryk did the research that led to the creation of the Czechoslovak Republic after World War I.

The most monumental of all the public buildings of the Upper East Side is the Metropolitan Museum of Art on Fifth Avenue at 82nd Street. Actually the building of this great pile has taken almost a century, and it is still far from finished. It consists of some fifteen separate but connected units in quite different styles. It extends four city blocks on land that was set aside for it in Central Park. The original unit faced the park. It was begun in 1874 and finished in 1880 and was designed by Calvert Vaux and Jacob Wrey Mould in the Victorian Gothic style. In 1888 a south wing, also facing the park, was designed by Theodore Weston in the neo–American Classic style, and in 1894 a similar one by Arthur L. T. Tuckerman was built to the north. Weston's design, which Tuckerman closely copied, predates the Columbian Exposition by five years and, together with the Williamsburgh Savings Bank in Brooklyn, could be considered a harbinger of the great classical movement that was soon to burst on the country as a result of the exposition. Both of these architects were closely involved with the museum—Weston as a trustee and Tuckerman as the museum's resident professor of architecture.

Later additions were designed by various architects, but the most familiar part, and the section that changed the museum's orientation from the park to Fifth Avenue, was the great central pavilion with its triple-arch motif which Richard Morris Hunt designed and which his son, Richard Howland Hunt, and George B. Post carried through to completion by 1902. In composition it is suggestive of the great triple arch that Thomas Hastings designed for the New York Public Library, but lacks the latter's three-dimensional drama. The museum's arches are restricted to the plane of the façade instead of being deeply

26. METROPOLITAN MUSEUM OF ART

a. Fifth Avenue Façade
Fifth Avenue, 80th to 84th Street
Center: 1902, Richard Morris Hunt
Wings: 1911–26, McKim, Mead & White
Steps and fountains: 1970, Kevin Roche John Dinkeloo Associates

recessed. Four pairs of Corinthian columns are brought forward from the façade, each pair originally standing on its own high pedestal. Stylistically, one feels that Hunt was trying to create a façade that would do credit to Imperial Rome, but that he had not quite escaped the effects of his early training at the École des Beaux-Arts. The strong articulation of the paired columns betrays his ingrained feeling that a monumental façade should provide a dramatic play of light and deep shadow and that sculpture was an integral element of architecture. He intended to crown the columns with allegorical groups of figures

b. South Façade (early view)
Fifth Avenue at 81st Street, in Central Park
1888, Theodore Weston

representing Egyptian, Classical, Renaissance and Modern Art, but funds have never been made available to carry this out, and the columns support nothing but large uncarved blocks.

The north and south wings on Fifth Avenue, which were subsequently added by McKim, Mead & White between 1911 and 1926, suggest that by this late date much of the fire had burned out of the famous firm. After the death or retirement of the original partners and designers, the firm continued for a long time to run on its initial impetus, but the designs, as here, were often merely dry, correct and dull.

c. West Façade (early view)
Central Park
Center: 1874–80, Calvert Vaux and Jacob Wrey Mould
South wing: 1888, Theodore Weston
North wing: 1894, Arthur L. T. Tuckerman

d. Old Assay Office Façade   (originally at 15 Wall Street)
American Wing, Metropolitan Museum of Art
Fifth Avenue and 82nd Street (inner courtyard)
1823, Martin E. Thompson
Relocated 1924

The best that can be said for the bland north and south wings is that they are not incompatible with Hunt's central pavilion and that their flatness enhances its richness.

The Hunt design has been further cooled in recent years by a great flight of steps added by Kevin Roche and John Dinkeloo Associates. While the museum certainly needed a more adequate entrance, this particular design reduces the articulation of the paired columns by pulling their separate pedestals into a continuous base. The new flight of steps literally spills onto Fifth Avenue and is flanked by two linear

fountains. The trees have been pushed back to the extreme north and south ends of the otherwise open plazas.

In 1970 the museum announced plans for some grandiose expansion, in particular a west wing to house the fabulous Robert Lehman collection of paintings, a north wing to shelter the Temple of Dendur, given to the United States by the Egyptian government before the Aswan High Dam flooded its site, and an extension to the south to take care of the unique collection of primitive art given to the museum by Governor Nelson A. Rockefeller.

The Landmarks Preservation Commission, whose power in connection with public Landmarks is only advisory and not absolute as with private buildings, expressed serious objections to the proposed Lehman pavilion and to details of the enclosure for the Temple of Dendur. As a result, although the museum is going ahead with both, it now plans to preserve all that remains of the earliest façade—the five Vaux and Mould arches facing the park—inside the new monumental entrance lobby to the Lehman wing. Also to be preserved is the south face to the Weston wing. Nothing will remain of the Tuckerman wing; it had already been seriously eroded by successive alterations. The 1823 façade of the old United States Assay Office will also be preserved. Martin E. Thompson designed this for the Second Bank of the United States on Wall Street. In 1853 the building became the home of the Assay Office. When it was demolished in 1915, I. N. Phelps Stokes, (who had spent a good part of his fortune and most of his life in assembling, editing and publishing the great six-volume *Iconography of Manhattan Island*) arranged for the stone-by-stone salvage of the façade. It was reerected in 1924 on the south face of the American Wing, which had just been added to the museum. This is the handsomest example we have of a monumental building in the Federal style.

The Metropolitan Museum was incorporated in April 1870 through the efforts of some civic-minded members of the Union League Club. It had no money, no works of art and no building. A few months later the purchase of 174 Dutch and French paintings started the collection, and it found temporary quarters on Fifth Avenue in what had been Dodworth's Dancing Academy. After one other temporary home, the Douglas mansion on 14th Street, it moved in 1880 to its glossy new quarters in Central Park, which were formally opened by President Rutherford B. Hayes. The City leases the land to the museum and makes contributions for maintenance, but the works of art come from generous donors, by bequest, gift or contribution. In the last one hundred years the Metropolitan has burgeoned into the finest museum in this country, and among the greatest in the world. Even though the museum has changed mightily since 1905, the words that Henry James used that year to describe it are still very apt: "It is a palace of art, truly, that sits there on the edge of the Park, rearing with a radiance, yet offering you expanses to tread."

A far cry—geographically, historically and architecturally—from the Metropolitan Museum is the Harlem Courthouse on East 121st Street at Sylvan Place. This 1891–93 building, by Thom & Wilson, seems in some ways a distant echo of the Jefferson Market Courthouse that Withers had done some twenty years earlier in Greenwich Village. Essentially neo-Romanesque in style, it retains Victorian Gothic overtones. It has a great round tower on the corner which is crowned with eight miniature gables and a multiplicity of gables with pinnacles on both streets. Though it lacks the freedom and exuberance of

27. *Harlem Courthouse*
172 East 121st Street,
at Sylvan Place
1891–93, Thom & Wilson

the Jefferson Market Courthouse, it is nevertheless a handsome and romantic structure. Its function as a courthouse terminated in 1961. Today it houses units of the City's Department of Air Pollution Control, Sanitation Department and Parole Board.

Quite different from the Harlem Courthouse is the building that Joseph Freedlander designed for the Museum of the City of New York on Fifth Avenue between 103th and 104th Streets. This is a restrained, elegant and formal example of the neo-Georgian style carried out in red brick and white marble. Its U-shaped plan, and the approach across a marble-balustraded terrace, is expressive of both its civic and its museum character. Yet somehow one feels that the building is just too big to be quite comfortable in the style it is wearing. If it is compared, for example, with the equally formal but considerably smaller Independence Hall in Philadelphia, one appreciates that there are very real aesthetic limits to the size of a building to which a particular style can appropriately be applied. Independence

28. *Museum of the City of New York   Fifth Avenue, 103rd to 104th Street 1929–30, Joseph H. Freedlander*

Hall seems perfectly at ease in its Georgian dress; the Museum of the City of New York is a little like an overweight dowager in a miniskirt.

This museum has a special appeal to true New Yorkers—whether native or by adoption. It is the country's first museum to be devoted exclusively to the life and times, the growth and the spirit, of a great city. It houses priceless collections of silver, costumes, furniture, portraits, old fire engines, toys, prints, ships' models, which hundreds of thousands flock to see every year.

It has embarked on a major new program to present the history of New York in chronological sequence, illustrating each period with the appropriate costumes, furniture, silver, household utensils and related items. The first exhibit of the new order was a mélange of taped narration, slides and artifacts, including a Revolutionary musket, an 1850 horsecar—the last surviving one in the city—and Opera Box No. 28, rescued from the old Metropolitan Opera House when it was demolished in 1966. The exhibit, entitled "Cityrama," traced the history of the city from 1524 (when Verrazzano first sailed into New York Harbor) to the present day. Other aspects of city life, including health, women's role and the future, will be treated in the same multimedia fashion.

Armories and a Watch Tower

Military and engineering structures of the Upper East Side provide some unexpected illustrations of how interesting purely utilitarian buildings can be. The oldest example is Martin E. Thompson's Arsenal begun in 1847 in Central Park at Fifth Avenue and 64th Street. It was designed in the style of an English manorial fortress with eight bristling towers.

This forbidding pile today contains nothing more aggressive than the hard-working staff of the Parks, Recreation and Cultural Affairs Administration, of which the Landmarks Preservation Commission is a component. It replaced an old arsenal downtown and predates Central Park itself. It was built by New York State to house its collection of artillery, rifles and ammunition. Although the old armory on Centre Street was in a most rickety state and pilferage of cannonballs and small arms was rampant, many good citizens opposed the transfer

29. *The Arsenal (early view)   (now Parks, Recreation and Cultural Affairs*
   Administration offices)
Fifth Avenue and 64th Street, in Central Park
1847–51, Martin E. Thompson

of the storehouse to a place "so far uptown." An official report to the
legislature in 1849 protested:

> A city with a population of half a million will always be liable
> to tumultuous assemblages. It is necessary therefore . . . that
> means shall be instantly afforded to quell the first indication of
> the riot. . . . If the cannon be all placed in the new Arsenal,
> distant four and a half miles from the present depot, they would
> be useless, for before the troops could march that distance to
> obtain them the object of a riotous mob would be accomplished.

Despite the objection, construction started in 1847, and when a
contemporary critic visited the building on its opening he commented, "Every arrangement indicates much taste and neatness."

By 1859 the City had acquired 843 acres of land for Central Park
for about $5,000,000—not a very good bargain, according to one
report that described the site as a "pestilential spot where rank
vegetation and miasmic odors taint every breath of air." It was a
shantytown for more than five thousand squatters. At this time the
city was built up to 34th Street, although horsecars found their way to
42nd Street.

Fortunately for New Yorkers today a few individuals foresaw

that the wilderness above 59th Street would be reached by the inexorable growth of the city, and they took steps to preserve it. A special committee, which included, among others, William Cullen Bryant and Washington Irving, decided that there should be an open competition for the design of a new park. The winners, Frederick Law Olmsted and Calvert Vaux, called their plan "Greensward," a name that fortunately did not stick. Their design provided for glades, copses, rock outcroppings, footpaths, bridle paths and carriage drives. The four transverse roads for crosstown traffic were sunk below the level of the park to be as inconspicuous as possible, while the roads and paths of the park itself crossed the transverses on bridges. It took nearly twenty years to complete the work, but every New Yorker believes that the wait was worth it. Central Park incorporated so many innovative ideas, it epitomized so perfectly a new realization of the necessity for urban recreation, and its influence across the country and around the world has been so extensive, that it has been placed on the National Register of Historic Places. Its design is considered by many to be one of the most important cultural contributions of nineteenth-century America.

While the long and arduous task of creating Central Park was in process, the City bought the Arsenal from the State and installed the Eleventh Police Precinct in it. Later, the Municipal Weather Bureau moved into the top floor, while the American Museum of Natural History found its first home on the second and third floors. In 1934 the building was renovated, and it has since that time been the headquarters of the Parks Department.

Another armory is that of the Seventh Regiment on Park Avenue, between 66th and 67th Streets. It is interesting on two counts. Its Park Avenue front, with its machicolated towers—that is, fitted with openings through which molten lead could be poured on an enemy trying to scale the walls—is a vigorous Victorian interpretation of a medieval French fortress. Its Lexington Avenue end, enclosing a great drill hall, 187 by 290 feet, demonstrates the same sort of engineering ingenuity that the late Victorians achieved in covering over their huge railroad stations and markets. Beneath the drill hall is a rifle range. The Veterans' Room and the library were decorated by a group of well-known artists under the direction of Louis Comfort Tiffany. The interiors, except for the purely utilitarian areas, are those of an exclusive club. They are handsomely furnished in a somber masculine style and very well maintained. The building, designed by Charles W. Clinton, was opened in 1880, an occasion marked by a great inaugural ball attended by everybody who was anybody, for the Seventh Regiment of the New York National Guard has been a proud organization in New York City for many generations.

30. *Seventh Regiment Armory   Park Avenue, 66th to 67th Street 1877–79, Charles W. Clinton*

All that remains of John R. Thomas' Squadron "A" Armory, which was built in 1895 to cover the block bounded by 94th and 95th Streets and Madison and Park Avenues, are the paired towers on the two Madison Avenue corners and the wall that connects them. This building was quite similar in plan to the Seventh Regiment Armory and also served a distinguished military organization for many years.

The armory was the home of a band of rugged gentlemen volunteers who served in Squadron "A" of the "First New York Hussars." The troop saw service in the Spanish–American War and, reorganized as the 105th Machine Gun Battalion, was called into the

United States Army during World War I. The building continued in use for polo matches and horse shows until 1966, when the Board of Education started plans for razing it to make way for a new intermediate school. It was actually in the process of being demolished when, with the intervention of the local community and the Landmarks Preservation Commission, the westerly wall and towers were saved just in time to be designated a Landmark. This was the most interesting part of the building from an architectural point of view.

The architect of the new intermediate school, Morris Ketchum, Jr., and Associates, has designed the school building to harmonize with the existing towers and wall. After years of study and successful battles over the budget, Ketchum produced an ingenious solution whereby the Landmark towers and wall form the screening backdrop for a combination park and playground that will also lend itself to outdoor concerts, theatricals and other community activities. A private donor made possible the construction of this facility in lieu of the usual asphalt-paved and chain-link-fenced school playground. The salvage of the best part of the armory and its imaginative reuse in connection with the school are an illustration of how new life can be found for old Landmarks.

31. *Squadron "A" Armory—Madison Avenue Façade*
Madison Avenue, 94th to 95th Street
1895, John R. Thomas
Restoration: 1972–73, Morris, Ketchum, Jr., and Associates

A purely utilitarian structure that has both historic interest and considerable charm is the last remaining fire watch tower in the city. It is set on a high, rocky outcropping in Mount Morris Park recently renamed Marcus Garvey Memorial Park. It was built around 1855 and is attributed to James Bogardus, the great proponent of cast-iron construction. The tower has an interesting octagonal framework, supporting two intermediate levels and a balcony at the top from which a fire watch could be maintained. At one time such towers were widely scattered throughout the city. When a fire was sighted, the tower watchman would strike his bell, indicating the number of the district where the fire was, and the signal was picked up by watchmen in other towers. Thus the volunteer fire companies got the word and dragged their equipment through the streets in the general direction of any blaze or smoke that could be seen.

32. Watch Tower
   Mount Morris Park at
      122nd Street
   1855,
         attributed to James Bogardus

By 1851 some of the towers were connected with a telegraphic warning system. In 1878, when the fire-alarm boxes and the telephone began to take over, and after a paid Fire Department had replaced the volunteers, the use of watch towers was discontinued. But the bell at

Mount Morris Park was rung for years after that, at 9 A.M. and noon. The community had become so used to the sound of the bell that local citizens insisted on having this daily reassurance that "all's well."

Historic Districts

The Upper East Side contains two small Historic Districts, quite different from one another.

TREADWELL FARM

Treadwell Farm with its four mid-block rows of houses dates from 1868 to 1876. The houses extend along both sides of East 61st and 62nd Streets between Second and Third Avenues, mostly on land that once formed part of Adam Treadwell's twenty-four-acre farm. Adam Treadwell was a wealthy merchant, born at Hempstead, Long Island, in 1772, the son of a Loyalist. He was a senior warden of Trinity Church, his fortune in 1845 was estimated at $400,000, and he owned considerable property downtown. A younger brother, Seabury Tredwell (who chose this spelling), built what is known as the Old Merchant's House at 29 East 4th Street, which is also a Landmark.

Adam Treadwell's heirs subdivided the farm property. Purchasers started to build in the late 1860s. Before plans had advanced very far, a voluntary protective covenant was entered into among twenty of the owners that is a remarkably farsighted example of cooperative city planning. While Clement Clarke Moore in the subdivision of his Chelsea property had imposed certain standards on buyers and builders, the twenty individuals who signed the Treadwell Farm covenant voluntarily imposed restrictions on themselves and their heirs in the realization of how much it was in their common interest to establish standards.

Some of the terms of the covenant are worth repeating. No building should be less than fifteen feet wide; all houses should be set back exactly five feet (an exception was made for churches and Sunday schools, which could be set farther back); and this space in front of the houses should always be kept unencumbered except for such necessities as steps. Furthermore, the houses were to be at least three stories

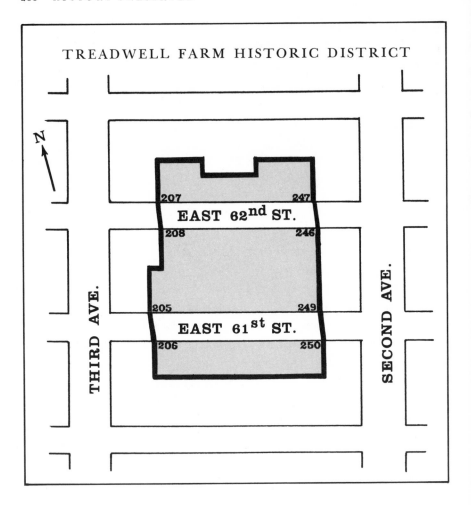

high and constructed of brick or stone. No little wooden houses like those uptown on 92nd Street were to go up in this elegant neighborhood.

The list of prohibited uses is an interesting commentary on the industrial and urban developments which mid-nineteenth-century homeowners considered objectionable. The covenant specified that

> no livery or other stable, slaughter house, smith shop, forge, furnace, steam engine, brass or other metal factory or foundry, or any manufactory of gunpowder, glass, glue, coal, oil, gas, varnish, vitriol, soap, friction matches, ink or turpentine or for tanning, or dressing, or keeping of hides, skins, or leather or any

tallow, chandlery, brewery, distillery, lager beer or refreshment saloon or tavern, or any establishment for the sale of liquors whether distilled or fermented, or any establishment for games or gambling house, tenement house, museum, circus, menagerie, police station, railroad depot, engine or car house, or railroad track or any establishment, business or occupation known as nuisances in the law which may be dangerous or offensive to the neighboring inhabitants shall ever be made, erected or permitted on said lots of land.

It is interesting to note that the objections are partly on the grounds of noise, partly of smell, partly of danger and partly of morality. The covenant was maintained, and the results are reflected in the character of the neighborhood as a whole rather than in the architecture of any particular building.

Almost all the houses in the Historic District appear to have been originally designed in the then fashionable French Second Empire style. They were formal, substantial and elegant brownstones, and some of the designs came from the offices of such distinguished architects as Richard Morris Hunt, Samuel A. Warner, James W. Pirsson and George F. Pelham. Despite the fact that the houses of Treadwell

North Side of East 62nd Street   Treadwell Farm Historic District

Farm were planned for individual owners and by different architects, the initial effect was one of considerable uniformity. Many of the exteriors have been substantially altered and many have lost their original high stoops, heavy doors, window enframements and cornices; nevertheless, an impression of cohesion has survived. This is in part due to the fine proportions of the wall openings, the uniform setback and the usually continuous cornice line. But, above all, it is the consistently high standards of maintenance, the pleasant flower boxes, trees and hedges, as well as the generally tasteful character of the alterations that give the district its charm.

John Gunther described the community in his foreword to the "Report of the East Sixties Property Owners Association," written in 1961 (it might have been entitled *Inside Treadwell Farm*) :

> . . . at one time or another and coming right up to the present, our roster, representing not more than a quarter of a mile or so of houses, includes men with public interests like Howard Cullman, Allen W. Dulles and Conger Goodyear, a covey of writers (Clifton Fadiman, Geoffrey Hellman, Walter Lippmann, Paul Gallico, Major George Fielding Eliot, Clementine Paddleford), bankers like Gilbert W. Kahn, dieticians (Gayelord Hauser), judges like the late Alfred C. Coxe, and artists, lovers of the arts, and architects ranging from Margaret Osborn and the late Savely Sorine to Aymar Embury, John H. MacFadyen, Perry Coke Smith and Christopher LaFarge.
>
> Surely few streets have—or had—so many pretty women in show business (Tallulah Bankhead, Vera Zorina, Kim Novak, Anne Baxter, Jane Wyatt, Faye Emerson, Barbara Bel Geddes, and the late Gertrude Lawrence) as well as such male counterparts as Montgomery Clift. Then—again I am picking and choosing almost at random—we have (have had) opera stars like Frances Alda, editors (C. D. Jackson, Allen Grover, and the late Geoffrey Parsons), fashion columnists like Tobe Davis, figures from the world of music and broadcasting (Goddard Lieberson and Murray Taylor), colorful ornaments of society (Julia Giles, Alice Astor Bouverie), publishers like Ivan Obolensky and Charles Duell, businessmen of various categories (Beardsley Ruml, Arthur Bunker, John Elliott, Oscar S. Strauss, II, Thomas A. Morgan, Louis Timmerman), lawyers (Carl W. Painter, Grayson M. P. Murphy, Royal Riggs, Charles Gleaves, and Thomas J. Blake), surgeons (Dr. William G. Cahan and Dr. Hans H. Zinsser), and such distinguished personalities as Fairfield Osborn, Stephen Galatti and Eleanor Roosevelt.

HENDERSON PLACE

Quite a different sort of Historic District, and one with quite a different history, is Henderson Place. It extends along East End Avenue between 86th and 87th Streets, along both the side streets and down the short dead-end alley that gives the district its name. This land once belonged to John Jacob Astor, who had a country place nearby, while Archibald Gracie's house was just a block away. Other families that bore famous old New York names—Bayards, Foulkes, Rhinelanders, Schermerhorns—also had country seats in the neighborhood. Between 1827 and 1829, the road that later became East 86th Street was made an important east-west thoroughfare, and five years later the New York and Harlem Railroad Company opened service to Yorkville through the countryside north of 14th Street. All this helped to break up the estates and accelerate the development of the area. In the second quarter of the nineteenth century, some of the well-to-do brewers such as the Ehret and Ruppert families moved in. The Ringlings had also made their home here. But it was not until about

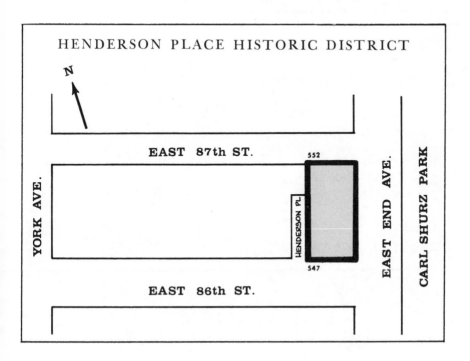

1900 that a heavy influx of Germans from the Tompkins Square section of the Lower East Side moved into Yorkville, establishing its *Bierstuben* and its *gemütlich* character.

Long before this development, however, the Astor property came into the hands of a man named John C. Henderson, who had made a fortune in furs and fur hats. In 1881 he decided to build some small row houses to sell to "persons of moderate means." He selected as his architects the firm of Lamb & Rich, who completed thirty-two houses within a couple of years. Twenty-four of the thirty-two still remain. They are fine examples of what is known, for some strange reason, as the Queen Anne style.

These houses, however, are notable for more than their style. The group represents an early example of an entire block front designed by an architect in a carefully composed way, with a beginning, a middle and an end. Turrets have been placed to emphasize where the row turns a corner; entranceways have been paired within a single sweeping arch; roof lines, bay windows and the detail and direction of each stoop have all been considered for their effect on the composition as a whole. Unfortunately, the houses along East End Avenue have

Henderson Place

individually been considerably altered. The original intent can best be appreciated along 87th Street and along the east side of Henderson Place itself. The eight matching houses that once faced these from the west side of the alley were torn down recently to make way for a towering apartment house, and much of the character of this little cul-de-sac was lost.

Though John Henderson had planned his block of houses for persons of moderate means and the houses themselves are tiny—the typical lot is only eighteen by forty-six feet, and some are as small as fourteen by forty feet—their charm is inescapable. In the general rediscovery of the East River that took place in the 1920s, Sutton Place, Beekman Place and East End Avenue evolved into fashionable enclaves. Henderson Place was considered a find, and the little houses have since been occupied by such prominent personages as Dean Millicent McIntosh of Barnard College, the Duke and Duchess de Richelieu, and Alfred Lunt and Lynn Fontanne.

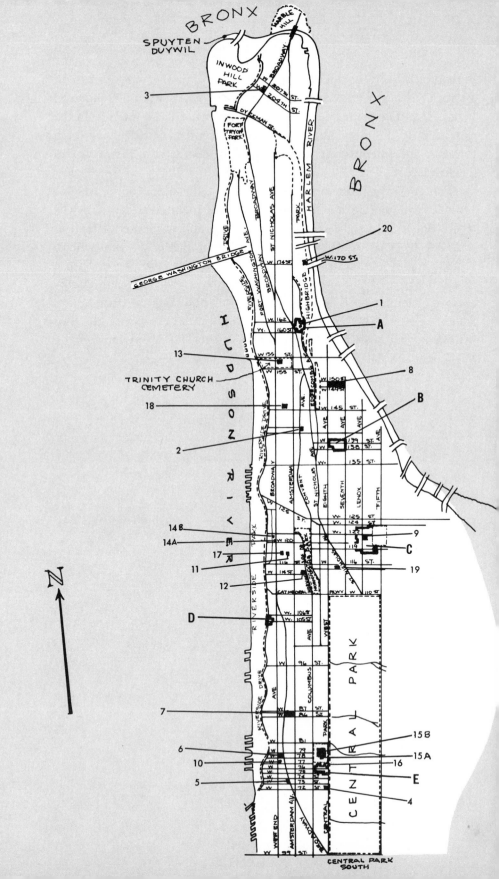

MANHATTAN

West Side Above 59th Street

CHAPTER SIX

MANHATTAN

West Side Above 59th Street

A LARGE PART of this area was known in the days of the Dutch as Bloemendael (Vale of Flowers) in memory of a town in Holland, and was the antecedent of the many places today named Bloomingdale. That it was an apt name is attested by Washington Irving, who, in his *Knickerbocker's History of New York,* described the Upper West Side as "a sweet rural valley, beautiful with many a bright flower, refreshed by many a pure streamlet, and enlivened here and there by a delectable little Dutch cottage, sheltered under some sloping hill; and almost buried in embowering trees."

From farms the area progressed to country estates. After the Revolution, development was steady but slow. The real push came in 1851 when the Hudson River Railroad opened its line to Albany, with several local stops in upper Manhattan. In 1867 the old country road from the city, the Bloomingdale Road, which had been made an extension of Broadway up to 59th Street, became "the Boulevard" north of that point, and in 1899 the Boulevard in turn became an extension of Broadway, thus further opening up the area.

This section of the city provides both parallels and contrasts with the East Side. It was built up later, and, although for a while it enjoyed a certain fashion, it never quite achieved the opulence of its competitor across the park. Rather, it became a monument to middle-class respectability. Many immigrants, particularly Jews from Eastern Europe, first settled in the Lower East Side ghettos. As they prospered they moved to the Upper West Side. (No one knows quite why; perhaps some unknown adventurer took the giant stride and members of his family and friends followed as they could.)

For many years the Upper West Side was *so* middle-class, *so* respectable, that sons and daughters moved as fast as possible to the lures of Greenwich Village or the chic of the East Side. In one of those great reversals that occur so frequently in New York, the area now is becoming popular among theater people, writers and artists who find the solid well-built houses great fun to restore and fine for growing young families.

Except for the former Charles M. Schwab château on Riverside Drive between 73rd and 74th Streets, and two or three other more modest mansions, also on Riverside Drive, the West Side was never able to boast of such a series of private palaces as still characterize many blocks just east of Fifth Avenue. Instead, there are rows and rows of quietly substantial houses, dating from the late nineteenth and early twentieth centuries. They are usually better preserved individually and the blocks are generally less broken up than their counterparts on the East Side.

There are also some notable apartment houses built around the turn of the century that, with their pomp and flourishes, give the West Side a very special character. But most interesting of all are three houses, survivors of a very early period, that cannot be matched anywhere else on Manhattan. Their survival can be attributed to the lack of pressure to get ahead that has always infected the rival to the east.

Country Mansions, a Farmhouse, Apartments and a Hotel

First and foremost is the Morris-Jumel Mansion near West 160th Street on Jumel Terrace. This great Georgian house was built by Colonel Roger Morris in 1765 on his large country estate on the highest elevation of Manhattan. The area was called Harlem Heights during the days of the Dutch. When the English held sway it was Mount Morris, and after the Revolution it received its present name,

Washington Heights. Morris and Washington had known each other since Morris had come to the New World as an aide-de-camp to General Braddock, on whose staff Washington also served. When the Revolution broke out, Morris, a Loyalist sympathizer, returned to England, but he came back in 1777 and served the British as inspector of refugees' claims. In 1783 he and his branch of the family returned to England for good.

Washington took refuge in the Morris house for a month, from September 14 to October 18, 1776, when he retreated to Harlem Heights after the disastrous Battle of Long Island. He used the house as his military headquarters in the vain defense of Harlem Heights before he had to abandon Manhattan altogether. There is an ironic little footnote to this story. Rumor has it that Washington had assiduously courted Morris' wife before her marriage, when she was Mary Philipse, daughter of a wealthy family that owned great estates farther up the Hudson River.

After the American forces evacuated the house, the British moved in, and they stayed there for the seven years they occupied New York City. The house then passed through a number of hands, finally becoming a tavern in 1796. In 1810 it came into the possession of a wealthy French merchant, Stephen Jumel. Under the demanding direction of the imperious and ambitious Madame Jumel, several alterations were made in the then fashionable Federal style. The doorway and the attenuated columns of the pedimented portico were probably added at this time. They are in contrast to the square massiveness of the original Georgian house.

1. Morris-Jumel Mansion
   Jumel Terrace between
      160th and 162nd Streets
   c. 1765
   Portico: c. 1810

Madame Jumel, who had been born Betsy Bowen in Providence, of doubtful antecedents and more doubtful youthful activities, was a very handsome woman. It was said that after some ten years of being Jumel's mistress she finally tricked him into marriage by staging a touching deathbed scene, the tenor of which was that her last wish was to be married. But even marriage did not bring her the social recognition she craved, and she spent a good deal of time in France, where her less than perfect French accent brought her some small and kindly tolerance. When Jumel discovered that his bride had had an illegitimate son, George Washington Bowen, the couple lived more and more apart, Jumel in Paris and Betsy in New York.

Jumel died in 1832, and the next year Betsy brought her intended bridegroom, Aaron Burr, then almost eighty, to the family mansion. They were married in the small parlor to the left of the main hall on the ground floor. A few months later they were divorced, and not long afterward Burr died. But widowhood, grass or otherwise, did not abash Betsy, whose activities became more and more eccentric. She urged some neighbors to name their twin sons Stephen Jumel and Aaron Burr, and was furious when they refused. She continued to use Burr's name, on the theory that it was a good name to travel under. Once in France when a body of troops impeded her way, she rose in her carriage and commanded, "Make way for the widow of the Vice-President of the United States!" She lived on in the old house until her death in 1865, at the age of ninety-three, having spent the last three years as a complete recluse.

After an endless series of lawsuits, the house was put on the market in 1903 for sale for a real-estate development. Fortunately, the City of New York bought it. A branch of the Daughters of the American Revolution restored the house and now operates it as a museum. It has been beautifully maintained and is furnished with many of the personal belongings of Colonel Morris, George Washington, the Jumels and Burr. It sits high in a park with a magnificent view over the city, and is one of the most attractive house museums that have survived.

Of comparable importance—but unfortunately in nothing like the same condition—is Alexander Hamilton's house, the Grange, on Convent Avenue north of 141st Street. This was one of the first Federal-style homes of its day, designed in 1801 by John McComb, Jr. After Hamilton returned to New York from Philadelphia, the then national

2. *Hamilton Grange (early view)*   *287 Convent Avenue between 141st
    and 142nd Streets   (formerly at 143rd Street off Convent Avenue)
1801, John McComb, Jr.*
Moved 1889

capital, where he had been the country's first Secretary of the Treasury, he resumed his practice of law in lower Manhattan, but because
of his uncertain health he wanted to live in the country. The location
in Harlem where Convent Avenue is today was ideal. It was near both
the Bloomingdale Road and the Albany Post Road, so he could reach
either New York City or the state capital with ease.

Hamilton took particular pride in his garden. "A garden, you
know, is a very usual refuge for a disappointed politician," was his
realistic evaluation of his hobby. He planted a grove of thirteen sweet-
gum trees symbolizing the original states of the Union.

However, tragedy stalked the Grange. Before the house was even
completed, Hamilton's eldest son, Philip, was killed in a duel defend-
ing his father's political views. Hamilton moved into his new place in
1802, but lived there less than two years, for his fatal duel with Aaron
Burr occurred in 1804. It was ironic that Burr, his archenemy, should,
many years later, move into the neighboring Morris-Jumel Mansion.
Hamilton's widow, Elizabeth, who was a daughter of General Philip

Schuyler, kept the Grange in the family for thirty years before she sold it.

Hamilton Grange was moved to its present location, which is about a hundred yards from the original site, in 1889, at the time it was donated to St. Luke's Episcopal Church, the successor to the little St. Luke's downtown on Hudson Street. It is now jammed in between an apartment house and the church, which was put up after the Grange had been moved. The church is only inches away from what was formerly the front of the house. In the process of moving, the front and rear porches were removed. The house was used as a temporary chapel and later as a rectory by the church. Until 1924, when the house was bought by George F. Baker, Sr., and J. P. Morgan, it was the victim of serious vandalism. Baker and Morgan gave the Grange to the American Scenic and Historic Preservation Society, which set up a trust fund of $50,000 for its permanent maintenance as a memorial to Hamilton. In 1961 the society turned the shrine over to the National Park Service, and it is now open to the public. It is hoped that eventually the house can be moved to a more appropriate site in the neighborhood.

The Park Service is slowly restoring the house as nearly as possible to its original appearance and acquiring furnishings that either belonged to the Hamilton family or are of the period. One of the portraits in the house today is of Mrs. Hamilton by an artist who was in debtor's prison. Mrs. Hamilton made periodic trips to the prison for sittings and persuaded some of her rich friends to do likewise. In this way at least one debtor was enabled to pay his way out of jail.

Not at all in the tradition of these two great mansions is the charming little Dyckman House on upper Broadway between 204th and 207th Streets, which was built in about 1783. It is a typical Dutch Colonial farmhouse, the last one left on Manhattan. It was once the center of a prosperous farm. The Dyckman family had settled in the northern end of Manhattan Island in 1661 and had helped to build the Free Bridge—sometimes called Dyckman's Bridge—over the Harlem River in 1758. This bridge, connecting Manhattan and what is now The Bronx (then Westchester), was built by irate commuters in competition to the so-called King's Bridge, controlled by the powerful Philipse family, which charged a stiff toll. This act of defiance was hailed by the New York *Gazette* as "the first step toward

Freedom in this state." The Dyckman family eventually owned about three hundred acres, which were farmed for two hundred years, until 1868. During the Revolutionary War, the Continental Army, in its retreat from Harlem Heights, occupied the Dyckman farmhouse, and subsequently the British used it during their occupation of Manhattan. When they withdrew in 1783 the British burned the building and the orchards. But the Dyckman family came back and reconstructed the house, using some of the original material from their former home. The building, as it stands today, is of fieldstone, brick and wood, with the gambrel roof, spring eaves and porch so characteristic of this style. In the grounds, surrounded by well-tended flower beds, are a smoke house and a military hut that had been used by the British during their occupation.

Descendants of the Dyckman family purchased the house in 1915 when it was threatened with demolition to make room for an apartment house. They restored it, filled it with family heirlooms and furniture and presented it to the City, which now runs it as a museum.

It requires a great leap of the imagination to jump from the New York of the Dyckman farm, of George Washington, Alexander Hamilton and Aaron Burr, to the New York of the apartment house, the only way of life the majority of present-day New Yorkers—at least Manhattanites—have ever known. The apartment-house tenant is, in fact, now so nearly synonymous with the urban dweller that it is hard to realize how recent and how radical this way of life really is.

There was, of course, an intermediate stage between the open farmland and country estates of the eighteenth century and the twentieth-century multiple dwelling, and that was the great era of single-family row houses that covered block after block of nineteenth-century New York. Vast areas of them still survive in Brooklyn. In Manhattan, like an endangered species, some of the best remaining blocks of row houses are now being protected within the preserves of Historic Districts. Manhattan seems to have altogether escaped the suburban phase of ticky-tacky houses, each freestanding on its own little private parcel of land, that characterizes so much of Queens and Staten Island today.

In Manhattan, squeezed as it is between two rivers, there has always been great pressure to use its limited land with maximum efficiency. This has made it much easier for Manhattanites to adjust

3. Dyckman House   *Broadway and 204th Street*
  c. 1783

psychologically to the shift from the single-family row house to the multiple dwelling. After all, if one is already accustomed to sharing a party wall with neighbors on either side, it is not too difficult to get used to the idea of a ceiling and a floor shared with neighbors above and below. The idea that your floor is someone else's ceiling and that your ceiling is someone else's floor involves only a shift in thinking from the long-accepted fact that only a few inches of brick, plaster and lath separate your bedroom from your neighbor's.

At all events, the acceptance of "French Flats," as they were called to distinguish them from tenements, was far more rapid in Manhattan than it is in Queens or Staten Island today, a century later. The earliest was built in 1869. But what made the new development really popular was the construction, from 1880 to 1884, by Edward S. Clark, heir to the Singer Sewing Machine fortune, of the Dakota Apartments on Central Park West, between 72nd and 73rd Streets.

The Dakota was the city's first luxury apartment house from the point of view of date and still can hold its own from the point of view of quality. The story goes that some of Clark's friends said that he was

4. *The Dakota Apartments*
1 West 72nd Street, at Central Park West
1880–84, Henry J. Hardenbergh

crazy to make such a sizable investment way out in the country, in the middle of run-down farms and shanties. He might just as well build "out in Dakota in the Indian Territory." The name "Dakota" stuck, rather than "Clark's Folly," as those same friends were calling it. But Clark proved wise in his investment. He employed a great architect, Henry J. Hardenbergh, who later designed the Plaza across Central Park. Both buildings have the same romantic feeling, rather more German than French in this case, but still in the tradition of the Renaissance. With its fine materials and superb scale, its gables, its dormers, its bay windows, balconies and turrets, the Dakota has the indestructible air and grandeur of a large European château. It would not seem out of place overlooking the Rhine. The exterior is faced with yellow brick, with stone trim and terra-cotta ornament. Its thick load-bearing walls, heavy interior partitions and massive floors of rolled iron beams and masonry arches make it one of the quietest buildings in New York. The high ceilings, the parquet floors, the mahogany wainscoting and paneling and the solid bronze hardware give the Dakota the unique qualities that still make it one of the most sought-after places of residence in the city. It was one of the first buildings in the city to have elevators, and the original mechanism is still in use although its cars have been somewhat modernized. Another first was the installation of service elevators behind the kitchens at each bank of apartments.

Though it followed the Dakota by a score of years, the Ansonia, on Broadway between 73rd and 74th Streets, continued the same standard of luxury. It too took years to build—from 1899 to 1904—and, when the richness of its detail and finish is examined, it is surprising that it could have been built so quickly. For the Ansonia was designed in the full flowering of the late Beaux-Arts style. The monumental aspects of this style are demonstrated by such public structures as Grand Central Terminal and the main building of the New York Public Library, but the purely decorative aspects of the style are given full expression in the Ansonia. The architect in this case was actually a Frenchman, Paul E. M. Duboy, but the design was very much under the personal control of the owner-builder, William Earl Dodge Stokes, who was responsible for much of the early development of Riverside Drive and the Upper West Side. The building, planned as a residen-

5. *The Ansonia Hotel*
   (*from a drypoint by Richard Haas*)
   2101-2119 Broadway,
   from 73rd to 74th Street
   1899–1904, Paul E. M. Duboy

tial hotel, incorporated many of Stokes's original ideas. He was an early advocate of all-masonry, fireproof construction with heavy interior partitions to separate the apartments. This had two interesting consequences—one planned, the other unexpected. Stokes did not approve of fire insurance and never carried any on the Ansonia. The heavy construction was also virtually soundproof, a factor that, from the start, made the building particularly attractive to musicians. They could practice their own performances fortissimo or give lessons to agonizingly inept students without disturbing their neighbors.

Among the notables who have lived at the Ansonia are Leopold Auer, Karin Branzel, Enrico Caruso, Gatti Casazza, Bruna Castagna, Feodor Chaliapin, Alessio De Paolis, Mischa Elman, Geraldine Farrar, Herbert Janssen, Lauritz Melchior, Yehudi Menuhin, Ezio Pinza, Lily Pons, Tito Schipa, Friedrich Schorr, Antonio Scotti, Igor Stravinsky and Arturo Toscanini. It has also attracted theatrical personalities like Billie Burke, Florenz Ziegfeld, De Wolf Hopper and Sol Hurok, as well as authors like Theodore Dreiser, Elmer Rice and W. L. Stoddard. Another Ansonia resident, who used the hotel as his U.S. base while plotting phases of the Mexican Revolution, was General Victoriano Huerta, Provisional President of Mexico in 1913–14, whose "government by assassination" President Wilson refused to recognize.

Even apart from its star-studded tenancy, the Ansonia was from the start a highly individual sort of enterprise. When it first opened, it included such unheard-of attractions as shops in the cellar and two swimming pools, as well as a roof garden where Stokes kept goats, ducks, chickens and even a small pet bear. He sold eggs to the tenants at half price until a lawsuit terminated this enterprise.

Though the Ansonia has subsequently declined from this peak of grandeur and, with changing mores and a radically different neighborhood, has gone through a fair share of financial difficulties, it is still inhabited by a number of prominent musical performers and particularly by their teachers and coaches. With the construction of Lincoln Center only a few blocks away, the auguries are good for a new lease on life for this flamboyant *grande dame* of the musical and theatrical world.

Somewhat later, a lot more sober and built within a couple of years of each other are two very dignified and quite similar apartment houses. Each takes up an entire city block; each is built around an inner courtyard, entered through monumental archways. These are the Apthorp Apartments, the earlier of the two, by Clinton & Russell, built in 1906–08 on Broadway between 78th and 79th Streets, and the Belnord Apartments by H. Hobart Weekes, 1908–09, on Broadway between 86th and 87th Streets. They have many similarities in style. Both are neo–Italian Renaissance, with all the details one would expect to find on a Florentine palazzo. The fact that the apartments are entered from a private driveway that circles the courtyard gives them a particular elegance. The Apthorp is the finer of the two in architectural detail, with its Broadway entranceway flanked by four sculptured figures.

These four structures, the Dakota, the Ansonia, the Apthorp and

6. *The Apthorp Apartments*
2201-2219 Broadway,
from 78th to 79th Street
1906–08, Clinton & Russell

7. *The Belnord Apartments*
201-225 West 86th Street,
between Broadway and Amsterdam Avenue
1908–09, H. Hobart Weekes

the Belnord, are fine examples of how the grandeur and the conspicuous display of the private home were transferred to the multiple dwelling. No luxuries were omitted—fireplaces, balconies, bathrooms, maids' rooms, guest suites, gardens. No guest or tenant needed to feel underprivileged.

Different from these four, in both design and intent, are the Dunbar Apartments, on 149th and 150th Streets between Seventh and Eighth Avenues, which John D. Rockefeller, Jr., launched in the 1920s as a prototype garden apartment-house complex for low-income families. These were the first garden apartment houses built in Manhattan and the first cooperative ever built for blacks. The complex was designed by Andrew J. Thomas in the neo–Spanish Renaissance style and took the form of six independent U-shaped buildings clustered around a large interior garden court.

8. Dunbar Apartments   149th to 150th Street, 7th to 8th Avenue 1926–28, Andrew J. Thomas

Rockefeller, who had long been interested in housing for low-income families, was approached by the Urban League in 1925 to finance second mortgages in Harlem. He responded by a decision to build his own cooperative. The Dunbar, named for the famed black poet Paul Lawrence Dunbar, resulted. Tenant stockholders were required to pay $150 down plus $50 a room in the larger apartments. The monthly payment averaged $14.50 per room, of which fifty-five percent represented interest and principal and forty-five percent maintenance, taxes and insurance. The idea proved so popular that all the apartments were sold within a couple of months after the development opened.

Rockefeller, who felt that the project should be self-supporting, was disappointed that the cost of the apartments made them prohibitive for the truly low-income family. But he was gratified that, for the first time in Harlem's recent history, there was a new development in which local residents could take pride. Furthermore, the Dunbar served as a model for future public and quasi-public housing by providing what was then considered very generous open spaces, as well as locations for community needs such as shops, banks and other services.

The Dunbar continued to thrive for several years, but the depression of the 1930s finally caught up with it. Tenants lost their jobs and were unable to keep up their mortgage payments. If they had to move, Rockefeller returned their original equity to them. Finally, in December 1936, he foreclosed, returned each tenant's equity and put all the apartments on a rental basis. Although the cooperative plan had to be abandoned, it was destined to reemerge after World War II in many middle-income housing projects all over the city as well as in Harlem.

Churches and a Seminary

The Landmark churches of the Upper West Side were all built between 1887 and 1914. Looking back at this quarter century of halcyon days seems almost like looking at another planet. It presents, from our perspective, an apparently unbroken stretch of peace and plenty, of unshaken faith in material progress and in the perfectibility of the human race. The French call the period *la belle époque;* for the

British it runs from Victoria's Golden Jubilee through her Diamond Jubilee to the Edwardian Age; in America the administrations of Cleveland, Harrison, McKinley, Theodore Roosevelt and Taft were a time of hitherto unknown prosperity and of high optimism for social and economic reform. Of course there were minor disturbances—the Boer War to many did not seem quite "right," others were bothered by the Spanish–American War and the Boxer Rebellion, and, in remote Russia, there was some sort of suppressed revolution after we helped settle their war with Japan—but these were like little ripples on a tranquil sea. The era as a whole, and the buildings it produced, exudes an atmosphere of solidity and self-esteem.

Nowhere is this more strongly felt than in the half-dozen churches that were built to serve the eminently respectable and comfortably well-to-do population that lived in this area at the time. Structures, and particularly religious edifices, were built to last. And they could, because labor costs were still low and an ample pool of highly skilled craftsmen was still available. No trouble or expense was spared to enrich the buildings with fine materials and refined details. Stylistically, the churches are conservative but sophisticated. They were designed by a generation of architects who had been well trained in their profession.

St. Martin's Episcopal Church on Lenox Avenue at 122nd Street was erected in 1888 from plans by William A. Potter. (His family produced another architect, a specialist in ecclesiastical design, as well as several distinguished churchmen.) This interesting group, which includes a rectory and a parish house, is perhaps the finest example we have of the scholarly neo-Romanesque style as distinguished from the earlier Romanesque Revival that is exemplified by St. George's on Stuyvesant Square, built more than thirty years before. A comparison of the two buildings will illustrate the difference in approach between the somewhat naïve Revivalist and the sophisticated Eclecticist.

While St. George's illustrates how the Romanesque Revival concerned itself with superficial details, what we call the neo-Romanesque, under the inspiration of H. H. Richardson, was searching for the inner spirit of the Middle Ages. The rows of little round-arched corbels that run along beneath the cornice and up the rake of the main front gable of St. George's are simply applied details. At St. Martin's the roughhewn stonework and the heaviness of the round-

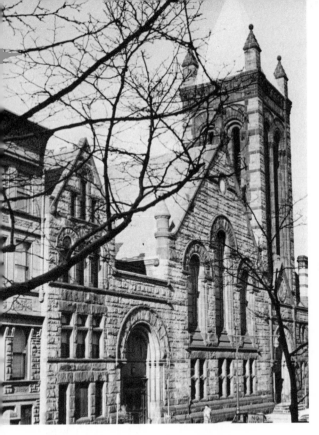

9. *St. Martin's Episcopal Church*
230-236 Lenox Avenue,
at 122nd Street
1887–88, William A. Potter

arched windows are expressive of a time when even churches had to be built like fortresses.

St. Martin's is notable for the unusual arrangement of its elements. The church itself, with its T-shaped plan, is entered from 122nd Street. A tall bell tower is tucked in next to the nave. Its carillon of forty-two bells, cast in Holland, is one of the finest in the country. The parish house with its more domestic scale extends along the full length of the Lenox Avenue frontage and makes a pleasing transition to the rows of neo-Romanesque houses that give the surrounding Mt. Morris Park Historic District so much of its character.

From its completion in 1888 this church has played an important role in the Episcopal Diocese of New York. After the original interior of the church was damaged by two fires, new mosaics, paintings, stained glass and church furniture were donated by loyal parishioners. As one church official remarked, "Some persons have wondered why such beautiful works of art should be placed in such a poor community." He goes on to say, "In all men there is the need to form, to find harmony and to make order; when these needs are not allowed expression man becomes defeated, dehumanized and confused. . . . This is why, then, that the people of this parish, this community, of whom many are poor in the material goods of life, nevertheless deserve the enrichment these great works of art afford."

Totally different from the massiveness of St. Martin's are the West End Collegiate Church and the Collegiate School, on West End Avenue at 77th Street. They were designed by Robert W. Gibson in his own romantic combination of Dutch and Flemish Renaissance elements. The result is delightfully fresh and flamboyant. The yellow-brown brick of the basic church structure is interrupted by a number of stone stringcourses. Its windows, its doorway, its corners, and, above all, the eighteen steps of its characteristic Dutch gable are all enriched with stonework, frequently alternating with stripes of brick. The steps of the main gable and the dormer windows that thrust out from the red tile roof erupt into a frenzy of terra-cotta brackets and pagodalike pinnacles. The choice of this style, with its reminiscences of the Low Countries, seems appropriate to a church with deep roots in Dutch New Amsterdam.

The Collegiate Church, an arm of the Reformed Dutch Church, was organized in New Amsterdam in 1628. The Collegiate School was started in 1638 and is the oldest private school in the United States.

10. West End Collegiate Church and Collegiate School
77th Street and West End Avenue
1892–93, Robert W. Gibson

The first schoolmaster, one Adam Roelantsen, arrived one cold March day in New Amsterdam from Holland, to found what was to be for many years the only school in the colony. His pay, when he got it, was poor and he was driven to moonlighting to make a living; the record shows that he brought suit against one of the burghers for payment due him for "washing defendant's linen."

When the British took over the colony in 1664, there was some muttering about the Dutch school insisting on teaching in the "Netherlandish tongue." Apparently these mutterings had little immediate effect, for it wasn't until 1773 that the school set out to find a bilingual master.

With the exception of the period when British forces occupied the city during the Revolution, the school has never suspended operations. In 1940, after more than three centuries of church control, the school became a separate entity, incorporated under the education laws of the state of New York.

Two churches within a few blocks of each other on Morningside Heights, St. Paul's Chapel at Columbia University and the Roman Catholic Church of Notre Dame, at Morningside Drive and 114th Street, make an interesting contrast in Eclecticism. The plans of the two buildings are almost identical, but their treatment is very different. Each is in the form of a Greek cross with a cylindrical drum rising over the square crossing. At St. Paul's, Howells & Stokes used Byzantine forms, combined in a very free way with a Florentine Renaissance gable and certain Romanesque elements. The fact that the chapel was built in a combination of brick and stone—which would have been appropriate to any one of the three styles—somehow pulls together this rather unlikely *ménage-à-trois*.

St. Paul's Chapel was built as a memorial to James Stokes and his wife, Caroline Phelps Stokes. The twenty-four windows in the drum of the dome bear the coats of arms of old New York families long associated with the history of the city and the university: Van Cortlandt, de Peyster, Beekman, Clinton and Rhinelander.

For Notre Dame, Cross & Cross went back for inspiration to austere prototypes of Napoleonic France. The garlanded band that runs around the entire church just beneath the entablature is very reminiscent of the Madeleine in Paris. Plans for a large dome over the crossing were unfortunately never realized. If they had been, the structure would have looked quite like Soufflot's Panthéon.

The interior of the Church of Notre Dame, which was built in honor of Our Lady of Lourdes, is notable for a well-lighted grotto in the apse that looks as though it had been hewn out of the rock of Morningside Cliff. That Cross & Cross too were not afraid to mix their styles is shown by the adjoining rectory, which, though designed in the neo–Italian Renaissance style, is perfectly compatible with the church.

11. St. Paul's Chapel,
Columbia University
Amsterdam Avenue between
116th and 117th Streets
1904–07, Howells & Stokes

12. Church of Notre Dame
Morningside Drive
and 114th Street
Apse: 1909–10, Dans & Otto
1914–28, Cross & Cross

The same free mixtures of styles is seen in some neo-Gothic structures: the Chapel of the Intercession with its adjoining vicarage, at Broadway and 155th Street, designed by Cram, Goodhue & Ferguson; and the Brown Memorial Tower, the James Tower and the James Memorial Chapel, at Union Theological Seminary on Broadway between 120th and 122nd Streets, all designed by Allen & Collins.

The 1911–14 Chapel of the Intercession at the edge of the uptown Trinity Church Cemetery, is a combination of late English Gothic elements with neo-Tudor details in the adjoining vicarage and cloisters. It is a particularly happy marriage, as the casual quality and intimacy of the Tudor details give a warm domestic character to the ancillary buildings that a consistent application of the Gothic style could hardly have achieved. The façade of the chapel itself is strongly suggestive of Goodhue's Church of St. Vincent Ferrer, built a few years later (one of the few instances in which this restlessly creative genius seems to have repeated himself). The chapel's high altar is inlaid with some fifteen hundred stones collected from the Holy Land and other places of early Christian worship. The ashes of Bertram Goodhue are contained in a marble memorial wall tomb in the north transept. The vault is deco-

13. *Chapel of the Intercession*
Broadway and 155th Street
1911–14,
   Cram, Goodhue & Ferguson

rated with reliefs of some of the famous New York buildings he designed.

The chapel is the successor of an earlier nearby Church of the Intercession, whose congregation was founded in 1846 as an independent Episcopal parish. In 1908 the church became a chapel of Trinity Parish, which had opened its uptown cemetery here in 1843, after its burial grounds in lower Manhattan became too crowded. In the cemetery—the largest in Manhattan—lie many important people, among them John James Audubon, Madame Jumel, and Clement Clarke Moore, whose body was moved here in 1889 from St. Luke's on Hudson Street. Every Christmas Eve a procession of children, each carrying a lighted lantern, makes a pilgrimage down the hill to Moore's grave. Here a giant wreath is reverently laid to honor the poet who gave us " 'Twas the night before Christmas . . ." Alfred Tennyson Dickens, son of Charles Dickens, is also buried here. The younger Dickens had come to the United States from his home in Australia in the fall of 1911 to make a lecture tour of the country and to take part in the one-hundredth-anniversary celebration of his father's birth, in February 1912, but on January 2 he was suddenly stricken with a heart attack in the Hotel Astor and died immediately. The funeral took place at Trinity Church, with a distinguished list of honorary pallbearers.

Union Theological Seminary's structures combine the same late English Gothic elements with the so-called Collegiate Gothic style. The neo-Gothic details of the James Memorial Chapel and the Brown and James Towers go well with the Collegiate style of the academic, administrative and residential halls around their quadrangles. Both the towers, with their delicate stone carving, are fine examples of the type of craftsmanship that could be obtained in this country before the First World War.

Union Theological Seminary was founded in 1836 as a graduate school for training in the Christian ministry. It has consistently been in the forefront of liberal causes—academic freedom, ecumenism and church involvement in social protest. Its faculty has included such liberal thinkers as Reinhold Niebuhr and Harry W. Ward, while its graduates have included Harry Emerson Fosdick, Ralph W. Sockman and Norman Thomas.

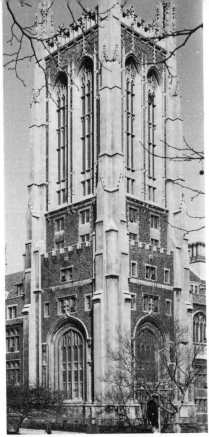

14. UNION THEOLOGICAL SEMINARY

a. Brown Memorial Tower
Broadway and 120th Street
1908–10, Allen & Collins

b. James Tower and
*   James Memorial Chapel*
Claremont Avenue,
*   120th to 122nd Street*
1908–10,
*   Allen & Collins*

Museums and Libraries

The West Side experienced a number of wide swings between high expectation that Central Park West and Riverside Drive would become as fashionable as Fifth Avenue and deep depression when it was found that they had not. The result of these speculative spasms was that between blocks of spotty development there remained great stretches of open land, spurned by the fashionable and wealthy, but ideal as sites for medical, cultural and educational institutions.

The American Museum of Natural History, which fills the equivalent of four blocks from 77th to 81st Streets between Central Park West and Columbus Avenue, is a counterpart to the Metropolitan Museum that balances it at the same latitude on the opposite side of Central Park. They were founded within a year of each other. Both soon became involved in the developing plan for Central Park. The American Museum opened in 1871 on the upper floors of Martin Thompson's old Arsenal, but started its own building three years later at its present site on Manhattan Square. This square had been intended by Olmsted and Vaux as an annex to Central Park, connected to it by a pedestrian bridge across Central Park West. There were also early plans for the development of a menagerie in Manhattan Square. With the abandonment of this idea, Olmsted was at least able to get the new museum to build outside the boundaries of Central Park itself. He was apparently less alert to the consequences of allowing extraneous encroachments onto his "Greensward" when, in 1876, the state legislature set aside, without protest, the site on which the Metropolitan was permitted to build. Olmsted was later to regret this lapse. In 1882 he stated, "Building can be brought within the business of the Park proper only as it will aid escape from buildings. Where building for other purposes begins, there the Park ends. The reservoirs and the museum are not a part of the Park proper: they are deductions from it."

Both institutions retained Calvert Vaux and Jacob Wrey Mould as their first architects. The earliest portion of the Natural History Museum, finished in 1877, is a five-story red-brick and stone structure in the Victorian Gothic style. It is now completely invisible, hidden in the midst of some seventeen interconnecting units that have been added all around it during the past hundred years. The earliest part that we see now is the central pavilion along 77th Street. Its long, low, seven-arch arcade in the Romanesque Revival style, begun in 1889, is flanked by heavy towers. Two sweeping stairways frame a central archway that once led to the carriage entrance on a lower level. The building is constructed of rough-faced pink granite and is crowned by a steep red slate roof. The architects, Cady, Berg & See, apparently met with a favorable response, because all the subsequent work they carried out for the museum continued to be in the same style—along the whole 77th Street block front and the wing that turns north on Columbus Avenue.

In 1922, when the museum was extended along Central Park West, Trowbridge & Livingston, while continuing the scale of Cady, Berg & See's work, and using the same pink granite, greatly simplified the design by eliminating details. This transition to something quite impersonal, and most especially the shift from rock-faced to smoothly dressed ashlar, enabled John Russell Pope to develop a great triumphal arch for the central unit on Central Park West (the Theodore Roosevelt Memorial) in the neo–American Classic style.

Trowbridge & Livingston actually carried through the execution of Pope's design and then continued the Central Park West façade northward with an approximate repetition of their rather impersonal wing which flanks it on the south. They also completed in 1935 a functional design for the Hayden Planetarium, with an expressive dome rising from the encircling Copernican Hall. Since that time, the museum has concentrated on internal reconstruction so that its extraordinarily rich collections can be shown to the public with all the advantages of modern display techniques.

These collections go back to the 1860s, when the country began to be stirred by the great advances that were being made in the natural sciences. Charles Darwin, Thomas Huxley and Charles Lyell, with their new views of the age of the earth and the theory of evolution, were opening up perspectives to the past that had hitherto not been dreamed of, even by exercising the wildest imagination. Pasteur and Lister, with their germ theory of disease and how antisepsis could prevent infection, were revealing a future in which man might control his environment. Under the energetic prodding of Albert Smith Blackmore, a young naturalist from Maine, a group of civic-minded New Yorkers, in 1869, secured a state charter for the American Mu-

15. AMERICAN MUSEUM OF NATURAL HISTORY

a. *77th Street Façade*
West 77th Street between Central Park West and Columbus Avenue
1889–1900, Cady, Berg & See

seum of Natural History and dug into their own pockets to purchase
the first exhibits—a collection of stuffed birds and mammals owned by
the German naturalist Prince Maximilian zu Wied-Neuwiebl.

From that modest beginning, the museum has grown to become
one of the world's greatest and most exciting showcases, where more
than 2,300 habitat groups, mounted specimens, dioramas and scientific
exhibits fill fifty-eight great halls. Here fascinating things can happen:
the Star of India, a 563-carat star sapphire, along with a 116-carat
sapphire and a 100-carat star ruby, were stolen from the fabulous gem
collection and later recovered; you can hear the weird sounds and
smell the hot odors of the rain forest of Peru; and you can see what the

b. ***Theodore Roosevelt Memorial***
Central Park West between 77th and 81st Streets
1931–35, John Russell Pope

sky looked like the night of Christ's birth. The museum is also a research laboratory, a school for advanced study, publisher of scientific material and sponsor for innumerable field explorations.

On the block below the Natural History Museum on Central Park West is the New-York Historical Society, a formally classical structure, built in two stages by two different architects. The central pavilion was erected between 1903 and 1908 by York & Sawyer, in the neo–American Classic style. Thirty years later the north and south wings were added by Walker & Gillette as flanking pavilions to the original central colonnade. The building as a whole has great unity, and it would be difficult to guess that it had been designed by two different

16. *New-York Historical Society*
  170 Central Park West, from 76th to 77th Street
  Center: 1903–08, York & Sawyer
  Wings: 1937–38, Walker & Gillette

firms a generation apart. The hard gray granite used for its construction imposed a limitation on ornamentation, and, except for the imposing entrance portals and the handsome cornice, the detailing is very severe.

The society was founded in 1804 and is the proud possessor of a uniquely valuable collection of books, manuscripts, maps, prints, paintings and decorative arts relating to American history and particularly to the history of New York State and New York City. Its collections include all of the known original water colors that John James Audubon painted for his monumental *Birds of America,* outstanding collections of Early American silver and glassware, and even equipment used by New York City's once important volunteer fire companies. It also has frequent special exhibits—not so long ago it displayed a rare and historic collection of New York speakeasy cards.

Much the most impressive example anywhere in the city of the neo–American Classic style is the Low Memorial Library, which McKim, Mead & White designed as the focus of the campus they planned for Columbia University when it moved to Morningside Heights in the 1890s. The library itself was inspired by the Pantheon in Rome, but with a Greek-cross plan and an octagonal transition to the flat, saucer-shaped dome. The imposing scale of the building is greatly enhanced by the way it has been placed at the top of a series of terraces and steps leading up from the level of 116th Street, which, in recent years, has been closed to traffic and converted into a tree-lined pedestrian mall. There are no buildings in New York City—and few anywhere—that have an approach that is so heroic and at the same time so gracious. The library was conceived as an integral part of the over-all campus plan, which opens out to the left and right as the library is approached. The flanking buildings, fountains, urns, balustrades and ornamental lighting standards are essential components of the design. They are like the successive wings of a classical stage set

17. *Low Memorial Library, Columbia University*
  116th Street between Amsterdam Avenue and Broadway
  1895–97, McKim, Mead & White

which gradually lead the eye inward and upward toward a central climax. This is urban planning on the grand scale. The relationship of one building to another and the definition of the open spaces between them are as carefully composed as the façades of the buildings themselves. It is New York City's major inheritance from the "City Beautiful" ideals that were inspired by Chicago's Columbian Exposition of 1893.

It was named in honor of his father by Seth Low, a former mayor of Brooklyn, who was the university's president from 1889 to 1901 and subsequently led an anti-Tammany reform movement in the city. The mayoral campaign of 1897 was one of greatest importance, because in January 1898 the creation of Greater New York was to take place. Adding the four boroughs to Manhattan would produce a patronage plum for the mayor second only to that of the President of the United States. Low was persuaded by the reform groups to run, but his campaign apparently did not get off the ground; the New York *Daily Tribune* said he was "designed by nature as a first-rate Sunday school politician." He ran second to the Tammany candidate, but graft and corruption became so flagrant that he won handily four years later.

Not all the West Side's public buildings are on so grand a scale as these three examples. Among the sixty-five branch public libraries which Andrew Carnegie financed during the first decade of the twentieth century are some fine examples of how an Italian Renaissance palazzo could be adapted to a relatively small edifice. These buildings were generally on side streets and had to conform to their residential surroundings. They provide good illustrations of how the scale of public and domestic architecture can be sensitively juxtaposed.

Two fine examples are the Hamilton Grange Branch Library (so called because of its proximity to Hamilton's country home) on West 145th Street and the rather simpler West 115th Street Branch, both designed by McKim, Mead & White. The Hamilton Grange Branch maintains the three horizontal divisions of the typical Florentine palazzo with successive gradations in rustication and simplification of detail from the bottom to the top of the building. There is also a skillfully managed shift from what is apparently a five-bay building on the top story to a three-bay one on the lower story, achieved by the subtle suppression of the two intermediate windows. The rich quality

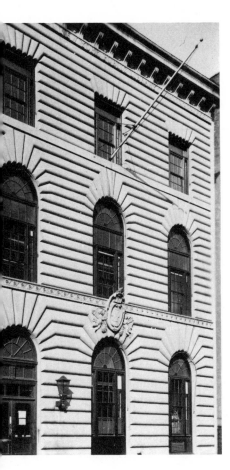

18. *Hamilton Grange Branch,*
New York Public Library
503-505 West 145th Street
1905–06, McKim, Mead & White

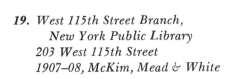

19. *West 115th Street Branch,*
New York Public Library
203 West 115th Street
1907–08, McKim, Mead & White

of both the Hamilton Grange and the West 115th Street Branches depends almost completely on the beautiful handling of the rusticated masonry. Decorative details are confined to the crowning cornices.

Both buildings have been renovated to meet modern library needs without jeopardy to their distinguished façades. At the time the Hamilton Grange Branch alterations were being considered, there were those who felt that the building should be demolished in the interest of efficiency and economy. They pointed out that the New York Public Library had already renovated the McKim, Mead & White Landmark branch on West 115th Street. The Landmarks Preservation Commission won this argument by pointing out that such reasoning was the equivalent of the old joke "Don't give him a book; he already has one."

An Aqueduct and a Water Tower

One of the great engineering triumphs of the nineteenth century was the creation of an adequate water supply for the City of New York. From the days of the Dutch, the city had been plagued by its lack. At the time of the Revolution the Tea Water Pump at the corner of Pearl Street and Park Row was the only source of unpolluted water in town, and frequently that ran only in a trickle. Vendors loaded casks of the water onto their carts and sold it at outrageous prices. Many times they substituted brackish water from the East River. Meanwhile, the city suffered from recurring and disastrous fires and had no effective way of fighting them. The polluted wells contributed to frequent epidemics of cholera and typhoid. A Swedish traveler in 1752, after having commented that he "found it extremely pleasant to walk in the town, for it seemed like a garden," added:

> There is no good water to be met with in the town itself; but at a little distance there is a large spring of good water, which the inhabitants take for their tea, and for the uses of the kitchen. Those, however, who are less delicate on this point make use of the water from the wells in town, though it is very bad. This want of good water lies heavy upon the horses of the strangers that come to this place for they do not like to drink the brackish water from the wells.

During the early 1800s many proposals were launched for providing the city with good and sufficient water: sinking artesian wells into Manhattan's bedrock; damming the Hudson to separate the salt from the fresh water; or using the Bronx, Croton or Passaic River as a source of supply. Croton was eventually chosen, and work was started in 1837 on an engineering scheme devised by Colonel De Witt Clinton, Jr. The plan included a dam across the Croton River (forty miles north of 42nd Street) to form a 400-acre reservoir; an aqueduct forty-one miles long, including sixteen tunnels; a 1,500-foot aqueduct bridge across the Harlem River; a receiving reservoir in Central Park; and a distributing reservoir at 42nd Street and Fifth Avenue where the New York Public Library now stands.

Five years later, on October 14, 1842, to the accompaniment of fireworks, parades and other jubilations, the first pure Croton water began to flow into the mains, hydrants and taps of the city. There was just one hitch: the high aqueduct across the Harlem River was not yet completed. Not to be daunted, the engineers had thrown up cofferdams in the river on which the water mains were temporarily installed. Work on the permanent bridge proceeded at a leisurely pace; it was finally completed in 1848.

Only three visible remnants of this great feat have survived within the city limits—the overdue High Bridge and aqueduct over the Harlem River that brought the water from The Bronx to Manhattan at 170th Street, the Water Tower in Highbridge Park, and the receiving reservoir of which Olmsted complained in Central Park.

The design of the system to bring Croton water across the Harlem River was the subject of long years of controversy: whether an inverted syphon resting on a low bridge would be cheaper and more effective than a high aqueduct bridge. Finally, High Bridge, as it has been known ever since and as designed by an engineer, John B. Jervis, was approved. Its elegant masonry construction and the severity of its lines constitute an architectural as well as an engineering triumph.

High Bridge has a strong resemblance to the remains of the lofty aqueducts that still dot the Roman Campagna. The problems faced in the first century A.D. by Roman engineers were essentially the same as those confronting New York engineers eighteen hundred years later. Their straightforward solutions, in terms of masonry construction,

20. *High Bridge and Water Tower in 1895*
   Bridge: from Highbridge Park at West 174th Street in Manhattan to
      West 170th Street in The Bronx
   1838–48, John B. Jervis
   Altered: 1923
   Tower: Highbridge Park opposite West 173rd Street and Amsterdam
      Avenue
   1872, attributed to John B. Jervis

were practically identical. In 1923 the Navy cut out some of the center spans of High Bridge and substituted a steel arch to provide a wider channel in the center of the river for greater navigability. This alteration, fortunately, did not greatly damage the effect of the rhythmic sweep of the original fifteen arches that spanned the river a hundred feet above the high-water level.

Originally there was a pedestrian walk across High Bridge, which has been closed to the public for many years because of vandalism and the problems of proper policing. The Parks Department, however, has recently embarked on a renovation program. When the walkway is reopened it will again afford a spectacular view, gentle breezes and modest exercise for those who wish to cross the river on foot or by bicycle.

Closely connected with the Croton system is the Water Tower in Highbridge Park which was built in 1872 from a design attributed to the same John B. Jervis. This is a vigorous neo-Romanesque structure that originally supported a 47,000-gallon tank. Water was pumped up to it in order to provide adequate gravity pressure to supply the upper parts of the city—in fact, as far down as Murray Hill. Similar water towers were later built in other parts of the city, but High Bridge Tower, the first, is the only one that remains, although it has not been used as a water tower for many years. In 1958 the Altman Foundation donated a carillon which now plays from the belfry of the tower as a memorial to Benjamin Altman and to the great engineering skill that established the city's first satisfactory water supply. This handsome campanile is an outstanding Landmark in upper Manhattan.

Historic Districts

ST. NICHOLAS

Far and away the best examples of row houses on the West Side and one of the best examples of planning for good urban living anywhere in the city are to be found in the St. Nicholas Historic District. The four rows, between Seventh and Eighth Avenues on both sides of 138th and 139th Streets, were planned as a whole and built in 1891 by David H. King. He employed three of the city's most distinguished architectural firms to design the rows. Each block front has its own individuality, and yet they get along together quite harmoniously. Each is designed as a single composition. The ends of each row are emphasized by such devices as a forward break in the building plane or by special enrichment of the terminal houses. This is the sort of "composed" block front that can now only be guessed at in Henderson Place, where subsequent alterations have seriously altered the original design. Except for minor details, the 1891 composition remains almost intact in the St. Nicholas Historic District.

The south side of 138th Street was designed by James Brown Lord in the neo-Georgian style in red brick with brownstone trim. The effect is restrained and in good taste. By pairing the entrances of adjoining houses to share a common stoop, Lord achieved a more rest-

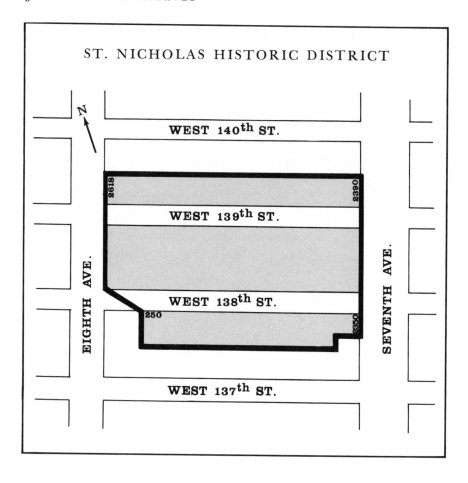

ful rhythm than the usual staccato of isolated stoops. The use of light wrought-iron railings, instead of heavy balusters, still further emphasizes the sense of continuity.

Quite different in spirit, though still neo-Georgian, are the houses on the north side of 138th Street and the south side of 139th Street which were designed by Bruce Price and Clarence S. Luce. They are carried out in buff-colored brick and enriched with a profusion of limestone and terra-cotta trim and decoration. Their splayed lintels, elongated keystones, garlands, wreaths, inset panels, quoins, balconies and balustrades give an over-all effect of elegance.

In sober contrast, on the north side of 139th Street, is a magnificent row of McKim, Mead & White houses of dark-brown brick in the neo–Italian Renaissance style. The entire row has a rusticated-brown-stone first story, and the houses are entered directly at the sidewalk level in the English manner. On the second story, a central window, emphasized by a heavy enframement, opens onto a balcony supported on stone brackets. Above it a round medallion is set into the brick-work, much in the Florentine manner.

The four rows of houses share a feature that is very rare in New York: a central service alley runs down the middle of the block and is entered from the avenue ends and at various points in the middle of the long frontages. These entrances are closed with ornamental iron gates. This feature, which is quite common in Baltimore, Boston's Back Bay and Chicago, never caught on in New York, perhaps because property values were too high or perhaps because the east–west streets of Manhattan are close together and residents preferred rear yards or gardens to alleys. However, the alleys serve the very useful and aesthetic purpose of concealing garbage cans and service deliveries.

The exceptional quality of the entire development was immediately recognized. Such an astute contemporary critic as Montgomery Schuyler commended King for "the employment of three architects of

North Side of West 138th Street   St. Nicholas Historic District
1891
Bruce Price and Clarence S. Luce

the first rank to compete with each other, not on paper, but in actual brick and mortar . . . in the most extensive building operation that has been carried out on the West Side." He added (prophetically) that "they have supplied but a small fraction of the demand that exists for such dwellings."

Even though these blocks were put up by a commercial builder for sale to individual buyers, the interests of all the property owners were protected by stipulations against building additions or alterations. In a way, this was a precursor of the Landmarks Preservation Law, and, despite subsequent economic difficulties, the integrity of the original design has survived.

The houses were originally intended for well-to-do buyers who were expected to flock north and make Harlem the city's most elegant neighborhood. But they were built in a period of overoptimistic speculation. The panic of 1904 forced owners to sell, often at a great loss. Many of the houses, in fact, had never been occupied. Black realtors persuaded Harlem property owners to sell or rent their houses to Negroes who were seeking better housing. By 1919 the King houses became available to blacks.

Many of the most distinguished professional and civic leaders of the community have lived in the St. Nicholas Historic District, including Abram Hill, who was one of the collaborators in the play *Anna Lucasta* and a founder of the American Negro Theater. He wrote a play about the Historic District and called it *On Striver's Row*. This name has been a popular designation for the area ever since.

At the initiative of the Landmarks Preservation Commission the City has recently appropriated funds for research and planning to insure that Striver's Row be preserved intact as part of the proposed St. Nicholas Park Urban Renewal plan. The plan will provide detailed recommendations for all exterior architectural renovations. Their execution will be carried out in cooperation with the 160 owner-residents. Of special concern is the treatment of the unique service alleys to provide an attractive and practical solution to the parking problem.

JUMEL TERRACE

Jumel Terrace Historic District was not as self-consciously planned as St. Nicholas, and yet the general effect is quite homogeneous, pri-

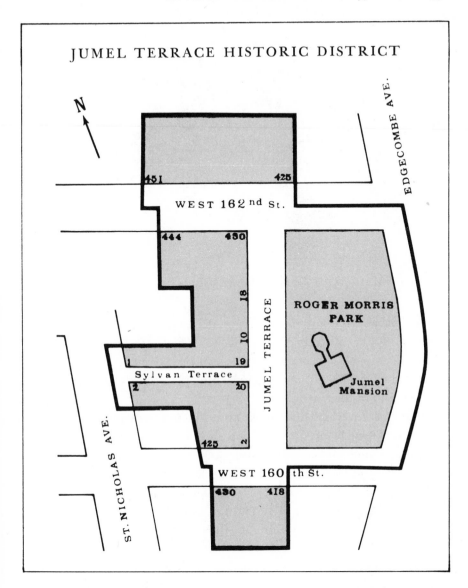

JUMEL TERRACE HISTORIC DISTRICT

N

EDGECOMBE AVE.

451   425

WEST 162nd St.

444   430

ROGER MORRIS
PARK

18

JUMEL TERRACE

10

Sylvan Terrace

1   19

Jumel
Mansion

2   20

ST. NICHOLAS AVE.

425   2

WEST 160th St.

430   418

marily because of the economic conditions under which its houses were built and the relatively short period of time during which the entire development took place.

After the death of Madame Jumel in 1865 and after sixteen years of litigation among her heirs, the extensive Morris-Jumel estate was finally sold off except for a two-block park which surrounds the mansion. The little wooden houses that still face one another across the dead-end Sylvan Terrace were constructed in 1882. This little

Sylvan Terrace   Jumel Terrace Historic District

street follows roughly the carriage drive that once led from the
mansion to the old Kingsbridge Road, which at this point is now
called St. Nicholas Avenue. The houses on Sylvan Terrace have all
been changed beyond recognition, but plans are currently under
discussion to restore them.

The real development started around 1890 with the brick houses
on 160th Street, facing north toward Jumel Terrace. They are characteristic of the Queen Anne style and are almost exactly contemporary with the Henderson Place houses. They are romantic and full
of interesting detail. About five years later some much more severe
neo-Romanesque houses, of limestone, were built along Jumel Terrace and on 162nd Street, and in 1902 some neo–American Classic
houses were constructed along 162nd Street. The fact that all of these
were built within a dozen years makes the difference in style of little
significance. They were substantial middle-class houses and still are.
They are well maintained and give a dignified background to the great
mansion they surround.

MOUNT MORRIS PARK

The influence of a park or open space on the formation of what is now
an Historic District is seen in the fine houses that grew up around

Washington Square, Gramercy Park and the grounds of the Morris-Jumel Mansion. The same beneficial effect of an open space on the development of its surroundings may be traced in the history of the Mount Morris Park Historic District. Only this time it was the laws of nature rather than of economics that shaped the future of the area.

After the adoption of the Commissioners' Plan for Manhattan in 1811 (which, incidentally, went only as far as 155th Street), the city engineers proceeded to open up street after street, avenue after avenue, along the inexorably straight lines that had been laid out. Such was the situation when Fifth Avenue was being pushed northward in the 1830s. Squarely in the line of its advance, between what are now 120th and 124th Streets, arose a seventy-foot-high rocky eminence, which, as the Common Council put it on June 22, 1835, was "unsuitable for building lots. However, there is the possibility of converting it into a place of ornament and beauty. No public place has as yet been laid out in Harlem."

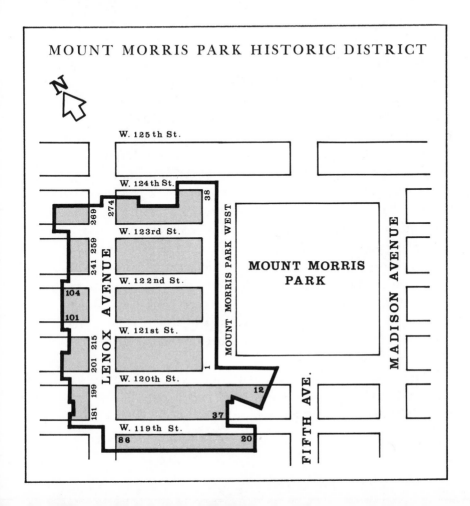

Mount Morris Park, now Marcus Garvey Memorial Park, was duly acquired by the City, but the expected development did not take place for a long time. Despite its original name of Snake Hill (Slang Burg to the Dutch), the area proved to be popular for country walks and picnics. The nearby racetrack for trotting horses on the flat land adjoining the Harlem River was undoubtedly an added attraction.

With the coming of the Third Avenue El in 1878, Harlem became a suburb of the city. Speculative building started about the same time and continued into the early twentieth century under the stimulating prospects of an East Side subway line. William B. Astor, Oscar Hammerstein and Henry Morgenthau, among others, began to buy up lots and to build elegant row houses for sale. Fortunately, the land around Mount Morris Park had been restricted by earlier deeds to residential development, and early builders chose such distinguished architects as Arnold Brunner, Hugo Lamb, George F. Pelham, William A. Potter, J. R. Thomas and James E. Ware to design their houses and the churches that soon sprang up among them. In 1903, the *New York Herald* compared the houses along Mount Morris Park West favorably with the mansions along Fifth Avenue.

The same high standards spread westward through the abutting side streets and along the wide and sunny expanse of Lenox Avenue. Only a few, and relatively low, apartment houses were built here, so the spires of the many churches still dominate the skyline.

Most of the Mount Morris Park Historic District lies within the proposed Milbank-Frawley Urban Renewal Project being carried out by the City's Housing and Development Administration, which supported the community's request for designation. It was recognized that Historic District designation can have a strong stabilizing influence on a community and would give the whole redevelopment area a more interesting and varied pattern. After designation, the New York State Narcotics Addiction Control Commission started to demolish eight houses on Mount Morris Park West between 120th and 121st Streets in order to build a new treatment center for drug addicts. The Landmarks Preservation Commission, supported by local residents, opposed this action and secured a court injunction barring the State from destroying the buildings.

The architecture of the district ranges through many styles, including neo-Grec, Queen Anne, neo-Romanesque, Victorian Gothic, neo–Italian Renaissance and neo–American Classic. There are rows of

Mount Morris Park

neo-Grec townhouses along 119th and 123rd Streets west of Mount Morris Park. A notable example of the Queen Anne style is No. 42 West 119th Street, and the neo-Romanesque finds its finest exemplification in St. Martin's Episcopal Church, a Landmark in its own right, as well as the houses to the south of it along Lenox Avenue. Some later examples of this style are at Mount Morris Park West between 121st and 122nd Streets. A fine example of late Victorian Gothic, with its tall slender spire, is the Ephesus Seventh Day Adventist Church at the northwest corner of 123rd Street and Lenox Avenue. Like nearby St. Andrew's, it lacks the polychromy so characteristic of the earlier phases of this style.

A prime example of the neo-American Classic style is the Mount Olivet Baptist Church, originally built as a synagogue, at the northwest corner of Lenox Avenue and 120th Street. The neo–Italian Renaissance also found considerable favor at this time and is best exemplified by the handsome residence (now a church) built for John Dwight at the northwest corner of Mount Morris Park West and 123rd Street, and a row of bowed-front town houses on the south side of 120th Street. The Mount Morris Presbyterian Church, at the southwest corner of Mount Morris Park West and 122nd Street, is most striking and unusual, with its Byzantine dome and arches.

CENTRAL PARK WEST – 76TH STREET HISTORIC DISTRICT

This T-shaped district covers most of the buildings on West 76th Street between Central Park West and Columbus Avenue as well as two blockfronts of Central Park West between 75th and 77th Streets and one apartment house on the south side of West 77th Street. With the exception of a church, another apartment house and a museum (the New-York Historical Society, an individually designed Landmark), the district comprises some forty individual residences of varying architectural styles but all representative of late-nineteenth-century Eclecticism. Although the styles range through neo–Italian Renaissance, neo-Grec, Romanesque Revival and Beaux-Arts, the fact that construction took place between 1887 and 1889 and that the owners agreed to compatible setbacks, scale and general design character, give West 76th Street a singular sense of being all of a piece. It is a quiet, tree-lined oasis of great dignity and appeal even though many of the original metal roof cornices, fine wrought-iron door grilles and elegant stoops have gone. The entrance to the street from Central Park West is impressively flanked by the New-York Historical Society on the north and the Church of the Divine Paternity on the south.

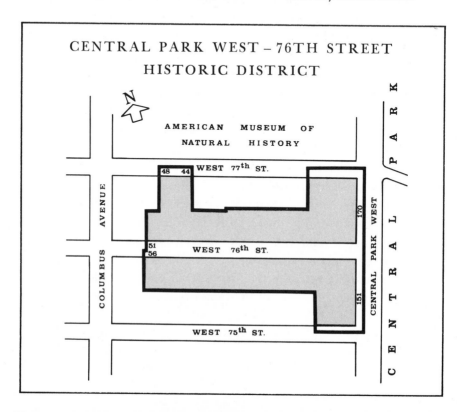

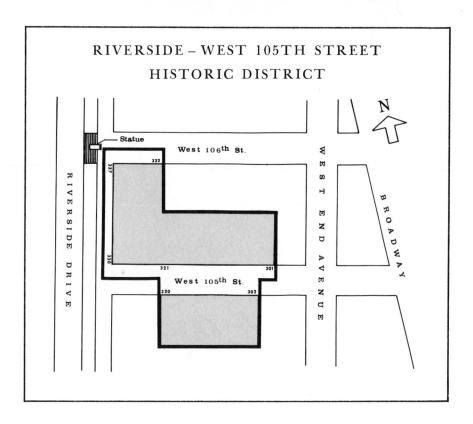

RIVERSIDE – WEST 105TH STREET
HISTORIC DISTRICT

This district extends along part of West 105th Street between West End Avenue and Riverside Drive, and along Riverside Drive to 106th Street. All of the residences here were built within three years (1899–1902) and under the terms of restrictive covenants which bound the owners to restrict the "character of the improvements to be placed upon said lots . . . so that the buildings . . . shall be of suitable character and such as are a benefit to the neighborhood." This has resulted in a remarkable stylistic unity.

The magnificent view of the Hudson River and Riverside Park give the area a suggestion of the openness and scale of Paris, a feeling that is intensified by the French Beaux-Arts style that marks all the houses. Those along 105th Street are all well preserved, of the same height and set back an equal distance from the building line; their billowing bay windows create a gentle rhythm as the street slopes toward the terrace above the drive.

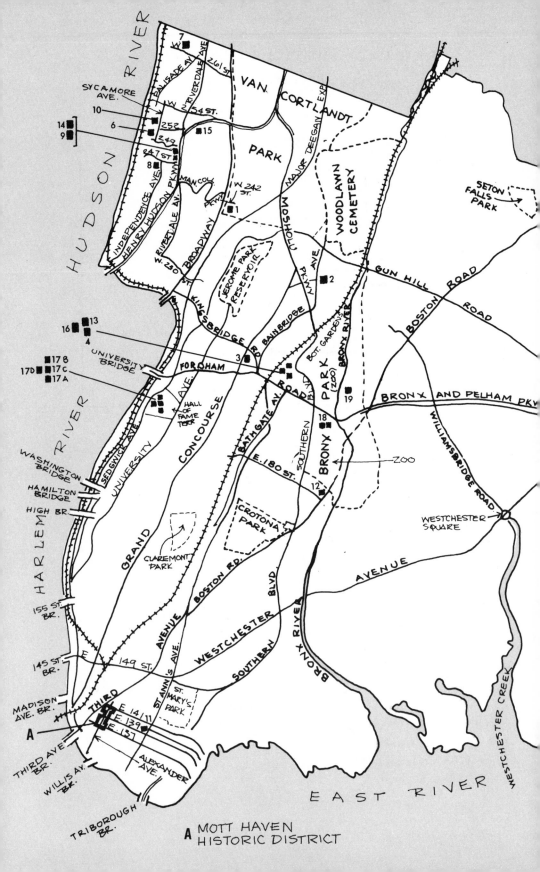

MOTT HAVEN
HISTORIC DISTRICT

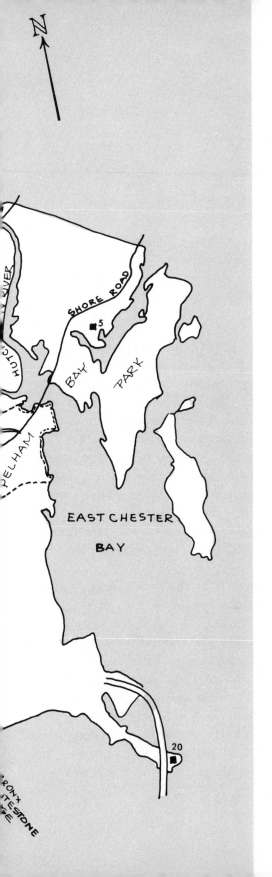

THE BRONX

CHAPTER SEVEN

THE BRONX

THE BOROUGH OF The Bronx is the only part of New York City that is geographically part of the United States mainland. All the rest of it is islands—fifty of them. And even The Bronx is surrounded on three sides by water: the Hudson River on the west; Spuyten Duyvil, the Harlem River and the East River on the south; and Long Island Sound on the east. Originally it was all part of Westchester County, but, beginning in 1874, bits and pieces were ceded to New York City until in 1898 Greater New York was created. It is also the only borough whose name is preceded by "The"—The Bronx, as though there could be another! The custom seems to have survived from the days when the whole area was known as "The Broncks' Farm." "The" endured even though "Farm" and the family for which it was named have vanished.

The borough was settled very early by the Dutch. A large stretch of land along the Harlem River was bought in 1639 by the Dutch West India Company from the Indians. A couple of years later a Danish Lutheran, Jonas Bronck, bought about five hundred acres between the Harlem River and what was to be named the Bronx River in his honor. He had moved from his native Scandinavia to Holland, where he married a Dutch woman, produced a family and prospered in general. But the lure of the New World beckoned, so he bundled up his brood and set sail. He settled in the borough that bears his name. It was said that Bronck paid two kettles, two guns, two adzes, two cows, one barrel of cider, six pieces of silver and two shirts for his property. This probably amounted to more than Peter Minuit paid for Manhattan, but was still a bargain.

The next settler was the doughty Mrs. Anne Hutchinson (history is very cloudy about her husband), who had migrated to Boston from her native England. But her liberal religious views and outspoken criticism did not sit well with the Puritans of New England, and she was declared "unfit for society" and banished. She settled, with a large family of children and a small band of followers, in the Pelham's Neck area in The Bronx. Not long after, the whole settlement, with the exception of one of Anne's small granddaughters, was wiped out in an Indian raid. The only reminders of this courageous lady, who was described by a contemporary as "a masterpiece of wit and wisdom," are the river and its parkway named after her.

The Anabaptist John Throckmorton, or Throgmorton, was the next. He brought thirty families to settle on a stringlike piece of land that was named Throgmorton's Neck—later shortened to Throg's Neck. However, the Indians also attacked this little settlement, and most of the colony fled to the safety of the fort in New Amsterdam.

Other refugees from the British colonies came to The Bronx, but, between the Indians and the antagonistic Dutch, they had a difficult time until the British occupation in 1664. Then the area was divided into large manors and country estates, the Van Cortlandt and Morris families between them owning much of it.

Physically, The Bronx is split by three prominent ridges that run through the borough from north to south. The westernmost is on the bank of the Hudson and is crowned by the Riverdale community. Broadway runs up the valley to the east of this. The crest of the second ridge is followed by the Grand Concourse. And the third, which is lower, includes Crotona Park, the Bronx Zoo, the Botanical Garden and the campus of Fordham University. To the southeast The Bronx gradually shelves off into a flat plain, salt marshes and a series of islands along the shore of Long Island Sound.

There is a geographical anomaly existing between Manhattan and The Bronx that is the cause of a chronic feud between their respective borough presidents. Just north of the Harlem River, after it turns west at the tip of Manhattan to reach the Hudson, there is a section called Marble Hill, otherwise known as No Man's Land. Originally, the Harlem River made a curving swoop around this fifty-odd-acre site to join Spuyten Duyvil Creek before it debouched into the Hudson. Using the river as its boundary line, Marble Hill was naturally attached to Manhattan. But in 1895 the channel of the Harlem was straightened to facilitate navigation, the old bed of the river was filled in and Marble Hill became just as firmly attached to The Bronx. It has never been redistricted, however, and today it is technically part of Manhattan although geographically in the southern Bronx. Residents pay taxes to Manhattan and look to Manhattan for police protection. A high-rise building, Marble Hill Houses, lies directly on the borough border, which runs along the bed of the old waterway. The telephone company finally gave in and listed all Marble Hill subscribers in both the Manhattan and Bronx directories. The status of Marble Hill has for years been a source of political discord in the area, the residents of the public housing being in favor of attachment to The Bronx, while the dwindling number of private homeowners on the "hill" keep their loyalty to Manhattan.

The Bronx is blessed with an impressive chain of parks; Van Cortlandt, Pelham Bay and Bronx Parks are among the largest. A grand plan for the New York City park system was devised by Frederick Law Olmsted, who fathered Central Park. He envisioned a whole series of green spaces, "parks," all through the city, linked together by tree-lined avenues, "parkways." The Bronx parks are linked together. It was also planned that they should be linked to the Manhattan parks by way of the Grand Concourse. Prospect Park in Brooklyn was to have been linked to Coney Island and also to Central Park by a tree-lined drive north to Ravenswood (where Queens Plaza is today) and across the East River to a wide and spacious 59th Street that was to have run past Central Park to the Hudson.

Henry Hope Reed, the great authority on Central Park, calls this idea "one of the rare visions in New York's city planning." Considering the constant competition of rising land values, it is almost miraculous that so much of the plan as originally conceived actually exists today.

The good fortune of The Bronx is due to the fact that its big development came late and came suddenly. A firm commitment to its great system of parks and parkways had already been made long before the overwhelming wave of speculative building arrived.

The Bronx grew slowly. A few little settlements developed along the old forest trail which became the Boston Post Road, and some industry sprang up beside the Harlem River after Jordan Mott opened his famous iron works in 1828. In time the towns of Mott Haven, Morrisania (settled in the area of Gouverneur Morris' estate), West Farms, Eastchester and Pelham grew up along the Boston Post Road. When the New York and New Haven opened its service in 1842 there was a rush of commuter settlers along the railroad. In the west, the Albany Post Road—built in 1669 and perhaps the oldest road in this part of the county—which ran north from Kingsbridge, where Broadway now crosses West 230th Street, opened up the area along the Hudson. But The Bronx remained essentially rural until late in the nineteenth century.

During the Civil War and the period following, there was a small development of comfortable row houses along Alexander Avenue in Mott Haven. At about the same time a quite different community was growing up in Riverdale; a few pioneers had taken early advantage of the beautiful views over the Hudson and the physical isolation of the locality. When the riverboats and the railroad made it more accessible, Riverdale became a favorite country retreat for wealthy New Yorkers. When the Third Avenue El reached 169th Street in 1888, The Bronx was opened up to a flood of new arrivals, which peaked around the turn of the century.

The ethnic composition of the million and a half present population of the borough has, in its brief and intense history, changed frequently as different minorities fled the old slums of Manhattan. First came the Irish and the Germans, then the Italians and the Jews. Today it is the blacks and the Puerto Ricans who are crowding into the southern part of the borough, again refugees from the ghettos of Manhattan and Brooklyn.

As a result of its unusual history, the forty-two square miles of The Bronx contain some of the city's wealthiest and some of its poorest districts. Riverdale can still boast of having New York's most spectacular sites and splendid private mansions; in fact, they are so elegant that the residents resort to all sorts of stratagems to avoid using "The Bronx" in their address. Morrisania, once the estate of the proud Morris family, and Hunts Point, once a fashionable country section with a fine view of the East River and its islands, now make up a central core of poverty and decay.

Between these extremes there are large areas occupied by middle-class families. They live primarily in the old-fashioned commodious apartment houses dating from the early 1900s that line the Grand Concourse and surrounding areas.

Stanley Milgram, of the City University of New York, made a study, *A Psychological Map of New York City,* which seeks to find what mental image New Yorkers have of their city. He flashed a picture of Gun Hill Road in The Bronx before his test audience. Among the responses was: "When I look at a neighborhood like this I think of baby carriages and *Reader's Digest.*" Another, more succinct: "Ick." However, these substantial apartment buildings were built to last and so far have escaped the demolition crews. There are even indications that their spaciousness and relatively low rents are attracting newcomers and even some who once left The Bronx for more elegant areas. Who knows, maybe baby carriages and *Reader's Digest* will become fashionable again.

Current efforts to improve living conditions for the most underprivileged and to meet the city's insatiable demand for more and more housing have resulted in another aspect of The Bronx. Acres of slums and every available inch of filled land have been covered with huge housing developments.

Manors, Mansions and a Cottage

The freestanding Landmark houses and mansions still remaining in The Bronx provide excellent illustrations of all the important styles of architecture that captured American taste from the pre-Revolutionary Colonial period down to the Civil War.

The earliest are two notable Georgian houses, the Van Cortlandt Mansion and the Valentine-Varian House. The Van Cortlandt Mansion, dating from 1748, is a handsome manor house, almost square, built of rough fieldstone with fine brick trim around the windows. The stone was quarried and dressed locally. The bricks, also made locally, form a neat transition between the irregular shapes of the stonework and the multipaned double-hung windows. The carved heads which form the keystones over the principal windows seem like a touch of unexpected Dutch whimsy in this otherwise very staid and

1. *Van Cortlandt Mansion*
East of Broadway at 242nd Street, in Van Cortlandt Park
1748

English-looking house. Such a mixture was not inappropriate for the home of a family which, by this date, was as much one nationality as the other.

The original Van Cortlandt, named Oloff, arrived in New Amsterdam in 1638 and founded a dynasty which at one time owned almost two hundred square miles of land. The Van Cortlandts were traders, merchants and shipbuilders, and they married into such families as the Schuylers, the Philipses and the Livingstons, thus doubling their wealth and influence.

Oloff's son Stephanus was appointed mayor in 1677, the first native-born American to hold that post. At the end of the Revolution, another descendant, an ardent Loyalist, escaped with his brother-in-law from the "Tory hunters" in the city. They were given refuge in a cowshed by a conscientious Dutch farmer who always walked backward when he brought them meals so that he could truthfully say he had never seen the fugitives. Still another descendant, Philip, was a general in the Continental Army, a member of Congress and a close friend of Lafayette, whom he accompanied on his triumphal tour of the United States in 1824. Van Cortlandt, who bore a striking resemblance to the French patriot, on more than one occasion took the place of the weary Frenchman in receiving lines to shake the hands of an enthusiastic and grateful populace.

Oloff's grandson Frederick built the family mansion only a couple of years before his death. Members of the family lived in the house continuously until 1889, when the building and the surrounding grounds were donated to the City as a public park. The National Society of Colonial Dames of the State of New York now has custody of the building, which it maintains as a museum.

In the Van Cortlandt burial ground slightly to the north of the house is a vault in which it is claimed the records of the City of New York were hidden during the Revolution. It was around the Van Cortlandt house that Washington kept campfires burning for several days to fool the British while he was withdrawing his troops across the Hudson.

Far less pretentious than the Van Cortlandt Mansion is the two-story Valentine-Varian House, also of rough-dressed fieldstone but

2. *Valentine-Varian House　3266 Bainbridge Avenue, at East 208th Street*
　c. 1775
　Moved 1965

without the refinement of the brick trim around the windows. It dates somewhat later. The land was acquired in 1758 from the Dutch Reformed Church by Isaac Valentine, a prosperous farmer. During the Revolution, Valentine and his family fled their property, which was the scene of several skirmishes and a memorable battle between British and American troops. In 1791 some 260 acres were sold to Isaac Varian, a prosperous farmer, for £1,500. The Varian family contributed a mayor and an alderman to the city administration.

The Valentine-Varian place was threatened in 1964 when the owner decided to put up an apartment building on the site. Fortunately, the will under which he had taken title to the property provided that the land could be sold but the house must be preserved. After agonizing months of delay, during which the weather, time and vandals took their toll of the old house, in 1965 it was moved with great care across the street onto city park land. It has been restored and is now the headquarters of the Bronx County Historical Society, a museum of artifacts, maps, documents and memorabilia tracing the history of The Bronx since Indian times.

The Van Cortlandt and Valentine-Varian houses and the Dyckman farmhouse, just across the river in Manhattan, provide a graphic cross section of the economic and social life of the second half of the eighteenth century. The elegant Van Cortlandt Mansion, home of prosperous large landowners, lacked no refinement or nicety to make life as gracious as possible; the Varian House, home of a middle-class, salt-of-the-earth family, provided a more modest way of living but still with a certain amount of comfort, even a luxury or two; and, finally, at the Dyckman House the hard-working farmer and his family had to make every necessity on the premises.

The little Poe Cottage on the Grand Concourse, which dates from about 1812, is typical of the small frame vernacular farmhouses that formerly dotted The Bronx countryside. Its importance as a Landmark is its connection with Edgar Allan Poe, who lived here from 1846 to 1848. Poe, who had married the beautiful Virginia Clemm in 1837, when she was not quite fourteen years old, lived in various places in Manhattan before coming to the little village of Fordham. Poverty and his own dour temperament, which led him to liquor and perhaps to drugs, had dogged him, even though he had had several major successes with such works as "The Raven" and "The Murders in the

3. *Poe Cottage   2640 Grand Concourse at Kingsbridge Road, in Poe Park*
   (*originally on Kingsbridge Road near Fordham Road*)
   c. 1812
   Moved 1913

Rue Morgue." His great tragedy occurred when Virginia contracted tuberculosis.

In 1846 the couple moved to this little farmhouse—then located on Kingsbridge Road near Fordham Road—in the vain hope that the open country and the clear air would restore Virginia's health. While Poe watched his young wife slowly die, he completed "Ulalume" and one of his finest poems, "The Bells," and probably started "Annabel Lee."

The City of New York acquired the house in 1913 and moved it to its present location in a city park. The building is now maintained as a Poe museum.

Rose Hill, now the administration building of Fordham University, and the Bartow-Pell Mansion, in the present Pelham Bay Park, were both built in the latter part of the 1830s in the Greek Revival style. They continue the Bronx tradition of random-fieldstone ashlar, though Rose Hill is rougher in texture than the Bartow-Pell house, whose stonework follows regular horizontal courses. Smooth-faced quoins at the corners of the latter house added further sophistication.

The window openings of Rose Hill are framed with brick, just as at the Van Cortlandt Mansion, and are surmounted by beautifully carved white marble lintels decorated with the typical Greek Revival palmetto leaf. The central window is entirely framed with dressed stone. Rose Hill's most notable feature is the very fine Ionic portico at the main entrance door. The house was built between 1836 and 1838 for Horatio Shepheard Moat, a Brooklyn merchant. In 1839 he sold Rose Hill and 106 acres of land to Bishop John Hughes of New York for use as a seminary. The building became the nucleus of St. John's College, opened in 1841; the college is now part of Fordham University, which was established in 1907.

The Bartow-Pell Mansion is both more delicate and more severe than Rose Hill. It stands on the land originally settled by the courageous but luckless Anne Hutchinson. Thomas Pell, an early English settler, signed a treaty with the Indians in 1654 under which he took possession of the property. Today a tree enclosed by an iron fence marks the spot where Pell signed the treaty. One of the Pells, lords of Pelham Manor, married a Bartow, and a descendant of both families, Robert Bartow, built his Greek Revival mansion between 1836 and 1842. The name of the original architect has never been documented. Some say it was Minard Lafever, and others say it was the Reverend

4. *Rose Hill* (*now the administration building
   of Fordham University*)
   *East 191st Street and Bathgate Avenue
   1836–38*
5. *Bartow-Pell Mansion
   Shore Road, Pelham Bay Park
   1836–42*

John Bolton, a clergyman, artist and architect, who designed the stained-glass windows for Lafever's Holy Trinity Church in Brooklyn Heights. Perhaps they worked on it together.

The City purchased the mansion in 1888 and in 1914 entered into an agreement with the newly established International Garden Club to restore both the house and the garden. In May 1915 the mansion was officially opened as headquarters of the club. It is now open to the public as a museum, as is the magnificent garden. The building belongs to the City and is under the jurisdiction of the Department of Parks.

The great Wave Hill mansion in Riverdale is also in the Greek Revival style. The central portion was built by William Lewis Morris in 1843–1844. It too is constructed of the same roughly dressed random-fieldstone ashlar that was so characteristic of The Bronx. Subsequent additions, though made much later, were carried out in the same material and maintain a certain uniformity of effect.

Wave Hill commands a magnificent view of the Hudson and the Palisades across the river and has been the home at various times of such diverse figures as Theodore Roosevelt, Mark Twain and Arturo Toscanini. Early in the twentieth century it was bought by the financier George Perkins, an early conservationist, whose daughter, Mrs. Edward Woolsey Freeman, gave it to the Parks Department, together with twenty acres of surrounding land, to be used as a center for the study of the environmental sciences, particularly as they relate to the city.

In vivid contrast to the austerity of these three houses is Fonthill, a Gothic castle overlooking the Hudson River at the extreme northwest corner of The Bronx. It is hard to believe that this extravagantly romantic building was built less than a decade after the restrained and elegant Bartow-Pell Mansion. It shows how rapidly and restlessly the nineteenth-century styles of architecture followed one another. The castle was built by Edwin Forrest, the renowned Shakespearian actor. His dream house on the Hudson was obviously inspired by William Beckford's Fonthill Abbey in England, that grandiose "folly" that inspired so much of the Gothic Revival. New York's Fonthill consists of six octagonal turrets, all of different heights and to each of which Forrest gave its own name. The windows are round-arched, flatheaded and ogival. The towers are battlemented and machicolated in the full Gothic tradition.

6. *Wave Hill   675 West 252nd Street,*
   at Sycamore Avenue, Riverdale
   Central section: 1843–44
   Two-story north wing:
      late 19th century
   North armor hall:
      1928, Dwight James Baum
   South wing: after 1933

7. *Fonthill*
   (originally Edwin Forrest House)
   College of Mount St. Vincent,
   West 261st Street
      and Palisade Avenue
   1846

An ecstatic reporter for the *New York Herald* on September 20, 1848, wrote a description of Mr. Forrest's new house, then under construction:

> Up the Hudson. Soon this will be as great an object of ambition to the man of taste, and of much interest to the traveller, as "up the Rhine." As it is, I doubt if the latter river can boast of more attractions than our own noble Hudson. In point of majestic beauty, it is greatly inferior. . . .
>
> Neither will the Hudson be deficient in that feature which lends to the Rhine so much of interest—its castles. About two miles south of Yonkers, Mr. Forrest, the celebrated tragedian, is building a castle, combining the Gothic and Norman styles of architecture that attracts the attention of all who pass up and down the river . . . presenting en masse a very unique and picturesque appearance.

Forrest must have been a difficult person to get along with, to say the least. His feud with the English actor William Charles Macready touched off the Astor Place Riot of 1849. When his in-laws took over his downtown home, he fled to the West 22nd Street house mentioned earlier, in the present Chelsea Historic District. He capped his career with a divorce from his wife, Catherine, which was a *cause célèbre* on both sides of the Atlantic. The Sisters of Charity of Saint Vincent de Paul bought Fonthill in 1856 and until very recently used it as the library of the College of Mount St. Vincent.

The next two examples of the Gothic Revival style are by James Renwick, Jr., architect of Grace Church and St. Patrick's Cathedral. One is the very grand house which is now the Greyston Conference Center of Teachers' College, Columbia University; the other is the little stone manse of the Riverdale Presbyterian Church.

Greyston sits majestically on a point above the Hudson, just south of Wave Hill. In the early 1860s when Riverdale began to open up as a country retreat for wealthy New Yorkers, one of the first to take advantage of the new fashion was William E. Dodge, who had Renwick design for him what was originally a simple stone Gothic Revival cottage for summer use. Subsequent additions—the romantic gables and dormers and the polychrome slate roof—gave it a Victorian Gothic flavor and turned it into a mansion.

The Dodge family was prominent in the copper and metal trade and in philanthropy. William Dodge's daughter, Grace, who con-

8. *Greyston (Conference Center of Teachers College,*
originally William E. Dodge House)
690 West 247th Street, at Independence Avenue, Riverdale
1863–64, James Renwick, Jr.

tinued to live at Greyston, was instrumental in the creation of
Teachers' College in 1887. Her nephew Cleveland E. Dodge, a grandson of the original owner, lived in the mansion for forty years. Following his aunt's interests, he became chairman of the board of trustees
of Teachers' College and in 1961 gave the building to the college,
which uses it for a conference center.

William Dodge had also been active in the Riverdale Presbyterian
Church, and it was probably through his influence that Renwick was
chosen to design the manse, now known as the Duff House, which
turned out to be rather an architectural oddity. Renwick found he
needed more headroom in the second floor than the typical dormers
would provide, so he added a French Second Empire mansard roof.
When he found that the roof overpowered the little one-story building, he tried to conceal it with Gothic gables and dormers. The result
is that practicality won the day but the roof totally eclipses the little
building it sits on.

9. *Duff House* (*originally the rectory of the Riverdale Presbyterian Church*)
4765 Henry Hudson Parkway West, Riverdale
1863, James Renwick, Jr. Dormers altered 1968

10. *Stonehurst* (*originally Robert Colgate House*)
5225 Sycamore Avenue, Riverdale
1860–61

The magnificent formal Italianate villa known as Stonehurst also dates from the 1860s. Geographically, it lies about halfway between the Greek Revival Wave Hill and the Gothic Revival Greyston, and it shares their sweeping view of the Hudson. Built by Robert Colgate, of the paint and lead (not the soap) branch of the family, it is now the home of Nicholas de B. Katzenbach, a former United States Attorney General and Undersecretary of State. As the name indicates, Stonehurst continued the Bronx tradition of great stone mansions, this time in superbly cut random ashlar of smoothly dressed gray granite imported from Maine.

To take maximum advantage of the view, a semicircular bay and wide porch project from the west front of the house. Both here and at Greyston there is strong evidence of the growing appreciation of scenery and interest in landscape architecture that were coming into vogue in the 1860s. The Hudson River School of painters reflects the same appreciation of the romantic beauty of the Hudson Valley. Both Greyston and Stonehurst display a sensitive response to their splendid setting. From all the porches and windows there are carefully planned and varying views, not only of the river but also of the lawns and gardens and of the immense oaks and copper beeches, some of which date back to the eighteenth century. Both houses have been superbly maintained and are unexcelled examples of what great country houses of the mid–nineteenth century were like at their best.

Churches and Cemeteries

The individually designated Landmark churches of The Bronx all fall within the quarter century from 1841 to 1866 and are all in the Gothic Revival style.

The earliest church building surviving in The Bronx is St. Ann's in the heart of Morrisania. The church was consecrated in 1841 and is constructed of fieldstone in a very simple Gothic Revival manner. It was built by Gouverneur Morris, Jr., in a field on his estate to serve for family worship. Today it serves a very different congregation—a crowded Puerto Rican community that now surrounds it.

Gouverneur Morris, Sr., father of the builder of St. Ann's, was the most famous member of the family. He was a member of the Constitutional Convention of 1787 and drafted the final version of the Constitution of the United States. A major economist and statesman of the American Revolution, he was the United States minister to France during the stormy days of the French Revolution, and was the only foreign representative who remained at his post during the Reign of Terror.

The younger Gouverneur Morris was described as brilliant, rough

*11. St. Ann's Church and Graveyard   St. Ann's Avenue at East 140th Street
1841*

and ready, often guilty of scandalous behavior. His father, perhaps foreseeing that he had a genius on his hands, directed that his son have

> the best education . . . to be had in England or America. But my express will and directions are that he never be sent for that purpose to the Colony in Connecticut, lest he should imbibe in his youth that low craft and cunning so incident to the people of that country which is so interwoven with their constitution that all their art cannot disguise it from the world, though many of them have endeavored to impose themselves upon the world of honest men.

The cemetery around St. Ann's Church and the crypts beneath it are much older than the building and contain the bodies of many of the members of the Morris family.

Another interesting cemetery, tucked away in the West Farms section just south of Bronx Park, is the oldest public burial ground for veterans in The Bronx. Veterans of four wars are buried here—the War of 1812, the Civil War, the Spanish–American War and World War I. The cemetery has been maintained by the Civil War Memorial Committee, which Bert Sack—himself a World War I veteran, a descendant of two Civil War veterans and a native Bronxite—founded in 1950. Under Sack's goading, damage caused by weather and vandals has been repaired and the Civil War soldier statue which mysteriously vanished in the early 1950s was located in a Department of Public Works warehouse and restored to its position of dignity. When a gun was finally restored to the arms of the statue, Sack wrote exultantly to the *Bronx Press-Review:* "Eureka! After five years of search, pleading and requests in this column, a gun has been procured and affixed in the hands of the Civil War Soldier statue in the West Farms Soldier Cemetery at 180th Street and Bryant Avenue. The lone sentinel is no longer empty handed." To avoid future vandalism, Sack cunningly announced that "the gun is not a Civil War gun, it's not a museum piece nor a collector's item. It is a dummy replica of a gun of the Civil War era."

The site of the cemetery has now been incorporated into the Bronx Park South Urban Renewal area, and, hopefully, its upgraded surroundings will ensure a safe future for this little plot of historic ground.

12. West Farms Soldier Cemetery
2103 Bryant Avenue,
at 180th Street
1815–1959

The present Fordham University Chapel was originally known as St. John's Church and was built in connection with the establishment of St. John's College, now part of Fordham University. It is in the early Gothic Revival style. The random ashlar of which it is constructed and the square central tower through which the chapel is entered suggest English prototypes. The original building, designed in 1845 by William Rodrigue, had no transept. In 1929 one was added in order to increase the seating capacity. At the same time an elaborately decorated copper lantern was added over the crossing. The church is notable for a series of stained-glass windows donated by Louis Philippe, King of the French, and for its altar, which had previously served in St. Patrick's Cathedral on Fifth Avenue for over sixty years.

Two small and quite similar churches that date from the 1860s are closely connected with the development of the major estates in Riverdale. They both nestle in wooded sections and continue to serve a wealthy clientele. The Riverdale Presbyterian Church was designed by James Renwick, Jr. It is a charming English parish church in the romantic Gothic Revival style. A few years later, Richard Upjohn,

13. *St. John's Church   (now Universi*
Chapel, Fordham University)
East 191st Street
and Bathgate Avenue
1845, William Rodrigue
Transept: 1928–29, Emile Perrot

14. *Riverdale Presbyterian Church*
4765 Henry Hudson Parkway West
1863, James Renwick, Jr.

15. *Christ Church   Riverdale Avenue*
and West 252nd Street
1866, Richard Upjohn

Renwick's great rival of the mid–nineteenth century, designed Christ Church on Riverdale Avenue. This has more of the Victorian Gothic qualities but still is very much the little parish church serving the estate owners on the bluffs overlooking the Hudson. How well these churches serve their parishes can be seen from a newspaper column, written in 1939, that advises that several Sunday services are conducted at the Riverdale Presbyterian Church, including "one at 8:00 A.M. for golfers and others who may attend in golf clothes, tennis or riding attire."

Universities, Gates and a Fountain

The Bronx contains three notable and quite contrasting groups of public structures. The first is the "Old Quad," now known as Queen's Court, on the Fordham University Campus. One side of this U-shaped group is formed by the University Chapel (St. John's), and by St.

16. St. John's Residence Hall,
Fordham University
East 191st Street and
Bathgate Avenue
1845, William Rodrigue

John's Residence Hall, which the same William Rodrigue designed in the same year, 1845. Judging from the size of this three-story dormitory, the college must have grown rapidly since the day in September 1841 when it opened with six students.

The first president of St. John's was the Reverend John Mc-Closkey, Archbishop of New York and the first cardinal to be named in the United States. St. John's Residence Hall is an early example of the Gothic style applied to a collegiate building, and can be compared to the West Building of the General Theological Seminary in Chelsea. It is an austere and rugged stone structure with buttresses terminating in a series of blunt pinnacles between the paired windows.

The second group is the former New York University campus on the height along Sedgwick Avenue, overlooking the Harlem River. Architecturally, this series of monumental buildings—all designed by McKim, Mead & White in the years from 1894 to 1912—is a great contrast to the Fordham group. The buildings are all in the uncompromising neo–American Classic style. The Hall of Languages is the earliest of the group and the Cornelius Baker Hall of Philosophy is the latest. These twin buildings, almost identical, are unadorned except for their tetrastyle Ionic porticos. Between them is the Gould Memorial Library, which has a hexastyle Corinthian entrance portico crowned by a pediment. All three buildings are framed by the semicircular open arcade known as the Hall of Fame. Here along a low parapet on either side of the walkway are the busts of eighty-nine

BRONX COMMUNITY COLLEGE CAMPUS,
CITY UNIVERSITY OF NEW YORK
(formerly New York University)
Hall of Fame Terrace,
between Sedgwick and University Avenues

a. Hall of Languages
1894, McKim, Mead & White

c. Gould Memorial Library,
circled by the Hall of Fame
1900, McKim, Mead & White

b. Cornelius Baker Hall of Philosophy
1912, McKim, Mead & White

d. Hall of Fame
1900, McKim, Mead & White

famous Americans, alternating with square piers which support a vaulted roof.

Elections to the Hall of Fame are held every five years on nominations made by the public. Final selections are made by a college of electors chosen by the university and representing all states and a wide variety of professions. To be eligible for nomination one must have been dead at least twenty-five years and have contributed in some major way to the history, culture or development of the United States. Those whose stern bronze busts stud the colonnade today are inventors, statesmen, scientists, philanthropists, even poets. All four structures have recently been purchased by City University of New York to serve as its Bronx Community College campus.

Quite different in spirit, the Rainey Memorial Gates and the Rockefeller Fountain form a monumental entrance to the New York Zoological Garden—Bronx Zoo—off Fordham Road. Heins & Lafarge were the architects for the original buildings of the zoo, and they laid out the formal Baird Court, which still exists. As a fitting central motif, William Rockefeller presented to the Zoological Society an early-18th-century fountain which he had had disassembled and brought over from Como in Italy in 1902. In 1910 the fountain was moved from the Baird Court to the circular turnaround at the main entrance to the zoo.

More than a quarter of a century later, Mrs. Grace Rainey Rogers completed the composition by donating an extraordinarily handsome pair of bronze gates designed by the sculptor Paul Manship, who worked on them for five years. They are interesting as one of the examples in New York of the French Art Deco style. The architectural portions of the project—the massive pink granite gateposts and decorative gate lodges—were designed by Charles A. Platt to complement Manship's work. The animals and plants that surround the gates were designed in profile so as to look equally well from either side. The gates were cast in Belgium and were installed in 1934 as a memorial to Mrs. Rogers' brother, Paul J. Rainey, a big-game hunter and generous patron of the zoo.

A Mill, a Fort and a Greenhouse

The two examples of utilitarian architecture that have been declared Landmarks in The Bronx are very different in appearance and func-

18. BRONX ZOO (NEW YORK ZOOLOGICAL GARDEN)

a. Rainey Memorial Gates
East Fordham Road
1934, Paul Manship, sculptor;
Charles A. Platt, architect

b. Rockefeller Fountain East Fordham Road
Basin: 1910, Heins & La Farge

tion. Yet each is an honest expression of its purpose, and each, in its own way, has found a useful new life.

One of the few early examples of an industrial building to have survived in the entire city is the Lorillard Snuff Mill, built around 1840 on the Bronx River. It is in such unpretentious buildings, whether used as warehouses or as manufactories, that many of the great New York fortunes had their roots. Often the uses to which the money was put have survived—the great mansion that was lived in, the church that was supported, the fine cultural edifice named for the donor, the funerary monument that memorialized the man of wealth— but rarely do we have any physical reminder of where and how the money was made.

19. *Lorillard Snuff Mill   Bronx River, New York Botanical Garden*
c. 1840
Restored: 1954

The first Pierre Lorillard in New York had started a tobacco business in the 1760s on what is now Park Row in Manhattan. Snuffing and sneezing were at the height of their popularity, and Pierre made a great success by grinding his snuff between huge millstones, thus making a better-quality product than by the usual method of rubbing tobacco over a grater. He originated the idea of packaging the snuff in animal bladders, tanned and dried like parchment. The first advertisement that Pierre published introduced the ever popular money-back guarantee: "If not found to prove good, any part of it may be returned, if not damaged."

Pierre's sons, Peter and George, moved the business to The Bronx in 1792, just as many of today's large companies are moving out of the city to find more space and better working conditions. They bought an old gristmill, powered by a waterwheel, at a dam across the Bronx River. Eventually the old mill was replaced with a larger one where the famous Lorillard millstones were installed to grind out the snuff. The mill was kept in operation until 1870.

When Peter died in 1843 at the age of eighty, ex-Mayor Philip Hone wrote in his diary: "He led people by the nose for the best part of a century and made his enormous fortune by giving them to chew that which they could not swallow."

The snuff mill is a fine example of carefully worked fieldstone with brick trim, very simple and straightforward. In 1884 the City acquired the building together with 661 acres of land which later became part of the New York Botanical Garden. The building has been restored and is now used for park services. A large conference room and a public cafeteria have given the old structure a new life.

Quite a different sort of structure and one which has found an even more unexpected new use is the huge massive Fort Schuyler, which was built in stages between 1833 and 1856. It is at the tip of Throgs Neck, which juts out into Long Island Sound. The structure consists of two levels of enclosed gun galleries topped by an open and battlemented deck, which surrounds a pentagonal courtyard open to the sky. At each of the salient angles that faces the water, a bastion projects to protect the fort with crossfire. The walls of gray Connecticut granite range in thickness from five to eleven feet.

Fort Schuyler originally mounted 312 guns. Paired with Fort Totten, on Willets Point in Queens, it was designed to protect the city with gunfire that could rake the lower part of the Sound. Like all the forts of New York, Fort Schuyler's bristling armaments were never called on for the purposes of warfare. But the story is that Fort Totten did fire one shot, so badly aimed that it plugged a hole in the wall of its sister fort across the Sound.

The need to defend this "back door" to New York did not arise until after steam propulsion of warships became a practical reality.

20. *Fort Schuyler (now New York*
Maritime College)
Throgs Neck
1833–56,
Captain I. L. Smith
College library:
1966–67, William A. Hall

Until then the hazards of navigating a sailing ship through treacherous Hell Gate were considered to be a sufficient natural deterrent to any naval attack from this quarter. It was thought that belligerent warships approaching New York down Long Island Sound would be forced to land their troops sufficiently far out on Long Island to give the city adequate warning of any attack on land.

Fort Schuyler has most successfully faced its technological obsolescence. After having been garrisoned but never put into action during the Civil War, it was finally abandoned in 1870, but it has in recent years taken on a new lease on life. In 1934 the WPA restored and converted it into the New York Maritime College, which is now part of the State University of New York system. In 1966–67 the architect William A. Hall converted some of the old gun galleries into one of the most interesting and handsome academic libraries in the county, thus demonstrating at least one instance in which the pen has supplanted the sword.

The system of forts that has defended New York City for over three centuries tells a fascinating story of the relationship between geography and advances in military technology. The better the technology, the more far-flung the defenses.

Originally "the Fort" on the tip of Manhattan—subsequently called Fort Amsterdam and Fort George—was considered sufficient protection for the tiny colony.

After the American Revolution came the system of pairing forts so that they could assail the enemy from two sides. Castle Clinton at the Battery and Castle Williams and Fort Jay on Governor's Island were built to defend the entrance to the East River—at that time considered more important, or at least more defensible, than the wide entrance to the Hudson.

The next stage was a pair of forts to defend the entrance to the Upper Bay—Fort Hamilton in Brooklyn and, facing it across the Narrows, Fort Wadsworth (of which Battery Weed is a Landmark) on Staten Island. When steam propulsion came in, Fort Schuyler and Fort Totten were built.

With the development of long-range coastal artillery came the far-distant Fort Tilden on the Rockaway Peninsula and Fort Hancock on Sandy Hook, to defend the Lower Bay. Today, with the development of guided missiles and without attempting to penetrate classified information, the present defenses of New York City may well be located in Idaho.

A far cry from the massiveness of a military establishment is the glassy and graceful Conservatory in the New York Botanical Garden (not pictured). It is made up of a central rotunda, the Palm House, and ten connecting greenhouses arranged in the shape of a giant letter *C*. This, the largest and most elegant horticultural house in the city, was the brainchild of Dr. Nathaniel L. Britton, one of the country's most eminent botanists, who had been inspired by a visit to the Royal Botanic Gardens at Kew in England. Even though half a century separates the two structures (Kew was built in 1845–47 and the New York Conservatory in 1899–1902), there is a strong relationship between the two.

The design of the New York Conservatory was provided by Lord and Burnham, then, as now, specialists in greenhouse construction. The firm, which had been founded in Syracuse, moved to Irvington in 1872 to be near the opulent Hudson River estates that provided them with most of their business. One of their most noteworthy early works is the greenhouse built in 1881 at Lyndhurst, the home of Jay Gould in Tarrytown, New York.

The 100–foot-diameter Palm House retains its original windows and elaborate transoms which create the effect of round-arched fan lights. The slender cast-iron columns are surmounted by a pressed-metal frieze of garlands and swags. The great central dome, soaring ninety feet into the air, is supported on curved steel trusses that spring from the ground and are gathered together at the top by a steel ring. Above this rises a drum and a smaller glass dome capped by a tiny cupola. Secondary glass domes cover the four corners of the *C* and are connected by typical greenhouse wings.

This type of metal and glass construction is part of a distinguished tradition—one of the really innovative contributions of nineteenth-century architects and engineers. Siegfried Giedion traces it back to the 1833 glass house of the Paris Jardins du Musée d'Histoire Naturelle. Sir Joseph Paxton's Crystal Palace, which housed London's Great Exposition of 1850–51, was the most famous example, and New York City's modest copy, which once stood at the west end of what is now Bryant Park, created a local sensation. The metal and glass railroad train sheds, the armory and library reading room roofs, the shopping arcades or gallerias that were built here and abroad all illustrate what sometimes happens when architects forget about creating architecture. One has only to stand in the Bronx Botanical Garden Palm House to experience an exultant sense of light, air and space, when what Lord and Burnham really had in mind was to devise the least expensive and most effective way of protecting tropical plants from New York City weather.

Mott Haven Historic District

The one Historic District in The Bronx runs from East 137th to East 141st Street, along Alexander Avenue and for varying distances down the side streets.

The district is named for Jordan Mott, inventor of the coal-burning stove, who established the Mott Iron Works at 134th Street and the Harlem River in 1828. Mott bought the land, which was part of Morrisania, from the aristocratic Gouverneur Morris, Jr. When the latter was asked whether he would object if the parcel were to be named Mott Haven, he snapped, "I don't care what he calls it; while he is about it, he might as well change the name of the Harlem and call it the Jordan."

The Mott Haven Historic District, like the rest of the South Bronx, has experienced successive waves of immigration as various minority groups have moved in. Today it is largely Puerto Rican.

Between 139th and 140th Streets on the east side of Alexander Avenue is a row of ten three-story brick houses that is certainly one of the earliest examples of row houses in The Bronx. They were built between 1863 and 1865, and one of them, No. 280, is known to have belonged to Edward Willis, a major developer of Bronx land, for whom Willis Avenue is named. They are very simple houses in the local vernacular style with a certain French Second Empire feeling. They were originally lived in by well-to-do Irish families and were known as "Irish Fifth Avenue" or "Politicians' Row."

A considerably later row of twelve three-story brick houses is immediately across Alexander Avenue. They were designed by the architect Charles W. Romeyne, who later created the highly original old Grolier Club. This time he worked in a mixture of styles that

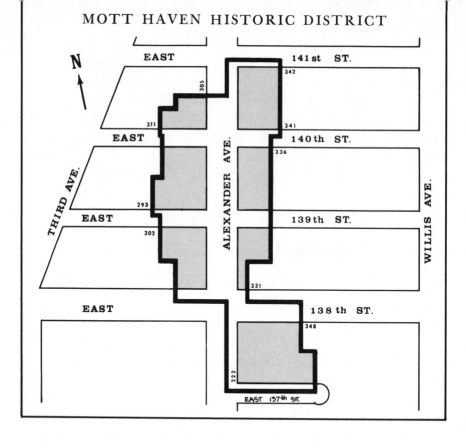

were fashionable in the early 1880s. They can best be described as transitional between neo-Grec and Queen Anne. Romeyne's design is particularly interesting in being one of the early examples, like Henderson Place in Manhattan, of a row of houses conceived as a unified whole rather than as a series of repetitive units. Here, as at Henderson Place, many houses have paired doorways and stoops and many retain their original hand railings and cast-iron newel posts.

The rest of the Historic District contains later rows of private houses and some apartments. It is a very harmonious district and has a quiet dignity of its own. Alexander Avenue conveys much the same mood that Edward Hopper has captured in his famous painting "Early Sunday Morning" that hangs in the Whitney Museum. Even the intrusion of a shop in one of the residences has been handled with such discretion that it does not detract from the quality of the street.

Both ends of the east side of Alexander Avenue terminate with a church. At the southern end, St. Jerome's Roman Catholic Church, of 1898, is in the neo–Italian Renaissance style but with strong Spanish influences. At the northern end the Third Baptist Church, which Ward & Davis designed, was an extraordinarily bold and modern piece of architecture for its time, 1902. Here too, however, the tower has many Baroque and Spanish features. Three quarters of a century ago no one could have foreseen that both of these churches were to be used primarily by Spanish-speaking congregations. In fact, today the Baptist church is officially known by its Spanish name, Tercera Iglesia Bautista.

Both ends of the west side of Alexander Avenue terminate with a public building. At the north end is the earliest branch library to be located in The Bronx. It was designed by Babb, Cook & Willard, the same firm that Andrew Carnegie selected to design his own mansion on Fifth Avenue, and, like so many of the branch libraries of this period, is in the style of an Italian Renaissance palazzo. The building at the south end of Alexander Avenue, also in the neo–Italian Renaissance style, is Thomas O'Brien's Fortieth Precinct Police Station—a very handsome structure in brick and limestone, completed in 1924.

East 139th Street   Mott Haven Historic District

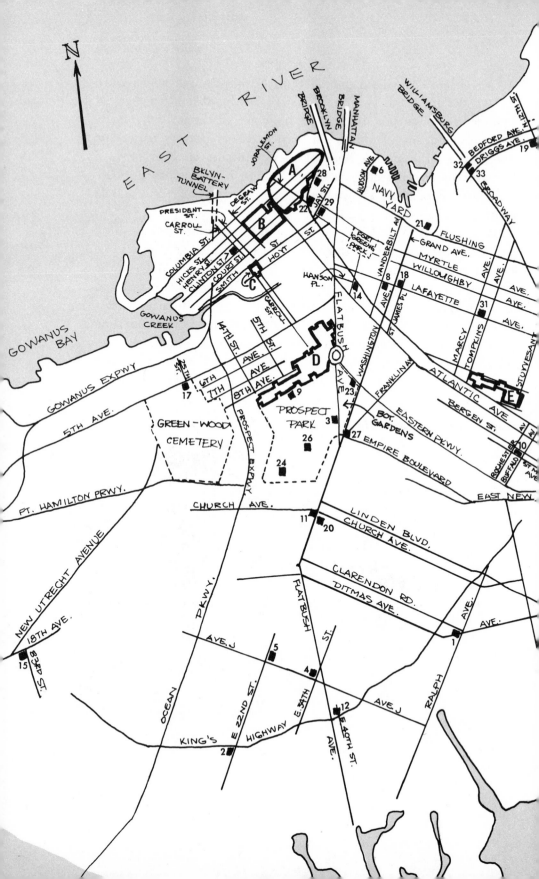

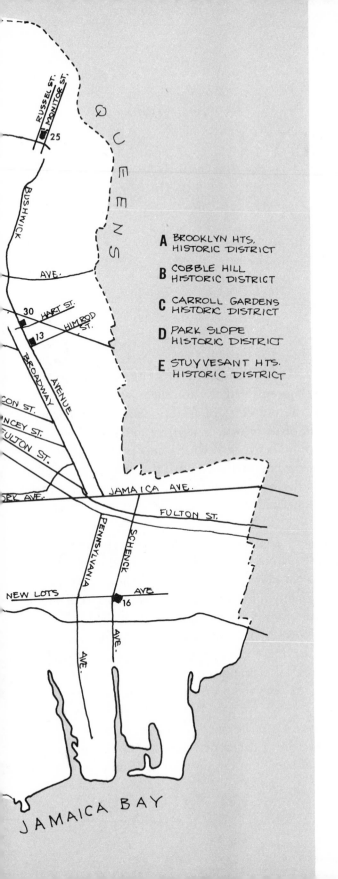

BROOKLYN

A BROOKLYN HTS.
HISTORIC DISTRICT

B COBBLE HILL
HISTORIC DISTRICT

C CARROLL GARDENS
HISTORIC DISTRICT

D PARK SLOPE
HISTORIC DISTRICT

E STUYVESANT HTS.
HISTORIC DISTRICT

CHAPTER EIGHT

BROOKLYN

T HE DANISH ANATOMIST of cities, Steen Eiler Rasmussen, compares Paris with London to illustrate the difference between what he calls the concentrated city and the scattered city.

Paris, like most of the old cities of Europe, had to be defended during the early period of its growth by walls studded with fortifications. Of necessity, people had to live within this protection. As the population increased, crowding increased until the need to expand became imperative. So additional walls were built in concentric circles, but the populace always remained concentrated within a clearly defined outer ring.

London, on the other hand, had a natural defense in the fact that Britain was an island. Relatively free of fear, at least throughout the Middle Ages and the Renaissance, a series of separate towns grew up at various crossroads. Originally these towns were quite independent and distinct from one another. Gradually, as the towns inched along the connecting roadways, borders became less distinct until finally the whole mass coalesced into the metropolis which we now know. However, the names of almost all of the original villages that are listed in the Domesday Book of the year 1086 survive as borough names in the county of London today.

The same comparison can be made between Manhattan and Brooklyn, although for quite different reasons. Manhattan is concentrated, and always has been, but not for reasons of military defense.

The swift waterways that completely surround this narrow and rocky island—"the oceanic amplitude," as Whitman calls it—have the same effect as the walls of Paris. The only difference is that the waterways could not be extended indefinitely to encompass more and more territory. From the earliest settlement on the southern tip of Manhattan, there was no direction in which to grow except up—that is, up the island. The wall on Wall Street, a defense against Indian incursions, was early leaped over in the search for more room, and the march north began. When the northward reach gave out, the march was still up—up in the air this time, into skyscrapers and high apartment complexes where more and more people could be concentrated in the strictly limited area available.

The analogy between Brooklyn and London is even closer. The physical geography of Brooklyn permitted unlimited expansion. The land is dead flat except for some low hills on the north and northwest. Brooklyn is part of the terminal moraine of the glacier that formed Long Island. Its natural boundaries are the East River, the Upper Bay, the Narrows, the Lower Bay and the Atlantic Ocean. Unbounded on the east, the urban growth could expand, as it has, indefinitely in this direction.

Like London, Brooklyn started as a series of separate villages that sprang up naturally at important crossroads. In time, they grew along the roadways until their borders merged. Eventually they became part of the City of Brooklyn, which was, in the beginning, simply one of many villages. In 1898 the City of Brooklyn, in turn, was incorporated into Greater New York. Although Brooklyn has no Domesday Book, the names of all six of the original towns are still in current use—Flatlands, Flatbush, New Utrecht, Gravesend, Bushwick and Brooklyn itself. The few high points of Brooklyn are so distinctive that their names reflect their geography—Cobble Hill, Brooklyn Heights, Bay Ridge, Park Slope, Prospect Heights, Clinton Hill, Boerum Hill and Stuyvesant Heights.

Brooklyn is a city of many faces. A stranger is bewildered as he turns from a tree-shaded street of small houses, each with a neat little front yard, and finds himself surrounded by false-fronted pizza parlors and an infinite variety of mom-and-pop stores. Another turn will find him in one of the most idyllic green spaces of which any city can boast, while the next corner will find him among massive blank-eyed warehouses, punctuated by small factories that do not seem very busy. And after one final turn, he will be dazzled by some of the proudest public buildings that have been built in this country or among rows of impeccably kept town houses that look as elegant today as Manhattan's famed Fifth Avenue did a hundred years ago.

The stand-up comic believes that Brooklyn is a state of mind, and for years has been getting a laugh and a hand by poking a tentative finger into a psyche he's not sure is there. In a way, Brooklyn has been fated to be an ugly duckling, always in the shadow of Manhattan. And Brooklyn as a dormitory for Manhattan cannot compete with the palaces of finance, communication and industry across the East River. These factors have contributed to alternating moods of inferiority and of aggressiveness.

Brooklyn first became part of the New World in 1636 when the Dutch bought some land from the Indians around what is now known as Red Hook on Gowanus Bay. There is some question about how Red Hook (which was destined to spawn some of the country's most unsavory characters) got its name—whether from the color of its soil or from the fields of cranberries that grew there. By 1642 a rather unreliable ferry service had been established from Manhattan to the other side of the East River, and fairly soon a little settlement called Breuckelen (Broken Land) appeared around what is now the inter-section of Fulton and Smith Streets. The homesick settlers named it after a village in the Netherlands. It was granted a municipal form of government by the Dutch West India Company in 1646, four years before New Amsterdam itself.

It did not take the Dutch long to discover the farming value of the fertile acres to the east of the settlement. Many of the leading New Amsterdam burghers, including Peter Stuyvesant, bought land there which they cleared and usually cultivated on an absentee landlord basis.

In 1816, Brooklyn, with a population of about six thousand and an area of one square mile, was incorporated as a village. The main street, Old Ferry Road (now Fulton Street), was by then solidly lined with taverns, stores and houses as far as the present Borough Hall. In 1834, when Brooklyn was given a city charter by the state legislature, it covered twenty-five square miles, and soon it began to absorb neighboring villages. By 1898, when Brooklyn became a borough of

Greater New York, it had nearly a million inhabitants and an area of seventy-five square miles.

The opening of the Brooklyn Bridge in 1883 had given the real impetus to the consolidation with Manhattan. As one local leader put it, the bridge would "so affiliate the two in heart and sympathy" that they would seek this "municipal marriage." Like any marriage, this has not been one of unadulterated bliss, and today there are serious Brooklyn voices raised in favor of divorce—not to marry another but to gain independence. Brooklyn has certain assets that could qualify it for a return to cityhood. It has a population of over 2,600,000 and would be the fourth largest city in the United States; it has ten institutions of higher learning; it has some of the city's worst slums; and its docks handle a quarter of the general cargo coming into New York City.

Farmhouses, Mansions and Cottages

Five Dutch farmhouses that have survived in Brooklyn have been designated Landmarks. The style varies little from the earliest to the latest, though there is more than a century and a half between them.

The Pieter Claesen Wyckoff House, at Clarendon Road and Ralph Avenue in the Flatlands section, is the oldest building in the city and in the state and one of the oldest wooden structures in the United States. It is a one-story building, but with a fully usable attic reached by a boxed-in stair. The "ski-jump" curve of the overhanging roof is characteristic of the Dutch Colonial vernacular. The house stands on land which four men, including Wouter Van Twiller, Peter Stuyvesant's predecessor as director general of New Netherland, bought in 1636 from the Canarsie Indians. Stuyvesant confiscated the land from Van Twiller—because the latter had injudiciously put it in his own name rather than that of the Dutch West India Company—and turned the farm over to Pieter Claesen to run on his behalf. Pieter had bought an adjoining piece of land on which, according to the most recent research, he built his house in 1652. Other studies have claimed that parts of the house, possibly built by Van Twiller, predate 1641.

Pieter Claesen was an indentured servant who had arrived in the New World in 1637. Pieter worked hard for six long years and finally

*1. Pieter Claesen Wyckoff House   Clarendon Road and
   Ralph Avenue, Flatlands
   1652 with sections possibly before 1641*

in 1643 fulfilled the terms of his contract and became a free man. In
1649 he settled in the area of today's Flatlands. At that time many of
the Dutch settlers had no fixed surnames: the name Claesen only indicated that Pieter was the son of Claes, or Nicholas. After the English
took over in 1664, the Dutch began adopting the English fashion of a
permanent family surname. Pieter chose Wyckoff, a combination of
wyk, meaning parish, and *hof,* meaning a court. Since Pieter was a
local judge at the time, this seemed a fitting appellation.

In 1937 Pieter's numerous descendants formed the Wyckoff
Family Association in America "to promote just pride in ancestry and
family tradition" and "perpetuate ancient landmarks associated with
the family." The original farmstead, which had remained in the hands
of Wyckoffs until 1901, actually was the main target of the organization. Members of the association tried repeatedly to buy the house,
which had never been moved from its original site, but the owners
refused to sell. In 1959 a number of members of the family formed the
Wyckoff House Foundation, which, in 1963, finally succeeded in
buying the property.

In 1969 the foundation conveyed the house to the City of New York with the understanding that the Parks Department would restore and preserve it while the family association would endeavor to raise an operating endowment as well as round up as much of the original Wyckoff furniture and furnishings as could be discovered. At the moment the house presents a sorry picture, boarded up and fenced in for protection. The only indication of its Landmark status is a sign that the City has erected and a neighbor that proudly proclaims itself the "Landmark Car Wash." Ambitious plans, however, are being made not only to restore the house but also to surround it with a park in order to convey some idea of what a seventeenth-century Dutch farm looked like.

Pieter Claesen Wyckoff had ten children who grew to adulthood, and his family has increased exponentially ever since. Today there are thousands of living descendants, of whom about nine hundred, from every state in the Union, are members of the association. They are listed by their line of descent from Pieter's children, and there are eight "line" vice-presidents of the association to represent the descendants of Cornelius, Annatje, Garret, Geertje, Jan, Marten, Mayken and Nicholas. The association holds annual meetings, which generally draw several hundred family members. An annual *Wyckoff Family Bulletin* gives news of the family, genealogical notes and a directory of members. A recent issue listed five different variations in spelling: Wicoff, Wikoff, Wyckoff (the most common) , Wycoff and Wykoff.

The Wyckoff-Bennett Homestead, at East 22nd Street and King's Highway, dating a century later than the Pieter Claesen Wyckoff House, is believed to have been built by Henry and Abraham Wyckoff, descendants of the prolific Pieter. The date 1766 carved into a beam of the old barn indicates that the house was standing at that time. Other souvenirs of the past are two little glass windowpanes which bear the name and rank, scratched with a diamond, of two Hessian soldiers who were quartered in the house during the Revolution and who thus hoped to achieve immortality of a sort. In 1835 the house was purchased by Cornelius W. Bennett. Today's occupant is the fourth generation of Bennetts to have lived here.

The Wyckoff-Bennett house is considered the finest example of Dutch Colonial architecture in Brooklyn. Despite the long period of time that separates them, there are many similarities between it and the Pieter Claesen Wyckoff House. The projecting roof has the same upturned sweep, though here the overhang is supported by six slender columns and dormers were added in the nineteenth century. Rural vernacular styles change very slowly; it is the city dweller who feels that he must keep up with the latest fashion.

2. *Wyckoff-Bennett Homestead   1669 East 22nd Street, at Kings Highway*
1766

The Lefferts Homestead in northern Flatbush, built between 1777 and 1783, is quite similar in style to the Wyckoff-Bennett house. Just as the present Dyckman House replaced an earlier building destroyed by the British in the Revolutionary War, so the present Lefferts Homestead was rebuilt with materials salvaged from the family's seventeenth-century house after it had been burned by the Americans during their defense of Flatbush in August 1776. Peter Lefferts, who built the present house, was the fourth generation of his family to live on the Flatbush property. He was lieutenant of militia of Flatbush, a judge and a state senator. Peter's son was also a man of parts—a member of the United States House of Representatives, a delegate to the New

3. *Lefferts Homestead*
Flatbush Avenue at Empire
Boulevard, in Prospect Park
(formerly at
563 Flatbush Avenue)
1777, 1783
Moved 1918

York State Constitutional Convention and a judge. He was also a man of stature—six feet four—and was said to have lifted up bodily a balky mule and set it down where he wished it to be.

The house formerly stood at 563 Flatbush Avenue, but in 1918 it was given to the City and moved into Prospect Park, opposite Empire Boulevard, where it is now maintained as a museum by the Daughters of the American Revolution. It is notable for its fine front doorway, obviously added much later; the design of this doorway has been attributed to Major L'Enfant. This elegant Federal detail, with characteristic leaded transom and sidelights, though superb in itself, seems somewhat out of place as the entrance to a little Dutch farmhouse.

The Coe House at 1128 East 34th Street, near Flatbush Avenue, is more properly known as the Van Nuyse House, after Johannes Van Nuyse, who completed it by 1806. The low extension at one side is reminiscent of the Lefferts house, but, unlike the latter, the building has retained its original simple Dutch door. It also lacks the elegance of a front porch; the overhanging eaves simply jut out exactly as they do in the Pieter Claesen Wyckoff House built 150 years earlier. In the mid-1800s the house was rented to Ditmas Coe, by whose name it has been known ever since. The building has been beautifully maintained by its current owner. Set back from the street behind a white picket fence, it comes as something of a surprise in the midst of its present-day surroundings.

Last in this series of Dutch farmhouses is the Van Nuyse–Magaw House, now at 1041 East 22nd Street, which Johannes built in 1800 and which Magaw bought in the 1850s. It is also the only one of the series to have a gambrel roof, though it still retains the overhanging ski jump at the eaves. The Van Nuyse–Magaw House was moved to its present site in 1916, when dormer windows were added.

Totally different in its style and its scale is the Commandant's House in the Brooklyn Navy Yard, which was built as a home for the commanding officer of the post. This house is one of the city's great structures in the Federal style, which was at its peak of popularity when the house was built in 1805–06. The detail is very refined, both inside and outside. The delicacy of the porch columns and the balusters, as well as the arched tracery of the narrow dormers, are all typically Federal. The Commandant's House has sometimes been attributed to the Boston architect Charles Bulfinch, in association with New York's own John McComb, Jr.

The Brooklyn Navy Yard (officially known as the New York Naval Shipyard) has been an important economic factor in the life of Brooklyn ever since the federal government started to buy land for it in 1801. The first ship built there, the *Ohio*, came off the ways in 1820. The ill-fated *Maine*, the supercarriers *Saratoga*, *Independence* and *Constellation*, the *Arizona*, sunk at Pearl Harbor, and the *Missouri*, on which the Japanese signed their surrender in 1945, were all built here. At its peak, the Navy Yard employed seventy thousand people. In 1966 the government closed the yard, putting six thousand out of work. This hit all of Brooklyn very hard, and particularly some of the poorer sections.

For three years the area became progressively more ghostly. Piers fell into disrepair, metal rusted, giant cranes loomed crazily over the forlorn scene. Finally, in 1969, after three years of yeoman's work on the part of New York City representatives in Congress, the Navy Yard was turned over to a semipublic corporation for industrial development. Today twenty-five firms are installed in the area, with a total

5. *Van Nuyse-Magaw House*
   1041 East 22nd Street,
      between Avenues I and J
   (formerly at East 22nd Street
      and Avenue M)
   c. 1800
   Moved 1916

4. *Johannes Van Nuyse ("Coe") House*
   1128 East 34th Street, between
      Avenue J and Flatbush Avenue
   before 1806

6. *Commandant's House, New York Naval Shipyard*
   Hudson Avenue and Evans Street
   1805–06, attributed to Charles Bulfinch and John McComb, Jr.

employment of over four thousand. The Navy reserved nineteen acres for its own use, including the Commandant's house and the old United States Naval Hospital.

Brooklyn contains three other exceptionally fine examples of free-standing houses—one in a pure Greek Revival style, dating from 1840, one a romantic Italianate villa of 1856 and a third a fascinating transitional example halfway between the two.

The nearly square brick house at the southwest corner of Clinton and Carroll Streets (No. 440 Clinton Street) is without doubt the finest example of a Greek Revival town house in the city. Three-story brick pilasters on the corners of the Clinton Street front and the shallow projection of the center bay divide the façade into three equal parts. The pilasters have granite capitals. Granite is also used for the central stoop, the handsome newel posts, the cap-molded window lintels, the sills and the facing of the basement walls. The cornice is of white painted wood, as are the first-floor window shutters. The house is now occupied by an undertaking establishment and is in an excellent state of preservation, although there is no necessary connection between these two facts.

The Joseph Steele House at 200 Lafayette Avenue, although entirely of wood, is much more ornate and lacks the uncompromising symmetry of the Clinton Street house. It contains such a mixture of Federal, Greek Revival and Italianate elements that experts differ in deciphering its history. The most likely theory seems to be that the two-story wing was originally a Federal-style house dating back to about 1812. Then, in the 1840s, the main body of the house was built in the Greek Revival style; the earlier structure was attached as a wing and its details "Grecized." At that stage, the main building probably had the flat, boxy look characteristic of the Greek Revival period, with a simple cornice running all around it at one level. The little pairs of horizontal windows in the frieze would then have provided light and air to a low, hip-roofed attic. Under this theory, it was an 1854 alteration that raised the roof so as to gain headroom on the third story. The builder was obviously worried about what to do about his newly fashionable Italianate cornice on the side elevation. If he continued it, as heretofore, all around the house, he would have to sacrifice the valuable full-size third-story window which he wanted. If he formed a full pediment, then the long side of the house would look like a chopped-off Greek temple. So, in an ingenious manner, he formed a pediment with a broken bottom chord and avoided both pitfalls. The elaborate door enframement, the rather heavy turned spindles and wide handrail of the stoop, and the somewhat timid little Italianate pediments over the front windows were probably all added at the same time.

An opposing theory has it that all of the main house was built in 1854 with a mixture of Italianate and very late Greek Revival details. Such a combination would not be at all unlikely in what was, in mid–nineteenth century, still a semirural area. The problem is not simplified by the fact that the iron railing that surrounds the yard has a Gothic Revival suggestion in its details!

*7. No. 440 Clinton Street,
at Carroll Street
c. 1840*

*8. Joseph Steele House
(Skinner House)
200 Lafayette Avenue,
at Vanderbilt Avenue
Wing: c. 1812
Main building: c. 1840s
Alteration: c. 1854*

Much the grandest of the trio is the Litchfield Villa, which stands inside the west boundary of Prospect Park, approximately opposite 5th Street. The building was designed by Alexander Jackson Davis in the Italian-villa style of the mid-1850s. The details of the carved capitals and highly ornamented frieze and cornice are exceptionally fine. An interesting feature of the Corinthian capitals is the substitution of native corn and wheat for the classically traditional acanthus leaves.

The asymmetrical arrangement of the masses of the house, with its towers, balconies, bay windows, porches, terraces and turrets, is highly romantic. The general silhouette is almost identical to the Gothic Revival villa, Lyndhurst, which Davis designed for Jay Gould at Tarrytown. Davis actually submitted numerous watercolor sketches of the Litchfield house in both the Gothic and Italianate styles before the owners finally selected the latter. Style was, at mid-century, as superficial as the changes of women's fashions. Just as the same dress could be made to look quite different if made up in a different material or color, so the same house could be Italianate or Gothic, to suit the patron's fancy.

The Litchfield Villa was conceived and built in the 1850s, during that placid lull before the storm of the Civil War, for Edwin Clark Litchfield, a lawyer who had made a fortune in promoting the Michigan Southern Railroad, the first east–west line to enter Chicago. The line later became part of the New York Central system. Litchfield wanted a home befitting his position in the community and naturally turned to the outstanding architect of the day, Davis, who made a specialty of country homes. It is an index of changing economic conditions that Davis' bill for all his alternative studies and for full working drawings for this mansion amounted to $824.

After the Civil War, plans for the creation of Prospect Park were revived and Litchfield donated twenty-four acres of land to the public purpose. But the park commissioners, evincing what the Brooklyn *Eagle* termed "a craving like that of David for Naboth's vineyard for Mr. Litchfield's Castle," pursued their goal, and Litchfield finally sold the property to the City of Brooklyn but remained in residence, at an annual rent of $2,500, until 1882, when he moved to Europe. The following year his house became the headquarters of the Brooklyn Park Commission, and it still serves as the center for park operations in the

9. *Litchfield Villa*
Prospect Park West between
4th and 5th Streets,
in Prospect Park
1856, Alexander Jackson Davis

borough. Despite all the years of typing, filing and coffee-breaking by generations of Parks Department employees, many of the old mansion's more gracious features have survived: the magnificent central rotunda, the double staircase of cast iron and many of the handsome carved mantelpieces.

In contrast to the grandeur of the Litchfield Villa, there are four very modest houses in Brooklyn of great historic importance. These formed a group on Hunterfly Road, which was an important highway during Dutch Colonial days. The remains of the highway now survive in the middle of a block bounded by Bergen Street and St. Mark's, Rochester and Buffalo Avenues, on what was the eastern boundary of Weeksville, one of the earliest free-black communities in New York City. The surviving buildings date from about 1830, and their irregular placement in the center of the block illustrates the original alignment of Hunterfly Road, which used to run from Bedford to Canarsie.

Little is known about the history of Weeksville, but a local group from the Bedford-Stuyvesant area has teamed up with City University of New York for an archeological and historical investigation. They believe that Weeksville was established sometime around 1827, the year that slavery was legally abolished in New York State. Indications are that the community was a literate and relatively affluent one of some thirty to forty property-owning families. It seems to have been largely a black community until after the Civil War, and there is evidence that it served as one of the principal refuges for blacks fleeing from Manhattan during the 1863 Draft Riots. The members of the

10. *Hunterfly Road Houses*   (*from a drawing by Valerio Villanueva*)
1698, 1700, 1702–4, 1706–8 Bergen Street
c. 1830

Bedford-Stuyvesant group are hopeful that the Hunterfly Road houses can be restored and become a museum of a long-forgotten period in black history.

Churches and Cemeteries

It wasn't until 1654 that the first church appeared in the area that encompasses the present Borough of Brooklyn. Up to that time the devout had had to cross the river to Manhattan. Even after the earliest churches were built none of the small communities could afford a full time pastor. Peter Stuyvesant would send Dominie Johannes Polhemus to minister to the spiritual needs of the citizens scattered over the area in widely separated villages. In order to accommodate his dispersed flock, the dominie preached in Flatbush on Sunday mornings and alternately in Brooklyn and Flatlands in the afternoons. But the faithful were not satisfied. They paid their dues, but they felt they weren't getting their money's worth. "We are getting a prayer, not a sermon, and it is poor and meager," they complained. So they withheld payment of their share of the fee for the minister. Stuyvesant quickly put a stop to such recalcitrance by sending a sheriff to see that the dues were paid and that the minister received his fee. From that time forward churches proliferated.

Many of the borough's most notable churches lie within the boundaries of its Historic Districts and will be discussed in relation to the surrounding residential communities which they were built to serve. Those individually designated Landmarks that are outside the Historic Districts are almost equally divided stylistically between the Classical and Romantic Traditions, with one unclassifiable example that is a law unto itself.

The earliest example in the Classical Tradition is the Federal-style Flatbush Dutch Reformed Church at the corner of Flatbush and Church Avenues, built in the last decade of the eighteenth century. With its rough-fieldstone construction and use of Holland brick around the openings, it is not dissimilar to the contemporary St. Mark's-in-the-Bowery. The Federal character is most clearly seen in the beautifully proportioned spire with its delicate colonnettes surrounding the octagonal wood lantern pierced by oval and round windows.

The elegance of the spire makes it worthy of comparison to the better-known spire of St. Paul's in Manhattan. The steeple still has its original bell, which was donated in 1796 by a parishioner who imported it from Holland. The ship carrying the bell to its new home was captured by the British and taken to Halifax. However, it was reclaimed and brought to Flatbush in time to toll the death of the country's first President in 1799, a rite it has performed at the death of every succeeding Chief Executive.

This is the third church built on the site. The original was built in 1654 under the direction of Peter Stuyvesant when Flatbush was only a little huddle of Dutch farmhouses. The name of the village was originally 't Vlacke Bos, which meant "the wooded plain," but it soon became Anglicized to "Flatbush." For many years the community remained somewhat isolated from the mainstream of Brooklyn, al-

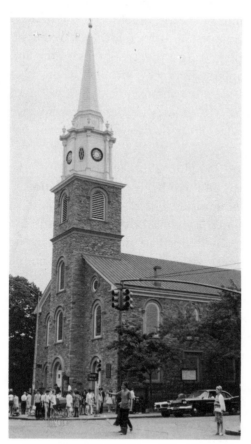

11. Flatbush Dutch Reformed Chu
866 Flatbush Avenue,
at Church Avenue
1793–98, Thomas Fardon

though it emerged in the late 1880s as a desirable residential area filled with comfortable middle-class homes. During World War I a popular song paid tribute to its domestic virtues—"Nesting Time in Flatbush." The advent of the subway in the 1920s finally succeeded in bringing the community completely into the orbit of the city.

The Flatlands Reformed Church of 1848, also the third to be built on its site, on Kings Highway at East 40th Street, is quite different in feeling from the Flatbush church. Built of white painted clapboard, it looks more like a church one would expect on a New England village green than in a metropolis like New York City. It is pure Greek Revival in design and a fine example of the austere dignity that could be achieved in this rather reticent style. Church records show that the building cost $5,506.29 to erect, including sixty pews, each with its own door.

The earliest church to have been constructed on the site, complete with stocks and a whipping post in the churchyard, was an octagonal edifice. It was dedicated in 1663 with Pieter Claesen Wyckoff in

12. Flatlands Reformed Church
Kings Highway and
East 40th Street
1848

attendance. Wyckoff, whose house is nearby, had moved with his young bride to Flatlands, then called Amersfoort, in the late 1640s and had promptly set about organizing a congregation.

The British soldiers who occupied Kings County during the American Revolution were required to attend church every Sunday. Those in Flatlands filed dutifully into the little octagonal church and just as dutifully listened to Dominie Ulpianus Van Sinderen exhort his congregation in Dutch, the official language of the Dutch Reformed Church until 1824. The soldiers, whose knowledge of Dutch was less than rudimentary, were quite unaware of the fact that the good Dominie was praying for the total disintegration of the British forces and the success of the struggling little Continental Army.

The remains of Wyckoff and his wife, Margaret, rest under the pulpit of the present church, and Dominie Van Sinderen is buried in the adjoining churchyard.

The Reformed Church of South Bushwick, though built only slightly later than the present Flatlands church, begins to reflect the rising affluence of mid-nineteenth-century Brooklynites. Stylistically the building belongs to the Greek Revival period, but its central tower over a massive front portico suggests the great Georgian churches of Wren and Gibbs in London. The over-all spirit is far grander than what we normally associate with the Greek Revival style. There is a certain cost-is-no-object air about it that contrasts strongly with its Flatlands contemporary.

The same late persistence of Greek Revival detailing is seen around the front doors and the small windows of the Hanson Place Seventh Day Adventist Church. This building, which was opened in 1860, was originally a Baptist church. The Seventh Day Adventists bought it in 1963. Its Greek Revival details seem perfectly at home with what is essentially an Italianate design. The heavy pediment and the cornice supported on carved modillions, the elaborate Corinthian columns and the arcaded nave windows are typically Italianate.

The same sort of "Gothic Survival" that was noted in Manhattan at the Church of the Transfiguration of 1801, the Sea and Land Church of 1817 and St. Augustine's Chapel of 1829 can be found in two Brooklyn churches, the New Utrecht Reformed Church at 18th Avenue and 83rd Street, and the New Lots Reformed Church at 620 New Lots Avenue.

13. *Reformed Church of South Bushwick*
855-867 Bushwick Avenue,
at Himrod Street
Main section: 1853
Wings: 1883

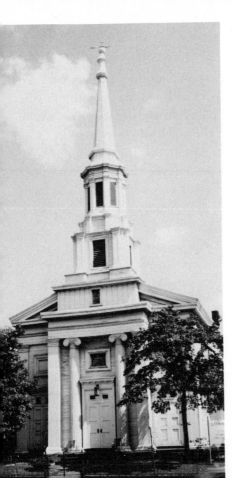

14. *Hanson Place Seventh Day Adventist Church*
(originally the Hanson Place Baptist Church)
88 Hanson Place, at South Portland Street
1857–60

The New Utrecht Reformed Church, with its rubblestone walls, its pointed windows outlined with bands of brickwork, its projecting square central tower and its classical cornice, is almost the exact counterpart of St. Augustine's Chapel and was built in the same year. It can be called Georgian-Gothic, or, if particular note is made of the spider-web round window over the main door, perhaps Federal-Gothic would be more exact.

The fieldstone of which the New Utrecht Church is built came from the 1699 church the congregation demolished in order to replace it with the present structure. During the Revolution, the British used the earlier church as a hospital and later as a stable for riding horses. In the grounds today stands a liberty pole to mark the spot over which the American flag first waved above the town of New Utrecht. The original pole was erected by the forefathers of the present church members on the occasion of the evacuation of the British in November 1783, amid the firing of cannon and shouts of joy. The pole has been frequently replaced over the years to celebrate continuously our hard-won liberty.

The New Lots Reformed Church, which dates back to 1824, could, except for its pointed windows and their simple lancet tracery, be accurately described as late Federal in style. While other churches in the city may be older, none built of wood has stood as long, unchanged from its original form. The story of its construction is also unique.

In 1821 the farmers of New Lots, tired of traveling all the way to Flatbush to go to church, decided to build their own. They felled the necessary oaks, cut them into boards, shaped them for framing and then let them weather. In May 1823 they started to work under the

15. New Utrecht
Reformed Church
18th Avenue and
83rd Street
1828

16. *New Lots Reformed Church   620 New Lots Avenue,*
   at Schenck Avenue
   1824

direction of a building committee. The timbers were notched, joined and secured by pegs with such care and attention to detail that the structure still stands in testimony to their craftsmanship. The records show that the out-of-pocket expenses were thirty-five dollars, which would seem to be a good investment under any circumstances for a building that has held its own for a century and a half.

From these early "Gothic Survival" details on essentially classical buildings, the chronological course of the true Gothic Revival as well as the Romanesque Revival and Italianate styles will be traced in the discussion of well over a dozen important churches that dot Brooklyn's large Historic Districts. To reach the next independently designated Landmark requires a long leap—a full generation in time, from 1828 to 1861, and an even longer leap in stylistic evolution: from the earliest tentative fumblings to the full flower of what is called the Victorian Gothic style.

The gatehouse, chapel and office that were built during the Civil War, from designs by Richard Upjohn & Son, as the main entrance to Green-Wood Cemetery at Fifth Avenue and 25th Street provide a remarkable introduction to what was in itself quite a remarkable innovation in the history of landscape design. Though preceded by a decade by Mount Auburn Cemetery in Cambridge, Massachusetts, the 478 acres of Green-Wood Cemetery, opened in 1840, represented a sharp break with what had hitherto been considered an appropriate setting for the interment of mortal remains. Until this time, people had been buried in or under churches, in compact little churchyards around the church of their affiliation, or, if in separate burying ground, then in compact isolated enclosures such as the First Shearith Israel Cemetery and the Marble Cemeteries, or in private family burying grounds. Green-Wood with its hills, ponds, handsome plantings, winding roads and superb views over New York Harbor was created in the form of a beautiful natural landscape as an assuagement of personal

17. Green-Wood Cemetery Gates   Fifth Avenue and 25th Street 1861–65, Richard Upjohn & Son

18. *Emmanuel Baptist Church   279 Lafayette Avenue, at St. James Place 1883–87, Francis H. Kimball*

grief. Many of Brooklyn's and New York City's dignitaries lie buried here: Elias Howe, De Witt Clinton, Henry Ward Beecher, Peter Cooper, Horace Greeley, James Gordon Bennett and countless others.

The flat pierced gables of tracery, the multiplication of little turrets, crockets and spires, and particularly the multicolored slate roofs on the adjoining lodges of Upjohn's entrance gates are all typical of the Victorian Gothic. The ensemble is held by many to be the finest example we have of this highly dramatic style.

Quite different in its approach is the design by Francis H. Kimball for the Emmanual Baptist Church on Lafayette Avenue. Again another full generation has gone by—it is now 1887—and the attitude toward architecture is much more scholarly and sophisticated. We are well into the Eclectic period. The square twin towers that flank the triple entrance doors certainly indicate that Kimball had looked long and carefully at the great French cathedrals. Here, however, he was building quite a small church, and he knew what to omit and what to simplify. That he also combined Gothic elements with late French Romanesque details shows what a sophisticated period we have reached. Though the church and the flanking chapel together took only four years to build, the mixing of the two styles was done deliberately to suggest that the building might have been under construction for a century or more, as so many of its transitional French prototypes actually had been.

Another example of Eclecticism illustrates how far afield architects could wander in their choice of models. The Russian Orthodox Cathedral of the Transfiguration of Our Lord was built between 1916 and 1921 by Louis Allmendiger on North 12th Street in Greenpoint. This is a scholarly reproduction of the Byzantine style so characteristic of Russian churches. A Greek cross is surmounted by a great central dome sitting on a drum. The onion shape of the dome is a hallmark of

19. Russian Orthodox Cathedral of the Transfiguration of Our Lord, 228 North 12th Street, at Driggs Avenue, Greenpoint 1916–21, Louis Allmendiger

the style. The four corners, between the arms of the cross, are filled with small towers, each capped with a domed octagonal cupola housing the bells no Russian church would be without. The combination of the five copper-covered domes, each surmounted by a gilded patriarchal cross, makes a very picturesque silhouette against the sky. The main mass of the church is extremely severe, its light walls being pierced by simple openings with round-arched heads. The whole composition is tied together by a massive cornice that runs continuously around the entire structure.

Public Buildings, Park Structures, a Triumphal Arch and a Tree

Whatever Brooklyn may lack in comparison to Manhattan in the abundance and magnificence of its commercial structures it more than makes up in a proud tradition of great public buildings and social and cultural institutions.

The original building for Erasmus Hall Academy, on the present Flatbush Avenue near Church Avenue in Flatbush, is the earliest public building to have survived in Brooklyn. The school, which is one of the oldest in the United States, was started in 1786 with funds contributed by John Jay, Alexander Hamilton and Aaron Burr, among others. The old building is now completely surrounded by the Collegiate Gothic structures of the modern Erasmus Hall High School and has been preserved in the courtyard as a museum. It is one of the finest examples we have of a monumental Federal building made of wood. The corner quoins are there purely for decorative effect, in imitation of stone prototypes that had the very real function of tying the exterior walls together. The slender porch columns, the chinoiserie railings—just like those on the roof of Gracie Mansion—the half-round window in the pediment, the dormers with their interlacing tracery are all characteristic of this elegant style that immediately followed the American Revolution.

Erasmus Hall was originally a private academy for boys. It was the earliest secondary school chartered by the Regents of New York State. Land for the school was given by the Flatbush Dutch Reformed

20. *Erasmus Hall* (*now in courtyard of Erasmus Hall High School*)
911 Flatbush Avenue, near Church Avenue
1786

Church across the street. When Erasmus Hall Academy opened, Flatbush was a quiet farming village just beginning to emerge from the effects of the long British occupation. The Battle of Long Island had swept over much of the area, and there is a legend that General Washington once had pitched his tent under a linden tree at the corner of the present Church and Flatbush Avenues. In any event, the new academy chose as its school colors the buff and blue of the uniform of Washington's men and as its name that of the great Dutch liberal scholar Desiderius Erasmus. The school started with twenty-six students. Ten years later its enrollment was 105; in 1823 a Female Department was organized; and today the high school, as part of the city's school system, has over six thousand students.

While it would be possible to make a long list of distinguished graduates of this venerable institution, it is easier to name its most famous dropout. Bobby Fischer, now chess champion of the world, quit Erasmus High in his junior year in order to concentrate on his game.

Today's pupils and faculty must wonder what the good old days could have been like when they read Rule 9, promulgated in 1797: "No student shall be permitted to practice any species of gaming nor to drink any spiritous liquors nor to go into any tavern in Flat Bush without obtaining the consent of a teacher."

The Flatbush Town Hall, on Snyder Street near Flatbush Avenue (not pictured), is a charming reminder of the days when Flatbush was an independent village. With the nearby Flatbush Dutch Reformed Church and Erasmus Hall it completes an important and nostalgic group.

The rugged individualism of the people of Flatbush was illustrated in 1873 when the citizens decisively defeated an annexation proposal that would have made Flatbush a part of Brooklyn. Following this show of independence a campaign for a proper town hall and for court sessions, town elections and other public functions was begun by the local papers. In 1874 the village fathers engaged John Y. Culyer to draft plans. Culyer, who was associated with Frederick Olmsted and Calvert Vaux in the creation of Prospect Park, designed a Victorian Gothic building somewhat reminiscent of Vaux's Jefferson Market Courthouse in Greenwich Village, although more modest in its scale and detail. The hall was completed in 1875 and was turned over to the town authorities on February 7, 1876.

Until Flatbush was finally annexed to Brooklyn in 1894, the town hall served the community well—as police headquarters, courthouse and social center. The grand ballroom on the second floor was the scene of all sorts of gay festivities, including the celebration of the centennial of Erasmus Hall Academy in 1886.

The red brick exterior with its buff stone trim is enhanced by a series of pointed arches accented by carved drip moldings ornamented with bosses. The arch on the first floor of the corner tower is supported by triple colonnettes, a typical Victorian touch. The front of the building is crowned by a large central gable which emphasizes the triple-arched entranceway at the first-floor level. There are two handsome cast-iron lamp posts flanking the front steps.

Perhaps one of the most enduringly satisfying buildings in all of New York City is Martin E. Thompson's United States Naval Hospital in the Brooklyn Navy Yard. It was built during the decade of the 1830s of smoothly dressed gray granite. Granite is an extremely hard material to work, and perhaps the very difficulty of handling it dictated the austerity of the design. The fact that it was a utilitarian structure for military use no doubt also influenced Thompson in selecting this rather astringent treatment. The net result, however, is a building of great restraint and strength. While technically classifiable in the Greek Revival style, the structure is so utterly simple that it is timeless in its appeal.

Brooklyn's Borough Hall, originally Brooklyn City Hall, on the north side of Joralemon Street between Fulton and Court Streets, was designed by Gamaliel King, who was a builder and a grocer until 1830, when he took up carpentering. It is much grander than the U.S. Naval Hospital but is still in the Greek Revival style. This is Brooklyn's oldest government building. The cornerstone was laid in 1836, and original plans called for the structure to occupy all of the little triangular park which extended as far as the present statue of Henry Ward Beecher. But financial woes intervened. The partially built structure was demolished, and the more modest present building was completed fifteen years after the original cornerstone had been set in place. Even on a reduced scale, the building was initially able to house all the municipal functions, including the courts. The building was designed to be approached from the north across what is now known as Borough Hall Plaza, toward which its handsome Ionic portico faces. With the construction of the Municipal Office Building across Joralemon Street and particularly with the placing of the subway entrances on Joralemon Street, almost everyone nowadays enters Borough Hall through its much less impressive basement rear door. Today, the building houses the office of the Brooklyn borough president and an interesting collection of portraits of former mayors of Brooklyn. The present neo-Georgian cupola, which is out of keeping with the austerity of the Greek Revival structure, was added much later.

It is instructive to compare the portico of Borough Hall with McKim, Mead & White's central portico for the Brooklyn Museum, built just about half a century later on Eastern Parkway at the edge of the Brooklyn Botanic Garden. This imposing pile, which is only partially completed, was designed in the neo–American Classic style, then at the peak of its popularity. Though both of the six-column porticos employ the Ionic order, the difference between Roman and Greek Ionic is at once apparent. The Roman capitals have a strongly

21. *United States*
 Naval Hospital
 Hospital Road,
  New York Naval Shipyard
 1830–38, Martin E. Thompson

22. *Brooklyn Borough Hall*
 209 Joralemon Street
 1846–51, Gamaliel King
 Cupola: 1898, C. W.
  & A. A. Houghton

23. *Brooklyn Museum (early view)*
 Eastern Parkway and
  Washington Avenue
 1894, McKim, Mead & White
 Removal of steps:
  1936, William Lescaze

emphasized line of horizontal ornament, as contrasted to the subtle curves of the Greek Revival Ionic capitals. The Roman entablature is heavier, the cornice has a greater overhang, the pediment is steeper, and—even apart from the group of sculptured figures that fill it—is far more richly ornamented. Not only is the pediment crowned by a confection of scrolls, fronds and rosettes, but the cornice of the typically Roman attic behind it is decorated with alternating lions' heads and swags. Yet there is an impersonal dryness to all of this profusion; it is as though the decoration had been squeezed like icing from a pastry bag. The twenty-eight heroic statues standing on top of the cornice on either side of the portico are suggestive of the free-standing figures that crown the Appellate Division Courthouse in Manhattan, which was built only a few years later.

The museum is one of three great cultural institutions adminis-tered by the Brooklyn Institute of Arts and Sciences; the others are the Children's Museum and the Botanic Garden. The Brooklyn Institute was established in 1823 as the Apprentices' Library, with a nucleus of 724 books and 150 pamphlets which enthusiastic and altruistic citizens trundled in wheelbarrows down to the reading room on Fulton Street. In 1843 the library was reorganized into the Brooklyn Institute for the purpose of "enlarging the knowledge in literature, science and art," and received a large endowment from Augustus Graham, a wealthy Brooklyn distiller. Today the Institute is largely supported by the City, although its three components receive substantial private con-tributions.

It is perhaps unfair to judge McKim, Mead & White's museum as it stands today. In 1936 the building underwent drastic remodeling under the sponsorship of the WPA. It was at this time that the giant flight of stairs that led up to the portico was removed. Two opinions of this alteration reflect as much on the shift in taste between the two periods in which they were written as they do on the work itself:

> During the past few years a WPA project has been making the museum one of the most modern and pleasantly arranged in the country. The most striking change has been the removal of a monumental stairway which originally gave access to the third story and the building of a new entrance hall at the ground level. [New York City Guide, by the Guilds' Committee for Federal Writers' Publications, Inc., Works Progress Administra-tion, 1939.]

The austere architecture of the museum lobby dates from its remodeling in the 1930s . . . during which the lobby was moved down one floor and the monumental exterior stairway removed; stark functionalism replacing the Classical impressiveness. [*A.I.A. Guide to New York City,* by the American Institute of Architects, New York Chapter, 1967.]

To us one of the most interesting sections of the museum is the Frieda Schiff Warburg Memorial Sculpture Garden, where some architectural ornaments salvaged from New York City buildings that have been demolished now find a home. A privately sponsored organization, the Anonymous Art Recovery Society, has been quietly retrieving gargoyles, keystones, carved plaques, masks, heroic statues and bits of ironwork from the doomed buildings in all five boroughs and presenting them to the museum. The stone carvers who created these architectural embellishments were unsung craftsmen, mostly English, Scottish and Irish. They were poorly paid and died young of "galloping consumption," now known as silicosis. But their art is a constant source of pleasure. Some of it is still *in situ;* for example, an apartment house on Park Avenue in Manhattan built forty years ago sports four carvings over the ground-floor windows, immortalizing figures common to apartment dwellings in those days—a stingy iceman, a lazy superintendent, a furnace tender feeding in one coal at a time and a doorman engrossed in a newspaper.

McKim, Mead & White made a more graceful and lyrical use of Eclecticism in their Grecian Shelter in Prospect Park, built in 1905. Unfortunately, the limestone columns terminate in terra-cotta capitals which support a terra-cotta entablature and balustrade. Terra cotta was popular in the late nineteenth and early twentieth centuries because it was cheap, permitted easy reproduction once a mold had been made, and lent itself to good polychrome effects. Often, however, it has proven to be vulnerable to the rigors of New York's climate with its extremes of temperature and its heavy rains and snowfall. The shelter was allowed to deteriorate sadly until 1966, when the Parks Department undertook an extensive restoration. Thanks to this work, the shelter can once more be enjoyed as one of the most beautifully proportioned structures in any of the city's parks.

In the original plans it was called the Croquet Shelter, but nobody knows why, since it was nowhere near the croquet grounds, which are

24. *Grecian Shelter*
Prospect Park between Park Circle and Ocean Avenue entrances
1905, McKim, Mead & White

at the other end of Prospect Park. It is nowadays officially known as the Grecian Shelter, another misnomer according to Clay Lancaster, who points out that the structure, with its Corinthian capitals, its highly decorated frieze and its swags and garlands, is much closer to Italian Renaissance prototypes than to anything that could be found in Greece.

Similar in its purpose as a temporary refuge from sun or rain is the gently curving Shelter Pavilion which Helmle & Huberty, a prominent Brooklyn firm, designed in 1910 for Monsignor McGolrick Park in the Greenpoint section. Their design was largely inspired by the Trianon at Versailles with its paired columns and the arrangement of arched windows in the two end pavilions. Unfortunately, this shelter has fared badly. It has been so seriously damaged by fire, vandals, the elements and the ill-advised addition of a comfort station that it is in all likelihood past redemption.

Fortunately, Helmle & Huberty's Boathouse on the Lullwater, back in Prospect Park, has fared much better. The design of the ground floor of this charming structure of 1904 is closely modeled on the loggia of Sansovino's Library of Saint Mark on the Grand Canal in Venice. The second story, however, is set back on all sides and

25. *Shelter Pavilion   Monsignor McGolrick Park,*
   Nassau Avenue and Monitor Street, Greenpoint
   1910, Helmle & Huberty

26. *Boathouse on the Lullwater (early view)*
   Prospect Park, East Drive near Lincoln Road
   1904, Helmle & Huberty
   Restoration: 1972–73, Brown, Lawford & Forbes

subordinated to the ground story. This too was a terra-cotta structure and suffered much deterioration over the years, but the Parks, Recreation and Cultural Affairs Administration, in a piece-by-piece restoration that can only be compared to the meticulous replacement of the stone facing of New York's City Hall, has recently restored the structure to its original condition. Technically the restoration was more difficult than that of City Hall, since terra cotta, a hard-baked high-glazed clay product, shrinks about ten percent in the firing. Hence molds had to be made larger than the existing units, so that the new pieces would fit. This was true restoration rather than mere reconstruction—a nice distinction, and one not always made by harassed municipal agencies. The result, however, has been worth the effort and expense, and the festive little building can now look forward to delighting as many generations in the future as it has in the past.

Another pavilion which Helmle designed in 1913 is the Fire Department's Brooklyn Central Communications Office on Empire Boulevard near Flatbush Avenue, adjacent to the Botanic Garden. This simple, utilitarian building is surprisingly similar to the magnificent Morgan Library in Manhattan. Both are neo-Italian Renaissance one-story structures which, for quite different reasons, required more wall space than windows. The architectural solution, in both

27. *Brooklyn Central Office, Bureau of Fire Communications*
35 Empire Boulevard
1913, Frank J. Helmle

cases, was to dramatize the contrast between blank flanking wings and an open central loggia.

The grandest of Brooklyn's classical Landmarks is the Soldiers' and Sailors' Monument in the Grand Army Plaza (not pictured). Seth Low, when he was mayor of Brooklyn (1882–1885), proposed that the city erect a fitting memorial to the men who fought in the Union forces during the Civil War. But it wasn't until 1889 that the idea took hold and funds for its construction were solicited by veterans of the Grand Army of the Republic. Eventually the state contributed a quarter of a million dollars to the cost.

John Hemingway Duncan, who later was the architect of Grant's Tomb in Manhattan, won the $1,000 prize for the design of the arch and the country's leading sculptors were commissioned to decorate it. Frederick William MacMonnies, a native of Brooklyn, who had studied under Augustus Saint-Gaudens, was the sculptor of the heroic groups on the south side of the arch and of the magnificent triumphal quadriga on top. The bas-reliefs on either side, below the arch, were the work of Thomas Eakins, who is perhaps better known as a painter than a sculptor, and William R. O'Donovan. Eakins is responsible for the horses, O'Donovan for the figures of Lincoln and Grant.

Despite the presence of these distinguished examples, Brooklyn architects did not always turn to the Classical Tradition when designing public buildings. They were not altogether immune to the romantic mood and the search for novelty that ran through so much of the nineteenth century. Three important public buildings in Brooklyn illustrate this point of view.

Mifflin E. Bell's Brooklyn General Post Office, on the corner of Cadman Place East and Johnson Streets, is a fine example of neo-Romanesque design. It is faced in polished and rough rock-faced granite and is elaborately carved. Techniques in stone cutting had so far advanced by 1885, when this building was started, that it seems almost to be showing off what could be done with granite. The general composition of the building, with its projecting half-round turrets, its steep slate-covered roof and dormers, its massive and squat ground-story arcade and the interesting play of round-arched and flatheaded windows, is quite similar, on a smaller scale, to the contemporary work of Cady, Berg & See at the American Museum of Natural History in Manhattan. Bell was supervisory architect for the

28. *Brooklyn General Post Office*
271 Cadman Plaza East
at Johnson Street
1885–91, Mifflin E. Bell
Extension: 1933,
James A. Wetmore

United States Treasury Department, which in those days designed and built all the post offices across the country. Some forty years after Bell completed his work, the acting supervisory architect for the Treasury, then James A. Wetmore, made an extensive addition to the building which blends agreeably with the original.

The man who was probably Brooklyn's greatest architect, and whose originality is only recently being recognized, was Frank Freeman. In much the same way as his famous predecessor Henry Hobson Richardson, he used the Romanesque style as a starting point for some wonderfully imaginative compositions. Two examples of his work have been designated Landmarks.

The old Brooklyn Fire Headquarters on Jay Street, between Willoughby Street and Myrtle Avenue, has until very recently been used as a firehouse, and a viable new use for it is currently being sought. The building was built in 1892 in a rich combination of rock-faced granite, red sandstone and dark-brown Roman brick, with terracotta details relieving the smooth surfaces. The red-tile roof is flashed with copper that has turned green, and the whole bold composition introduces a colorful note in an otherwise rather drab neighborhood. The great archway, through which dashed clanging fire engines drawn by excited horses, and the tower, which was formerly used to spot fires, were both functional and wonderfully expressive of their function.

The building that Freeman designed in the same year and in the same spirit for the Bushwick Democratic Club is quite different in scale from his firehouse. It is now occupied by the Bethesda Pentecostal Church, even though the intertwined initials "B.D.C." can still be deciphered in the terra-cotta ornamentation. The building is almost residential in scale and could very easily have been a rich man's mansion. The imaginative interplay of Roman brick, terra cotta and stone, the dramatic modeling of the surface with semicircular, segmental, rectangular and triangular recesses and projections, and,

29. *Old Brooklyn Fire Department*
Headquarters
365-367 Jay Street
1892, Frank Freeman

30. *Bushwick Democratic Club*   (*now the Bethesda Pentecostal Church*)
719 Bushwick Avenue, at Hart Street
1892, Frank Freeman

above all, the virtuosity that keeps such a complicated mixture from getting out of control places Freeman at the top of his profession. As his work becomes more widely known, Freeman will eventually be recognized as one of the great forerunners in the development of twentieth-century architecture.

If Freeman's work points to the future, another Brooklyn Landmark brings to the city a venerable past record, one dating back some forty to sixty million years. This is the magnolia tree (*Magnolia Grandiflora*) that stands in front of a house at 679 Lafayette Avenue, in the Bedford-Stuyvesant section. This species is believed to have developed in the Eocene period. The magnolias are members of the Ranales order, and the irregular number of their petals, sepals and stamens show them to be one of the earliest species of flowering trees to have evolved. *Magnolia Grandiflora* is indigenous to the United States and was one of the first exotic trees to be introduced to Europe from North America in the early eighteenth century. It was named after a French botanist, Pierre Magnol, who collected and identified the species.

While its design considerably predates any man-made structure in New York City, this particular specimen is also notable for its history and its vitality. In 1885 William Lemken had a slip sent to him from North Carolina. He planted it in his front yard, where it throve. This was unusual, because *Magnolia Grandiflora* rarely flourishes so far north. By good fortune, there had been just the right degree of protection from the north wind, of moisture and of sunlight, to allow the tree to live for almost a century. It is now over seventy feet tall and each spring delights its admirers with a dazzling display of large white, lemon-scented flowers.

This is *not* the "tree that grows in Brooklyn." That is the ailan-

31. Magnolia Grandiflora
679 Lafayette Avenue
c. 1885

thus, or tree of heaven, which is so hardy and prolific that it thrives not only in Brooklyn but in every back yard and vacant lot in the city. It was first imported from China and was supposed to dispel the soggy vapors that rose from marshes and were believed to cause a variety of illnesses.

The Brooklyn magnolia tree was adopted by a local resident, Mrs. Hattie Carthan, almost twenty years ago. When it was threatened by a housing development, she rallied neighbors, schoolchildren, public officials and the press to support her plea to save this magnificent and rare specimen. She was successful. The Landmarks Preservation Commission, in designating the tree, spelled out in the greatest horticultural detail the safeguards needed to preserve it for future generations to enjoy. The tree is important not only as a botanical rarity; the popular reaction to its designation as a Landmark illustrates how valuable such symbols are in fostering community pride and in providing people with a sense of continuity with the past.

Commercial Buildings

Since Brooklyn never developed the concentration of wealth that Manhattan did and remained predominantly a city of homeowners, there never developed in Brooklyn the great pile of commercial construction that looms so dramatically just across the East River. In fact, only three commercial structures have been designated as Landmarks in Brooklyn. Two are banks on Broadway in the Williamsburg section, near the eastern end of the Williamsburg Bridge.

The Kings County Savings Bank, designed by King & Wilcox in 1868, is a fine example of the French Second Empire style. It represented a period of conspicuous display in which it was not considered vulgar, at least by the people in power, to boast openly of one's wealth. The post–Civil War period in the United States, with its carpetbaggers and robber barons, was quite similar in spirit. From its scale and general character there is nothing, on the outside, that would distinguish the Kings County Savings Bank from a millionaire's mansion. Somehow, it seems quite suitable that in Brooklyn, the city of homes, even a bank could be domesticated.

Not much later, but totally different in feeling, is George B. Post's

Williamsburgh Savings Bank of 1875, in which he has anticipated by a full generation the great American Classical resurgence that was not to come into full flower until after 1893. Not only does the style mark a sharp break with its Kings County neighbor, but the entire spirit has changed. Whereas the earlier building, though rather palatial in size, was thoroughly residential in character, the Williamsburgh Savings Bank, with its gigantic entrance portal and towering dome, does everything possible to impress the visitor with the power, stability and wealth of its resources. It is hard to realize these days, when banks try to outdo one another with their friendly-neighbor approach, that there was a long period in which just the opposite effect was the goal. In the

32. Kings County Savings Bank
135 Broadway, Williamsburg
1868, King & Wilcox

33. Williamsburgh Savings Bank
175 Broadway, Williamsburg
1875, George B. Post

fifty years from 1875 to 1925, bank architects outdid one another to create a father image in the mind of the timid depositor and to overawe the diffident supplicant for a loan.

The Brooklyn City Railroad Company Building (not pictured), now known as 8 Cadman Plaza West, at the intersection of Fulton and Furman Streets, was built in 1860–61 and is a much simpler example of a business building in the French Second Empire style than the Kings County Savings Bank. It was built for the railroad company on the site of the home of Judge William Furman, one of Brooklyn's leading citizens. In Judge Furman's day the property was on the water's edge directly in front of the ferry stairs, and he was reputed to have kept an oyster house in his basement where the succulents from the East River could be shucked and consumed while they were still fresh. The building is five stories high and constructed of brick with granite trim and at present is being converted into artists' studio apartments.

Historic Districts

In terms of Landmarks, and in relation to the other boroughs, Brooklyn has its fair share of rare survivals of rural farmhouses, of fine churches and mansions, of imposing public buildings, but the real *genius loci*—the peculiar character of the place that makes the most abiding impression—lies in its residential neighborhoods. This is why the paragraph of New York City's Landmarks Preservation Law that provides for the protection of areas which "have a special character or special historical or aesthetic interest or value; and represent one or more periods or styles of architecture typical of one or more eras in the history of the city; and cause such areas, by reason of such factors, to constitute a distinct section of the city" is so particularly important to Brooklyn. These are the words that permit the designation of Historic Districts. Stripped of their legal formality, they mean simply that in a few parts of the city certain areas have survived with a distinct character that distinguishes them from their surroundings and that this character in and for itself alone is something worth preserving. The whole is considered to be greater than the sum of its parts. It is through the survival of such distinctive islands in the city that Brooklyn achieves its unique character.

Thus far, five such Historic Districts have been designated in Brooklyn; others impatiently await their turn for designation. Surprisingly enough, what was almost an afterthought in the drafting of the Landmarks Law has proven to be its most popular aspect. People like to feel that they are living in special and historic surroundings, and the majority gladly accept the restraints put on exterior changes to their buildings, in exchange for the stability such controls ensure for the whole neighborhood. Brooklyn Heights, Cobble Hill, Stuyvesant Heights, Carroll Gardens and Park Slope—each represents a different period, and each has its notable architecture, its own history and its individual character. All consist predominantly of two-, three- and four-story row houses, extending block after block, on tree-lined streets, interrupted only by an occasional school or church or apartment house. While there is some overlap, both of time and of tradition, taken together these Historic Districts graphically illustrate the best of the Brooklyn way of life for a century and a half.

BROOKLYN HEIGHTS

Brooklyn Heights, the oldest and best known of the districts, changed from a rural to a suburban area following the opening, in 1814, of steam-powered ferry service between the foot of Fulton Street in Brooklyn and the foot of Fulton Street in Manhattan. By 1845 the proprietors were boasting that a passenger waited no more than three minutes for a ferry and paid two cents for the three- to five-minute ride.

The new ferry received the financial backing of such owners of Heights farmland as Hezekiah Pierrepont and the Middagh and Hicks families, who promptly had their land surveyed and sold off in 25-by-100-foot lots. Pierrepont, an enterprising brewer, as early as 1820 advertised property suitable for families "who may desire to associate in forming a select neighborhood and circle of society, for a summer's residence or a whole year." With rare foresight he touted the property as eminently practical for gentlemen whose duties required "their daily attendance in the city." The speed with which their investment paid off may be measured by the rate of building of new homes for the businessmen, shippers and merchants who had offices in lower Manhattan, but who appreciated the amenities of the Heights as an easily

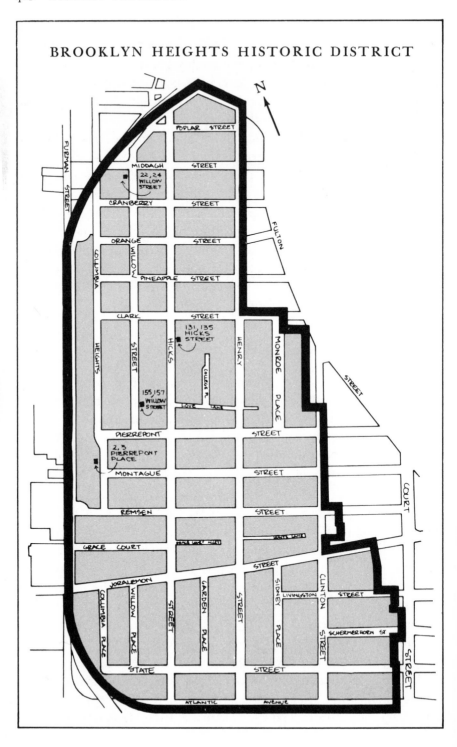

BROOKLYN HEIGHTS HISTORIC DISTRICT

Esplanade, Brooklyn Heights Historic District

accessible place in which to live. While records of 1807 show only seven houses on Brooklyn Heights, by the outbreak of the Civil War there must have been well over seven hundred if we are to judge by the 684 pre-1861 houses that survive today.

Brooklyn Heights is on a bluff above the East River cut off from the rest of the borough by Brooklyn's Fulton Street. It is thus isolated on its high eminence with a breathtaking view of the tip of lower Manhattan. Its geographical isolation is what set it apart initially— from the shipping, warehouses and industry along the waterfront to the west and from a spreading commercial district along Fulton Street to the east. Its popularity as a prosperous residential community was what preserved it through most of the nineteenth century.

After the 1883 opening of the Brooklyn Bridge, the 1908 advent of the IRT subway under the river, and, above all, the rapidly increasing use of the automobile, the Heights lost its hitherto unique combination of advantages: splendid isolation and ready accessibility. The result was a slow and sad change in the aristocratic neighborhood of the 1880s and 1890s. Feeling their privacy invaded, the patrician inhabitants fled. Their mansions were cut up into rooming houses. Hotels spread and apartment houses appeared. Property values fell and several blocks began to look and act like slums.

Around 1955, Brooklyn Heights began to be rediscovered. Wall Street workers who had scorned Brooklyn for the Upper East Side, Riverdale and Westchester suddenly woke up, as their Fulton Street Ferry ancestors had done in 1814, to the charm and convenience of this little community. During the acute housing shortage in the years right after the end of World War II, adventurous young families began to move in, buying the fine old houses, restoring them and getting deeply involved in the Brooklyn Heights Association, an active and vigorous community organization that was determined to preserve the Heights at all costs. It was the effective pressure of this organization, under the leadership of William R. Fisher, that in no small way deserves credit for getting New York City to enact its Landmarks Preservation Law.

At his appearance before the Landmarks Preservation Commission in November 1965, Otis Pratt Pearsall testified that a census of Brooklyn Heights revealed that at least half of the then existing buildings dated from before the Civil War and ninety percent of them from before 1900. There were, furthermore, 60 good examples of Federal houses, 405 Greek Revival, 47 Gothic Revival and 201 Italianate houses. In addition, 216 buildings were described as Eclectic or miscellaneous. Sixty-one carriage houses had survived, a surprisingly high number for these easily dispensable structures, and 190 buildings were described as indescribable, though "of generally conforming scale."

With such a wealth of varied material to select from—and undoubtedly every critic and every resident would have a different list of favorites—it is possible to mention only a few representative examples of the typical styles.

On Willow Street, Nos. 155, 157 and 159 are well-preserved examples of the Federal row house. The Flemish bond of their brickwork, their flat lintels with incised panels, the eight-paneled front doors with flanking Ionic colonnettes, leaded-glass transoms and sidelights, as well as the open-cage wrought-iron newels at the foot of the stoop steps, are all characteristic and well preserved. So are the roundheaded dormer windows set beneath little pediments.

Nos. 155 and 157 Willow Street
Brooklyn Heights Historic District
1826, 1829

There are fine Greek Revival houses at Nos. 22, 24 and 26 Willow Street, in which running bond has replaced Flemish bond, the lintels are no longer paneled but are capped with a simple molding, the doors have four panels and are flanked by flat pilasters, and the sidelights and transoms are no longer leaded. Decorative details in cast iron have been added to the stoop and area railings. At the top of the houses there is a cornice with a wide, plain fascia board below it; the pitch of the roof has been reduced. There are no dormers. Finally, the front door has been emphasized by a stone enframement capped by a very low pediment. The slight inward taper of the door enframements, almost Egyptian in feeling, and the projecting Greek ears where the jambs meet the lintel are also in character.

Most delightful, and dating from the same period, is the group along Willow Place (quite distinct from Willow Street), Nos. 43 through 49, which were built in 1846. Their two-story wooden colonnade is an early attempt to treat a row of houses as a unit, a single composition, as was done in a much grander manner at about the same time in Colonnade Row on Lafayette Street in Manhattan. In fact, the Willow Place buildings are sometimes referred to as the "poor man's Colonnade Row."

The Gothic Revival is well represented by the handsome pair of houses at Nos. 131 and 135 Hicks Street. Built in 1848 of smoothly dressed brownstone, they are practically contemporaneous with the Willow Place Greek Revival row. The squareheaded double-hung windows are divided by heavy vertical mullions, the window openings topped by inverted-U label moldings—a late Gothic detail. The doors are divided into narrow vertical panels ornamented with carved tracery and are flanked by pointed-top sidelights and clustered colonnettes. These are repeated in the stonework of the deep door embrasures, which terminate in a low pointed arch. The railings consist of cast-iron tracery. No. 131 retains its original newel posts, though the finials are gone.

These three styles, Federal, Greek Revival and Gothic Revival, overlapped to a certain extent as architects in the first half of the nineteenth century sought to find an idiom expressive of their time and place. But these styles were not magnificent enough for the emerging millionaires, who felt that only the opulence of the Italian Renaissance fitted the grandeur of their way of life. Among the very grand houses, Nos. 2 and 3 Pierrepont Place were designed in the Italianate style by Frederick A. Petersen, architect of the Cooper Union Foundation Building in Manhattan, and not by Richard Upjohn, to whom they are frequently attributed. Originally there was a third house, subsequently demolished. These four-story double-width houses, set on high basements, are much the most magnificent of any in Brooklyn Heights.

One of the most interesting public buildings in Brooklyn Heights, perhaps as interesting for what is inside as for its outer architecture, is the Long Island Historical Society at 128 Pierrepont Street. The architect of the building was George B. Post, whose design was selected over those submitted by such eminent contemporaries as Alexander Jackson Davis, J. Cleveland Cady and Richard Upjohn. Begun in 1878, the building is a fine example of Eclecticism. Its exterior blends the earth tones of Philadelphia pressed brick with terra cotta. High-relief terra-cotta busts of noted historical figures decorate the façade, the work of the sculptor Olin Levi Warner.

Nos. 131 and 135 Hicks Street
Brooklyn Heights Historic District
c. 1848

Nos. 24 and 22 Willow Street
Brooklyn Heights Historic District
c. 1846

Nos. 2 and 3 Pierrepont Place
Brooklyn Heights Historic District
1856–57, Frederick A. Petersen

The Long Island Historical Society, which was established in 1863, is unique in the city. Its collection of books, manuscripts, maps and prints presents a complete record of the history and times of the island that has played such a dominant role in the development not only of New York City but of the whole Eastern seaboard. It even has documentation on the dates of construction and the names of occupants of most houses in Brooklyn.

An illustration of the way in which the Landmarks Preservation Commission functions within an Historic District is the story of the modern building designed for the Jehovah's Witnesses, also known as the Watchtower and Bible Tract Society, at the southeast corner of Columbia Heights and Pineapple Street, for which a proposal for a twelve-story office building was presented to the Commission for approval. Such a height would, of course, have been totally out of scale with its five-story neighbors. After considerable negotiation, the applicant agreed to a building five stories high on the street line. The architect, equating the word "historic" with "Georgian," produced a design that the members of the Commission felt was inappropriate, and they asked for something simpler. They were then presented a Greek Revival version and, subsequently, one which could only be defined as a transition between the Federal and the Grand Concourse styles. These also were rejected. Finally the applicant engaged as consultant an architect who designed a building totally contemporary with its period of 1969 but—and this is the crucial point—aesthetically compatible with its surroundings. This one was approved. Its tower is skillfully used to turn the corner, and it relates well with the buildings beyond it.

Historic Districts are not frozen immutably in the past. Life goes on and changes occur. The preservationist strives to ensure that such changes will be appropriate to their neighborhood. After all, the charm of New York City's Historic Districts depends both on the quality and on the variety of their architecture. The really important point—and one that is often missed by zealous antiquarians—is that the buildings worthy of preservation represent the best that have come down to us from widely different periods and in widely differing styles. When a new building, for one reason or another, is to be built in an Historic District it should be the best possible representation of our own day; it should speak our own idiom. But in mass, color (texture and materials) and scale, it must be compatible with its surroundings. A good contemporary building that observes these good-neighbor policies is a more appropriate addition to an Historic District than a poor copy of something, which, at best, can be nothing more than a stage set.

In the roughly fifty blocks of the Brooklyn Heights Historic District there are twelve churches, of which eight were built in the six years between 1844 and 1850. As might be expected, these are almost all Gothic Revival in style, and they include two fine examples of the work of Minard Lafever, the 1844 Church of the Savior (or First Unitarian Church), at Pierrepont Street and Monroe Place, and the 1847 Holy Trinity Protestant Episcopal Church, at Montague and Clinton Streets. Lafever, who used the Greek Revival style for his residential work, chose the Gothic Revival style for his churches. This is a good illustration of how strongly the nineteenth-century attitude toward architecture was influenced by what we would think of as nonarchitectural considerations. That the same architect— and he was one of the best—could work simultaneously in two such different traditions as the Gothic and the Greek shows how strongly he, and his patrons, were controlled by an abstract ideology—namely, that only the Gothic style could provide an appropriate setting for Christian, and particularly for Protestant Episcopal, worship.

In 1854 Lafever also used the Gothic Revival style for Packer Collegiate Institute at 170 Joralemon Street. It would be interesting to know just what led him to this choice. Perhaps Lafever in his collegiate building, like James Renwick, Jr., in his almost contemporary Smallpox Hospital on Roosevelt Island, identified higher education and the care of the sick with the church as in the medieval tradition. In any event, Gothic architecture soon became strongly identified with collegiate architecture and, to a lesser extent, with hospitals.

Four other churches in Brooklyn Heights deserve a special word. Richard Upjohn's Congregational Church of the Pilgrims at Remsen and Henry Streets (now the Maronite Rite Roman Catholic Church of Our Lady of Lebanon) has a small projecting stone in one of its walls that is said to be a fragment of Plymouth Rock. Furthermore, the west and south doors are salvage from the ill-fated liner *Normandie,* which burned at its Hudson River dock in 1942. The church was planned in 1844 and is supposed to have been the first church in the United States in the Romanesque Revival style. It predates by a decade the Marble Collegiate Church in Manhattan, whose description by its architect as "Romanesque" was a rather misleading label. Upjohn, whatever he called his work, was certainly ahead of his time with the rugged vigor of his Pilgrim Church design. Even with the loss of its spire and other minor modifications, it still makes a powerful impression. Three years later, with his brownstone Grace Church on Hicks Street at Grace Court, Upjohn returned to the safer fold of the well-established Gothic Revival style. But even what seems to us a rather innocuous work could be vehemently attacked by a contemporary. Robert Cary Long, Jr., writing of Grace Church in 1849, complained of its "thinness and meagreness" as well as its "ponderosity." Needless to add that Long was also an architect.

James Renwick, Jr.'s St. Ann's Church, at Clinton and Livingston Streets, is known as the "mother of Brooklyn churches," because its parishioners helped to organize at least six other Protestant Episcopal congregations. It is a good example of post–Civil War Victorian Gothic, similar to the Green-Wood Cemetery gates which his great competitors, Richard Upjohn & Son, had designed just a few years earlier.

J. C. Wells's huge Italianate Plymouth Church on Orange Street, built in 1849, is very early for this style. Plymouth Church merged with the Pilgrim Church in 1934 and has since been known as the Plymouth Church of the Pilgrims, but the piece of Plymouth Rock still remains in the Remsen Street church. Plymouth Church's political history is almost more interesting than its architectural history, for this was where the famed and flamboyant Henry Ward Beecher, violent abolitionist, presided for forty years, 1847–87. He and his sister Harriet Beecher Stowe, whose book *Uncle Tom's Cabin* probably did more for the antislavery movement than all her brother's eloquence and showmanship, were among the thirteen children of Lyman Beecher, of whom it was said that "he was the father of more brains than any other man in America." Henry Ward Beecher was a man of tremendous vitality who could shout down all the proslavery hecklers that sought to silence him. Beecher once brought a beautiful mulatto girl to the church with the announced intention of auctioning her off to the highest bidder. Crowds stormed the church and thousands had to be turned away while Beecher extolled the beauty of the girl, who was dressed in virginal white. His eloquence roused the crowd to a fury of indignation, and he soon had a healthy sum of money and a collection of jewels with which to buy the girl's freedom.

The later years of Beecher's life were clouded by a suit for $100,000 brought in 1874 by one Theodore Tilton, a former associate, who charged the minister with having had improper relations with Mrs. Tilton. After a trial that lasted six months and that titillated the whole country, the jury could not agree. Although his own church exonerated Beecher, his reputation and influence, which had previously been nationwide, suffered considerably from the scandal.

COBBLE HILL

The Cobble Hill Historic District is really an extension of Brooklyn Heights, both geographically and in time sequence. Just as Brooklyn Heights was developed after the 1814 opening of the Fulton Street steam ferry to Manhattan, so Cobble Hill, south of Atlantic Avenue, began to develop when what came to be known as the South Ferry from Atlantic Avenue began to operate in 1836. Cobble Hill also follows Brooklyn Heights in the sequence of its architectural styles. There are no Federal houses and only a few of the Greek Revival, but there are many in the Gothic and Romanesque Revival and Queen Anne styles.

In the process of dating the earliest examples of each of these styles, it was discovered that new architectural fashions generally made their appearance on Cobble Hill anywhere from five to fifteen years after they were first introduced in Manhattan. This is particularly true of the builder-designed houses, which represent by far the largest number. Such a consistent time lag suggests that perhaps the builders in this rather quiet backwater were not quite sure of their own taste. They would wait to see whether or not a new style caught on before risking their money to build a row of houses that the public might not fancy. This supposition is supported by the fact that the few architect-designed houses on Cobble Hill are usually as up-to-the-minute as any; after all, it was only their clients' money they would be risking.

Cobble Hill, with its predominance of three-and-a-half-story brick or brownstone houses along tree-lined streets, has a homogeneity that

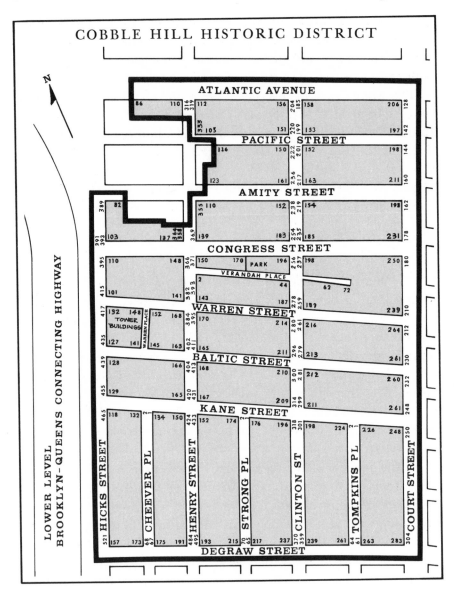

Brooklyn Heights, with the intrusion of high-rise buildings, lacks. Some people have called it the poor man's Brooklyn Heights, and in many ways it is. But its very simplicity and modesty give it a particular integrity.

Cobble Hill can boast of extraordinarily fine ironwork. Nowhere else in the city have so many interesting designs survived, some of them unique to Cobble Hill. This is particularly true along Tompkins Place and Cheever Place, in addition to good individual examples elsewhere.

Fine illustrations of the various architectural styles exist, either singly or in short rows, interrupted occasionally by interesting churches. Nos. 228 to 238 Warren Street, a row of six Greek Revival houses, are particularly fine examples of this style and have some outstanding ironwork. A good example of Gothic Revival in domestic architecture is No. 271 Degraw Street. Three very fine Italianate houses are located at 166–170 Congress Street, while No. 179 Amity Street is a good example of a French Second Empire town house. A small clubhouse at 162 Pacific Street is an example of Romanesque Revival. Of later styles, Nos. 143–153 Amity Street retain their original neo-Grec appearances and Nos. 33–43 Strong Place are a charming row of little town houses in the Queen Anne style. No. 219 Clinton Street on the corner of Amity Street is an imposing example of the Eclectic period. Its combination of neo-Romanesque and neo–Flemish Renaissance makes it unique.

Perhaps the most momentous event ever to have taken place on Cobble Hill was its use by General Washington as an observation post during the disastrous Battle of Long Island. After the American evacuation of Brooklyn, the British are supposed to have cut off the top of Cobble Hill so that it would not command their headquarters on Brooklyn Heights.

For most of its subsequent history, and after its transformation from open estates and farmland, Cobble Hill was a quiet, comfortable suburb. The Upjohns, both father and son, lived in the district, and so did Leonard Jerome after he moved from Rochester in the 1850s. Before he built his Madison Square mansion he occupied in succession two rented houses here. His glamorous daughter Jennie, mother of Sir Winston Churchill, was born in the house now known as No. 197 Amity Street. But most of the Cobble Hill residents, through the second half of the nineteenth century, were modestly prosperous solid citizens.

As in Brooklyn Heights, there came a gradual change at the end of the nineteenth century and well through the first half of the twentieth. The original native-born Americans and the English and the Germans were gradually succeeded by Irish, Swedes, Norwegians,

Italians, Syrians, Greeks, Lebanese and Puerto Ricans. These relative newcomers have, however, been among the most active instigators of the Cobble Hill renaissance. The Cobble Hill Association, incorporated in 1959, and the considerably older Syrian Young Men's Association have spearheaded the movement. It is most appropriate that this should be so, for Cobble Hill is the site of one of the earliest and most interesting sociological experiments in the history of American architecture.

In 1876–77, Alfred Tredway White, a Brooklyn businessman and

No. 219 Clinton Street   Cobble Hill Historic District

philanthropist interested in tenement-house reform, decided to put his theories to the test. He based his plans on English models, but was also influenced by some American idealists such as Walt Whitman, who, as early as 1856, had urged builders to "mingle a little philanthropy with their money making and to construct tenement houses with a view to the comfort of the inmates as well as the maximum of rent." White believed that this could be done; he built a project at Hicks and Baltic Streets designed to be rented to working people at modest rentals and also designed to bring him a five percent return on his investment. White, to his death, claimed that he was no philanthropist and that he always made his five percent. No sooner had he finished his first project, the Home Buildings, than he started another, the Tower Buildings, on the next block—on Hicks Street from Baltic to Warren Street. William Field & Son were the architects for both projects. They provided central courtyards for recreation as well as light and air for the tenants. They designed central stair towers that could be entered only from open balconies that gave access to the individual apartments. This arrangement ensured that in case a fire started in any of the apartments the stairwell would not become filled with smoke. This simple but highly effective safety provision was later, after the First World War, hailed as a great innovation in Holland and Germany, where it was called the *Ausgang* method of apartment planning.

White followed his apartment houses with an enchanting group of two-story houses, only eleven and a half feet wide and thirty-two feet deep, on Warren Place, behind the Tower Buildings. The twenty-six narrow houses face one another across a center island of greenery and flowers. Each has six rooms, while eight larger houses at the ends of the court have nine. Each of these houses, like the apartments in the Home and Tower Buildings, had its own toilet facilities, an unusual feature in those days, particularly in low- and middle-income housing. White thus, several generations ahead of his time, provided a truly modern and ideal complex—flats, small one-family houses, green spaces, recreation areas and even indoor plumbing. The small houses on Warren Place today are all privately owned and are priced far beyond the means of those members of the "laboring classes" for whom they were intended, but the apartment rentals are still within the means of low- and middle-income groups.

Tower Buildings, 417-435 Hicks Street
Cobble Hill Historic District
1878–79, William Field & Son

Warren Place
Cobble Hill Historic District
1878, William Field & Son

Both Minard Lafever and Richard Upjohn built notable churches on Cobble Hill, less imposing, perhaps, than those on Brooklyn Heights, but still important. Lafever designed what is now St. Frances Cabrini Roman Catholic Chapel of Degraw Street. It was originally the Strong Place Baptist Church and was designed in the Gothic Revival style in the early 1850s. In 1841–42, Upjohn did his Christ Episcopal Church at Clinton and Kane Streets in the same style. With its rectangular plan and square entrance tower set in the center of the front façade, Christ Church and the slightly earlier Church of the Ascension in Greenwich Village were, in a sense, Upjohn's exercises for the famous Trinity Church he was to design a few years later on Broadway at the head of Wall Street. Christ Church is particularly noteworthy for its interior furnishing designed by Louis Comfort Tiffany in 1917.

One other large church in Cobble Hill, St. Paul's, at the corner of Congress and Court Streets, has had an interesting history. The original portion, which was built in 1838, was designed in the Greek Revival style. However, in 1860, in order to bring it up to date and into fashion, it had a tower added and was refaced in the Gothic Revival style.

STUYVESANT HEIGHTS

For most of its early history, Stuyvesant Heights was part of the outlying farm area of the small hamlet of Bedford, which had been settled by the Dutch during the seventeenth century within the incorporated town of Breuckelen. In time Bedford Corners, near the present Historic District, became an important crossroads of the growing network of roads leading from the East River to the eastern part of Long Island. By the 1860s the gridiron street system of the district began to be built. In a frenzy of patriotism, many of the new streets were named after prominent figures in American naval history— Thomas MacDonough, Stephen Decatur, William Bainbridge, Isaac Chauncey—while avenues were named for New York governors: Peter Stuyvesant, Morgan Lewis, Enos T. Throop, Daniel D. Tompkins. (Sumner Avenue was originally Yates Avenue, after Governor Joseph C. Yates.)

By 1869 the area was still largely rural, with a few freestanding country homes. But the next year saw the introduction of masonry row houses which were destined to change the whole section into an urban community. By the 1890s building development was in full swing. But even under the pressure of real-estate promotion there

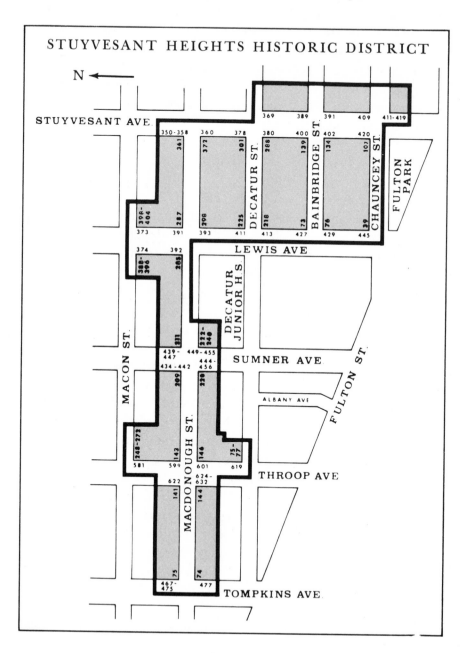

were some sober and far-seeing community leaders who laid down ground rules. For example, the owner of the property on the south side of Decatur Street sold his land to the Embury Methodist Church, now the Mount Lebanon Baptist Church, with the stipulation that the church "must have plenty of room for both air and light to breathe and worship in." The rear of the street he insisted be "for townhouses only."

Middle-class merchants and shopkeepers with a sprinkling of professionals, mostly German and Irish, were the original owners of Stuyvesant Heights homes. When the Williamsburg Bridge opened in 1903 the area attracted the Manhattan commuter. With the influx the area became increasingly elegant.

But, as elsewhere, the depression of the 1930s took its toll of the original property owners, who were either too old or too poor to keep up their homes. Blacks, from Harlem and the South, refugees from the ghettos, both urban and rural, sought a new way of life in Stuyvesant Heights. Real-estate speculators inaugurated a vicious block-busting campaign between 1930 and 1950. They bought houses at depressed prices from panic-stricken white owners and sold them at such inflated prices to blacks that the new owners had to convert them to multifamily units.

Today, Stuyvesant Heights has reverted to a stable community of proud middle-class folk, predominantly black. Residents take tremendous pride in their homes, most of which are still owner occupied. If the houses are divided into apartments, they are generally rented to other members of the family.

In contrast to the row houses of Cobble Hill, which were usually built three or four at a time, the rows in Stuyvesant Heights are generally longer, sometimes extending for a whole block. Moreover, and this is their particular distinction, these rows were often designed as unified architectural compositions, with a beginning, a middle and an end, rather than as so many identical units being turned out of a machine. Examples of this approach have been seen in the four magnificent block fronts of the St. Nicholas Historic District in Manhattan.

Most of the rows were built for speculative purposes by local Brooklyn builders and by local Brooklyn architects. All the builders and almost all the architects lived in or near the district and took great

pride in their work. They built well. It was a period of good craftsmanship, and that these blocks have survived and retained their
integrity is a credit to the way in which they were conceived and
constructed.

French Second Empire and neo-Grec were the dominant styles of
the 1880s. Here, as at Cobble Hill, the fashions ran about ten to
fifteen years behind the times. By the end of the decade almost all of
the four blocks of MacDonough Street were built up on both sides,
very much as we see them today.

The 1890s saw the development of block fronts along Lewis and
Stuyvesant Avenues and the cross streets between them. They also
saw the introduction of the L-shaped front stoop, a gracious and
opulent feature which first appears in the row from No. 106 to 116
Bainbridge Street. The more up-to-date neo-Romanesque and Queen
Anne styles began to catch on at the same time and often with

Bainbridge Street, corner Lewis Avenue
Stuyvesant Heights Historic District

romantic mixtures of the two, either from house to house in a particular row or combined in a single façade.

After the turn of the century, neo–Italian Renaissance elements added spice to an already rich mixture, and the classical influence of the Chicago Exposition inevitably began to be felt. The latter is first seen along the west side of Stuyvesant Avenue, between Bainbridge and Decatur Streets, in a row in which round and polygonal front bays alternate and where some neo-Romanesque traces are still to be found. Purely neo–American Classic designs in white limestone followed, by 1910, along both sides of Stuyvesant Avenue in the most southerly block of the Historic District. The last row to be built in Stuyvesant Heights was on the south side of Bainbridge Street, where fifteen brick houses alternate the neo-Georgian and neo–Spanish Renaissance styles.

Three notable churches punctuate the otherwise purely residential character of Stuyvesant Heights. They are as active today in serving the community around them as they were at the time they were built.

The neo-Romanesque Mount Lebanon Baptist Church on Decatur Street near Lewis Avenue, with its adjoining parsonage, was originally built in 1894 as the Embury Methodist Episcopal Church. It is a boldly asymmetrical composition with a strong arched entrance balanced by a round tower and a great flat gable. St. Philip's Episcopal Church, which was erected in 1898–99 on MacDonough Street as the Church of the Good Shepherd, is an academically correct neo-Gothic building carried out in rough ashlar. A red-brick and polychrome parish house and Sunday school, which runs through to Decatur Street, was added in 1905.

Most picturesque of the three is the late Victorian Gothic group that runs from MacDonough Street along Throop Avenue to Macon Street. It includes Our Lady of Victory Church, built in the 1890s of dark-gray random ashlar with strongly accented quoins and decorations around the windows in lighter stone. This building was designed by the Brooklyn architect Thomas Houghton, while the rectory, the convent and the school were added in the 1920s by Helmle & Corbett, another famous Brooklyn architectural firm that continued in the Houghton spirit. Incidentally, the Corbett of this firm later was to be associated with the group of architects who made the first plan for Rockefeller Center.

CARROLL GARDENS HISTORIC DISTRICT

This district, which includes over 158 buildings, covers the areas of Carroll and President Streets between Smith and Hoyt Streets. It is an outstanding testimonial to the intelligence, cooperativeness and civic imagination of an early group of real-estate developers. The area was built up betwen 1859 and 1884 by a series of developer-builders, including William J. Bedell and his family, Edward P. Crane, Theodore Pearson and John Layton. They used brownstone facing shipped from quarries in New Jersey and a wide variety of ornamental elements manufactured in small local factories. They combined these elements in various ways but displayed a rare sense of community consciousness by using for each house a design that would be in harmony with its neighbors.

The two- and three-story houses are built in long rows, set far back behind carefully tended gardens. They conform to the slope of the streets, with gradual adjustments in the height of stoops and roof and cornice lines. The nearby Carroll Park and the offset layout of the surrounding streets give the district a delightfully deceptive air of self-containment.

PARK SLOPE HISTORIC DISTRICT

This district is a roughly inverted L-shaped area adjacent to Prospect Park and the Grand Army Plaza and is bounded approximately by the park on the east, Flatbush Avenue on the northeast, Park Place on the north, Sixth, Seventh and Eighth Avenues on the west and Fourteenth Street on the extreme southern end.

The Park Slope Historic District contains over 1,900 structures which present an important cross section of the trends in American architecture during the five decades between the Civil War and World War I. The late Italianate, French Second Empire, neo-Grec, Victorian Gothic, Queen Anne, Romanesque Revival, neo-Renaissance, neo-American Classic, neo-Federal and neo-Georgian are all represented by well-designed examples. Yet, despite this mixture, the row houses in Park Slope provide a good example of self-generated town planning. Even long rows of twenty or so houses are given interest through dis-

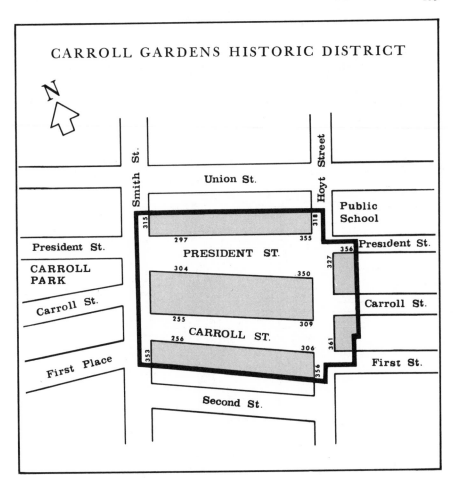

CARROLL GARDENS HISTORIC DISTRICT

N

Smith St.

Union St.

Hoyt Street

Public
School

President St.

315

318

297

355

356

President St.

CARROLL
PARK

PRESIDENT ST.

304

350

327

Carroll St.

255

309

Carroll St.

256

CARROLL ST.

306

361

First Place

353

356

First St.

Second St.

ciplined variety. Three-sided bay windows may alternate with curved fronts; materials, colors, details and the depths of front yards may have subtle variations—and yet the whole district has a wonderful quality of homogeneity and coherence.

Builders began to take an interest in the area in the late 1860s and early '70s, but it was the opening of Brooklyn Bridge in 1883 that brought the high tide of development. The well-to-do concentrated in the upper tier, and particularly along the park frontages in what became known as "the Gold Coast." Houses and walk-up apartment houses below Eleventh Street were built for people of more modest means. Today the entire Historic District attracts a cross section of

PARK SLOPE HISTORIC DISTRICT

Prospect Pl.

Park Pl.

Park Pl.

Sterling

Flatbush Ave.

Sterling Pl.

Park Pl.

Butler Pl.

St. Ave.

John's Pl.

Plaza St.

Underhill Ave.

Lincoln Pl.

SIXTH AVE.

Pl.

ST. JOHN'S PL.

LINCOLN PL.

BERKELEY PL.

SEVENTH AVE.

Grand
Army
Plaza

Eastern Parkway

FIFTH AVE.

Flatbush Avenue

UNION ST.

PRESIDENT ST.

POLHEMUS

FISKE PL.

CARROLL ST.

M'TGM'RY PL.

SIXTH AVE.

EIGHTH AVE.

PARK WEST

GARFIELD PL.

1st ST.

N

2nd ST.

SEVENTH AVE.

3rd ST.

4th ST.

5th ST.

PROSPECT
PARK

6th ST.

PROSPECT

7th ST.

8th ST.

EIGHTH AVE.

9th ST.

10th ST.

11th ST.

12th ST.

13th ST.

14th ST.

Bartel
Pritchard
Sq

15th St

Prospect Park Southwest

people who appreciate the nearby park, the substantial well-built houses and the relative tranquillity of the neighborhood.

Unique not only in Park Slope but in the whole city is the Montauk Club, designed by Francis H. Kimball and completed in 1891. While it was clearly inspired by the Gothic palaces of Venice, it is not a slavish copy of any particular one. The architect, by the introduction of American Indian motifs and details drawn from native flora and fauna, has endowed it with its own special character. It is one of the few survivors of the many private clubs that once abounded in Brooklyn.

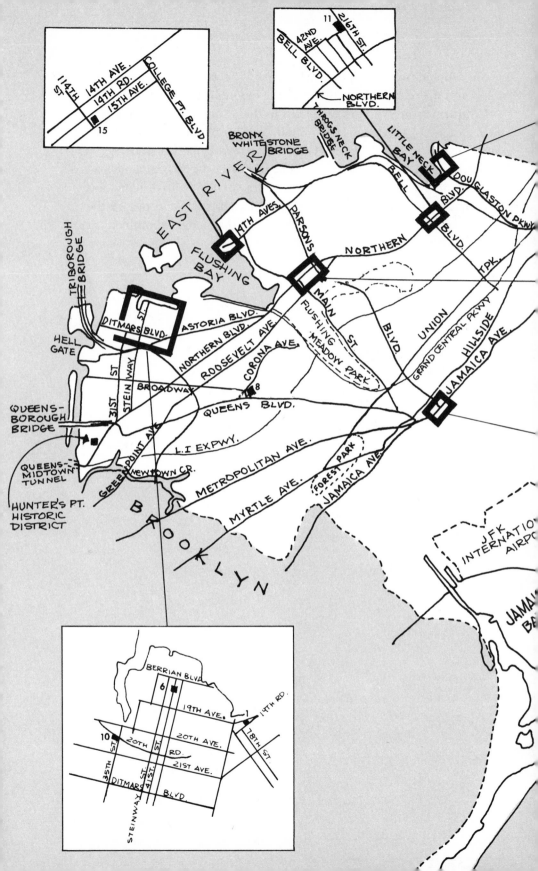

Inset (top left):
114TH ST.
114TH AVE.
114TH RD.
115TH AVE.
COLLEGE PT. BLVD.
15

Inset (top right):
11
216TH ST.
42ND AVE.
BELL BLVD.
NORTHERN BLVD.

Main map labels:
BRONX WHITESTONE BRIDGE
THROGS NECK BRIDGE
LITTLE NECK BAY
DOUGLASTON PKWY.
BELL BLVD.
EAST RIVER
14TH AVE.
PARSONS
NORTHERN
FLUSHING BAY
MAIN ST.
UNION
GRAND CENTRAL PKWY.
HILLSIDE AVE.
JAMAICA AVE.
TK.
TRIBOROUGH BRIDGE
DITMARS BLVD.
ASTORIA BLVD.
NORTHERN BLVD.
ROOSEVELT AVE.
CORONA AVE.
FLUSHING MEADOW PARK
BLVD.
HELL GATE
31ST ST.
STEINWAY
BROADWAY
QUEENS BLVD.
8
QUEENS-BOROUGH BRIDGE
L.I EXPWY.
METROPOLITAN AVE.
FOREST PARK
JAMAICA AVE.
9
QUEENS-MIDTOWN TUNNEL
GREENPOINT AVE.
NEWTOWN CR.
MYRTLE AVE.
HUNTER'S PT. HISTORIC DISTRICT
BROOKLYN
JFK INTERNATIONAL AIRPORT
JAMAICA BAY

Inset (bottom):
BERRIAN BLVD.
6
19TH AVE.
14TH RD.
10
20TH ST.
20TH AVE.
18TH ST.
20TH RD.
21ST AVE.
35TH ST.
41ST ST.
DITMARS BLVD.
STEINWAY ST.
1

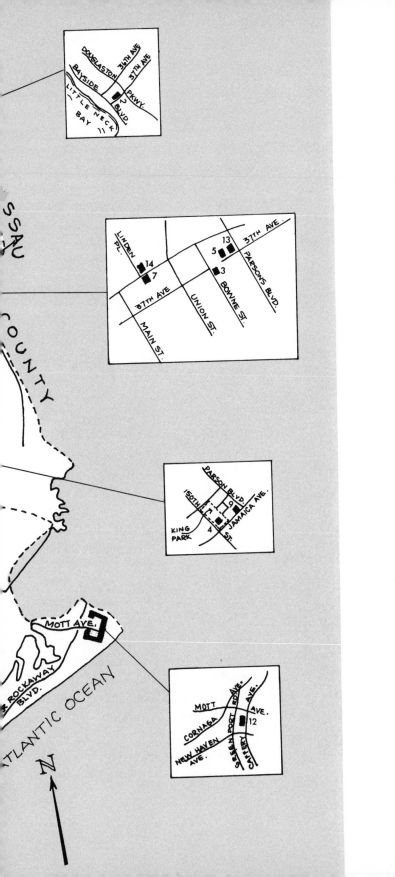

QUEENS

CHAPTER NINE

QUEENS

PHYSICALLY, Queens is the largest of the five boroughs of the City of New York and the second largest in population, with two million inhabitants. It is hard to realize that less than a century and a quarter ago Queens was a semirural, rather gentle and relaxed area of barely twenty thousand people. Until the end of World War I whole sections of the eastern part of the borough were still completely rural.

The exact date and place of the first settlement in Queens are a matter of controversy. We know that Maspeth received a charter from the Dutch in 1642 and that Middleburg, later known as Newtown, was settled in 1652 under the same patent. The patent for Flushing (corrupted from the Dutch Vlissingen) dates from 1645 and for Jamaica from 1660.

The Dutch were liberal in permitting English migrants from New England to settle in sparsely inhabited areas of New Netherland. When the English took over the colony in 1664, they confirmed the Dutch grants to the early villages, and in 1683 they organized Queens County, named in honor of Catherine of Braganza, queen of Charles II of England. It was one of the twelve counties in what at that time constituted the British province of New York, which included such farflung areas as parts of Maine and Vermont and islands off the coast of Massachusetts.

The early Queens settlements remained completely isolated, not only from one another but also from New Amsterdam. They did not coalesce naturally, as did those of Brooklyn by growing along the interconnecting roads. Rather, they remained essentially independent until quite recently– in fact, until the 1920s. Since then they have been forcibly homogenized by vast real-estate developments, mainly of single-family or semidetached two-family houses. Since World War II huge multifamily housing developments have risen to dominate parts of the landscape.

A single continuous ridge, part of the glacial terminal moraine that starts in Brooklyn, runs slightly north of east like a backbone along the center of Queens, through Cypress Hills, Kew Gardens, Jamaica Hills, Fresh Meadows and up into Little Neck. North of the ridge the ground is broken and rolling, while to the south it is un-relievedly flat. It terminates in the great Jamaica Bay. This remark-able body of water, with its wildlife refuge, has long been under threat of encroachment by the neighboring Kennedy International Airport, which is constantly seeking more and longer runways. The bay is protected from the open Atlantic by the long Rockaway Peninsula, which, with Coney Island in Brooklyn, marks the westernmost of the series of sand spits that protect the whole southern shore of Long Island. With the creation of the Gateway National Park, not only are the superb beaches at the western end of Rockaway Peninsula to be preserved for public enjoyment, but Jamaica Bay itself will be saved for the undisturbed tenancy of its native and migratory birds.

There is a staggering network of highways that lace the borough in all directions, connecting Manhattan, Brooklyn and The Bronx with the city's two great airports, Kennedy and La Guardia; with its two racetracks, Aqueduct and Belmont (which is technically in Nassau County but whose western gate is just within the Queens County line) ; and with the suburbs and playgrounds of Long Island. In addi-tion, Queens is famous for its "Cemetery Belt." Anyone who has driven along the Interborough Parkway will not wonder why this route is known as the "terminal moraine." It passes through what seems like endless acres of graveyards, one following another without interruption: Calvary, New Cavalry, Mount Zion, Mount Olivet, Lutheran, St. John's and dozens of others.

Since there is no real tradition of Queens as a whole, its people give imaginary attributes to the names of their local communities in order to have something with which they can identify. Often, these individual localities cannot be physically distinguished from one another. Stanley Milgram, in his study on how New Yorkers "see" their city, found that a resident of Queens is four times more likely to recognize a street location in Manhattan than one in his home borough. People rarely say they live in Queens; they live in Rego Park or Jackson Heights or Fresh Meadows. These place names have more reality to their residents than the sprawling, amorphous mass that "Queens" represents. And yet many of these names are of recent origin; only a handful, such as Newtown, Maspeth, Flushing, Jamaica or College Point, have roots in history.

William I. Thompson, in his book *At the Edge of History*, might almost be describing Queens when he says, writing about Los Angeles:

> If the urban sprawl is without order, [man] will see patterns in it even if these patterns are paranoid signs of a conspiracy. . . . Precisely because there is no real tradition, the elders create fantasies of mother, country, God (who is really Uncle Sam in more heavenly attire), private property, flag and family and on and on in the litany of the atavist.

Queens today is becoming the stronghold of the middle class. It is the haven of those, both black and white, who flee the ghettos and crime of other parts of the city. Of its two million inhabitants, 250,000 are black, and the borough has more individual homes owned by blacks than the rest of the city combined. The whole borough has 205,000 one-family homes, 77,000 two-family homes and 313,000 apartment units, many of them in small buildings. It has 16,278 acres of parks—more acreage than the entire island of Manhattan.

The very youth of Queens explains why there is a paucity of structures that can qualify as Landmarks. Its rural origins are represented by a few remaining farmhouses. In the old towns there is some fine civic and ecclesiastical architecture. Some isolated examples of great mansions also survive.

Farmhouses and a Manor

Two strains can be traced through what survives of the vernacular rural architecture of Queens—the so-called Dutch Colonial type and the English. They are roughly contemporary, and an Englishman was as likely to be found living in a "Dutch Colonial" house as was a Dutchman.

Two "Dutch" farmhouses, the Lent Homestead in Steinway and the Cornelius Van Wyck House in Douglaston, offer a contrast in the integrity of their preservation. The Lent Homestead was built in 1729 and still retains almost all of its original stonework, hewn timbers and shingles. The dormer windows are products of a later period. On the other hand, the Van Wyck House, which was built around 1735, is the victim of a number of additions, the earliest going back to the eighteenth century and the most recent and disastrous to 1930: asphalt shingles on the roof and scalloped shingles on the exterior walls.

Lent Homestead
78-03 19th Road, Steinway
c. 1729

2. Cornelius Van Wyck House
37-04 Douglaston Parkway, Douglaston
c. 1735–40
South and west extension: c. 1770
Alterations and kitchen wing: 1920–30

The Lent house retains the typical overshot Dutch Colonial roof, sloping steeply and with a slight lift at the overhang, both front and rear, just like a modern ski jump. It was built by Abraham Lent, a grandson of Abraham Riker, of the family that gave its name to Riker's Island, the prison compound in the swirling East River just north of La Guardia Airport. When Abraham Lent died, his will provided: ". . . my plantation where I now dwell is to be sold among my children to the one that shall give the most for it." His youngest son, Jacobus, bought the property. This house illustrates how the early farmers built with the materials at hand—stone from the fields, timber, trim and shingles cut from the surrounding forests.

The earliest part of the Van Wyck House was built by Cornelius Van Wyck, who sired three sons. One was a fervent Revolutionary patriot who died as a result of a year's confinement on board one of the notorious British prison ships. The youngest son was an ardent Tory who remained loyal to the British Crown to the very end and joined the Loyalist exodus to Nova Scotia. One of Cornelius' descendants was the first mayor of New York to be elected by popular vote; another was the first bishop of the Protestant Episcopal Church in the United States.

The English vernacular tradition is well illustrated in the Bowne House in Flushing. The earliest portion consisted of a kitchen with bedrooms upstairs and was built by John Bowne in 1661. Various additions were made in 1680 and 1691. In 1830 the roof was raised and the north wing added. But the house still retains much of its original appearance. Its steep roof and shed dormers suggest medieval British traditions. It is notable not only for its architecture and age (it is the oldest house in Queens) but also for its identification with the struggle for religious freedom in this country.

John Bowne, an Englishman who settled in Flushing in 1651, was originally a member of the Church of England, but sometime before 1662 he joined the Society of Friends, or Quakers—so called because the English founder, George Fox, frequently and with vehemence called upon his congregation to "tremble at the word of God." Defying the orders of Governor Peter Stuyvesant, who called the society "an abominable sect," Bowne offered the use of his kitchen as a meeting place for the hounded Friends. Bowne was arrested, fined and imprisoned in September 1662. In December of that year, Stuyvesant,

3. Bowne House   37-01 Bowne Street, Flushing
  c. 1661
  Additions: 1680, 1691
  Roof raised: 1830

whose only wish was to be rid of the intransigent and troublesome Friends, deported him to Holland.

The ship carrying Bowne docked at Dublin, and, heaping injury upon insult, its master demanded that Bowne pay for his passage, which the authorities in New Netherland had somehow neglected to provide for. Bowne refused, with some heat, to pay for his own exile. With the help of Quaker friends, he made his way to Amsterdam, where he argued for religious tolerance before the Dutch West India Company with such eloquence that the astounded Peter Stuyvesant received instructions from the home office to see to it that the "people's conscience should not be forced by anyone but remain free in itself." With this, the principle of freedom of worship was established in the New World—a principle that was subsequently written into the Bill of Rights.

The Bowne House, in which nine generations of Bownes have lived, is today called "a shrine to religious freedom" and is operated as a museum by the Bowne House Historical Society. It stands in an

4. *King Mansion   King Park, 150th Street and Jamaica Avenue, Jamaica*
Rear cottage: 1730
West front and connection: 1750
East front, entrance and porch: 1806

attractive, well-kept garden, not far from the Friends' Meeting House
that Bowne helped establish in 1694 after his reunion with his family
in Flushing.

Totally different in its character and history is the King Mansion
in Jamaica. The oldest part, which still contains the original kitchen,
was a one-story cottage built in 1730. It was used as a parsonage by the
Reverend Thomas Poyer of the nearby Grace Episcopal Church. His
successor, the Reverend Thomas Colgan, bought it from Poyer's
widow and, in 1750, added the westerly portion of what is now the
main body of the house. He also connected this with the old kitchen
by a one-and-a-half-story link. Rufus King bought the property in
1805, and the next year he added the eastern section and unified the
whole with the present porch and handsome Federal-style entrance
door with its leaded sidelights and transom. Though built of wood
rather than of brick or stone, this house provides a good picture of

what the country seat of a wealthy gentleman of the early nineteenth century looked like.

Rufus King, statesman, diplomat, friend of Presidents, four times senator from New York, and an unsuccessful Presidential candidate in 1816, was a born aristocrat, went to the best schools, joined the best law firms, had all the right things going for him, and yet history seems to have passed him by. The probable reason is that it was his misfortune to live (1755–1827) in an era of giants. Not only were Washington, Adams, Hamilton, Jefferson and Franklin giants; they were colorful and they were movers of men. They were hard to compete with.

King's actual accomplishments, however, were many. He helped draft the Constitution by "revising the style and arranging the articles," according to a contemporary account. His tact and resourcefulness as minister to London during the years 1796–1803 are largely credited with having smoothed relations between the recent enemies and with having averted or, perhaps more properly, with having postponed another war. He was a strong opponent of the extension of slavery into the new territories, and an important contributor to the Missouri Compromise.

Today the King Mansion is under the jurisdiction of the Parks Department, and its interior is maintained by the King Manor Association. It is open to the public as a museum.

No connection of the aristocratic King family of Jamaica was Joseph King, dashing English sea captain who settled in Flushing in the latter part of the eighteenth century. His comfortable farmhouse, which he called Kingsland, had been built in 1774 by his father-in-law, Charles Doughty, a wealthy Quaker farmer who is reputed to have been the first person to free a slave in Queens—his servant Sarah. Captain King had been captured by French privateers during the French Revolution and imprisoned in Paris. Through the intercession of an unknown American he was smuggled out of France to New York, and eventually he settled down in Flushing to the life of a well-to-do farmer.

The house is an interesting mixture of Dutch and English vernacular traditions. The central chimney, the gambrel roof and the quadrant windows in the gable suggest New England. The split front door is typically Dutch.

Almost more significant than its simple architecture or its early history are the twentieth-century adventures of the Kingsland Homestead. In 1968 the little farmhouse, which was then located on 155th Street, found itself about to be gobbled up by the expansion of an adjoining supermarket parking lot. Through the agitation of local community groups, the intervention of the City Planning Commission, the active participation of the newly established Landmarks Preservation Commission and the cooperation of the Parks Department, arrangements were ultimately worked out, after a few cliff-hanging crises, to lift the old building from its foundations and roll it a dozen blocks to Weeping Beech Park, where it has now been restored, largely through private funds, as a congenial neighbor to two other Landmarks—the Weeping Beech Tree itself and the Bowne House. It is open to the public as a museum.

Different, as though from another world, as indeed it is, is the

5. *Kingsland Homestead   37th Avenue between Parsons Boulevard and*
   Bowne Street, Flushing (formerly 40-25 155th Street)
   1774
   Moved 1968

6. *Steinway Mansion*
18-33 41st Street, Steinway
c. 1850s

great Steinway Mansion of the 1850s in the northwest corner of Queens. The house was built by Benjamin Pike, a prominent optician. In the 1870s it was bought by William Steinway, who in 1881 moved his piano factory to Queens to escape the labor problems of Manhattan. The family occupied the house until the 1920s. It has twenty-seven rooms, elaborately carved ceilings, a four-story tower and a domed entrance rotunda. A grandson of William, John Steinway, recalls that in the skylight of the dome there was a huge stained-glass eye. "I thought it was the Eye of God, and it wasn't until many years later that I realized it was probably the trademark of the optician who built the house."

The mansion is typical of the great nineteenth-century country houses that are so characteristic of Riverdale but rare in Queens. It can best be described as a romantic Italianate country villa. It is Italianate in its details but wildly romantic with its roughhewn stone-work, its asymmetrically placed tower, its porches, its bay windows, terraces and arcades. The Corinthian columns which support its main entrance porch are made of cast iron rather than stone or wood. These mass-produced structural elements were just then coming into wide use for commercial buildings, and it is surprising to find them in so magnificent a mansion.

Originally, the house, from its eminence, had an expansive view over the East River and was surrounded by lawns and tennis courts, stables and orchards, as well as a village of homes for piano plant workers. The whole area eventually became known as Steinway. Now its neighbors include a sewage plant, a packing-materials factory, a contractor's garage and several junkyards.

A Meeting House, Churches, Graveyards and a Tree

The Friends' Meeting House on Northern Boulevard in Flushing is not only the oldest house of worship standing in New York City, but one of the oldest in the country. It has been continuously used by the Society of Friends since 1694 except for the period between 1776 and 1783, during which the British used it successively as a prison, a store-house for hay and a hospital. The meeting house was built on land held in the names of John Bowne and John Rodman. Their title to the property was a piece of legal fiction. The Society of Friends could not own property in the province of New York, so Bowne's and Rodman's names appeared on the deed in order to circumvent the law.

The meeting house is just around the corner from Bowne's own home, which had been used for Quaker meetings until the new building was ready. The original section is the easterly third of the present building. It has tiny windows and a very steep hipped roof— both medieval characteristics.

In 1716–19 the building was enlarged to its present size, but the original chimney was not rebuilt. Rising on the line of the original west wall, it gives the present roof its asymmetrical appearance. The roof is almost as high as the two stories below it. There are separate double entrance doors for men and for women under the south porch, which was added in the nineteenth century. The interior with its hardwood benches and total lack of adornment is typical of the restraint and austerity that has always characterized the Quakers.

7. *Friends' Meeting House   137-16 Northern Boulevard, Flushing*
1694
Enlarged 1716–19

The meeting house stands with its back to Northern Boulevard, along which now thunder day and night the cars, trucks and buses of the twentieth century. It faces south so that the faithful, spartan though they were, might profit from what warmth the winter sun could give them. It wasn't until 1760 that two iron stoves were installed to fend off chilblains. In 1956, after 195 winters, the two stoves were finally replaced by a central heating system.

South of the Friends' Meeting House is a very old and very peaceful cemetery. Until the mid–nineteenth century the graves were not marked at all, and even after 1835 they were identified merely by small, uniform stones, on the theory that everyone is equal in death. John Bowne is buried here, as well as William Burling and John Farmer, who, among the first in America, spoke out against the institution of slavery as early as 1716. Also buried here is John Murray, who was the founder of both the New York Society for the Manumission of Slaves and the New York Public School Society. Through his work with the latter organization, he is considered to be the father of public education in New York City. Samuel Leggett is also buried here. In 1823 he organized the New York Gas Light Company, and his home in Manhattan was the first house in the city to be lighted by gas.

The Reformed Dutch Church of Newtown and its adjoining Fellowship Hall form a delightfully unsophisticated pair of structures that were not actually united until 1906, when Fellowship Hall, built as a chapel in 1854, was moved to line up with the church, which dates from 1831. The latter is one of the oldest wooden churches in the city, though unfortunately the original wood clapboards have recently

8. Reformed Dutch Church of Newtown and Fellowship Hall
85-15 Broadway, Elmhurst
Church: 1831
Fellowship Hall: 1854
Fellowship Hall moved and buildings joined: 1906

been covered with an aluminum imitation. It was built in the Greek Revival period, but the steepness of the pediment, the modillions supporting the cornice, and the bull's-eye window are reminiscent of the Georgian period. The graceful octagonal belfry with its slender colonnettes and its roundheaded windows is quite Federal in feeling. In the main body of the church what were originally squareheaded windows were later "Gothicized" by label moldings and tracery. Fellowship Hall, in the same independent spirit, though half the size of the adjoining church, has a portico twice the height of the church porch. Yet, taken altogether, this naïve mixture of styles and scale has a certain rural charm and gives the impression of long, active and affectionate use.

Grace Episcopal Church in Jamaica is totally different in spirit, though the original portion was built within a year of Fellowship Hall. The church is a good example of the Gothic Revival style at its height. Handsomely constructed of stone, with a spire set on a chunky tower, the structure exudes a sense of power, dignity and pride. It was designed by Dudley Field, a New York architect. In 1902 the rear chancel was added by Cady, Berg & See, but so completely in the spirit of the original as to be hardly distinguishable from it.

The congregation was founded in 1702 by an English missionary who was sent out by the Society for the Propagation of the Gospel in Foreign Parts. In those days the remote little village of Jamaica apparently qualified as a foreign part. But the community was large enough to have religious dissensions among the Presbyterians, who made up the majority, the few members of the Dutch Reformed Church, the Quakers and the handful of Anglicans. The latter were forced out of the Old Stone Church, which the community shared, and had to hold their services in the Town Hall until 1734, when the first Grace Church was built on the present site. This was followed in 1822 by a larger church which burned in 1861, to be succeeded, still on the same site, by the present structure.

Today's congregation is comprised of about eighty percent middle-class West Indians and twenty percent whites. The congregation is proud of its long tradition of amiable racial amalgamation. Rufus King, whose Landmark house is just down the block, is buried in the church cemetery, as are several other prominent figures in the emancipation movement.

9. *Grace Episcopal Church*
155-03 Jamaica Avenue, Jamaica
1861–62, Dudley Field
Chancel: 1901–02, Cady, Berg & See
Graveyard: c. 1734

Queens contains three other cemeteries of considerable historic interest. The Lawrence Family Graveyard in the Steinway section of Queens was a private burial ground for members of the distinguished Lawrence family. The earliest Lawrence to be buried there, in 1703, was Major Thomas Lawrence, and the last was Miss Ruth Lawrence in 1956. To have over two and a half centuries of family history concentrated on one half-acre plot of land is unique in the city. The graveyard contains twelve high-ranking military officers who served their country from the Dutch Colonial days to the Civil War. Most famous among them is Major Jonathan Lawrence, statesman and soldier of the American Revolution. Also buried here are seven members of the family who held high government posts.

The Lawrences also had a second and larger graveyard in Bayside. The site was a wooded area overlooking Little Neck Bay. The family had owned the property since the days of Dutch patents. For many years it was their favorite picnic ground. In 1832 it was decided to use it as a burial ground for members of the large and growing family. The last interment was in 1925. Members of the family who are buried here include a mayor of New York City, a president of the Stock Exchange and a county judge, as well as an Indian named Mocassin who, as a token of affection, was given the first name of Lawrence and buried with the family. The Lawrences were related to George Washington, whose half brother's name, Lawrence Washing-

10. *Lawrence Family Graveyard*
   20th Road and 35th Street, Steinway
   1703–1956

11. *Lawrence Graveyard, Lawrence Memorial Park*
   216th Street and 42nd Avenue, Bayside
   1832–1925

ton, reveals the family connection. It was through this half brother that George Washington came into his Mount Vernon estate in Virginia.

In recent years the graveyard was seriously vandalized and allowed to deteriorate. The Bayside Historical Society and descendants of the Lawrence family joined forces to restore and preserve the site. Inspired by the "Don't give up the ship" motto of their naval-hero ancestor, Captain James Lawrence, their efforts succeeded and the area is now well maintained as the Lawrence Memorial Park.

Much less fortunate is the tiny eighteenth-century burial plot of the Cornell family in Far Rockaway. Richard Cornell and his wife, Elizabeth, with their five sons and two daughters, settled in Far Rockaway in 1690 and lived in a large frame house overlooking the ocean near the present Beach 19th Street, on a site now occupied by the Hebrew Institute of Long Island. This was the first house built by white settlers in the Rockaways. Their only neighbors were the Indians. The family graveyard contains the resting place of Thomas Cornell, who lived from 1703 to 1764 and represented the county of Queens in the General Assembly of New York Province for twenty-seven years. Other descendants include Ezra Cornell, founder of Cornell University, and his son Alonzo, who was governor of New York State from 1879 to 1884. The cemetery survives in the center of a block, completely overgrown, long neglected and forgotten.

12. *Cornell Graveyard Adjacent to 1463 Greenpor Road, Far Rockaway c. 1700*

A popular motif that was carved on many American tombstones of the eighteenth century was a weeping willow. In fact, this symbol of grief, as well as other conventionalized ornaments, has been used by folk-art authorities to trace the careers of the anonymous stone carvers who moved up and down the Eastern seaboard plying their sepulchral trade. Thus it is not inappropriate to conclude this discussion of

13. *Weeping Beech Tree   37th Avenue between Parsons Boulevard and Bowne Street, Flushing, in Weeping Beech Park*
1847

Queens cemeteries with a description of one of the borough's most famous, most mournful and most magnificent trees.

The Weeping Beech Tree, which flourishes in its own neatly land-scaped park in Flushing, was the first tree designated by the New York City Landmarks Preservation Commission as an official Landmark. At the time some members were a bit apprehensive concerning the popular reception of designating a non-man-made object. Their fears were happily allayed when a representative of the New York Chapter of the American Institute of Architects testified, "This is a nomination of rare perception. We, as architects, realize the great importance of nature to man's environment and wholeheartedly endorse this tree for designation as the great Landmark it is."

The cutting from which this specimen was grown came from Beersal, Belgium. A Baron de Mann had planted an avenue of beech trees on the driveway of his estate. He spotted a droopy little seedling and ordered it destroyed. But a kindhearted gardener transplanted it in a secluded spot, where it grew and grew and grew until it became an object of deepest interest to horticulturists all over the world. Apparently the "weeping" form that the branches assumed was the result of a spontaneous and totally unexpected mutation. In 1847 Samuel B. Parsons, a Flushing nurseryman who supplied Central and Prospect Parks with many of their trees and shrubs, took a trip to Europe in search of rare plants. He succeeded in purchasing a shoot of the Belgian wonder tree, which he brought home in a flower pot. From that slip grew today's Landmark: over sixty feet high, with a spread of about eighty-five feet and a trunk that measures fourteen feet in circumference.

Public Buildings

Since the borough of Queens has never had a well-defined center and is, in fact, still searching for a physical focus, its public architecture is largely of local interest.

The two Landmark examples of civic buildings in Queens both date from the Civil War period. The Flushing Municipal Courthouse was built in 1862, just across Northern Boulevard from the Friends' Meeting House; the Poppenhusen Institute was built in 1868 in nearby College Point.

The old Flushing Town Hall, now the Flushing Municipal Courthouse, is an example of the early Romanesque Revival style, as shown by its roundheaded windows, its corbeled brickwork and the closely spaced brackets that support the cornice. But the spirit of the building, the contrast between the light painted yellow brick and the dark-brown painted trim, the heavy cornice, the gables and the turrets give an unmistakably Victorian cast to its character.

The Town Hall was the scene of every function that was of any importance in Flushing from 1862 to 1900. Community meetings, fancy-dress parties, opera productions, firemen's balls, all were held here. Tom Thumb performed in the auditorium. President Ulysses S. Grant addressed the Flushing citizenry from the balcony, and Teddy Roosevelt gave a Presidential campaign speech from the steps of the portico.

In its Victorian architectural feeling the Poppenhusen Institute in College Point, designed by Mundell & Teckritz, is quite similar to the

14. *Flushing Town Hall* (now the Flushing Municipal Courthouse)
137-35 Northern Boulevard, Flushing
1862

15. *Poppenhusen Institute*
114-04 14th Road, College Point
1868, Mundell & Teckritz

old Flushing Town Hall, although the Institute should technically be classified as an example of the incoming Italianate style with a French Second Empire roof, while the Town Hall is technically Romanesque Revival. They both have the same contrast of painted yellow brick with dark-brown trim, the same horizontal bandings, the same heavy cornices, the same central gable, the same feeling of solidity. The influence of the period can be basically more important than stylistc labels.

The Poppenhusen Institute was a private school built by Conrad Poppenhusen, a German-born immigrant destined to become the founder of the hard-rubber industry in this country. He built his Institute primarily as an adult evening school where the poor could learn a vocation and the immigrant could learn English. The motivation and aims were not unlike those that led to the establishment of Cooper Union in Manhattan. When Poppenhusen Institute opened, it housed the first free kindergarten in the United States, a free library, the village offices, the College Point Savings Bank, the town jail and a youth center. Today the Institute still functions as a vocational school open to all. It conducts English classes for foreign-language-speaking people—largely Puerto Ricans. Tuition fees are minimal.

And, in its basement, today used for storage space, are the two small airless cells which were installed when the Institute was the town jail. College Pointers loyally proclaim that the cells were used only to dry out roistering Manhattanites who came to this salubrious point of land for outings and vacations.

Hunter's Point Historic District

The one block on 45th Avenue between 21st and 23rd Streets in Hunter's Point is probably the most complete and best-preserved example of the Italianate row houses that at one time dominated block after block of Manhattan and Brooklyn. Most of these houses were built in the early 1870s for well-to-do families by two developers, Spencer Root and John Rust.

It is ironical that the high-stooped Italianate style that is now generically referred to as "brownstone" should have its outstanding surviving exemplars built of something called Westchester stone—a

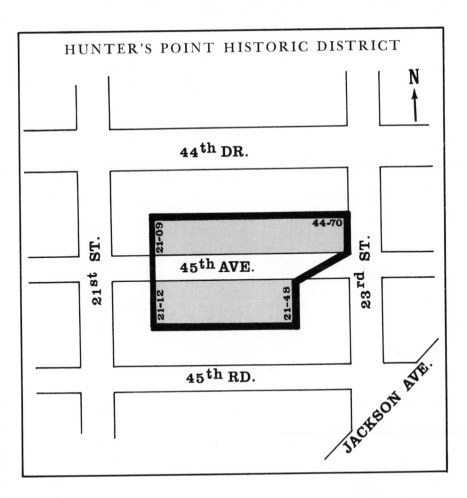

considerably harder material than the flaky brown sandstone that was so much more widely used. This is perhaps why ten houses in the Hunter's Point Historic District—five on the north side of 45th Avenue (Nos. 21–21 through 21-29) and five across the way (Nos. 21-12 through 21-20)—remain in almost perfect condition.

The noted architectural critic Vincent Scully has recognized the post–Civil War era as

> the true urban culmination of the century [when] the somber brownstones appeared, stately and marvelous, looming above the iron-speared sidewalks, bold and warm in their presences, varied in their forms. They were the strongest definers of the domestic streets ever produced in America. . . . They were the very blood and fiber of New York; wherever they appeared they brought with them something of its special physical arrogance and its pride.

North Side of 45th Avenue   *Hunter's Point Historic District*
1871–72

The Hunter's Point Historic District also contains examples of some other nineteenth-century architectural styles, including French Second Empire houses with mansard roofs, some neo-Grec and even some small Queen Anne houses. But it is its late Italianate rows that give the district its unique distinction.

Hunter's Point had originally been purchased by the second minister of the Dutch Reformed Church in New Amsterdam, Dominie Everardus Bogardus. The point of land jutting out into the East River just north of Newtown Creek was known as Dominie's Hook. When the British came, in 1664, it became a part of Newtown, and later it passed into the hands of the family of a British sea captain, George Hunter. In 1825 the name of the estate was changed to Hunter's Point.

Its real transition from a rural to an urban community came in 1860 when the Long Island Railroad was forced by local protest to move its principal terminus from Atlantic Avenue to Hunter's Point. The tunnels and bridges now crossing the river were still a long way in the future, so travelers from Manhattan had to disembark from the 34th Street Ferry at Hunter's Point and transfer to the railroad. Just as the development of Brooklyn Heights dates from the opening of the Fulton Street Ferry and that of Cobble Hill from the inauguration of the South Ferry at Atlantic Avenue, so the development of Hunter's Point dates from the opening of the 34th Street Ferry. A prosperous community soon grew up, as inns, taverns and other amenities were opened to accommodate the commuters. This led to the urbanization of the area and to the construction in the 1870s of the distinguished groups of houses that made it such a fine residential neighborhood.

As traffic and urbanization increased, the original owners slowly drifted away and government workers, largely Irish, from Long Island City, moved in. Most colorful among these was the last mayor of Long Island City, "Battle-Axe" Gleason, who had earned his name when he headed a direct-action delegation that chopped down a fence erected by the Long Island Railroad and resented by the local citizenry.

The Queensborough Bridge, with its trains roaring overhead, opened in 1909. While this improvement greatly facilitated communication between Manhattan and Queens and led to the intense industrial development of Long Island City, it struck a death blow to what had been a quiet residential area. The houses on 45th Avenue were converted into the multifamily dwellings that they are today. Subsequent subway and vehicular tunnels literally and figuratively still further undermined Hunter's Point. The mainstream of traffic and progress pushed over and under Hunter's Point into the rapidly growing central and eastern portions of the borough. It is to this accident of technological geography that the city owes the survival of these handsome houses in their tree-shaded setting.

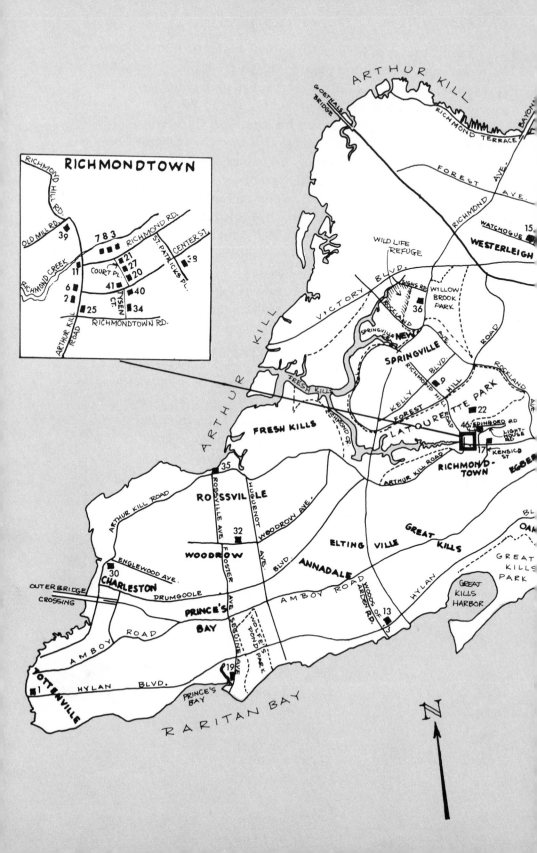

RICHMONDTOWN

ARTHUR KILL

RICHMOND HILL RD.

OLD MILL RD.

39

783

RICHMOND RD.

ST. PATRICKS PL.

CENTER ST.

9

RICHMOND CREEK

11

COURT PL.

21
27
20

ARTHUR KILL ROAD

6
2

41

TYSEN CT.

40

25

34

RICHMONDTOWN RD.

ARTHUR KILL

GOETHALS BRIDGE

RICHMOND TERRACE

BAYONNE

FOREST   AVE.

RICHMOND

AVE.

WATCHOGUE

15

WESTERLEIGH

WILD LIFE REFUGE

VICTORY   BLVD.

SIGNS RD.

ROCKLAND

WILLOW BROOK PARK

36

SPRINGVILLE

ROCKLAND

NEW SPRINGVILLE

RICHMOND   BLVD.

FOREST   HILL

9

LATOURETTE PARK

22

ROCKLAND   AVE.

FRESH KILLS

KELLY

RICHMOND CR.

EPINBORO RD.

46

LIGHT HOUSE RD.

17

KENSICO ST.

RICHMOND-TOWN

EGBER

FRESH KILLS

RICHMOND RD.

ARTHUR KILL ROAD

ARTHUR KILL

35

ROSSVILLE

HUGUENOT AVE.

WOODROW AVE.

ROSSVILLE AVE.

GREAT

OAK

BL

32

FOOSTER AVE.

WOODROW

AVE.

BLVD.

ELTING VILLE

KILLS

GREAT KILLS PARK

ARTHUR KILL ROAD

ENGLEWOOD AVE.

ANNADALE

WOODS OF ARDEN RD.

GREAT KILLS HARBOR

OUTERBRIDGE

30

CHARLESTON

DRUMGOOLE

AMBOY   ROAD

HYLAN

13

CROSSING

PRINCE'S BAY

SEGUINE AVE.

WOLFE'S POND PARK

TOTTENVILLE

1

AMBOY   ROAD

HYLAN   BLVD.

19

PRINCE'S BAY

RARITAN   BAY

N

STATEN ISLAND

CHAPTER TEN

STATEN ISLAND

A NYONE TAKING a first glance at a map of the New York metropolitan area would very naturally assume that Staten Island is a part of the state of New Jersey, not of the state of New York. It is separated from Manhattan by five miles across Upper New York Bay, and from Brooklyn by a full mile across the Narrows, but New Jersey lies less than a quarter of a mile away along most of the length of Kill van Kull and Arthur Kill.

When the English captured New Amsterdam in 1664 the pear-shaped island (13.9 miles long by 7.3 miles wide at its broadest point) became part of the province of New York. It was named Richmond after the Duke of Richmond, a son of Charles II. The Lords of Berkeley and Carteret, proprietors of New Jersey, contested the decision, and a dispute arose between New York and New Jersey. Tradition has it that the Duke of York decided to settle the argument by awarding the prize to the province of the citizen who could circumnavigate the island in twenty-four hours, and that a Captain Christopher Billopp, representing New York, succeeded in 1687. In any event, the island remained in New York, a fact finally confirmed in 1833 by a joint commission that agreed that New Jersey's claims to Staten Island be exchanged for New York's claims to South Jersey.

The relationship between Richmond and her sister boroughs has always been of a somewhat casual nature. The rest of the city has had little influence on the island until quite recent years. For most New Yorkers, Staten Island has been primarily the terminal of the world's greatest bargain—a glorious one-hour round-trip ferry ride for only ten cents.

Physically, Staten Island is bisected by a ridge of hills that runs from northeast to southwest down the middle, with the highest point being Todt Hill, 409 feet above sea level. This is not only the highest point on Staten Island, it is the highest point on the entire Eastern seaboard between Maine and Florida. The Dutch called this eminence Yserberg, or Iron Hill, from the iron mines they and their successors worked. Later, the peak became known as Todt (i.e., Death) Hill. Historians have never found a satisfactory explanation for this ghoulish appellation.

From this central ridge the land slopes off in both directions: toward the Lower Bay and Raritan Bay on the southeast and toward Arthur Kill, Newark Bay and Kill van Kull on the west and north. Much of the western part of the island consists of salt marshes, which are gradually being reclaimed by what is euphemistically called "sanitary fill" and more accurately described as garbage dumps covered with topsoil.

Giovanni da Verrazzano, the Italian-born navigator sailing under the French flag, discovered the island in 1524 when he stopped to take on fresh water from a spring near the site of the present Tompkinsville. Sometime between 1626 and 1630 it was given the name of Staten Eylandt, after the Dutch governing body, the States General of the Netherlands. With commendable impartiality the islanders have kept the two names—the English Richmond and the Dutch Staten Island. Richmond is the official name of the county and the borough, which are coextensive and which include not only Staten Island but also several small offshore islands. There is now a move on foot to change the name of the borough to Staten Island.

Beginning in 1639, several attempts were made to colonize Staten Island, but in each case the settlements were wiped out by Indians, not always without provocation. The Pig War in 1641, the Whiskey War in 1643 and the Peach War in 1655 were precipitated by the ruthless treatment of Indians by the colonists. Each time peace was concluded there were concurrent negotiations for the formal sale of land to the whites. The final sale was arranged in 1670, by which time it is figured the Dutch had bought the island five times over.

Perhaps another reason for the failure of these early attempts at colonization was the attitude of Peter Stuyvesant, director general of New Netherland. He could not have cared less about the distant and difficult island that was part of his domain, and he gave the settlers little help in their struggles with Indians and the wilderness.

The earliest permanent settlement was Oude Dorp (Old Town), which was established in 1661 near the site of the present Fort Wadsworth at the Narrows, that dramatic stretch of water that connects the upper and lower parts of New York Harbor. By 1664 Peter Stuyvesant had relented somewhat; it can hardly be said of him that he softened. In any event, he acceded to the colonists' pleas to have a preacher, who reported later that the director general permitted him "to go to preach there every two months and administer the Lord's Supper. This I have done for about a year, in the winter season it is troublesome on account of the great water, or bay, which must be crossed, and the showers and storms which occur."

The first real village to develop was Richmondtown, almost exactly in the geographical center of the island. It became the seat of government in 1729 and remained so until 1920, when the county seat was moved to St. George. Richmondtown was originally called "Coccles Town," probably from the quantities of oyster and clam shells (cockles) that were dug out of the nearby Fresh Kills. It was probably when the name became corrupted to the ignominious "Cuckoldstown" that the town fathers decreed the name should be changed to Richmondtown.

The Staten Island Historical Society has long been interested in the value of Richmondtown as an historic site, to illustrate the evolution of a small American village during the seventeenth, eighteenth and nineteenth centuries. In 1939 the society purchased and restored its first building. In 1952 the restoration of Richmondtown became a joint undertaking of the New York City Department of Parks and the Staten Island Historical Society. Surviving original buildings have been supplemented by others moved to the site from elsewhere on the island, particularly when they were threatened with destruction by highway or real-estate improvements. The entire project, when completely restored, will give a rounded picture of two centuries of life in a small but important county seat, comparable to the Williamsburg Restoration. So far, thirteen structures in Richmondtown have been designated as individual Landmarks, and it is expected that the whole village will eventually be designated an Historic District.

Staten Island, which had a large Loyalist population, was occupied by the British two days after the signing of the Declaration of Independence and has the dubious distinction of having been the target of the last shot fired in the Revolutionary War.

Long before this time, a sailboat ferrying service was set up between Manhattan and Staten Island, but it was irregular and hazardous. Cornelius Vanderbilt, the "Commodore," who was born near Stapleton, established the first regular service for ferrying goods to Manhattan in 1829.

Except for a flurry in 1812 when New Yorkers became aware of the possibilities of Staten Island in the defense of the city, the island remained chiefly a farming and fishing community, little concerned with the goings-on across the bay. But in 1830 the island was discovered as a fashionable bathing resort. Prominent New York families began to appreciate the bucolic and scenic joys it offered. The island even spawned a literary colony, including James Russell Lowell, Francis Parkman and Bill Nye, while Henry David Thoreau and Ralph Waldo Emerson were frequent visitors at the home of the latter's brother, Judge William Emerson, who had moved to Staten Island from Massachusetts in 1837. Thoreau, who had come as a tutor to the judge's children, wrote of his experiences on Staten Island in 1843:

> I have already run over no small part of the island, to the highest hill and some way along the shore. . . . But it is rather derogatory that your dwelling-place should be only a neighborhood to a great city. . . . I do not like their cities and forts, with their morning and evening guns, and sails flapping in one's eye. I want a whole continent to breathe in and a good deal of solitude and silence, such as all Wall Street cannot buy nor Broadway with its wooden pavement. I must live along the beach, on the southern shore which looks directly out to sea and see what that great parade of water means, that dashes and roars, and has not yet wet me, as long as I have lived.

Isolated as it has been from the rest of the city throughout most of its history, the borough of Richmond has preserved its unique character to a greater extent than any other part of New York. It still consists of a series of quite distinguishable villages and communities whose names retain distinctive associations. They have not as yet been entirely merged as in Brooklyn, nor have they thus far been completely homogenized as in Queens. The old Staten Islanders are loyal to their home towns—to Tompkinsville, Rosebank, Richmondtown, Tottenville or Annadale—rather than to New York City or even to their own county. The opening in 1964 of the Verrazano-Narrows Bridge (the official spelling of the bridge uses only one "z"), the longest single span in the world, is changing all that, however. The population has increased from 221,000 in 1960 to 330,000 in 1972. The newcomers have not had time to strike deep roots, and the character of the housing developments that have sprung up to receive them gives little hope that they will ever have the chance. The dire warnings of the city planners against repeating the costly errors of the other boroughs go largely, but not entirely, unheeded. By valiant efforts and heroic local support, it does seem that a magnificent and continuous green belt will be preserved along the spine of the island's hills; that the best of the south-shore beaches which Thoreau so deeply appreciated will become part of the federally financed Gateway National Park; that the rest of the shorefront will be saved from an unnecessary highway; and that here and there, if you can find them, there will actually be a few intelligently planned cluster developments and a few sections of sensitively laid-out streets. But generally the Cassandra-like pleas of the planners are drowned out by the cries of two opposing choruses: of the old guard who feel that by opposing any governmental intervention they will be able to turn the clock back to the wonderful days of unhampered independence; and of developers who want nothing to stand in the way of "progress" and quick profits. Actually, of course, each group is playing right into the other's hand.

In the midst of this crucial battle, the designation of Landmarks as psychological anchors to history and as the nuclei around which viable new uses can grow has a more critical role to play than anywhere else in the city. The character of the other four boroughs is, for better or worse, already fixed. That of Staten Island is still in the balance.

A Manor House, Farmhouses, Cottages and Villas

The architecture that has survived on Staten Island to be preserved by Landmark designation is, as one would expect, very largely residential and rural. The examples are, moreover, so numerous and so varied, and many have such long histories of additions, alterations and restorations, that they cannot readily be classified in the neat stylistic packages used to describe the architecture of other sections of the city. The design of country houses was very rarely—at least until quite recent days—the work of an architect. A local builder, a master carpenter or occasionally a gifted "amateur" would be in charge of construction, and he or the owner would make whatever design decisions there were to be made. These would be based on other nearby houses or on features of other houses that they happened to have seen and liked. In the nineteenth century there were also a number of carpenters' guides, such as *The Architect—A Series of Original Designs for Domestic and Ornamental Villas,* by William A. Ranlett, a Staten Island resident, and more sophisticated "pattern books" for country cottages, such as Andrew Jackson Downing's *Cottage Residences* and *The Architecture of Country Houses,* that had wide circulation and helped spread the new fashions as they succeeded one another.

The net result, while difficult to catalogue, is, perhaps for that very reason, the more intriguing. There is an unsophisticated freshness about many Staten Island houses that is particularly appealing. In order to appreciate them in relation to one another and to what was going on elsewhere, they will be discussed here in two broad groupings: a vernacular series and stylistic series. While these categories, like all such classifications, are bound to be somewhat arbitrary, they may help as a guide through a rather complicated situation.

The vernacular group may be broken down into seventeenth-century houses, eighteenth-century houses (roughly 1725 to 1775), turn-of-the-century houses (1775–1845), and, finally, a mixed category of houses that have been altered and added to over such long periods as to be partly classifiable in more than one of the three groups.

The stylistic group is somewhat simpler. It falls quite easily into successive periods, each peaking for about fifteen years, but on Staten Island there is considerable overlap. The peak periods are: Federal, 1815–30; Greek Revival, 1830–45; Gothic Revival, 1845–60; Italianate, 1860–75; "Stick style," also 1860–75; and, finally, Eclectic, 1875 and later.

THE VERNACULAR GROUP

SEVENTEENTH-CENTURY HOUSES The Conference House at Tottenville dates back to about 1680 and is a fine example of a seventeenth-century manor house, not too different in its substantial and lordly character from the eighteenth-century Van Cortlandt Mansion in the Bronx, but much less sophisticated in its details. The stone gable ends, with their squared-off shoulders and towering chimneys, the steep roof, small windows and random-fieldstone masonry, all seem closer to the Middle Ages than to the Georgian England of the elegant Van Cortlandts. Yet this house was once the seat of the manor of Bentley. It was built by the same Captain Christopher Billopp who was said to have circumnavigated the island. Billopp was appointed head of customs of New York City by King Charles II, who was his good friend, and who had granted him extensive acreage at the southernmost tip of the island where Tottenville is today.

1. *Conference House   (Billopp House)*
Foot of Hylan Boulevard, Tottenville
c. 1680

Captain Billopp's grandson Colonel Christopher Billopp was, as were many wealthy landholding citizens, an ardent Tory. His house and lands were confiscated at the end of the Revolutionary War, and he emigrated with other Loyalists to Canada.

The house received its present name from the famous conference that took place there on September 11, 1776, between Benjamin Franklin, John Adams and Edward Rutledge, representing the American side, and Vice-Admiral Lord Richard Howe, commander of the British fleet which was then anchored off the shore of Staten Island. The purpose of the meeting was to seek a peaceful settlement of the war that had started with the Battles of Lexington and Concord in 1775.

The conference started serenely, even elegantly. John Adams wrote that Lord Howe "had prepared a large handsome room by spreading a carpet of moss and green sprigs, from bushes and shrubs in the neighborhood, till he had made it not only wholesome but romantically elegant; and he entertained us with good claret, good bread, cold ham, tongues and mutton."

Lord Howe protested his deep affection for America and offered "to extend the royal clemency and full pardon to all repentant rebels who would lay down their arms and return to their allegiance to the King." Franklin said this was impossible, since the colonies had, just two months earlier, declared their independence. The conference ended with a few polite remarks, and the American delegation returned to Perth Amboy aboard Howe's barge. As they were leaving the boat, Franklin offered some gold and silver coins to the sailors, but the commanding officer forbade the sailors' accepting them. "As these people are under the impression that we have not a farthing of hard money in the country," explained Franklin later, "I thought I would convince them of their mistake. I knew at the same time that I risked nothing by an offer, which their regulations and discipline would not permit them to accept." Was Poor Richard the author of "How to Eat Your Cake and Have It, Too"?

The Conference House continued as a residence after the Revolutionary War, then became a factory and finally fell into neglect until 1926, when it was acquired by the Conference House Association and turned over to the City. The house was finally restored and is now open to the public as a museum.

Dating also from the late seventeenth century and as modest as the Billopp manor house is imposing, the little wooden Voorlezer's House was built in 1695. It has been restored on its original site in Richmondtown. The *Voorlezer* was a lay reader and schoolteacher. In this little two-story frame house, which is the oldest known elementary school still standing in the United States, the *Voorlezer* conducted his school, led religious services and also lived with his family. When the building was threatened with destruction, the Staten Island Historical Society purchased it in 1939 and restored it, and thus began the Richmondtown Restoration.

2. Voorlezer's House   59 Arthur Kill Road, Richmondtown
   c. 1695

EIGHTEENTH-CENTURY HOUSES   Dating almost half a century later is the Lake-Tysen House, also in Richmondtown, where it was moved in 1962 when it was threatened with demolition. It was built in Oakwood about 1740 by Joseph Guyon. Guyon was a descendant of one of the many French Huguenots who settled in Staten Island after the 1685 Revocation of the Edict of Nantes. They found here the freedom to practice their religion that they had lost at home.

The Lake-Tysen House is a fine example of the so-called Dutch Colonial style, with the characteristic gambrel roof and spring eaves. It is one of the earliest examples we have in which the overhanging roof is supported by a series of columns to form a veranda. The kitchen was added in 1800, but otherwise the Lake-Tysen House retains most of its

3. Lake-Tysen House   3711 Richmond Road, near Court Place,
    Richmondtown   (formerly in Oakwood)
    c. 1740
    Kitchen addition: c. 1800

original features and demonstrates how a prosperous farmer lived in the mid–18th century.

Quite similar, except that it was built in fieldstone rather than wood, is the Christopher House. Formerly on Willowbrook Road in Willowbrook, it was dismantled in 1970 and removed to Richmondtown, where it is awaiting reassembly in the restoration. The central large room and attic date back to 1756 and are believed to have been built as a tenant house by Colonel Thomas Dongan, great-nephew and namesake of Governor Dongan, on whose 5,100-acre manor of Cassiltowne the little house stood. Later it passed into the hands of Joseph Christopher, who enlarged it to its present size in 1764. Christopher, an ardent revolutionary, was a member of the Committee of Safety during the Revolution and held secret meetings in his home. The nearby "Great Swamp," so they say, proved useful as an escape route in case of a raid. The swamp has since been partly filled in and is now Willowbrook Park.

The Neville House of 1770, on Richmond Terrace in New

Brighton, on the north shore of the island, is more monumental than the Lake-Tysen House. A two-story veranda with columns running through both the first and second stories is reminiscent of the eighteenth-century architecture of the West Indies and may have been inspired by visits to the Caribbean by Captain John Neville, who built his Staten Island mansion when he retired from the sea. Later the house was used as a tavern and became known as the Old Stone Jug. It prospered primarily due to its proximity to Sailors' Snug Harbor, a home for retired and indigent old salts.

4. Christopher House   *(early view)*
Future location: Richmondtown
  (formerly at 819 Willowbrook
    Road, Willowbrook)
c. 1756
Dismantled 1970; now awaiting reassembly

5. Neville House   *("Old Stone Jug")*
  806 Richmond Terrace, between Clinton
    and Tysen Streets, New Brighton
  c. 1770

TURN-OF-THE-CENTURY HOUSES Back in Richmondtown there are some very modest houses that illustrate how simple people lived in the late eighteenth century and on into the nineteenth. To varying degrees, they reflect English or Dutch antecedents, but the rural vernacular character which they all share seems more significant than the small differences of detail and date that distinguish one from another.

The Boehm-Frost House of about 1770 is a wooden building with brick end chimneys. An 1845 addition is distinguishable by the neatly sawed narrow clapboards which contrast with the wide boards of the earlier portion. The house is interesting in having its upper window sash larger than the lower. In the cold winters more than sufficient ventilation could be obtained by raising a small portion of the lower sash. On the present site of this house, Dr. Thomas Frost, a prominent Staten Island physician and storekeeper, had built a home which was destroyed in 1883. In 1965 the Boehm house, which was located in the Fresh Kills land-fill area, was threatened with demolition. Since it was similar in style and size to the Frost house, it was moved by the City to the Richmondtown Restoration and set up on the foundations of the Frost house.

The Cooper's Shop, of 1790, was moved to Richmondtown from nearby Egbertville in 1966. It consisted originally of one room with a

6. *Boehm-Frost House*
   43 Arthur Kill Road,
   (formerly in Fresh Kills)
   Richmondtown
   c. 1770
   Addition: 1845

garret above. In 1800 a one-room extension was added and later a small addition for a cooper's shop.

The Basketmaker's Shop, of 1810, was moved to Richmondtown from the Fresh Kills land-fill area. It is a one-story frame building with an attractive spring eave extending over a veranda. The high stone cellar may have been planned as a protection against the marshy ground around Fresh Kills. This cellar was used for the family kitchen as well as for the basket-making shop of the owner.

On the crest of the New Springville hill that overlooks the Richmondtown Restoration is the Sylvanus Decker Farmhouse of 1810. It has some later additions, including the sweeping spring eaves. The farm, with its eleven acres and six outbuildings, was left to the Staten Island Historical Society in 1955 by Richard Decker. It is operated in conjunction with Richmondtown Restoration, is planned to show present-day visitors how nineteenth-century farmers made their livelihood, and is probably the last place in the city where New York children will be able to learn where eggs, milk, chickens, bacon and vegetables come from before they reach the supermarket.

HOUSES OF MIXED PERIOD That Staten Island was a conservative and stable community is nowhere better illustrated than in the seven houses next to be described. All of them, through the span of one or two centuries, have undergone so many alterations and additions that it is impossible to assign any of them to a particular period or style. They all share, however, the distinctive character of belonging to Staten Island and of having deep roots in its history. Some of them have been occupied during their entire existence by a single family, and, while the houses just grew, like Topsy, the unselfconscious architectural outcome often has a charm all its own.

Oldest of the group is the Billiou-Stillwell-Perine House in Dongan Hills, whose earliest section goes back to 1662. The original fieldstone section contains an enormous Dutch fireplace with a huge chimney head supported on two wooden posts, perhaps unique in this country. One can walk right into the fireplace without stooping, and the hearth was big enough for roasting a whole ox. This part of the house, with its steep medieval roof, was built by Pierre Billiou, leader of the 1661 settlement of Oude Dorp. Various stone and frame additions were made about 1700, 1750, 1790 and 1830. The triple hyphenated name

7. *Cooper's Shop*
   3747 Richmond Road, Richmondtown
   (formerly in Egbertville)
   c. 1790
   One-room addition: c. 1800
   Conversion to shop: after 1800

8. *Basketmaker's Shop*
   3741 Richmond Road,
   Richmondtown
   (formerly in Fresh Kills)
   c. 1810

9. *Sylvanus Decker Farmhouse*
   435 Richmond Hill Road,
   between Kelly Boulevard
   and Forest Hill
   Road, New Springville
   c. 1810
   Extended, porches added and
   windows changed: c. 1840

10. Billiou-Stillwell-Perine House   1476 Richmond Road, between
*   Alter and Cromwell Avenues   Dongan Hills*
1662
Additions: c. 1700, 1750, 1790, 1830

of the house reflects only a part of its complicated history. Today there are seven rooms on the ground floor and seven bedrooms upstairs. An unusually early paneled chimney breast of the 1700 section still survives.

The so-called Treasure House in Richmondtown dates from 1700. The original clapboard building was raised in 1770, a rubblestone cellar built underneath it and a north wing added. An extension to the south was added a century later. The house gets its name from the discovery in 1850 of about seven thousand dollars in British coins which had been secreted in its walls during the American Revolution.

Contemporary, in its earliest part, with the Treasure House, the Alice Austen House—in the Rosebank section about a mile north of where the Verrazano Bridge now spans the Narrows—hid a treasure which, when finally discovered, far surpassed in drama and lasting value any possible cache of coins. Originally the house was nothing more than a one-room Dutch farmhouse, but later, as with so many houses like it, it was added to again and again until it had become transformed into a long, low, rambling cottage. Located at the top of a meadow sloping down to the water, it commanded a magnificent view across Upper New York Bay toward the tip of Manhattan.

When John Austen, a wealthy and cultivated New Yorker, saw it in 1844, he fell in love with the place. His was one of the first of the prominent families from the crowded city to find a peaceful refuge on Staten Island—at first only to stay at hotels during the summer months, but later to buy land and become part of the fashionable local society that flourished there between the end of the Civil War and the opening of the twentieth century. He named his new home "Clear Comfort" and spent no end of time and energy in improving the house and its grounds. He is certainly responsible for the Gothic

11. *Treasure House*
 37 Arthur Kill Road, Richmondtown
 1700
 Raised and north extension added:
  c. 1770
 South addition: c. 1860

12. *Alice Austen House   2 Hylan Boulevard, Rosebank*
 c. 1691–1710
 North extension, porch and dormers: 1844

Revival details added to the low veranda and the three peaked dormer windows. There is even a legend, not entirely impossible, that Austen's friend, James Renwick, Jr., advised him on the design of these improvements. Certainly Austen took great pride in them.

A frequent traveler to Europe, he generally booked the best cabin on the steamer and always managed to be on deck to signal his family as the ship steamed past Clear Comfort. This was not lost on his fellow passengers, who, he wrote, spoke of the property as "being most lovely. The fact of being the owner of such a spot gave me quite a position among them at once." And in 1867 he wrote to his wife from London: "How does the grass look? I shall never forget the day I passed out of the Narrows how lovely the old cottage looked. It was much admired by the passengers who stood near me. The Captain ordered the ship run close to our side when I told him I wished to make a signal to you." A couple of years later, he reported that a chance acquaintance he had met in Switzerland had told him that Clear Comfort was "without any exception the most lovely place on the Island."

It was into this idyllic setting that the two-year-old Alice, Austen's granddaughter, moved in 1868. Her father, Edward S. Munn, had deserted the infant girl and her mother shortly before this. The wronged wife resumed her maiden name and returned to her father's home. It was here that Alice lived until she was seventy-nine, when, ill and destitute, she was forced to sell her few personal possessions for six hundred dollars and to move first to an apartment, then, with the charitable help of a few friends, for four or five years into nursing homes, before becoming a pauper inmate of the City Farm Colony.

However, Alice Austen's importance in the history of New York City and in the history of women's liberation far transcends her tragic personal story. By the age of eighteen, and with the encouragement of her grandfather and two uncles, Alice had become a highly skilled photographer, expert in all the technical aspects of what was then a new art and a new science. It was a most unlikely career for a young lady brought up in sheltered circumstances, yet she pursued it with passion and rare creativity for more than fifty years. Working with heavy and unwieldy equipment and doing all her own developing, she left an unparalleled legacy of some seven thousand glass negatives that show what the world around her looked like from 1880 to 1930. Fortunately, the precious plates were rescued by Loring McMillen, director of the Staten Island Historical Society and director of the Richmondtown Restoration, just as Miss Austen was being ousted from her home.

And there is a happy, or at least a happier, note on which her life ended. From 1945 to 1948 volunteer members of the Historical Society staff, led by C. Coapes Brinley, sorted out the photographic treasures stored in the basement of the Staten Island Historical Society Museum in Richmondtown. They realized their unique value and tried, at first without success, to sell some of the pictures to raise money for Alice Austen's support. Finally Oliver Jensen, now editor of *American Heritage*, sold an illustrated story on her extraordinary career to *Life* magazine. With the proceeds, Alice Austen was rescued from the poorhouse. From the publication of the *Life* story in September 1951 until her death six months later at the age of eighty-six, she was able to enjoy the comfort of a private nursing home. More important, she was able to see the value of her life work recognized. Celebrations were given in her honor. The children and grandchildren of her childhood friends came to see her. She did not, however, live to see her beloved Clear Comfort made a Landmark, nor to see the City acquire enough land to make a park around it, nor to know of current efforts to establish an Alice Austen photographic museum in her honor.

The Poillon House in Annadale was built about 1720, though remnants of a 1696 structure survive in the basement. The house was substantially enlarged in 1837, and in 1848 Frederick Law Olmsted, the noted landscape architect, added a one-and-a-half-story wood extension and raised the existing roof and inserted little horizontal windows at the attic-floor level.

The three periods of the Kreuzer-Pelton House in Livingston, on the north shore of the island, are distinctly visible to this day. The earliest part, a one-room cottage and garret of fieldstone construction, dates back to 1722, while the steep-roofed one-and-a-half-story central section of rough-cut stone, now sheathed with scalloped shingles, was added in 1770. In 1836 a two-story brick extension was added at the other side of this central section. A trapdoor in the oldest portion of the house leads down into a cellar which the romantically inclined call the "dungeon" but which was actually used to store wine.

More modest is the little Housman House in Westerleigh, which

13. *Poillon House*
   4515 Hylan Boulevard ne[
      Woods of Arden Road,
      Annadale
   c. 1720
   Enlarged: 1837
   Raised and extended: 18[

14. *Kreuzer-Pelton House   1262 Richmond Terrace,*
      between Pelton and Bement Avenues, Livingston
   One room and garret: 1722
   One-and-a-half-story center section: c. 1770
   Two-story brick extension: 1836

displays only two periods, a small one-room stone section of 1730 and a clapboard addition attached to it in 1760. Peter Housman was a prosperous millwright. He came to an untimely end in his little house when, in the year 1784, he resisted an attempted robbery by a party of Jersey raiders and was murdered. The problem of law and order, or, rather, the lack of it, is nothing new in New York.

Finally, in this group of mixed-period houses is the Scott-Edwards House in West New Brighton, in which the original 1730 building was happily wedded, a century later, to a formal Greek Revival porch. In the 1840s this house was the home of Judge Ogden Edwards, a descendant of Jonathan Edwards and a cousin of Aaron Burr. He has the distinction of being the first New York State Supreme Court justice to have come from Staten Island.

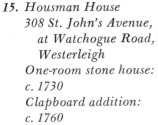

15. *Housman House*
308 St. John's Avenue,
at Watchogue Road,
Westerleigh
One-room stone house:
c. 1730
Clapboard addition:
c. 1760

16. *Scott-Edwards House   752 Delafield Avenue, between Clove Road*
and Raymond Place, West New Brighton
c. 1730
Alterations and portico: 1840

THE STYLISTIC SERIES

This group of houses demonstrates that even remote and rural Staten Island was not altogether immune to the influence of architectural fashion. Almost all the styles that succeeded one another with such dizzying rapidity in the more urbanized sections of nineteenth-century New York found an echo here. Sometimes, as might be expected, new fashions caught on locally rather later than they did in the heart of the metropolis. Sometimes, but by no means always, local interpretations by country carpenters lack subtlety or sophistication in comparison with their city cousins. But often their uninhibited approach has a freshness that is lacking in the work of those who built by the book.

FEDERAL STYLE   The simple Moore-McMillen House on Richmond Road, completed in 1818, is the only Landmark example on Staten Island of this elegant post–Revolutionary style. Accustomed as we are to seeing Federal buildings constructed in brick and stone and handsomely ornamented with ironwork, it is hard to recognize their characteristics in what seems at first glance a simple wood-shingled cottage. But they are all there: the attenuated proportions of the porch posts, the delicately carved dentils of the cornice, and, above all, the handsome enframement around the eight-paneled front door with its flanking colonnettes, its glazed transom and its pair of elongated side windows. The Moore-McMillen House was originally the rectory

17. Moore-McMillen House   (*originally rectory, Church of St. Andrew*)
3531 Richmond Road, opposite Kensico Street, Richmondtown
1818

of the Church of St. Andrew, which served a very wealthy congregation. It was known as the "Golden Rectory" and still boasts silver-plated hardware.

GREEK REVIVAL If the Federal style apparently never spread widely in Staten Island, the Greek Revival period hit it hard. Five examples, all built between 1835 and 1840, have been designated as Landmarks. A comparison among them, however, illustrates how varied the local interpretations could be.

18. Gardiner-Tyler House
27 Tyler Street, between
Broadway and North Burgher
Avenue, West New Brighton
c. 1835

The Gardiner-Tyler House, for example, in West New Brighton, is a very grand mansion indeed. It was built about 1835 by Mrs. Elizabeth Racey, who sold it some years later to Mrs. Juliana Gardiner of New York and Easthampton. The latter eventually gave it to her daughter, Julia Gardiner Tyler, who had spent her youth in another Landmark, Colonnade Row in Manhattan, before she eloped with the middle-aged President John Tyler. After her husband's death in 1862, the flamboyant Mrs. Tyler returned with her seven children for six more years in Colonnade Row, but from 1868 to 1874 she lived in her handsome Staten Island mansion.

The extremely flat pediment over the porch of the Gardiner-Tyler House is characteristic of the finest period of Greek Revival architecture, though the columns that support the pediment are rather unusual. Their ornate Corinthian capitals are more Roman than Greek, but the fact that the columns spring directly from the ground without benefit of bases is more Greek than Roman and would be quite correct for the Greek Doric order.

Somewhat more austere, but no less imposing, is the Seguine House in Prince's Bay, built in 1840. A pedimented porch extends across the entire front and supports a second-story balcony. The small rectangular windows tucked under the cornice are particularly characteristic of the Greek Revival style. The simple square piers, with a rectangular panel recessed in each face, stand on block bases and are capped by similar blocks. This looks like the sort of compromise that a country carpenter might make if he did not feel quite capable of turning out the carved capitals, molded bases and round fluted shafts one would expect to find in a contemporary mansion in Brooklyn or Manhattan. The house was built by Joseph Seguine, whose estate extended along the waterfront around Prince's Bay. His ancestors had lived on Staten Island since early in the eighteenth century. The residence still commands a magnificent view of Lower New York Bay.

19. Seguine House
   440 Seguine Avenue,
      between Wilbur Street
      and Purdy Place,
      Prince's Bay
   c. 1840

20. *Stephens House and*
    General Store
    Center Street and Court Place,
    Richmondtown
    1837
    One-story addition:
    after 1837

21. *Bennett House*
    3730 Richmond Road,
    at Court Place,
    Richmondtown
    c. 1837

The Stephens House and General Store, which are now part of the Richmondtown Restoration, show what happened to the Greek Revival mode when it filtered down to less wealthy patrons. There are the same flat rectangular windows in the frieze below the cornice that the Seguine House has, and the same simple square piers on both the front and back porches. This house was built in 1837 and remains on its original site. The rear wing was a general store and has been faithfully restored and stocked with appropriate goods. The Bennett House of the same period, also in Richmondtown, is another example of how Greek Revival details were translated by a country carpenter into a down-to-earth clapboard dwelling.

Quite different is the nearby Latourette House, on a hill overlooking Richmondtown. This is a brick mansion built in 1836 by David Latourette, a prosperous truck farmer and planter. Latourette, and his father before him, had worked some five hundred acres of the finest farmland on Staten Island, which subsequently formed the nucleus of what is now Latourette Park and its public golf course. The mansion itself is now a clubhouse, and old Staten Islanders believe that the troubled ghost of David Latourette wanders about the spacious rooms in protest against the profanation of his home. In order to visualize the original appearance of the building, one has mentally to strip away the front porch and balcony, which were added in 1936. One can then see the fine paneled pilasters that flank the entrance door, with its narrow sidelights and transom. The small horizontal windows under the eaves still persist in this brick version of the Greek Revival style.

22. *Latourette House   Richmond Hill Road, Lighthouse Hill,*
   in Latourette Park
   c. 1836
   Porch: 1936

GOTHIC REVIVAL   Around 1845 the Gothic Revival manifested itself in a series of Staten Island houses with steep roofs, pointed window heads, trefoil scrollwork and a multiplicity of irregularly arranged gables, towers, dormers and chimneys.

23. *Pendleton House*
22 Pendleton Place,
between Franklin and
Prospect Avenues,
New Brighton
c. 1855

The fullest expression of the new style is to be seen in the Pendleton House of 1855, in New Brighton. The deeply overhanging eaves, the quatrefoil panels and cinquefoil or pointed window heads, the gables and dormers—sometimes decorated with pendant scrollwork—the oriel and bay windows, and, above all, the asymmetrically placed tower are all Gothic. The wood shingles are old American tradition. One detail illustrates delightfully how compromises were reached. The windows are quite "Gothically" glazed with diamond panes, yet, except in the dormers and the attics under the gables, the glass is set in traditional American double-hung sash. Only in locations where the windows were less likely to be opened did the builder risk setting his glass in the more picturesque, if less practical, "magic casements, opening on the foam of perilous seas, in faery lands forlorn."

Very much simpler and quite similar to each other are the Dr. Samuel MacKenzie Elliott House in Livingston and the Parsonage at Richmondtown. In both buildings the scrollwork and the pointed gable windows are the principal Gothic giveaways. The front door of the Elliott House has a flattened Tudor arch above its transom and quatrefoil panels in the lower portion of the door itself. The side

24. *Dr. Samuel MacKenzie*
Elliott House
69 Delafield Place, between Davis
and Bard Avenues, Livingston
c. 1850

25. *The Parsonage*
74 Arthur Kill Road,
Richmondtown
c. 1855

porch of the Parsonage, however, has a neo-Federal transom quite out of keeping with the rest of the house. The Elliott House is built of carefully dressed random ashlar, while the Parsonage is faced with clapboard.

Dr. Samuel MacKenzie Elliott was a man of many parts. He was one of the country's first oculists and eye surgeons and boasted among his patients John Jacob Astor, Peter Cooper, Henry Wadsworth Longfellow and Horace Greeley. He was an active abolitionist and harbored slaves in the cellar of his house, where he built a special fireplace for cooking. Not satisfied with these activities, he spent his spare time designing houses. The house at Livingston is of his own design.

Even more sparing in their suggestion of Gothic inspiration are the Garibaldi cottage in Rosebank and the one-room Grocery Store in Richmondtown.

What is now the Garibaldi Memorial is a starkly simple little house built in 1845. The only Gothic elements are the steep central gable and a rather naïve attempt to fill it with an ogival arched window. For a period in its history, this little cottage was completely covered over by an enormous, monumental lath-and-stucco baldachino whose classic columns and pediments did violence to the simplicity of the structure it was sheltering. The protective monument was subsequently removed. The order of the Sons of Italy in America maintain the memorial.

The great Italian liberator lived here in loneliness and poverty for about a year and a half after the collapse of the Roman Republic in 1849. He shared the house with his friend Antonio Meucci, who was one of the important early workers in the development of the telephone. The two men eked out a living making candles in the back yard. Garibaldi later returned to Italy and, in 1860, led the famous One Thousand in the liberation of Sicily and Naples. He lived to see his lifelong dream fulfilled—the unification of all Italy. In 1891 the house and its contents were put up for auction. Seventeen candles that Garibaldi had made brought $6.75.

26. GARIBALDI MEMORIAL
420 Tompkins Avenue, at Chestnut Avenue, Rosebank

a. Garibaldi Cottage *(as it is today)*
c. 1845

b. Former Baldachino *(now removed)*

27. *Grocery Store*
Court Place, Richmondtown
(formerly in Eltingville)
c. 1860

The little 1860 Grocery Store, now moved from Eltingville for preservation in Richmondtown, is much the simplest of all the examples and is barely identifiable as Gothic. Only its emphasis on the vertical wood battens and the steep pitch to the roof place it within the Gothic Revival style.

ITALIANATE   Overlapping the Gothic Revival, and outlasting it, was the Italianate style. It had an appeal to the newly prosperous class that was emerging in mid-century. It provided just the sort of spacious and imposing ambiance that was wanted for the opulent entertaining of the day. The two Italianate Landmark houses on Staten Island are both rather early examples of the style.

The Hamilton Park Cottage in New Brighton was built in two stages between 1859 and 1872. Its most notable feature is the central triple-arched porch flanked by two bays whose handsome Italian Renaissance details have been beautifully translated into wood. The formality of the three windows above the porch is typically Italianate, as are the heavy brackets which support the overhanging cornice.

New Brighton, named for the English seaside resort, was started in 1836 by a speculator, Thomas E. Davis, as a summer resort for Manhattanites. Then, as now, only half an hour from the Battery, it offered magnificent views. Then, but *not* as now, the air was salubrious and the beaches were clean and pure. Soon fashionable hotels arose along Richmond Terrace and handsome summer cottages cropped up on the hill above. Incidentally, any suburban or country house, regardless of its size, was called a "cottage." Hamilton Park Cottage was one of an enclave of such houses built by Charles K. Hamilton, a Manhattan merchant who saw the attractions of commuting by ferry across the bay. After the Civil War, developers began a campaign to promote the northern and eastern shores of Staten Island as a summer-vacation area. Their advertisements pulled no punches: "Glorious old Staten Island," "First Paradise of the old Patroons," "Choice Retreat of the Refined and Wealthy of New York," "Nothing in the Vicinity of New York is found to Surpass this most 'Beautiful Isle of the Sea' with its sea-girt shores, decked with costly villas and thrifty Villages." But health hazards, most serious of which was malaria, and poor and irregular ferry service deterred buyers, and it was not until around 1900 that the island became a truly popular resort.

Much simpler than the Hamilton Park Cottage is the Pritchard House of 1845, also in New Brighton. The strong projecting corner

28. Hamilton Park Cottage
105 Franklin Avenue,
between Buchanan
Street and Park Place,
New Brighton
1859, 1872

quoins, the eared moldings around the squareheaded windows, and the paired modillions that support the cornice are typically Italianate, as is the row of scroll brackets on which the second-story balcony rests. The scrollwork over the porches, however, seems to be a quaint survival of the Gothic Revival period.

29. Pritchard House
66 Harvard Avenue,
at Park Place,
New Brighton
c. 1845

STICK STYLE   The restless striving for new effects and romantic variety reached a sort of frenzied climax in what has been called the Stick style. This is purely American and is characterized by tall vertical proportions, irregular planes, overhanging eaves and a plethora of diagonal "stickwork," inserted like wooden lace in every available location. It is not dissimilar, in terms of exterior materials, from what was going on inside the parlors, reception rooms and dining rooms of the very same houses. A room was considered to be indecently undressed unless chairs and sofas were topped with antimacassars, mantels draped with fringed scarves, tables with embroidered and tasseled covers, pedestals with laces, and even paintings hung with fabric festoons. The Kreischer House in Charleston, overlooking Arthur Kill, is an excellent example of this style with its

30. *Kreischer House   4500 Arthur Kill Road,
    near Englewood Avenue, Charleston
    c. 1885*

octagonal corner tower and its assortment of gables, projections, porches, fretwork and scrolls.

Whether it was due to the fact that local families tended to hang on to their old houses or that there was not the same rivalry among new fortunes for novelty and display that existed in Manhattan, Staten Island seems to have escaped the dizzying series of Eclectic styles that bedeviled other parts of the city. There are few examples of neo-Romanesque, neo-Gothic, neo-Georgian, neo-Federal or neo–American Classic houses that were so prevalent elsewhere from the 1890s through the 1920s. In fact, the only Eclectic Landmark residence on Staten Island is so surprising in its choice of style and so personal in its treatment that it seems a law unto itself.

When Ernest Flagg designed his own home in the midst of the Dongan Hills section, he turned for inspiration to the Dutch colonies in the Caribbean. The great thirty-two-room mansion with its two-story porch and curved central pediment, with its big square chimneys brought boldly forward to the front of the house, with its round observation deck thrust right through the center of a gambrel roof, the

31. *Ernest Flagg House   209 Flagg Place, Dongan Hills*
1898, Ernest Flagg

building suggests the palace of an eighteenth-century governor of Aruba, Curaçao or Surinam. But it is actually a highly original creation, like everything this talented architect designed.

Churches and Graveyards

Where there are country houses there are country churches. Two of Staten Island's simple wooden churches exemplify nicely the poles of classicism and romanticism between which popular tastes oscillated throughout the nineteenth century.

The Woodrow Methodist Church is—if one ignores for the moment the tower and belfry—a pure Greek Revival building. Square-headed windows along the sides are the only interruptions to the simple white clapboarding. A severe flight of steps the full width of the church leads up to the Doric portico. The only concession to ornamentation is confined to the simple paneling of the pair of double entrance doors and the eared and pedimented moldings that enframe them. The belfry, with its columned arcade, and the rather stubby spire are obviously later additions.

The first Methodist church on Staten Island, dating back to 1787, was located on the site of the present building, which dates from 1842. Two outstanding preachers are associated with the Woodrow Methodist Church. Francis Asbury, the missionary whom John Wesley sent

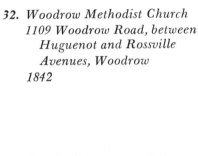

32. *Woodrow Methodist Church*
1109 Woodrow Road, between
Huguenot and Rossville
Avenues, Woodrow
1842

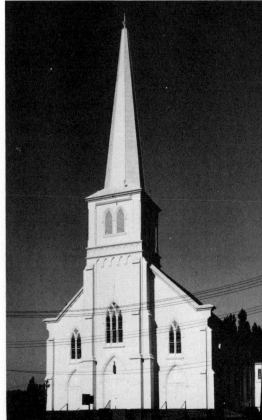

33. *Brighton Heights Reformed Church*
St. Mark's Place and Fort Place,
New Brighton
1864

from England in 1771 to spread Methodism in America, had as his first assignment the Staten Island circuit, which included the Woodrow church. The Reverend Henry Boehm, who devoted seventy-six years of his life to the Methodist ministry in Staten Island, is buried in the Woodrow Cemetery.

Dating a quarter of a century later, the Brighton Heights Reformed Church is a delightful interpretation in wood of the Gothic Revival style. The paired buttresses at the corners of the central tower and at the corners of the main body of the church imitate stone prototypes, though, of course, in wood construction, they are purely decorative. The pointed windows and multiple paneled doors, the band of quatrefoil decoration around the base of the tower and the little pointed corbels below it are a few of the typical Gothic Revival details. When simplified to the capability of a country carpenter, they take on a particular charm.

Country churches in the seventeenth and eighteenth centuries were almost invariably surrounded by churchyards, as is evident in the case of the Woodrow Methodist Church. But there were also private family graveyards which were known as "homestead" burial plots and which were usually found on a remote part of the family farm. One of the most interesting is part of the Richmondtown Restoration and is known as the Van Pelt–Rezeau Cemetery after the families that occupied the Voorlezer's House when it ceased being a school. Five generations of the families are buried there. This tiny plot, with its

34. Van Pelt–Rezeau Cemetery   Tysen Court, Richmondtown
c. 1780

simple old tombstones, is still partly surrounded by sections of some finely wrought iron fencing. Although their gravestones are missing, two young people, Ernst, a Hessian drummer boy who was serving in the British occupation forces, and a girl known as "Pretty" Van Pelt, were buried in this plot during the Revolution. Ernst had been billeted with the Van Pelt family in the Voorlezer's House, and the two young folk became fast friends. Ernst was killed during a skirmish, and during the action young Pretty, who had always been frail, died, presumably of a broken heart.

Of similar origin is the Sleight Family Graveyard in Rossville, on the west side of Staten Island just above the salt marshes that lead down to Arthur Kill. The plot was originally used as a graveyard for the Sleight family, but later it was shared by other families. Peter

35. *Sleight Family Graveyard (Rossville or Blazing Star Burial Ground) Arthur Kill Road at Rossville Avenue, Rossville 1750–1850*

Winant, the son of one of the original colonists who established the first permanent settlement on Staten Island in 1661, was buried here in 1758. In addition to Sleights and Winants, one finds here such names as Seguine, Perine and Poillon—families that have been identified with much of the island's early history and with many of the surviving Landmarks. This graveyard is also known as the Blazing Star Burial Ground because of its proximity to the old Blazing Star Ferry that used to cross Arthur Kill to New Jersey.

Though the stone and brick churches of Staten Island are sometimes more pretentious than the wooden ones, they share the same stamp of having been built to serve a country parish. Earliest of this group is the brick Asbury Methodist Church on Richmond Avenue, whose original side walls of 1849 remain but whose front and tower were rebuilt in 1878. This vernacular building with its squareheaded windows on the side and its round-arched windows on the front recalls such Federal antecedents as St. Luke's Chapel in the Greenwich Village Historic District in Manhattan. The curious shape of the openings in the wooden belfry would seem to make it unique in church architecture. When the openings are examined closely, however, they are seen to be simply the forthright expression of the cross-bracing that the carpenter inserted to stiffen his structure against the wind.

The church was named in honor of Bishop Francis Asbury, who was also associated with the Woodrow Methodist Church. When, in his early days as a missionary, he arrived on Staten Island he first stayed at the home of Peter Van Pelt and conducted his services there. He had the satisfaction of seeing the five hundred Methodists who were in America in 1771 grow to 214,000 by 1816, the year he died. It is estimated that this indefatigable circuit rider traveled 300,000 miles and preached 17,000 sermons during his forty-five years of ministering to the people of the Eastern seaboard.

The charming small chapel that was begun for the residents of Sailors' Snug Harbor in 1854 is much more sophisticated than the Asbury church, though it follows the same plan: a rectangular "meeting house" entered through the base of a square central tower. The detail represents the full flowering of the Italianate style. The paired brackets that support the cornice over each pilaster are particularly characteristic, as are what Sir Bannister Fletcher defines as "arcade-type" windows—i.e., roundheaded openings filled in with a pair of roundheaded arches, the space between the three heads being filled in with a small circle. In the case of the chapel, the small circles so fascinated the anonymous architect that he also used them to fill in the three bull's-eye windows just below the belfry. The delicate little free-standing colonnettes that support the round arches of the belfry itself are a Victorian touch.

An interesting footnote to the technology of transportation is an invitation issued in October 1856 to the city's bluebloods to attend the dedication of the chapel. The ceremony was scheduled for 2 P.M., and

36. (*Left*) *Asbury Methodist Church   2100 Richmond Avenue, between Signs Road and Rockland Avenue, New Springville*
  Side walls: 1849
  Tower and front rebuilt: 1878

37. (*Right*) *Sailors' Snug Harbor Chapel   Richmond Terrace between Tysen Street and Kissel Avenue, New Brighton*
  1854

the invitation carried the information that "a Steamboat will leave the Pier foot of Whitehall Street at 1:00 o'clock." This, in the days of steamboats and carriages, allowed just one hour for the trip, the same time that was allowed in 1972 for guests to get to the ceremony marking the City's taking title to Sailors' Snug Harbor.

St. Patrick's Roman Catholic Church, in the Richmondtown Restoration, is a good example of the Romanesque Revival style. It is almost exactly contemporaneous with the Gothic Revival Brighton Heights Reform Church—they date from 1862 and 1864 respectively. They are similar in plan, proportion, scale and general feeling. The differences between the two buildings are that the Brighton Heights

Reformed Church is built of white-painted wood and has pointed windows and some Gothic details, while St. Patrick's is constructed of brick, has roundheaded windows and employs such Romanesque details as a row of corbels following the rake of the front gable and a series of concentric archways to frame the deep-set front portal. A comparison of the two buildings demonstrates how much stronger the similarities are than the differences.

The 1872 Church of St. Andrew in Richmondtown is the first Landmark church on Staten Island whose architect—William H. Mersereau—can be identified. Its asymmetrical massings, its rough-cut random-fieldstone walls, its picturesque contrast of steep gables with battlements, its varied groupings of roundheaded and bull's-eye windows (all faced with brick), and, above all, its rugged solidity, clearly bespeak the scholarly aspect of the Eclectic period. This is an English parish church of the twelfth century. It has simply been transplanted

*38. St. Patrick's Church
53 St. Patrick's Place,
Richmondtown
1862*

39. Church of St. Andrew
Old Mill and Arthur Kill
Roads, Richmondtown
1872, William H. Mersereau

from the rolling English countryside to an equally romantic setting in Staten Island.

The Brighton Heights Reformed Church and St. Patrick's, essentially the same but superficially different, are respectively called Gothic Revival and Romanesque Revival. St. Patrick's Church and the Church of St. Andrew, superficially the same but essentially different, are respectively called Romanesque Revival and neo-Romanesque.

Public Buildings

With one notable exception, the public buildings in Staten Island follow the general pattern of its churches. They provide simple, quasi-vernacular examples of the styles that were popular throughout the nineteenth century, and illustrate, often with charm and individuality, country interpretations of urban fashions.

The earliest is the Third County Courthouse, which tops the hill at Richmondtown Restoration on Center Street and dates back to 1837. The strong Tuscan columns and the low pediment over them suggest the contemporary Woodrow Methodist Church, though the columns here are huskier and the pediment lower. The central pavilion is built with local traprock, while the rear and sides of the courthouse are brick. A square cupola surmounts the roof. The building is now used for the administrative offices of the Richmondtown Restoration and the Staten Island Historical Society. The large courtroom, now used as an auditorium, has been restored to its appearance during the eighty-two years of its use as the court of highest jurisdiction in Richmond County. It again contains the original judge's bench, the clerk's desk and the witness box.

40. *Third County Courthouse*
302 Center Street,
*   opposite Court Place,*
*   Richmondtown*
c. 1837

It was here that what has been called one of the country's ten most important lawsuits was conducted. Its importance lay in the fact that it helped to establish the principle of change of venue. Polly Bodine, of a prominent Staten Island family, was accused of setting fire to a house where she was baby-sitting for some young cousins. The children died and Polly was brought to trial in 1844. Because everybody was related to the defendant, it was impossible to secure an impartial jury, and the trial had to be moved out of town, where Polly was acquitted.

The County Clerk's and Surrogate's Offices lie diagonally across the way from the courthouse. This is an unpretentious two-story brick building in a vernacular interpretation of the Italianate style. The oldest section, built in 1848, was a one-story building. In 1858 a second story was added, in 1877 a wing, and in 1917 an extension to the wing. These additions are all in keeping with the original structure. Abandoned in 1920, when the county clerk's and surrogate's offices were moved to St. George, the building was renovated in 1933–35 and turned over to the Staten Island Historical Society for use as an historical museum.

More typical of the middle and latter parts of the nineteenth century are the New Brighton Village Hall of 1871 and the Edgewater Village Hall of 1889.

41. County Clerk's and Surrogate's Offices (now Staten Island Historical Society Museum) 303 Center Street at Court Place, Richmondtown
One-story building: 1848
Second story: 1858
Wing: 1877
Extension to wing: 1917

42. New Brighton Village Hall
(now Martin Luther King
Heritage House)
66 Lafayette Avenue,
New Brighton
1871

The New Brighton Village Hall, a three-story brick building, shows the influence of the French Second Empire style with its mansard roof, paired pilasters and ornate corbels. It is far simpler than contemporary prototypes in Brooklyn or Manhattan. The fact, however, that it is a freestanding building, and that when it was built it represented for the village of New Brighton all the majesty of government, gives it a dignity that is still apparent. After standing vacant for a number of years, the building was bought in 1971 by Heritage House, a community group, for use as its headquarters and also as a center for social programs for young people and the elderly. Heritage House was organized after the assassination of Dr. Martin Luther King, Jr., to provide services to the black community of Staten Island, which is concentrated in the area around the old Village Hall.

The Edgewater Village Hall in Stapleton is very similar in feeling and material to its counterpart at New Brighton, though it was built eighteen years afterward and reflects the Romanesque Revival style in the extensive use of brick corbels. The truth is that when such styles sift down to the local and amateur level, the differences in details, over which architectural historians would be willing to fight duels, are really of secondary importance. It is the "feel" of such buildings, their materials, their scale and their craftsmanship, rather than their correctness, that make them important to us.

One still senses the local pride with which the author of a "Descriptive Sketch of Stapleton" could write in 1893 that the Edgewater Village Hall "is one of the finest on the island, or, for that matter, anywhere in the immediate vicinity of New York." It is "substantial . . . of brick two stories in height and of a somewhat ornate style of architecture . . . well adapted to the purpose for which it is devoted." A considerable number of hair-splitting battles among historians of nineteenth-century architecture might well be avoided if, once and for all, they could agree on a catch-all category to be known

43. Edgewater Village Hall
   Tappan Park and Canal
   Street, Stapleton
   1889

as the "somewhat-ornate-but-well-adapted-to-the-purpose-for-which-it-is-devoted" style of architecture.

Definitely *not* to be included in this category (although when they were built they were considered to be well adapted to the purpose for which they were intended) are the five magnificent Greek Revival buildings that make up the main part of Sailors' Snug Harbor. It can also be said of them today, almost a century and a half since the earliest of the group was built, that they are not only the finest in Staten Island or in the immediate vicinity of New York, but, without question, the most impressive group of Greek Revival buildings in the United States.

These buildings stem from the generosity of the son of a Scottish ship's master who had amassed a fortune during the Revolutionary War from what has been variously described as "profitable commerce" or as "privateering." When his bachelor son, Robert Richard Randall, was considering how to dispose of his inherited fortune, he followed the advice of his lawyer friends Alexander Hamilton and Daniel D. Tompkins that a fortune made on the sea might well be left for the establishment and support of a home for "aged, decrepit and worn-out sailors." His property consisted largely of Manhattan real estate just north of the present Washington Square, in the area that is now bounded by Waverly Place, East Tenth Street, and Fourth and Fifth Avenues. The income on this property in 1800 was $4,000 a year; in 1848, $40,000; in 1898, $400,000; and by 1927 had risen to over $1,000,000. The income has not greatly increased since then, because most of the rents are tied up in long-term leases.

After years of litigation with disappointed collateral relatives of Randall, the trustees under his will—he had died in 1801—were at last able to buy, in 1831, a farm in Staten Island on a grassy knoll running down to Kill van Kull, which connects Upper New York Bay with Newark Bay. The old salts thus were never to be out of sight of the busy harbor which had played such an important role in their lives. The Manhattan property was kept for income-producing purposes.

The present complex of buildings was begun with the central one (Building C), the design of which has long been attributed to Martin E. Thompson, who is well known for his buildings in the Greek Revival style. Through research in the very recently opened archives of Sailors' Snug Harbor, I. Barnett Shepherd has made the surprising discovery that Minard Lafever was somehow involved in the design of the central building. The design would have been made at the crucial moment in his career when his listing in Longworth's New York City Directory changed from "carpenter" to "architect." He appears to have worked on the central building from September, 1831, when construction started, until August of the following year, when apparently the work was continued by Samuel Thompson & Son—listed as "architects and superintendents"—who constructed the inner pair of flanking buildings in 1839–40 and 1840–44 respectively and may have had a hand in the original design. In the nineteenth century the distinctions between "architect," "builder" and even "carpenter" were not as clearly defined as they are today. The same Samuel Thompson was associated with Town & Davis and John Frazee in connection with the old United States Custom House (now Federal Hall National Memorial) on Wall Street, and it is possibly the similarity of the names that led to the long-standing attribution of the Sailors' Snug Harbor buildings to Martin E. Thompson.

Further research will doubtless be necessary before credit can positively be given to Minard Lafever for the imposing design of an octastyle Ionic temple, approached by a broad flight of steps. Its low pediment is entirely devoid of ornamentation, and its marble columns, which in 1845 replaced the original brick and stucco ones, are unfluted. Whoever was responsible for the design can also probably be credited with at least the concept of the inner pair of flanking buildings (B and D), though the connecting corridors appear to have been somewhat modified from his original idea.

The incredible thing is that when the outer pair of buildings (A and E) was added, almost half a century later, by anonymous architects, the plan was carried through with such skill and subtlety that the entire composition looks as though it came from the hand of one master. The inner pair of flanking buildings seems to be set slightly behind the central structure, but this is only an optical effect resulting from the fact that they have no projecting porticos. Actually the front walls of all five buildings are in a single plane. The simple fronts of the first flanking pair are framed by corner pilasters. Small pedimented porches provide their only enrichment. The architects of the outer pair chose a hexastyle temple form in order not to compete with the eight-columned central building. This outer pair is also linked to its neighbors by a repetition of the one-story corridor.

There are two important Landmark components of the Sailors'

a. Main Buildings
Building C: 1831–33,
   Minard Lafever or
   Martin E. Thompson and
   Samuel Thompson & Son (?)
Building B: 1839–40
Building D: 1840–44
   Minard Lafever (?),
   Samuel Thompson & Son
Building A: 1879
Building E: 1880

b. Dedicatory Plaque

Snug Harbor complex that sometimes are overlooked by the visitor overwhelmed by the grandeur of the Greek Revival structures themselves. These are the handsome Greek Revival iron fence that runs along the boundary of the property and the delightful little pedestrian gatehouse on Richmond Terrace.

The fence, which dates from 1842 and thus is nearly as old as the

c. *Iron Fence*
Original portion:
1842, Frederick Diaper

d. *Pedestrian Gatehouse*
c. 1860, 1880

buildings it surrounds, was designed by Frederick Diaper, a fellow of the Royal Institute of British Architects and a founding member of the American Institute of Architects. It was fabricated by William Alexander, "smith and ornamental ironworker," of Manhattan. Except for the loss of some of the ornamental rosettes, it is in almost perfect condition. The purpose of the fence, it is said, was not so much to keep trespassers out of the property as to keep the old sailors in—or at least to discourage trips to such places as the Old Stone Jug.

The fence is interrupted by a number of gates, wide double gates for carriages and various single ones for pedestrians, including the gatehouse on Richmond Terrace. While individual details of this building could be labeled Italianate, Romanesque Revival and French Second Empire, it is in fact an exuberant example of the vernacular architecture of the day. Its crowning glory is a small square cupola. A visitor standing below can see that each of its four faces contains a pair of small roundheaded windows glazed in glorious ruby-red glass. Its big central archway frames a view of the obelisk erected in memory of Robert Richard Randall and of the octastyle portico of the main building. The rather cozy quality of the gatehouse provides a warm welcome to the severe stateliness of the Greek Revival buildings beyond it.

The Harbor's recent history is perhaps its most dramatic. After the designation of these buildings as Landmarks, the trustees of Sailors' Snug Harbor announced that they were going to build new and more efficient quarters for their elderly charges and tear down the old buildings because they would interfere with the view. As one member of the Landmarks Preservation Commission put it, this was the "most extraordinary example of institutional vandalism" he had ever heard of.

Thus began a long series of difficult and complicated negotiations which were to last nearly six years. The trustees argued that the structures were no longer suitable for good geriatric care, and that the maintenance of old buildings was a constant drain on their fixed income. They took the Landmarks Preservation Commission to court, and the case was decided in favor of the Harbor. The Commission appealed the case and established the constitutionality of the Landmarks Preservation Law in a memorable decision.

The issue of economic hardship, however, remained undetermined. While the question was in abeyance, numerous studies were made for modernizing the interiors of the structures, for making inconspicuous additions behind them or for the construction of an entirely new group of buildings on another portion of the property. The future needs, management and finances of the Harbor were all thoroughly studied. Finally, an amicable solution was negotiated. ·

With the active intercession of Mayor John V. Lindsay and Parks

Commissioner August Heckscher, the City of New York bought fourteen and a half acres of the property that included the five Greek Revival Landmarks, the charming little Italianate chapel and three very useful subsidiary structures, as well as enough of the surrounding grounds to ensure that the Landmarks will be preserved in their park-like setting. Plans are being made to convert the buildings into a cultural center, for which Staten Island's rapidly increasing population will soon have an urgent need. As a first step, the Staten Island Institute of Arts and Sciences, in need of expansion space, is currently moving its historical and art collections into space which the Harbor is making available.

Meanwhile, the Sailors' Snug Harbor trustees arranged to sell the balance of their property to a housing developer. Local protests, however, rose to such a clamor that the City again intervened to acquire the entire property as a public park. With the proceeds of both sales the Sailors' Snug Harbor trustees are planning to build a new home, designed according to the latest standards for geriatric care, on a site in North Carolina where they will be able to take advantage of the medical and research facilities of Duke University. While some of the "aged, decrepit and worn-out sailors" may miss their Landmark home and the view of New York Harbor, there is no question that their creature comforts will be well cared for.

On February 16, 1971, when a resolution of the fate of Sailors' Snug Harbor first seemed about to be realized, *The New York Times* carried an editorial entitled "All Snug in the Harbor," which commented:

> It has taken five years of negotiations between the City and the trustees of Sailors' Snug Harbor to save six landmark structures on the Staten Island waterfront from a fate worse than death known as modernization. . . . In a decision of major importance the [Landmarks] law was upheld. . . . There is no longer any doubt that the concept of preservation is not only in the public interest but is a decisive factor in the quality of the environment.

Lighthouses and a Fort

The utilitarian and military structures of Staten Island run the gamut from the simplest rural building to a structure of monumental proportions and power.

The 1854 New Dorp Lighthouse on Altamont Street is the simplest. It is little more than a clapboard cottage over which a stubby square tower and cupola have been raised. It depended for visibility on its elevation, for the hill on which it stands commands a magnificent view of both the Narrows and the Lower Bay. The lighthouse, also known as the Moravian Light, since it is close to the New Dorp Moravian Church, remained in operation for over a century, from the time of its construction until it was closed down in 1964.

45. *New Dorp Lighthouse*
(Moravian Light)
Altamont Street, New Dorp
c. 1854

Much more what one would imagine a lighthouse to look like is the Staten Island Lighthouse, built in 1912. It is the sort of structure that one would expect to find on a rocky New England headland or on a sandy storm-battered island rather than within the boundaries of New York City. It is located well inland, on Lighthouse Hill, which overlooks Richmondtown Restoration. The light shines out 231 feet above sea level and works in conjunction with the Ambrose Light Tower, which replaced the famous old Ambrose Light Ship to guide ships into the channels of New York Harbor. The structure is a strong and honest example of utilitarian architecture. Its octagonal tower of yellow brick rises from a deeply rusticated stone base. The tower

46. Staten Island Lighthouse
Edinboro Road,
Lighthouse Hill
1912

windows, framed with stone, follow the lines of the staircase that the lighthouse keeper must climb. Two octagonal lookout balconies project from the masonry walls, the lower and larger one being supported by sixteen massive cast-iron brackets.

The most impressive and the most historic of Staten Island's utilitarian structures is the fortification now known as Battery Weed and formerly called Fort Richmond. It is close to the shore of the Narrows just to the north of the Verrazano Bridge. Battery Weed is part of the Fort Wadsworth Military Reservation, the oldest continuously manned military post in the United States. Its antecedents go back to 1663, when a small wooden blockhouse was built by the

47. Battery Weed   Fort Wadsworth Military Reservation
1847–61

Dutch as a protection from the Indians. To this the British added more blockhouses and fortifications, and in the early 1800s the Americans stepped up the defenses, so that the Narrows was well protected by the time of the War of 1812.

Battery Weed itself is the successor to Fort Richmond, which dated back to 1812 and was served by thirty cannons. The fort that we see today was named after Stephen H. Weed, who was killed in the Battle of Gettysburg, in July 1863. It is built at the water's edge in the form of a trapezoid, with four tiers of guns set in the open-arched galleries that face the water. An octagonal stair tower at each of the salient corners leads from one gun gallery to another. The long inshore wall is lower than the gun galleries; its blank surface is interrupted only by a massively enframed central gateway. By the middle of the Civil War the 284 guns made it one of the strongest points on the East Coast of the United States. It was matched by Fort Hamilton on the other side of the Narrows in Brooklyn. This pair of forts guarded Upper New York Bay against the incursion of enemy ships.

While Lexington, Massachusetts, may boast of having been the place where the "shot heard round the world" was fired, Fort Wadsworth has the distinction of having been the target of the last shot fired in the Revolutionary War. When the British were evacuating New York City and its environs at the end of 1783, a crowd of jeering local citizens clustered on the hillside around what is now Fort Wadsworth to see them off. The sailors on the last of the British gunboats to sail out of the Narrows were so incensed at this derisive farewell that they lobbed a shot at the crowd. Fortunately, it fell short of its goal and landed in the water.

Glossary

Acanthus—An architectural ornament in the shape of the leaf of a thistle-like plant; used in particular to decorate the Corinthian capital.

Arcade—A series of arches supported on columns or piers, either attached to a wall or freestanding.

Arch Voussoirs—See Voussoirs.

Ashlar—Masonry composed of smooth rectangular building stones in regular courses.

Baluster—One of a series of short supports for a railing, as for a staircase or a balcony.

Balustrade—A series of balusters supporting a railing.

Band—A horizontal stripe, either raised, recessed or differentiated by material or texture from the main surface of a façade.

Batten—A narrow strip of wood, usually vertical, used to cover the joint between two boards behind it.

Battered Wall—A wall that slopes inward toward the top.

Battlement—A parapet interrupted by a series of openings.

Belt Course—A narrow raised horizontal band.

Bond—A general term describing the way in which the stones or bricks are laid so as to form a unified whole; in particular, the patterns that result from the various ways of laying brick so as to tie the face brick to the cheaper backing.

Bracket—A member projecting from a wall to support some overhanging element.

Buttress—A mass of masonry built against a wall to give it stability or to support the pressure of an arch or a vault.

Cap Molding—The projecting topmost molding on a lintel, pilaster or capital.

Chinoiserie—A type of decoration, popular in the eighteenth century, inspired by Chinese designs. It is characterized by diagonal elements and elaborately interlaced forms.

Chord—As applied to architecture, this geometrical term means the straight horizontal width of an arch or curved opening.

Cinquefoil—An ornament of generally rounded form, divided into five lobes.

Colonnade—A series of columns set at regular intervals, usually supporting an entablature, a roof or a series of arches.

Colonnette—A small slender column.

Compound Pier—A pier composed of several columns clustered together.

Console—An ornamental bracket in the form of an S-shaped scroll.

Corbel—A block or series of blocks stepping out from the face of a wall to support the beam of a roof or some other feature.

Corinthian Order—The classical column that is characterized by a bell-shaped capital covered with acanthus leaves; rarely used by the Greeks, but popular, in a slightly different form, with the Romans.

Cornice—A horizontal molded projection which crowns the top of a wall or a building or is used over a window or a door opening to shield it from the rain.

Course—A horizontal row of stones or bricks in a wall.

Crenellated—Furnished with battlements; by extension, a crenellated molding consists of squared indentations alternating between the top and the bottom of a band.

Cresting—Ornamental openwork, generally of metal, which surmounts a roof ridge, a wall, etc.

Crocket—An ornament in the form of a projecting clump of foliage spaced along a Gothic gable or spire.

Cupola—A small domed structure rising from a roof.

Dentils—A row of small square blocks beneath Ionic and Corinthian cornices.

Doric Order—Simplest of the classical orders, with unornamented saucer-shaped capital, fluted columns and, in the Greek form, no base.

Dormer—A vertical window, and the houselike structure containing it, that projects through a sloping roof.

Double-hung Sash—A window consisting of two counterweighted portions that slide up and down in parallel vertical tracks.

Double Keystone—A decorative treatment for the top center of an arch in which a narrow splayed stone extends above and often projects from the usual single keystone.

Dressed Stone—Stone that has been smoothly squared and finished.

Drip Molding—A projecting molding designed so that rainwater will fall free of the wall or opening below it.

Drum—A round, cylindrical form, often forming the support for a dome.

Eared Moldings—Moldings which surround and emphasize the extension of a lintel above a door or window opening.

Embrasure—An opening in a wall or parapet through which a gun was fired; also a recess or niche usually enframing a window or door opening.

Enframement—A frame or molding surrounding an opening.

Engaged Column—A column attached to the wall or to a pier behind it.

Entablature—The crowning portion of a classical order above the capitals; it consists of an architrave, a frieze and a cornice.

Fanlight—A semicircular or semi-elliptical window with radiating muntins or leads.

Fascia, Fascia Board—A rather wide, plain horizontal band which may form part of a classical entablature or cover the projecting ends of roof rafters.

Fieldstone—Rough undressed stone, usually from a local source.

Finial—An ornamental termination of a gable, a pinnacle or a post.

Flèche—A small slender spire rising from the ridge of a roof.

Flemish Bond—A method of laying bricks in which the ends and the sides of the bricks alternate horizontally and the ends and the sides are centered over each other vertically.

Fluting—Parallel vertical grooves in a column or pilaster.

Flying Buttress—A segmental arch carrying the thrust of the vault of the nave of a Gothic church outside the building to a detached pier.

Fret—A running design consisting of straight lines intersecting at right angles; often called a "Greek key."

Frieze—The central section of an entablature, frequently enriched with sculpture.

Gable—The vertical triangle at the end of a building formed by a sloping roof.

Gambrel Roof—A roof with two slopes of different pitch on either side of the ridge.

Guttae—Pendant ornaments, like small pegs, attached to the underside of the cornice in the Doric order.

Hipped Roof—A roof with slopes on all four sides.

Impost Block—The stone block on which an arch rests.

Ionic Order—A classical order distinguished by a double spiral scroll to form the capital.

Keystone—The topmost wedge-shaped stone that locks an arch into place.

Label—A molding that extends horizontally across the top of a flatheaded opening and vertically down each side for a short distance in the form of a hood.

Lancet Tracery—The ornamental patternwork in stone that filled in Gothic windows; its sharply pointed arches are characteristic of the early English period.

Lintel—The horizontal beam over the top of a window or door opening.

Loggia—A gallery or arcade open to the air on at least one side.

Lug—A small projecting part of a larger member, in particular the part of a windowsill that is built into the masonry at either side of the opening.

Lunette—A semicircular window or panel below a vault or a dome.

Machicolated—Provided with openings through which missiles or molten lead could be thrown on the enemy below.

Mansard Roof—A roof with a relatively flat upper portion but with a steep lower slope through which shallow dormers frequently project.

Modillion—An ornamental bracket or console under a cornice, usually in the Corinthian order; its horizontal dimension is greater than its vertical.

Molding—A strip of stone or wood, usually curvilinear, used for decorative purpose.

Mullion—A fixed vertical divider in a window, often serving a structural purpose.

Muntin—A thin member, of wood or lead, used to subdivide the glass area of a window into smaller panes.

Ogive, Ogival—An S-shaped curve—i.e., one that has both convex and concave portions.

Oriel—A bay window, especially one projecting on corbels from an upper story.

Overhang—A projecting upper part of a building, as a roof, a balcony or an upper story.

Overshot Roof—A roof which projects, often in a concave curve, beyond the face of the wall below it.

Palladian Window—A three-section window, with the center one arched.

Pediment—The triangular gable end of a roof in classical architecture, or a similar form used decoratively over door or window openings.

Pier—An upright support, usually rectangular, as contrasted to a column, which is round.

Pilaster—A flat pier projecting slightly from the wall to which it is attached.

Pinnacle—A small upright ornament or spire capping a gable or other roof projection.

Polychromy—Work executed in many colors.

Porch—An outside appendage to a building, forming a covered approach to the door.

Portico—A roofed structure supported by columns or piers, usually attached to a building as a porch, but extending along an entire side.

Pylon—A monumental mass of masonry flanking the entrance to a building, a bridge, etc.

Quadrant Windows—Windows in the shape of a quarter circle.

Quatrefoil—An ornament of generally rounded form, divided into four lobes, like a fourleafed clover.

Quoins—Stones at the outside corners of a building laid with their long dimensions in alternate directions. They serve structurally to tie together two walls that meet at right angles, but are often emphasized for purely decorative purposes.

Radial Brick—Brick ground to a wedge shape and used to form a structural arch, which may be semicircular, elliptical or flat.

Rake—Inclination from a perpendicular direction—applied to the slope of a roof or a gable.

Random Ashlar—Rectangular stones of varying sizes set in an irregular pattern.

Random Fieldstone—Rough-surfaced undressed stones of varying sizes set in an irregular pattern.

Rock-faced—The weather-worn face of stone left as it comes from the quarry; only the joints are squared.

Roman Brick—A special-shaped brick, larger and longer in proportion than common brick.

Rubblestone—Rough, undressed stone, usually of smaller and more uniform sizes than that referred to as "fieldstone."

Running Bond—A method of laying brick with no "headers," or short ends, showing on the face of the wall.

Rustication—Stonework in which the joints are strongly emphasized by being recessed; often the stone surface is also roughened.

Sash—A distinct portion of a window, either fixed, hinged, pivoted or sliding.

Segmented, Segmental—Consisting of a portion of a circle less than a semicircle.

Sidelights—Narrow vertical windows at either side of a door.

Spandrel—The triangular space between the curve of an arch and its rectangular enframement; also the rectangular portion of a wall between the head of one window and the sill of a window directly above it.

Spire—A slender tapering feature surmounting a tower.

Splayed—Sloping outward, wedge-shaped.

Spring Eave—A roof which extends over the wall below it (i.e., an overshot roof) and which rises in a concave curve.

Steeple—The main vertical feature of a church, comprising a tower and a spire.

Stoop—A raised platform reached by steps and leading to the entrance of a building.

Tracery—Ornamental openwork of stone or wood, characteristic of Gothic windows.

Transom—A window over a door; sometimes, also a fixed pane of glass over an operable window.

Trefoil—An ornament of generally rounded form divided into three lobes, like a clover.

Trophy—A sculptured collection of symbolic objects, often used to enrich a gable or to crown a monumental entrance.

Tuscan Order—The Roman counterpart to the Greek Doric style; the column is not fluted and has a base.

Vault—An arched covering of stone or brick over a building.

Veranda—A raised open gallery, covered by a roof.

Vermiculation—Stone incised with short curved forms resembling the tracks of worms.

Voussoirs—The wedge-shaped stones or bricks composing an arch.

Water Table—A projection near the base of a building, designed to throw rainwater clear of the foundations.

Bibliography

AIA Guide to New York City, ed. Norval White and Elliott Wilensky; sponsored by the New York Chapter, American Institute of Architects. New York: Macmillan, 1967.

Asbury, Herbert, *The Gangs of New York.* New York: Garden City Publishing Co., 1927.

Barlow, Elizabeth, *Frederick Law Olmsted's New York.* New York: Praeger, 1972.

———, *The Forests and Wetlands of New York City.* Boston and Toronto: Little, Brown, 1969.

Belden, E. Porter, *New York, Past, Present and Future,* 2nd edition. New York: George P. Putman, 1850.

Bliven, Bruce, Jr., *Under the Guns.* New York: Harper & Row, 1972.

Brown, Eve, *The Plaza, Its Life and Times.* New York: Duell, Sloane & Pearce, Meredith Press, 1967.

Burnham, Alan, ed., *New York Landmarks.* Middletown, Conn.: Wesleyan University Press, 1963.

Carmer, Carl, *The Hudson.* New York: Rinehart, 1939.

A Church in History. Brooklyn, N.Y.: Plymouth Church of the Pilgrims, 1949.

Churchill, Allen, *The Upper Crust.* Englewood Cliffs, N.J.: Prentice-Hall, 1970.

Churchyards of Trinity Parish in the City of New York, 1697–1969. New York: The Corporation of Trinity Church, 1969.

Classical America, Vol. I, Nos. 1 and 2.

Delaney, Edmund T., *New York's Turtle Bay, Old and New.* Barre, Mass.: Barre Publishers, 1965.

Designation Reports, adopted on individual Landmarks and Historic Districts from Pieter Claeson Wyckoff House, Brooklyn, October 14, 1965, through The Conservatory, New York Botanical Garden, The Bronx, October 16, 1973. New York: New York City Landmarks Preservation Commission.

Dictionary of American Biography, 1944 edition.

Ditmas, Charles Andrew, *Historic Homesteads of Kings County.* Brooklyn, N.Y., 1909 (published by the compiler).

Dooley, P. J., *Fifty Years in Yorkville*. New York: Parish House, 1917.

Dunshee, Kenneth Holcomb, *As You Pass By*. New York: Hastings House, 1962.

Ellis, Edward Robb, *The Epic of New York City*. New York: Coward-McCann, 1966.

Fein, Albert, ed., *Frederick Law Olmsted's Landscape into Cityscape: Plans for a Greater New York City*. Ithaca, N.Y.: Cornell, 1967.

Feininger, Andreas, *The Face of New York*. New York: Crown, 1954.

Fifth Avenue. New York: Fifth Avenue Bank, 1915.

Fitzpatrick, Benedict, *The Bronx and Its People: A History, 1609–1927*. New York: Lewis Historical Publishing Co., 1927.

Giedion, Siegfried, *Space, Time and Architecture*. Cambridge, Mass.: The Harvard University Press, 1941.

Gilchrist, Agnes Addison, "Notes for a Catalogue of the John McComb Collection, N.-Y. H. S." *Journal of the Society of Architectural Historians*, Vol. XXIII, No. 3 (October 1969).

Gilder, Rodman, *The Battery*. Boston: Houghton Mifflin, 1936.

Headley, Joel Tyler, *The Great Riots of New York, 1712–1873*. New York: Dover, 1971.

Hone, Philip, *The Diary of Philip Hone*, 2 vols., ed. Bayard Tuckerman. New York: Dodd, Mead, 1889.

Humphreys, Hugh, and Regina Benedict, "The Friends of Alice Austen," *Infinity*, periodical of the American Society of Magazine Photographers, Vol. XVI (1967), No. 7.

Huxtable, Ada Louise, *Classic New York: Georgian Gentility to Greek Elegance*. Garden City, N.Y.: Doubleday Anchor Books, 1964.

Kouwenhoven, John A., *The Columbia Historical Portrait of New York*. New York: Doubleday, 1953.

Lamb, Martha J., *History of the City of New York: Its Origin, Rise and Progress*. New York, 1922 (reprinted from original plates of *Valentine's Manual*).

Lancaster, Clay, *Old Brooklyn Heights*. Rutland, Vt.: Charles E. Tuttle Co., 1961.
————, *Prospect Park Handbook*. New York: Walton H. Rawls, 1867.

Landy, Jacob, *The Architecture of Minard Lafever*. New York: Columbia, 1970.

Leng, Charles W., and William T. Davis, *Staten Island and Its People: A History, 1609–1929*. New York: Lewis Historical Publishing Co., 1930.

Lockwood, Charles, *Bricks and Brownstones*. New York, St. Louis, San Francisco, London, Sydney, Toronto: McGraw-Hill, 1972.

Lyman, Susan Elizabeth, *The Story of New York*. New York: Crown, 1964.

McCabe, James D., Jr., *Lights and Shadows of New York Life, or, The Sights and Sensations of the Great City*, an 1872 facsimile edition. New York: Farrar, Straus & Giroux, 1970.

McCullough, David, *The Great Bridge*. New York: Simon and Schuster, 1972.

McDarrah, Fred, *Museums in New York*. New York: Dutton, 1967.

Marcuse, Maxwell F., *This Was New York!* New York: LIM Press, 1969.

Maurice, Arthur Bartlett, *New York in Fiction*. Port Washington, N.Y.: Ira J. Friedman, 1969.

Mayer, Grace M., *Once upon a City*. New York: Macmillan, 1958.

Memoirs of the Long Island Historical Society, Vol. I (1867).

Morris, James, *The Great Port: A Passage Through New York.* London: Faber and Faber, 1970.

Neufeld, Ernest, ed., *The Renascence of City Hall.* New York: The City of New York, 1956.

New York, N.Y. New York: American Heritage, 1968.

New York City Architecture, Selections from the Historic American Buildings Survey, No. 7. Washington, D.C.: U. S. Department of the Interior, 1969.

New York City Guide, by the Guilds' Committee for Federal Writers' Publications, Works Progress Administration. New York: Random House, 1939.

New York City Landmarks. New York: New York City Landmarks Preservation Commission, n.d. (1972).

New York Community Trust, *The Heritage of New York.* New York: Fordham, 1970.

Olmsted, Frederick Law, Jr., and Theodora Kimball, eds., *Frederick Law Olmsted, Landscape Architect, 1822–1903,* Vol. II, *Central Park as a Work of Art and as a Great Municipal Enterprise.* New York and London: G. P. Putnam's Sons, Knickerbocker Press, 1928.

Opening Ceremonies of the New York and Brooklyn Bridge, May 24, 1883. Brooklyn, N.Y.: Brooklyn Eagle Press, 1883.

Ottley, Roi, and William J. Weatherby, *The Negro in New York.* Dobbs Ferry, N.Y.: Oceana Publications, 1967.

Plan for New York City: A Proposal. New York: New York City Planning Commission, 1969.

Pyke, John S., Jr., *Landmark Preservation.* New York: Citizens' Union Research Foundation, 1972.

Rasmussen, Steen Eiler, *Experiencing Architecture.* Cambridge, Mass.: The M.I.T. Press, 1959.

Reed, Henry Hope, *The Golden City.* New York: Norton, 1971.

———, "The Vision Spurned: The Story of City Planning in New York," *Classical America,* Vol. I (1971), No. 1.

———, and Sophia Duckworth, *Central Park: A History and a Guide.* New York: Clarkson N. Potter, 1967.

Seymour, Catryna Ten Eyck, *Historic Walking Tour Maps: Downtown New York* (1970), *Greenwich Village* (1970), *Madison Square and Gramercy Park* (1965). New York: The Seymours.

Shaw, Esmond, *Peter Cooper and the Wrought Iron Beam.* New York: Cooper Union School of Art and Architecture, 1960.

Shelton, William Henry, *The Jumel Mansion.* Boston and New York: Houghton Mifflin, Riverside Press, 1916.

Stewart, William Rhinelander, *Grace Church and Old New York.* New York: Dutton, 1924.

Stokes, I. N. Phelps, *The Iconography of Manhattan Island, 1498–1909,* 6 vols. New York: Robert H. Dodd, 1915.

Tieck, William A., *Riverdale, Kingsbridge, Spuyten Duyvil, New York City.* Old Tappan, N.J.: Fleming H. Revell Co., 1968.

Zook, Nicholas, *Houses of New York Open to the Public.* Barre, Mass.: Barre Publishers, 1969.

Chronological Charts

The following chronological charts list only individual Landmarks that had been designated as of March 14, 1972. Buildings in Historic Districts are not included. Structures are arranged according to the categories described in the Introduction. Architectural styles and fashions are discussed in Chapter One. Periods of extremely early and extremely late examples of a style are indicated by a bar of lighter tone. Where no style is indicated the Landmark belongs to the "miscellaneous" category, which defies classification. Except in the few cases where a later addition is significantly different from the original, a Landmark is listed only once—under the date of its earliest portion.

In addition to serving as an analytical index of Landmarks by date, by type and by style, the vertical bars in the right-hand columns illustrate graphically how architectural taste has swung back and forth for three centuries between the classical and the romantic traditions. The number of bars in any one decade shows how many different styles were concurrently being used. The number of dots in any one bar gives a rough idea of the relative popularity of the various concurrent styles.

	residential	ecclesiastical	public
1650	Pieter Claesen Wyckoff House ————		
1660	Bowne House ———— Billiou-Stillwell-Perine House ————		
1670			
1680	Conference House ————	Trinity Churchyard First Shearith Israel Cemetery	
1690	Alice Austen House ———— Voorlezer's House ————	Friends' Meeting House, Flushing ————	
1700	Treasure House ————	Cornell Graveyard Lawrence Family Grave- yard	
1710	Fraunces Tavern ————		
1720	Poillon House ———— Kreuzer-Pelton House ———— Governor's House ———— Lent Homestead ————		
1730	King Mansion (rear) ———— Scott-Edwards House ———— Housman House ———— Cornelius Van Wyck House ————	Grace Episcopal Graveyard	
1740	Lake-Tysen House ———— Van Cortlandt Mansion ————		
1750	King Mansion (west front and connection) ———— Christopher House ————	Sleight Family Graveyard	
1760	Morris-Jumel Mansion ———— Wyckoff-Bennett Homestead ————	St. Paul's Chapel ————	
1770	Neville House ———— Boehm-Frost House ———— Kingsland Homestead ————		

commercial	utilitarian	NON-STYL-ISTIC	THE CLASSICAL TRADITION	THE ROMANTIC TRADITION

VERN.

GEORG.

Bowling Green Fence

	residential	ecclesiastical	public
	Valentine-Varian House ———		
	Lefferts Homestead ———		
1780		Van Pelt-Rezeau Cemetery	
	Dyckman House ———		
	Edward Mooney House ———		
			Erasmus Hall ———
1790	Cooper's Shop ———		
		Flatbush Dutch Reformed Church ———	
	James Watson House (east part) ———		
		St. Paul's Chapel Tower ———	
	John McComb House (27 Harrison Street) ———		
	Gracie Mansion ———		
	Abigail Adams Smith House ———	St. Mark's-in-the-Bowery ———	
1800	Van Nuyse-Magaw House ———		
		Church of the Transfiguration (R.C.) ———	
	Hamilton Grange ———		
			City Hall ———
	Stuyvesant-Fish House ———		
	Jonas Wood House (25 Harrison Street) ———		
	Commandant's House ———		
	Johannes Van Nuyse House ———		
	King Mansion (east front, entrance and porch) ———		
	James Watson House (west part) ———		
	No. 2 White Street ———		
		Old St. Patrick's Cathedral ———	
1810	Basketmaker's Shop ———		
	Sylvanus Decker Farmhouse ———		
	Morris-Jumel Mansion, portico ———		
	Poe Cottage ———		
	Joseph Steele House (original wing) ———		
		West Farms Soldier Cemetery	
	Stephen Van Rensselaer House ———		

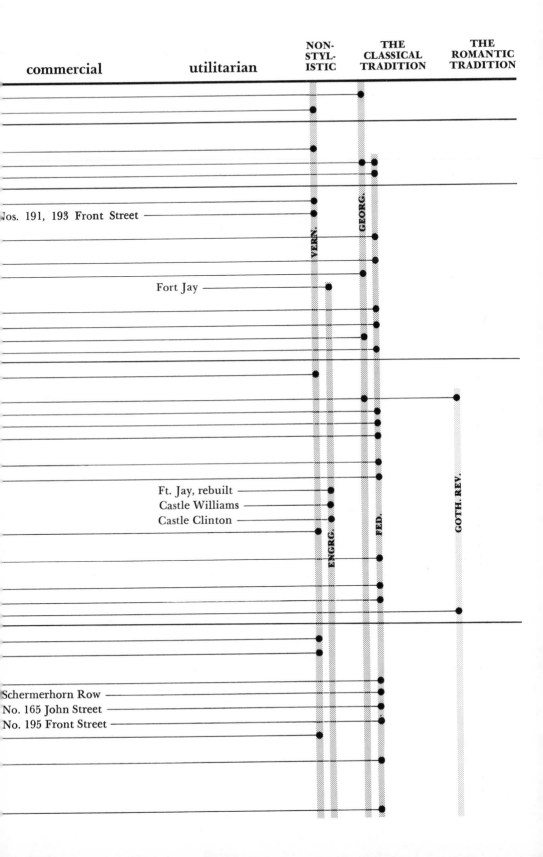

commercial utilitarian

Nos. 191, 193 Front Street

VERN. GEORG.

Fort Jay

Ft. Jay, rebuilt
Castle Williams
Castle Clinton

ENGRG. FED. GOTH. REV.

Schermerhorn Row
No. 165 John Street
No. 195 Front Street

	residential	ecclesiastical	public
	James Brown House ———		
		Sea and Land Church ———	
	Moore-McMillen House ———		
	John McComb, Jr., House (27A Harrison Street) ———		
1820		New Lots Reformed Church ———	
	No. 51 Market Street ———		
			Old Assay Office Building —
		Bialystoker Synagogue ———	
			Old St. Patrick's Convent and Girls' School ———
	Henry Street Settlement ———		
	Nos. 29, 31, 33 Harrison Street ———		
		St. Mark's-in-the-Bowery Steeple ———	
		New Utrecht Reformed Church ———	
	Nos. 37, 39, 41 Harrison Street ———		
		St. Augustine's Chapel ———	
1830		New York Marble Cemetery	
	Hunterfly Road Houses ———		
			Old United States Naval Hospital ———
			Sailors' Snug Harbor, Building C ———
		New York City Marble Cemetery	
	Old Merchant's House ———		
		Reformed Dutch Church of Newtown ———	
	Daniel Le Roy House ———		
	La Grange Terrace ———		
		Lawrence Graveyard, Lawrence Memorial Park	
	No. 131 Charles Street ———		
			Federal Hall National Memorial ———
	Gardiner-Tyler House ———		
		St. James' Church (R.C.) ———	
	Rose Hill ———		
		St. Peter's Church (R.C.) ———	
	Bartow-Pell Mansion ———		
	Latourette House ———		
	Stephens House and General Store ———		

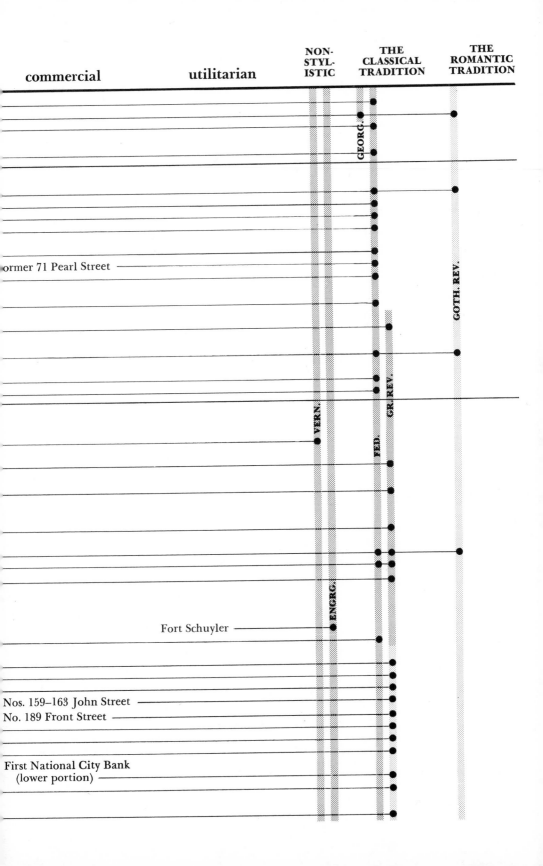

commercial	utilitarian	NON-STYL-ISTIC	THE CLASSICAL TRADITION	THE ROMANTIC TRADITION

former 71 Pearl Street

Fort Schuyler

Nos. 159–163 John Street
No. 189 Front Street

First National City Bank
(lower portion)

GEORG.

VERN.

ENGRG.

FED.

GR. REV.

GOTH. REV.

residential	ecclesiastical	public

Bennett House —

Third County Courthouse -

Sailors' Snug Harbor,
Building B —

1840

Admiral's House —

Sailors' Snug Harbor,
Building D —

Scott-Edwards House
  portico —

No. 440 Clinton Street —
Seguine House —

John Street Methodist
  Church —
St. Ann's Church —

Joseph Steele House
  (main part) —

Mariners' Temple —
Woodrow Methodist
  Church —

Grace Church, Manhattan —

Wave Hill —
Alice Austen House (porch
  and dormers) —
Nos. 26, 28, 30 Jones Street —

Church of the Holy
  Communion —

No. 37 East 4th Street —

St. John's Residence Hall —

Garibaldi Cottage —
Pritchard House —
The Players —

St. John's Church
  (Fordham) —
Trinity Church —

Grace Church Rectory —
Fonthill —

Church of the Holy
  Apostles —
St. George's Church —

Brooklyn Borough Hall —

Weeping Beech Tree

Flatlands Reformed
  Church —

County Clerk's and Surro-
  gate's Offices —

Theodore Roosevelt House —

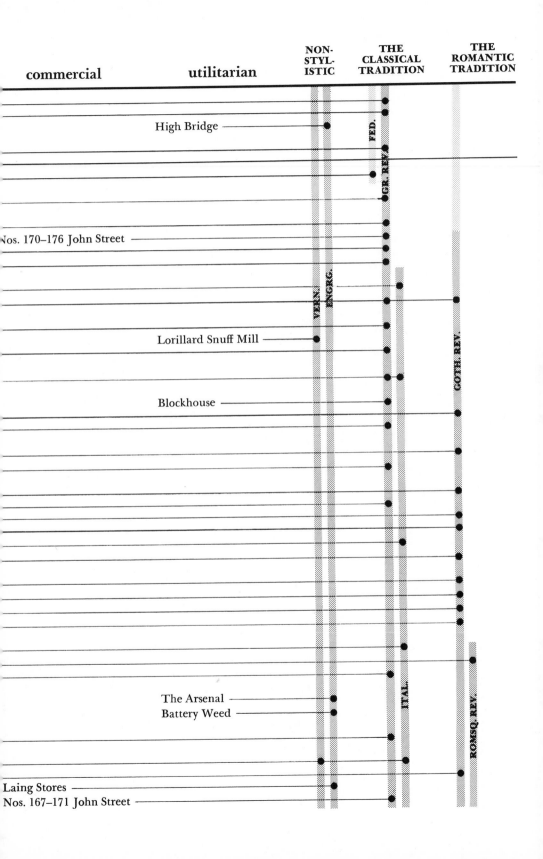

residential	ecclesiastical	public
Nos. 437–459 West 24th Street ————		
	Asbury Methodist Church ————	
	Church of the Transfiguration (Episcopal), Rectory and Guild Hall ————	
		Astor Library ————

1850

residential	ecclesiastical	public
	Beth Hamedrash Hagodol Synagogue ————	
Dr. Samuel MacKenzie Elliott House ————		
	Serbian Orthodox Cathedral of St. Sava ————	
Joseph Steele House (alterations) ————		
	Marble Collegiate Reformed Church ————	
J. P. Morgan, Jr., House ————		
Salmagundi Club ————		
		Foundation Building, Cooper Union ————
	Reformed Church of South Bushwick ————	
	St. Mark's-in-the-Bowery portico ————	
	Sailors' Snug Harbor Chapel ————	
	Fellowship Hall (Reformed Dutch Church of Newtown) ————	
Steinway Mansion ————		
The Parsonage ————		
Pendleton House ————		
Litchfield Villa ————		
Nos. 311 and 313 East 58th Street ————		
	Hanson Place Seventh Day Adventist Church ————	
	Church of the Holy Apostles, transepts ————	
	St. Patrick's Cathedral ————	
No. 152 East 38th Street ————		
	Friends' Meeting House, East 20th Street ————	
Hamilton Park Cottage ————		
No. 122 East 92nd Street ————		

1860

residential	ecclesiastical	public
Grocery Store, Richmondtown ————		
Stonehurst ————		

commercial	utilitarian	NON-STYL-ISTIC	THE CLASSICAL TRADITION	THE ROMANTIC TRADITION

o. 191 Front Street façade

dia House

New Dorp Lighthouse
Watch Tower

Haughwout Building

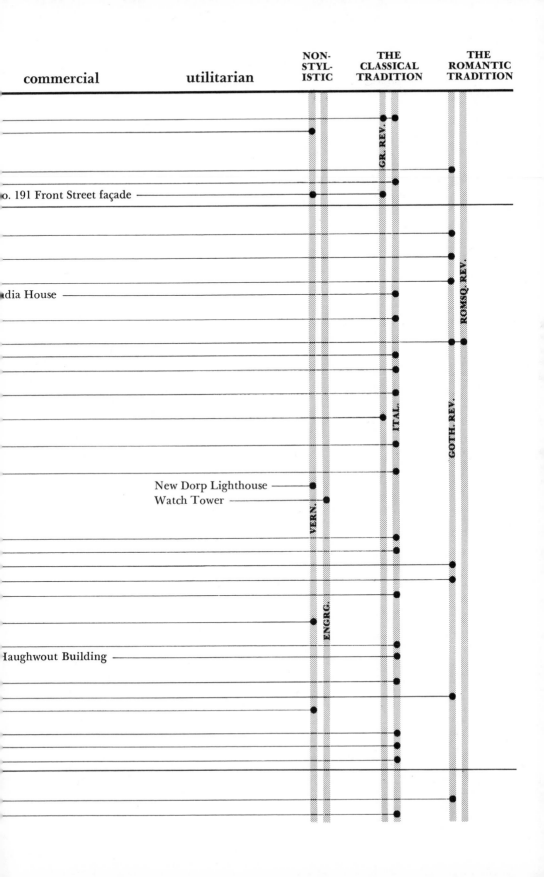

residential	ecclesiastical	public
	Serbian Orthodox Cathedral of St. Sava, Parish House ———	
	Friends' Meeting House and Seminary, Rutherford Place ———	
Nos. 157, 159, 161, 163–165 East 78th Street ———		
	Green-Wood Cemetery Gates ———	
	Grace Episcopal Church, Jamaica ———	
		Flushing Town Hall ———
	St. Patrick's Church, Richmondtown ———	
	Riverdale Presbyterian Church ———	
Greyston ———		
Duff House ———		
	Brighton Heights Reformed Church ———	
No. 312 East 53rd Street ———		
	Christ Church ———	
	Old St. Patrick's Cathedral, rebuilt ———	
		Poppenhusen Institute ———
1870		
		New Brighton Village Hall —
	Central Synagogue ———	
No. 120 East 92nd Street ———		
	St. Andrew's Church, Harlem ———	
	Church of St. Andrew, Richmondtown ———	
National Arts Club (new façade) ———		
		American Museum of Natural History, Central Wing ———
		Metropolitan Museum of Art, west façade, center —
The Judson ———		
		Sailors' Snug Harbor, Building A ———

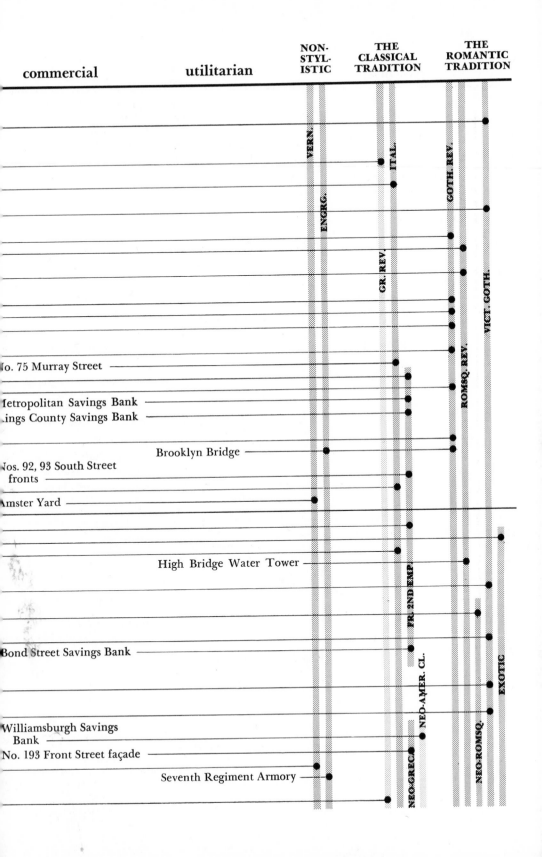

commercial   utilitarian   **NON-STYL-ISTIC**   **THE CLASSICAL TRADITION**   **THE ROMANTIC TRADITION**

VERN.

ENGRG.

ITAL.

GOTH. REV.

GR. REV.

VICT. GOTH.

ROMSQ. REV.

No. 75 Murray Street

Metropolitan Savings Bank

Kings County Savings Bank

Brooklyn Bridge

Nos. 92, 93 South Street fronts

Amster Yard

High Bridge Water Tower

FR. 2ND EMP.

Bond Street Savings Bank

NEO-AMER. CL.

EXOTIC

Williamsburgh Savings Bank

No. 193 Front Street façade

Seventh Regiment Armory

NEO-GREC.

NEO-ROMSQ.

residential	ecclesiastical	public
1880		
		Sailors' Snug Harbor, Building E
		Foundation Building, Cooper Union, three top stories
Cardinal's Residence and Rectory, St. Patrick's Cathedral		
The Dakota Apartments		
Villard Houses		
Hotel Chelsea		
	Emmanuel Baptist Church	
		Magnolia Grandiflora
Kreischer House		
		Brooklyn General Post Office
	St. Martin's Episcopal Church	
The Players porch		
		Metropolitan Museum of Art, west façade, south wing
		Edgewater Village Hall
	St. Andrew's Church, moved and enlarged	
		Carnegie Hall
		The Century Association
		American Museum of Natural History, 77th Street Façade
1890 Old Grolier Club		
	Judson Hall, Tower and Church	
		The American Fine Arts Society
		Harlem Courthouse
		Old Brooklyn Fire Department Headquarters
		Bushwick Democratic Club
	West End Collegiate Church and Collegiate School	
		The Harvard Club
		Hall of Languages, Bronx Community College
	Immaculate Conception Church	
		Metropolitan Museum of Art, west façade, north wing
		Brooklyn Museum

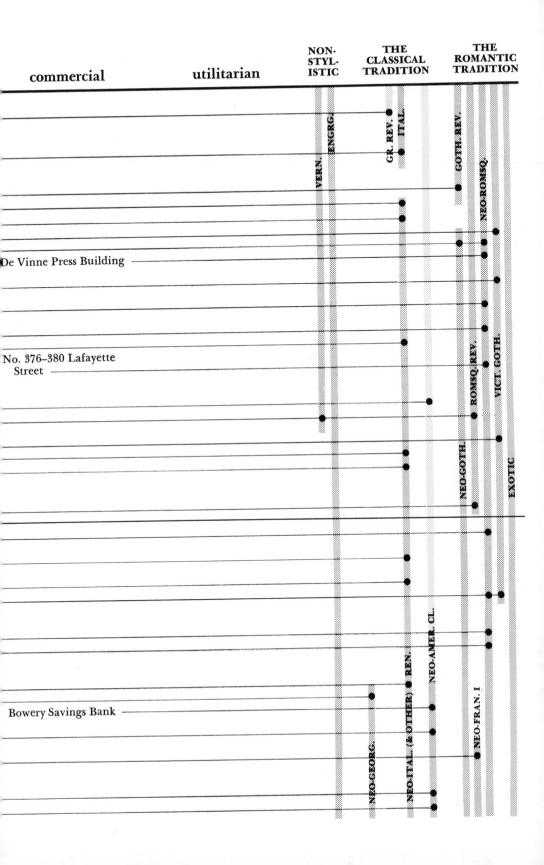

commercial   utilitarian

NON-STYL-ISTIC

THE CLASSICAL TRADITION

THE ROMANTIC TRADITION

VERN.

ENGRG.

GR. REV.

ITAL.

GOTH. REV.

NEO-ROMSQ.

ROMSQ. REV.

VICT. GOTH.

NEO-GOTH.

EXOTIC

NEO-AMER. CL.

REN.

NEO-ITAL. (& OTHER)

NEO-FRAN. I

NEO-GEORG.

De Vinne Press Building

No. 376–380 Lafayette
Street

Bowery Savings Bank

residential	ecclesiastical	public
		Firehouse, Engine Company No. 31 ———
		Association of the Bar of the City of New York ———
		Low Memorial Library ———
	Church of St. Ignatius Loyola ———	
		Appellate Division, New York State Supreme Court ———
	Church of the Transfiguration (Episcopal), Lich Gate ———	
	Holy Trinity Church and St. Christopher House ———	
		University Club ———
		Brooklyn Borough Hall, cupola ———
		Firehouse, Engine Company No. 33 ———
Ernest Flagg House ———		
William R. Moore House ———		
		New York Public Library ———
The Ansonia Hotel ———		
		Surrogate's Court (Hall of Records) ———

1900

residential	ecclesiastical	public
		Hall of Fame, Bronx Community College ———
		Gould Memorial Library, Bronx Community College ———
		New York Chamber of Commerce ———
		United States Custom House ———
		Yorkville Branch, New York Public Library ———
Payne Whitney House ———		
		Metropolitan Museum of Art, Fifth Avenue Façade, center ———
R. Livingston Beekman House ———		
Cartier, Inc. ———		
		Grand Central Terminal ———
		Morgan Library ———
		New-York Historical Society ———
	St. Paul's Chapel, Columbia University ———	
		Boathouse on the Lullwater ———

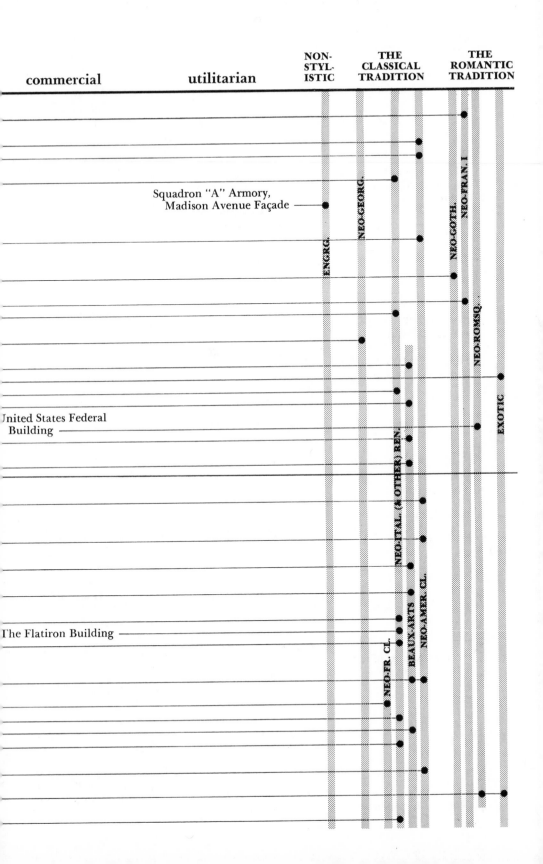

commercial	utilitarian	NON-STYL-ISTIC	THE CLASSICAL TRADITION	THE ROMANTIC TRADITION

Squadron "A" Armory, Madison Avenue Façade

United States Federal Building

The Flatiron Building

ENGRG.
NEO-GEORG.
NEO-ITAL. (& OTHER) REN.
NEO-FR. CL.
BEAUX-ARTS
NEO-AMER. CL.
NEO-GOTH.
NEO-FRAN. I
NEO-ROMSQ.
EXOTIC

residential	ecclesiastical	public
		Grecian Shelter ———
		Hamilton Grange Branch, New York Public Library
		American Academy of Dramatic Arts ———
The Plaza Hotel ———		
No. 131–135 East 66th Street ———		
	St. Patrick's Cathedral, Lady Chapel ———	
The Apthorp Apartments ———		
		West 115th Street Branch, New York Public Library
Alwyn Court Apartments ———		
Fraunces Tavern reconstruction ———		
Edward S. Harkness House ———		
The Belnord Apartments ———		
	Union Theological Seminary: Brown Memorial Tower, James Tower and James Memorial Chapel ———	
Percy R. Pyne House ———		
Villard Houses, East 50th Street addition ———		
James B. Duke Mansion ———		
	St. Thomas' Church ———	

1910

residential	ecclesiastical	public
	Church of Notre Dame ———	
		Rockefeller Fountain, Bronx Zoo ———
		Shelter Pavilion, McGolrick Park ———
		U.S. General Post Office ———
	St. Jean Baptiste Church ———	
	Chapel of the Intercession ———	
Vicarage, Chapel of the Intercession ———		
		Metropolitan Museum of Art, Fifth Avenue Façade, north and south wings ———
		New York County Courthouse ———
		Cornelius Baker Hall of Philosophy, Bronx Community College ———
Ogden Codman House ———		

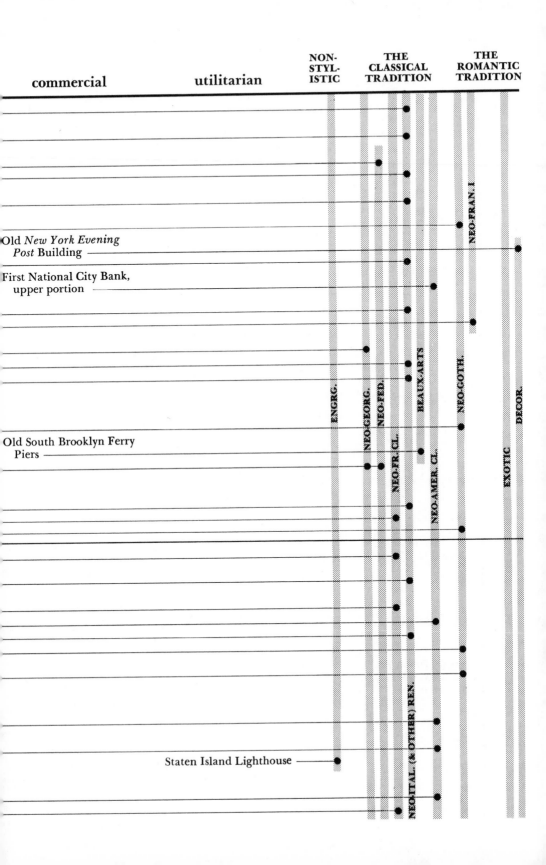

commercial   utilitarian

NON-
STYL-
ISTIC

THE
CLASSICAL
TRADITION

THE
ROMANTIC
TRADITION

Old *New York Evening Post* Building

First National City Bank, upper portion

Old South Brooklyn Ferry Piers

Staten Island Lighthouse

ENGRG.

NEO-GEORG.

NEO-FED.

NEO-FR.-CL.

NEO-CLASI. (& OTHER) REN.

BEAUX-ARTS

NEO-AMER.-CL.

NEO-GOTH.

NEO-FRAN.-I

EXOTIC

DECOR.

residential	ecclesiastical	public
		Brooklyn Central Office, Bureau of Fire Communications ——
Rectory, Church of Notre Dame ——		
Mrs. J. William Clark House ——		
Willard Straight House ——		
		The Regis High School ——
Henry P. Davison House ——		Municipal Building ——
The New York Society Library ——		
William Sloane House ——	Church of St. Vincent Ferrer (R.C.) ——	
Cartier Inc., remodeled as a shop ——	Russian Orthodox Cathedral of the Transfiguration of Our Lord ——	
George F. Baker, Jr., House ——		
	St. Bartholomew's Church ——	
1920		
Lewis Spencer Morris House ——		
Oliver D. Filley House ——		
Dunbar Apartments ——		
Vincent Astor House ——	St. Bartholomew's Church Community House ——	
No. 69 East 93rd Street addition to George F. Baker, Jr., House ——		
	St. John's Church (Fordham), transepts ——	
George Whitney House ——		Museum of the City of New York ——
1930		
		New York County Lawyers' Association ——
Clarence Dillon House ——		
Mrs. Graham Fair Vanderbilt House ——		
William Goadby Loew House ——		American Museum of Natural History, Roosevelt Memorial ——
No. 152 East 38th Street alteration ——		Rainey Memorial Gates, Bronx Zoo ——
		New-York Historical Society, wings ——

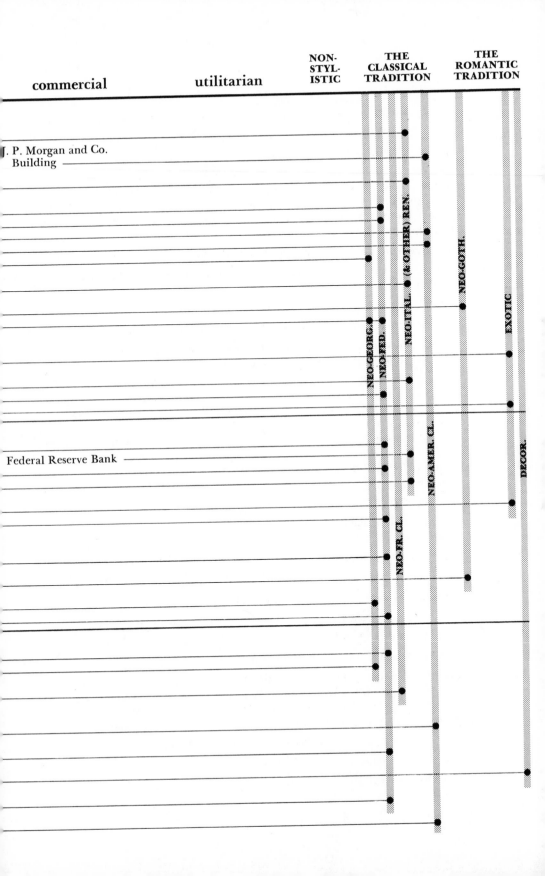

commercial   utilitarian   NON-STYL-ISTIC   THE CLASSICAL TRADITION   THE ROMANTIC TRADITION

J. P. Morgan and Co. Building

NEO-GEORG. NEO-FED. NEO-ITAL. (& OTHER) REN. NEO-GOTH. EXOTIC

Federal Reserve Bank

NEO-AMER. CL. NEO-FR. CL. DECOR.

Picture Credits

Grateful acknowledgment is made to the following for permission to reproduce photographs. Those not specifically credited come from the Landmarks Preservation Commission.

Mark Feldstein: Jonas Wood House, p. 59

The New-York Historical Society, New York City: Astor Library, p. 137; Conference House, p. 476; The Dakota, p. 302; Five Points, p. 78; Flatiron Building in construction, p. 227; Hamilton Grange, p. 298; High Bridge, p. 326; Jefferson Market Courthouse, p. 160; Metropolitan Museum of Art, p. 273; Saint Paul's Chapel, p. 63

The New York Public Library: Castle Williams, p. 101

The J. Clarence Davies Collection, Museum of the City of New York: Castle Clinton, p. 102

Avery Library: The Century Association, p. 211

The Pierpont Morgan Library, Ezra Stoller © Esto: Morgan Library, p. 215

Brooke Alexander, Inc., Eric Pollitzer: Flatiron in 1973—Haas etching, p. 227; Nathan Rabin: The Ansonia Hotel—Haas drypoint, p. 303

Herman Hong: Brooklyn General Post Office, p. 410; Christ Church, p. 359; Cornelius Van Wyck House, p. 447; Edgewater Village Hall, p. 513; Flatbush Dutch Reformed Church, p. 390; Flatlands Reformed Church, p. 391; Fort Schuyler Library, interior, p. 366; James Tower, p. 315; Jones Street houses, p. 118; West Farms Soldier Cemetery, p. 357; Reformed Dutch Church of Newtown, p. 456; Riverdale Presbyterian Church, p. 359; Squadron "A" Armory, p. 283; Staten Island Lighthouse, p. 521; 312 East 53rd Street, p. 175; Wyckoff-Bennett Homestead, p. 380

Manning Solon: "Little Church Around the Corner," p. 195

Herman N. Liberman, Jr.: St. Bartholomew's, p. 208; St. Thomas', p. 202; Notre Dame, p. 312

Museum of the City of New York: Nos. 122 and 120 East 92nd St., p. 249

Metropolitan Museum of Art: Litchfield Villa, p. 387; Old Assay Office, p. 275

Constance M. Jacobs: St. Martin's Episcopal Church, p. 309

New York University: Cornelius Baker Hall of Philosophy, p. 361

John R. Kennedy: Fort Schuyler, exterior, p. 366

The Staten Island Historical Society: Alice Austen House, p. 485

Peter Choy: Ernest Flagg House, p. 502; Gardiner-Tyler House, p. 491; Garibaldi Cottage, p. 497; Kreischer House, p. 501; Latourette House, p. 494; Pendleton House, p. 495; Pritchard House, p. 500; St. Andrew's, p. 509; St. Patrick's Church, p. 508; Sleight Family Graveyard, p. 505; Sailors' Snug Harbor Chapel, p. 507

Association of American Architects: Garibaldi Baldachino, p. 497

Greensward Foundation, Inc.: The Arsenal, p. 280

Brooklyn Museum: Brooklyn Museum, p. 403

Index

Architecture is a physical fact; history happened in actual places. We hope this book will stimulate the reader to explore the city on foot, to seek out and examine the many vestiges of its great and enduring past, and to acquire a discriminating and appreciative view of this heritage.

The Authors

"As world cities go, New York has had only a brief history, but that history is dear to New Yorkers, and is growing dearer every day that its remnants become rarer."

As early as the 1830s, some prescient New Yorkers were bemoaning the loss of the city's fine old architecture, slammed down by the wrecker's ball, sacrificed to what Walt Whitman called the city's "pull-down-and-build-over-again spirit." Fortunately for us, we now have the Landmarks Preservation Commission to protect the structures that survive. Since its establishment in 1965, it has designated some 378 buildings and twenty-three entire areas as Landmarks and Historic Districts. And now Harmon H. Goldstone, former Commission Chairman, and Martha Dalrymple have prepared this indispensable guide.

History Preserved brings together the architectural, cultural and social forces that have shaped the unique character of each borough of New York City. With district maps, chronological charts, discussions of the various styles, and lavish illustrations, the book points out every

(continued on back flap)